ENVIRONMENTAL

CARE & SHARE

Distributed by: **E TIP, Inc.**
PO Box 83, North Aurora, IL 60542-0083
(630) 966-8992 FAX (630) 801-9569
www.life-enzymes.com | sales@etipinc.com
(Veteran Owned Small Business)

DEDICATION

To all of the members of the "Changing of the Guard," Nature's Nobility.

ENVIRONMENTAL

CARE & SHARE

Working Model Constructs

which suggest

We Can Do Better

William R. Jackson, PhD

Jackson Research Center
Colorado Office
P.O. Box 1749
Evergreen, Colorado 80439

Library of Congress Cataloging-in-Publication Data
Jackson, William R. #94-096719
Environmental Care & Share
William R. Jackson, PhD-1st ed.

ISBN #0-9635741-2-4

Environmental Care & Share
1. Title 1995
CIP

Printed in the United States of America

Foreword

It was several years ago when an otherwise vibrant, involved, happily married young mother found herself suffering from daily headaches often described as "daggers" in her head. Each day started with numbness in her arms and hands, as well as a confused sense of reality and severe depression. Sleepless nights did not help matters.

"What it all meant" and "what to do about it" were questions that remained unanswered...until one afternoon, the day before Thanksgiving, 1991. Her doctor informed the young lady that the results revealed a deficiency in her immune system. It did not appear to be a case of AIDS, rather, an abnormality caused by an exposure to environmental toxins.

Relieved by the hope of finally resolving this "mystery condition," she was still at the depth of her dysfunction - unable to cook, clean, grocery shop, drive or even to care for her two small children. For years she experienced chronic breathing difficulty, flu-like symptoms (achy muscles, sore throats, swollen glands) and neurological problems. Through evaluations by specialists in environmental medicine, she learned that she was experiencing common symptoms of chemical hypersensitivity from an over-exposure to environmental chemicals. It was confirmed that her chronic fatigue, mental confusion, mood swings and depression were due to the "neurotoxic" effects of chemicals which actually altered her brain chemistry!

It took me five years to discover the source of the problem, for you see, I was that young woman. It was a relief to discover that the depression which accompanied gardening (toxic pesticides); headaches while changing diapers (fragranced diaper wipes); and irritability from housecleaning (harsh chemicals) - were, in fact, caused by reactions to everyday chemicals. My pains were not negative reactions to my circumstances! Just the simple awareness of the source of the exposures made the difference between merely "existing" with chronic illness - and enjoying life each day in good health.

May I encourage you to explore how common chemicals can affect each one of us - where we live, work and play. Even after what I have been through, I still believe some chemicals have enhanced the quality of our lives, and others, still cannot be avoided entirely. I believe that we can live in harmony with our ever-changing environment by: 1) choosing non-toxic substitutes whenever possible; 2) employing natural methods of remediation for environmental waste problems; and 3) seeking appropriate medical support for any damages caused by harmful exposures and rebuilding our immune systems to a greater level of chemical tolerance.

Giovanna De Santi-Medina*

---

*Giovanna De Santi-Medina is the past President of the Environmental Health Association. She presently works with the Price-Pottenger Nutrition Foundation as editor of the *PPNF Journal*, one of the most prestigious environmental/natural health publications nationwide. As an investigative journalist and health reporter, she has been published in various popular magazines and is a sought-after speaker on environmental health topics.

INTRODUCTION

BOOKS

Books for the Environmental Foundation
    And books for the public schools;
Books for the wise and the otherwise,
    And books for the dullard and fool.

Books that are fat or skinnier than that
    And books that are tall and thin,
Books for show with nowhere to go,
    And quite a few worth looking within.

Books for the baby and old Grandpa,
    And books for the working class,
Books for college and junior high,
    And for every grade we pass.

So give us books of every kind
    For the ignorant and the wise old sage,
There's something in this book for everyone
    If you put your heart in the printed page.

THE POET'S VOICE
Dr. William R. Jackson

The Environmental Health Foundation is a non-profit, for public benefit, corporation. As the Secretary of the Foundation stated, "May the advancement of knowledge never cease for lack of support. May the advancement of mankind never cease for lack of knowledge." The foundation is dedicated to furthering knowledge through:

1. EDUCATION: Scholarships, seminars, consultation, educational materials, including the publication of books; and
2. RESEARCH: Including grants for new technology and new products.

Relative to our responsibility to the publication of educational materials, we subscribe to the concept:

Books speak with thunderous tones from age to age,
Man has no power to match the printed page.

When the officers of the foundation commissioned the writing and publication of this book, it was with the intent of promoting research and education for the health and well being of all inhabitants of spaceship earth. The specific goals included demonstration of the following facts:

1. The generation of hazardous and toxic materials can be reduced substantially;
2. Safe substitution products are emerging; and

3. Safe chemical treatments are becoming more and more available through current research.

The author of this book, Dr. William R. Jackson, has presented a strong case for environmental care in the first half of the text, followed by the practical application of two working model constructs as demonstrative examples which indicate "we can do better." Environmental improvement and well-being are possible, and with your sharing and help, are probable. We trust you will enjoy this book, and take its truths to heart.

Jolynn K. Zapico
President of Environmental Health Foundation
Colorado Office
P.O. Box 1749
Evergreen, CO 80439

Brief Table of Contents

TABLE OF CONTENTS

ACKNOWLEDGEMENTS

In the development of any book, many more individuals are involved in the book's conception and birthing than those set forth on the title page. We express sincere appreciation to those who helped us during this project.

To Jolynn Kay Zapico for the computer input and formatting of the entire text of the book;

To Robbi Jo Jackson, JD, LLM, and Dr. Cindy Lynch, PhD, for their editorial assistance;

To the two ladies who advanced funds to the foundation for the first printing of this book: Evelyn Holcomb Megorden in memory of Ronald S. Megorden, and Gwendolyn Holcomb Venske in memory of Albert A. Venske;

To the Environmental Health Foundation and its officers who commissioned the book and who continued to assist from the book's beginning to its end;

To my family and friends who helped collect data, and who served as a support team;

To the experienced and capable printing company;

Thank you all!

PREFACE

We are all familiar with "bad news/good news" drama. Noting that the world is full of serious environmental problems is not a new observation. We are in the daily process of harming ourselves as well as destroying one another. It seems that our "today-oriented" civilization has ascended from the very ashes of battered, ill people by decimating our natural resources. The question is, how do YOU relate to this destructiveness, this evidence of a greed-motivated, self-centered social malignancy found among us? Ultimately, each person participates in a self-killing process of his or her own choice. Why do we make such choices? That we make these choices is the bad news. Can you identify harmful environmental issues? Yes. But can you implement protective alternatives to these issues in order to save your very own life?

The good news is, there are solutions to our accumulated environmental circumstances, problems and practices. You can accept the fact that our best defense against self-destructiveness lies in the courageous application of intelligence, to IDENTIFY our local ecosystem problems, to CLASSIFY possible answers to these problems, to COMPLY with present improvement programs, and by all means, to TRY to implement a strong personal philosophy and practical process for improving our environment.

This book includes two parts. The first part, Chapters 1-10, comprising the "HOW COME" part of the book. What are the problems? What are the consequences? What are our alternatives? The second segment of this book is the "HOW TO" portion of the presentation. It includes two working model constructs which suggest ways to improve our localized environmental inequities. The second part strongly suggests "WE CAN DO BETTER." The examples are not yet popular today, nor are they specifically exclusive. But our world-wide community is beginning to see many start-up solutions to help solve our enormous unsafe environmental encroachments.

The Environmental Health Foundation commissioned me to share my thoughts with you through this book. I hope that this sincere presentation will meet your needs and foster a better understanding of our ENVIRONMENTAL dilemma. I also hope you CARE enough about these health and welfare issues to SHARE answers with one another, and to become one of NATURE'S NOBILITY. You have my best wishes as you endeavor to make our world a better and healthier place to live.

William R. Jackson, PhD

ENVIRONMENTAL

CARE & SHARE

I

WILL YOU HELP?

Chapter Outline

The Big Spaceship
What Can I Do To Help?

The Big Spaceship

Our earth has been described as a spaceship. As intelligent thinking humans, we all live on board the 8,000 mile in diameter spherical spaceship, which is speeding around the sun at 60,000 miles per hour and spinning on its axis as it orbits. Thus we speak of flying by plane, "in" for a landing or "out" from the airport, to fly "around" the spaceship earth and come "in" again for a landing. Of the 4.5 billion people on this spaceship, what can you and I do to make it a safer place to live?

WHAT IS YOUR COMMITMENT TO HELP SOLVE OUR ENVIRONMENTAL PROBLEMS? The following is an example of the commitment and environmental philosophy of one group of spaceship earth inhabitants. The date was 1851, and the situation involved Seattle, the Chief of the Suquamish, and other Indian tribes around Washington's Puget Sound. The city of Seattle is named after the Chief, and legend has it that this speech was made in response to a proposal in which the Indians were asked to sell two million acres of land for $150,000.

As you read this thought-provoking example, you may wish to examine and further develop your own sense of responsibility toward the environment of our spaceship. Chief Seattle spoke:

> How can you buy or sell the sky, the warmth of the land? The idea is strange to us.
>
> If we do not own the freshness of the air and the sparkle of the water, how can you buy them?
>
> Every part of this earth is sacred to my people. Every shining pine needle, every sandy shore, every mist in the dark woods, every clearing and humming insect is holy in the memory and experience of my people. The sap which courses through the trees carries the memories of the red man.
>
> The white man's dead forget the country of their birth when they go to walk among the stars. Our dead never

forget this beautiful earth, for it is the mother of the red man. We are part of the earth and it is part of us. The perfumed flowers are our sisters; the deer, the horse, the great eagle, these are our brothers. The rocky crests, the juices in the meadows, the body heat of the pony, and man--all belong to the same family.

So, when the Great Chief in Washington sends word that he wishes to buy our land, he asks much of us. The Great Chief sends word that he will reserve us a place so that we can live comfortably to ourselves. He will be our father and we will be his children.

So we will consider your offer to buy our land. But it will not be easy. For this land is sacred to us. This shining water that moves in the streams and rivers is not just water but the blood of our ancestors. If we sell you land, you must remember that it is sacred, and you must teach your children that it is sacred and that each ghostly reflection in the clear water of the lakes tells of events and memories in the life of my people. The water's murmur is the voice of my father's father.

The rivers are our brothers, they quench our thirst. The rivers carry our canoes, and feed our children. If we sell you our land, you must remember, and teach your children, that the rivers are our brothers and yours, and you must henceforth give the rivers the kindness you would give any brother.

We know that the white man does not understand our ways. One portion of land is the same to him as the next, for he is a stranger who comes in the night and takes from the land whatever he needs. The earth is not his brother, but his enemy, and when he has conquered it, he moves on. He leaves his father's grave behind, and he does not care. He kidnaps the earth from his children, and he does not care. His father's grave, and his children's birthright are forgotten. He treats his mother, the earth, and his brother, the sky, as things to be bought, plundered, sold like sheep or bright beads. His appetite will devour the earth and leave behind only a desert.

I do not know. Our ways are different from your ways. The sight of your cities pains the eyes of the red man. There is no quiet place in the white man's cities. No place to hear the unfurling of leaves in spring or the rustle of the insect's wings. The clatter only seems to insult the ears. And what is there to life if a man cannot hear the lonely cry of the whippoorwill or the argument of the frogs around the pond at night? I am a red man and do not understand. The Indian prefers the soft sound of the wind darting over the face of a pond and the smell of the wind itself, cleansed by a midday rain, or scented with piñon pine.

The air is precious to the red man for all things share the same breath, the beast, the tree, the man, they all share the same breath. The white man does not seem to notice the air he breathes. Like a man dying for many days he is numb to the stench. But if we sell you our land, you must remember that the air is precious to us, that the air shares its spirit with all the life it supports.

The wind that gave our grandfather his first breath also receives his last sigh. And if we sell you our land, you must keep it apart and sacred as a place where even the white man can go to taste the wind that is sweetened by the meadow's flowers.

You must teach your children that the ground beneath their feet is the ashes of our grandfathers. So that they will respect the land, tell your children that the earth is rich with the lives of our kin. Teach your children that we have taught our children that the earth is our mother. Whatever befalls the earth befalls the sons of the earth. If men spit upon the ground, they spit upon themselves.

This we know: the earth does not belong to man; man belongs to the earth. All things are connected. We may be brothers after all. We shall see. One thing we know which the white man may one day discover: our God is the same God.

You may think now that you own Him as you wish to own our land; but you cannot. He is the God of man, and His compassion is equal for the red man and the white. This earth is precious to Him, and to harm the earth is to heap contempt on its creator. The whites too shall pass; perhaps sooner than all other tribes. Contaminate your bed and you will one night suffocate in your own waste.

But in your perishing you will shine brightly fired by the strength of the God who brought you to this land and for some special purpose gave you dominion over this land and over the red man.

That destiny is a mystery to us, for we do not understand when the buffalo are slaughtered, the wild horses are tame, the secret corners of the forest heavy with scent of many men and the view of the ripe hills blotted by talking wires.

Where is the thicket? Gone. Where is the eagle? Gone.

The end of living and the beginning of survival.*[1]

---

[1]*Chief Seattle's speech was submitted by Dr. Glenn T. Olds at Alaska's Future Frontiers conference in 1979. As quoted in Organic Soil Conditioning, 1993. Jackson.

What Can I Do To Help?

On May 30, 1884, Oliver Wendell Holmes, speaking before the Army of the Republic said, "Recall what our country has done for each of us, and ask ourselves, 'What can we do for our country in return?'" LeBarron Russel Broggs, in 1904, referring to his Alma Mater, paraphrased the proclamation: "Ask not what she can do for me, but what can I do for her?" The paraphrase of Oliver Wendell Holmes, used in John F. Kennedy's Presidential inaugural address on January 20, 1961 rang out, "Ask not what your country can do for you, but what you can do for your country."

As we consider the environmental effects of various hurtful and hazardous chemically caused problems, we ask, "Is this an inevitable situation? Does progress necessarily include negative effects? If our land and our health suffer from the results of our activities, is restoration and healing possible? If so, how? What will be required, and what must we do?"

Our lives have experienced major changes during the past 50 years. The acceleration of mechanical technology has precipitated ingenuity and economic change. Industry with its modifications, advancements, and its methods of sanitizing reflect questionable change. Health motivated experiments have included the risk of the unknown. These "advanced" methods, procedures and stimulants (including many man-made chemicals) have been employed in the struggle for technical, financial and medical survival. Many new ideas have been abused. In some cases, the long-term effects of these developments have not been researched adequately. Problems of environmental toxicity are becoming apparent around our global spaceship. Our food lacks the nutrients we need, fields are becoming sterile, dangerous chemicals threaten our industries and our personal work places, many of our waterways are contaminated, and much of our groundwater is becoming polluted.

What is the problem? Is anyone honest and brave enough to answer? Do PRIDE, PROPAGANDA, and PROFIT blind each one of us? This problem involves all economic strata, commercial, industry, and agricultural enterprises, as well as consumers. Landowners are losing the fertility of their soil. Many family farms are gone forever, or in numerous cases, they are only days from bankruptcy. Our rivers and lakes are polluted, and our work places are often compared to chemical war zones. Consumers are complaining of serious health problems. Is the dramatic battle for survival being lost?

Just who is the winner in this scenario? Is it possible that the few who might profit most in the short run influence government, research, and the dissemination of information in negative ways, and that the lives and the well being of the masses are unimportant to them?

But, if I am one among the masses and you are one, WHY DON'T WE come up with some answers for ourselves? Maybe our responsibility is not to change the world. Perhaps we must only make our little part of the world safer and more productive for ourselves, our family, and our neighbors. We must start where we are and make a difference in the lives of those around us.

The creation of our spaceship earth was perfectly balanced, and today our ecosystem can be restored to that same balance, if we choose. Perhaps, as trustees of our spaceship earth, our paraphrase today could be, "ASK NOT WHAT ELSE I CAN TAKE, NOR WHICH OF NATURE'S RULES MAY I BREAK, BUT RATHER, IN MY ENVIRONMENT, WHAT CAN I DO TO HELP?"

Our next chapter, IS MORE HELP ON THE WAY?, compliments our trend of thought. The victory can be won, our environment preserved, and our health restored if we all take an aggressive role in assisting nature's natural balance.

II

IS MORE HELP ON THE WAY?

Chapter Outline

Environmental Pollution

Our national economy is overly dependent upon hazardous and toxic related production. Approximately 16 million jobs are tied directly to the continued development and use of toxic materials in fields as diverse as agriculture, mining, electronics, chemicals, health care, food processing, transportation, and textiles. While gross domestic production and corporate profits grew moderately over the last decade, the United States lost more than three million manufacturing jobs and our standard of living dropped from third to thirteenth in the industrialized world. The apparent contradiction between the growth in gross domestic product and the decline in living standards can be explained, in part, by the replacement of human labor with capital for more equipment and chemicals for more powerful but questionable effects.

During the 1950s, over 30% of the work force was engaged in manufacturing. Now approximately 17% manufacture, and that work force percentage is steadily dropping. Our American businesses are closing shops in the United States and shifting these shops to other parts of the world to take advantage of cheaper labor costs, and more lax environmental laws and enforcement. Since 1965, U.S. corporations have erected more than 1,800 plants employing 500,000 people in the Third World alone.

Do you realize that as recently as 1965, every color television set purchased in the United States was made by an American owned company in one of our domestic plants? However, despite the sale of over twenty million television sets in this country, not one of our major manufacturers has dominated this industry recently.

Our economic decline has been accompanied by ongoing environmental degradation. At the same time, public health problems related to toxins are steadily increasing.

Pollution problems made worse by the development and widespread use of synthetic organic chemicals continue to cause an ecological and public health calamity of unprecedented magnitude. The Environmental Protection Agency (EPA), confirms the existence of more than 32,000 toxic dump sites around the country in need of cleanup. The EPA also estimates that close to 25 million Americans live within four miles of a Superfund hazardous dump site. According to their reports, cancer risks are as high as one in 100 for people living near the sources of this pollution. As much as 400 billion pounds of toxic chemicals are emitted annually into our communities.

The reported cases of cancer and other diseases related to toxic exposure continue to increase. Since 1950, the incidence of cancer per 100,000 U.S. citizens has climbed by more than 42%. Between 1980 and 1987 alone, the prevalence of asthma increased by close to one-third among Americans. The National Cancer Institute disclosed a 28% increase in the incidence of childhood cancer from 1950 to 1987. Recent studies have found decreases in fertility among young Americans in their twenties. Many of the synthetic chemicals reaching our bodies are capable of attacking virtually every human organ system and remain prime instigators for these deteriorating health conditions.

The use of chemicals by agricultural entities, as well as other businesses, has produced needed products such as manufactured goods, pharmaceutical products, fertilizers, herbicides, pesticides, and other agricultural chemicals. In addition, there are coatings, adhesives, and various other useful items. In all, we produce more than 100 million tons of synthetic chemicals each year. As a consequence of the use of these chemicals, tens of millions of tons of waste pollutants are produced. We do not yet know all the ill effects of these chemicals or the environmental imbalance they create.

Maybe the Government Can Help

Prior to the enactment of a number of federal laws, there was little control of the disposal of these pollutant wastes. As a result, many environmental disasters occurred. The increasing awareness of these kinds of tragedies raised public, governmental, and business concern about the management of toxic chemicals in the soil, water, and air, and about hazardous waste disposal and the transport of hazardous materials.

According to Sandra Tucker, Environmental Specialist, much U.S. legislation and regulatory activity has been aimed directly at improving the management of hazardous wastes. The following discussion of federal hazardous waste law is extremely important to business activities, such as real estate transactions. For example, if oil was drilled for on your ranch or farm in the past, are there hydrocarbon and oil residues from the mud pits or overflow pond, leakage from storage tanks, or transport spills? Perhaps that area is now unproductive because of the contamination. How about water table contamination? Who is responsible, by law, for cleaning up such pollution problems? The oil drilling company? The drilling investors? The title company? Your attorney? Your lender? A new owner of the property? You? These laws also affect business in general because much of the federal language has been incorporated into the drafting of state statutes regarding hazardous waste management and investigation. Below is an overview of six legislative actions that are significant in environmental pollution issues.

RCRA

1. The **RESOURCE CONSERVATION AND RECOVERY ACT** (RCRA, 42 USC, Sections 6901 through 6987), was enacted in 1976 as the first step in regulating the potential health and

environmental problems associated with solid hazardous and nonhazardous waste disposal. The RCRA and the regulations developed by the Environmental Protection Agency (EPA), to implement its provisions address the determination of whether hazardous wastes are being generated, techniques for tracking wastes to eventual disposal, and the design and permitted operation of hazardous waste management. This is the federal law governing all aspects of handling hazardous waste. It is often referred to as the "cradle-to-grave" law, and it established a tracking system for hazardous waste from generation to ultimate disposal.

HSWA

2. The **HAZARDOUS AND SOLID WASTE AMENDMENT** (HSWA, PL98-616) was enacted in 1984 to address regulatory gaps in the RCRA program regarding highly toxic wastes. For example, it includes regulation of carcinogens, listing and delisting of

hazardous wastes, permits for hazardous waste facilities, small quantity generators, leaking underground storage tanks, and the elimination of land disposal of hazardous waste, including regulation deadlines according to a congressionally mandated schedule.

CERCLA

3. The **COMPREHENSIVE ENVIRONMENTAL RESPONSE, COMPENSATION AND LIABILITY ACT** (CERCLA, 42 USC, Sections 6901 through 6957), also known as Superfund, was enacted in 1988 to ensure that a source of funds ($1.77 billion) is available to clean up abandoned hazardous waste dumps, compensate victims, address releases of hazardous materials, and establish liability standards for responsible parties.

SARA

4. The **SUPERFUND AMENDMENTS AND REAUTHORIZATION ACT** (SARA, PL99-499) was enacted in 1986 to increase the Superfund to $8.5 billion, to modify contaminated site cleanup criteria scheduling, and to revise settlement procedures. It also provides a fund for leaking underground storage tank cleanup and a broad, new emergency planning and community right-to-know program.

TSCA and CWA

5, 6. The **TOXIC SUBSTANCE CONTROL ACT** (TSCA) was enacted in 1976 and the **CLEAN WATER ACT** (CWA) was enacted in 1972. These were enacted to attempt to control the occurrence of various toxic pollutions.

Maybe the Legal System Can Help

As the number of laws and regulating agencies governing the cleanup of our spaceship earth's environment has increased, the total cost for such remediation and the complexity of environmental toxic waste safety requirements also have increased. Many recent statutes impose enormous retroactive liabilities upon individuals and companies for past actions that may have complied with previously applicable standards. Moreover, in private lawsuits, courts seem to have been increasingly willing to impose liability for personal injury and property damage upon a wide variety of parties whose actions have adversely affected the environment. It is interesting to note that this often includes land owners, business owners, corporations, and lenders; even real estate brokers have incurred this liability. Government agencies as well as private plaintiffs have sought to impose liability for environmental damage upon a wide variety of defendants.

What is Our Environmental Leverage?

1. Many hazardous wastes and toxic chemical pollutants are deadly, and our abuse of these materials is throwing

our spaceship earth as well as our universe out-of-balance.

2. The U.S. government has initiated laws and specific procedures regarding hazardous and toxic waste. Penalties include stiff cash fines and in some cases prison terms for those who violate these rules.

3. If there are continuous violations of the laws of nature, let us hope that the laws of our government will punish the violators before nature, while out-of-balance, destroys all of us. Thus, the environmental legal leverage of the law may assist in remediation.

4. Remember, we do not break rules without consequences. Often violated rules eventually break us. This principle is very applicable in nature.

5. Nature has its natural balance, but if it is forced out-of-balance, there are natural provisions for remediation. Humic and microbial balance has redeeming and cleansing ability.

6. There is good news: Nature has answers, and for a responsible, responding society, there can be HEALING FOR OUR LANDS, AS WELL AS OUR HEALTH!

The next chapter, INHERITED CHEMICAL ILLNESS, is of extreme importance to each of us. The people of the United States take pride in the fact that we have the freedom to make our own choices. With those choices comes responsibility. But, what if deadly choices are made for you? What if you have no choice? What if unborn children become victims, having had no choice regarding their deformities?

III

INHERITED CHEMICAL ILLNESS

Chapter Outline

The Chemical Patch

Do you know anyone that has been helped by using a physician-prescribed patch? Smokers can use a nicotine patch to break the smoking habit and still receive the nicotine their body craves! How simple. The patch supplies nicotine through the skin and the cell tissues in amounts that equal or exceed the nicotine from a cigarette. Women may adjust to menopause more easily by reducing hot flashes and other symptoms with the use of a hormone patch. Patches have also been developed to counter motion sickness and administer vaccines of many types. Further research is being conducted on many other types of patch-supplied medication, such as treatments for certain types of diabetes, asthma, and heart problems.

Isn't that amazing? A little patch can be placed on our skin which absorbs the medication. Then it passes through the tissue and circulates through the body to provide balance for a particular medical need. Modern technology can be wonderful. It is fun to watch a plan come together in such a helpful way. The concept has proven to have great merit.

On the other hand, what if you were a mechanic using a strong solvent to clean auto parts every day? Is your skin and your body tissue exposed to more deadly chemical exposure than if you had this material on a PATCH? How about your lungs when you inhale harmful vapors? Do you ever wash paint off of your hands with strong thinner? How about solvent-based hand cleaner? Is this as much exposure to your body as if you were using a PATCH containing harmful paint thinner or solvent-based hand cleaner? If you were a custodian, an employee of a hotel cleaning crew, or a sanitation engineer cleaning up a food plant, could you find chemicals involved that plainly state: "Do not ingest;" "Will burn the skin;" or "Will cause eye damage"? Would you wear a PATCH with this deadly chemical on it? Do you even know what chemicals you are using? Can you guarantee you will never get those chemicals on you or that you will never breathe the harmful fumes? Is your job worth the risk? What about the risk for your children? Your life? Are there safer products your employer could provide? How much chemical material was absorbed by Vietnam Veterans and Desert Storm troops? Was their exposure at least as significant as if the toxic matter had been applied through a small skin patch? Repeated exposures to hazardous chemicals in our work and living environments constitute the equivalent of HAZARDOUS CHEMICAL PATCHES.

Reproduction Hazards

The University of California at Berkeley, Wellness letter, April 1994, included this headline: FATHERING HEALTHY BABIES. The article confirmed that although 7% of all babies born in the United States are born underweight and about 3% have obvious birth defects, very little is known about the causes. We used to assume that fathers were only sperm donors and sperm is strong and invincible, thus not affected by environmental exposures. On the other hand, we have heard a lot about women needing to be so careful because the egg is "passive" and fragile. Remember, men *and* women create babies. The genetic involvement of both the male and female are critical. Yes, the egg and the female have received much attention relative to the need to give the child-to-be a fair chance to survive. What if the father-to-be is a custodian or a mechanic using solvents or harmful chemicals? It is now recognized that sperm, just like any cell, is susceptible to genetic damage, and as stated by the University of California Wellness paper, the seminal fluid or the sperm itself may carry harmful materials, such as drug residues or harmful chemicals.

According to a recent article, "Reproduction Toxicology", Dr. Derra Lee Davis, of the Department of Health and Human Services, indicated that over 60 different compounds or industrial processes have been identified as increasing defects in human sperm and potentially increasing the risk to offspring. As the University of California's quoted information further indicated, multiple studies have shown that wives of workers exposed to commonly used substances such as rubber, plastic, toluene, and benzene are more likely to miscarry. A study of the offspring of firemen conducted at the University of British Columbia found an increased risk of a congenital heart defect in firemen's children, perhaps because firemen are exposed to toxic chemicals in their line of duty. Whether or not they plan to become parents, workers should not be exposed to hazardous chemicals.

Environmental Illnesses

Dr. Bryan Smith is the Director of the National Information System for Vietnam Veterans. He published an article entitled "Environmental Illness and Vietnam Veterans' Children." The research findings carry heavy implications for all of us who carry the known or the unknown HAZARDOUS PATCH of commercial, war time, or industrial chemical exposure. Not only does it affect our present generation -- you and me, but it also affects innocent, yet unborn children. The following includes information from the article, reprinted here by permission.

> The staff of the National Information System for Vietnam Veterans and their families (NIS), a project of the Center for Developmental Disabilities of the University of South Carolina supported by the Agent Orange Class assistance Program, have been collecting client information as a part of their Information and Referral function for slightly over a year. They have interviewed parents of health care providers in an effort to connect over 1500 children with appropriate services

to meet their needs. Most of the children have multiple problems within and between categorical groupings of a variety of developmental disabilities, birth defects, genetic conditions that can be grouped into the area of immune response disorders. These include persistent skin rashes, infections, chronic fevers and asthma. The NIS staff has observed that these immunological dysfunctions, which may sound minor in relationship to the damage caused by a birth defect or developmental disability, are serious and often disabling. They occur in many members of the same family constellation and persist for many years. In fact, many veterans reported that their children have never lived a day without them.

These observations have prompted some relevant questions that need to be addressed and are the basis of this White Paper. These questions are posed as needs assessment issues to identify services that will further assist Vietnam veterans and their families rather than as research questions that may be searching for a cause and effect relationship.

1) Are alterations in immune functions a marker or a symptom of exposure to an environmental agent?

2) Are alterations in immune functions a teratologic effect?

3) Are these dysfunctions developmental disabilities by themselves, as opposed to conditions occurring concurrently with a developmental disability and do these children constitute an underserved population? and

4) Are these immunological problems medically treatable?

Are alterations in immune functions a marker or a symptom of exposure to an environmental agent?

The health impacts of environmental agents are mediated through effects on cells, the cell being the unit structure in the living organism. Recent developments in cellular and molecular biology have provided powerful new concepts and techniques for studying the normal behavior of cells and the response of cells to environmental agents. These developments can greatly improve our understanding of the mechanisms of environmentally provoked disease.

Environmental exposure to chemicals, both synthetic and natural, has altered human physiologic structure and function. Almost all Americans have a detectable level of synthetic chemicals like halogenated hydrocarbons, for example, in their bodies. Environmental concentrations of natural chemicals such as ammonia and formaldehyde also are many orders of magnitude higher than in the past. Humans have many biochemical scavenger systems that protect them from damage caused by chemically altered cells and proteins. However, since we are now exposed to much higher concentrations of natural chemicals as well as massive amounts of synthetic chemicals to which our ancestors were never exposed, it is easy to see that, with regard to chemical exposures, our protective resources are taxed to a much greater extent than were theirs.

Although allergic and hypersensitivity reactions have long been recognized as responses to environmental chemicals, other environmentally related disturbances in immunity--such as depression of immunity and dysregulation of immunity, (auto-immunity)--have only begun to receive significant attention from toxicologists. Traditional methods for toxicological assessment have implied that the immune system is a frequent target of toxic insult following chronic or acute exposure to environmental chemicals, therapeutic drugs, abused drugs, or radiation. Interaction of the immune system with these xenobiotics (allergens) may result in undesirable effects of three principal types:

1) those manifested as immunosuppression;
2) those manifested as immune dysregulation (auto-immunity);
3) those manifested as an immunologic response to the xenobiotic.

The extent of the chemical-induced hypersensitivity disease has been known for some time.

According to Levin and Byers (1987), the toxicology community has recently become aware that a broad spectrum of chemical xenobiotics can suppress the immune system and increase susceptibility to infectious agents or cancerous cells. Several clinical studies in humans have demonstrated a parallel effect on immune dysfunction. For example, it has been observed that individuals accidentally exposed to polychlorinated biphenyl contaminated rice oil exhibit immune dysfunction.

Disabilities Among Children

There are biochemical, cellular, and physiological markers that can signal whether an individual has been exposed to a toxicant, quantify the extent of exposure, characterize the susceptibility of the exposed person, and identify pre-clinical signs of any resulting injury or disease. Is the immunologic dysfunction seen in Vietnam Veterans' children a marker of exposure to a toxicant or is there another marker that could implicate an exposure?

Most Frequently Reported Developmental Disabilities in 1500 Children of Vietnam Veterans*

Skin disorders
Learning disabilities
Allergies
Attention deficit disorders
Asthma
Mental retardation
Speech disorders
Hearing problems
Emotional problems
Seizures
Cerebral palsy
Heart defects
Orthopedic problems
Visual disorders
Cancer
Renal (kidney) disorders
Cleft lip and palate
Scoliosis
Headache
Growth abnormalities
Chronic infections
Cysts

(*Listed by order of frequency)

Almost all Americans have a detectable level of synthetic chemicals like halogenated hydrocarbons in their bodies.

Susceptibility to the toxic effects of a foreign substance may vary widely, with profound implications for risk assessment. A major source of such diversity is variation in the manner in which substances are metabolized in different individuals. Factors contributing to this variation include heredity, age, sex, diet, drugs, smoking habits, occupation, lifestyle, and health status. The effects of heredity on such variations are particularly marked but are often outwardly unapparent. Relatively little study has been devoted to this issue thus far.

The toxicity of a substance depends on the concentration and time in which its active form is present at its biological site of action. These factors, in turn, depend on such variables as the route of exposure, dose, dose rate, handling of the substance, its metabolism, and its excretion. This interaction is referred to as the pharmacokinetics relationship.

Ironically this relationship has been used systematically in the development and testing of drugs, but has not been incorporated in the design, interpretation, and analysis of toxicological studies.

Intense exposure to high levels of toxic chemicals often causes cell deaths. The clinical symptomatology associated with this type of damage has long been recognized as the acute toxic effects of chemical exposure and has been well documented in the medical literature (Asher, 1978; Dean and Padarathsing, 1981; Koller, 1985; LaDou, 1985; and Sharma, 1986). More recently, physicians have become aware of the effects of chronic low-level exposure to toxic chemicals and related influences on the biological regulatory mechanisms of the body. These factors serve as a foundation for the recognition of the disease called environmental illness.

The long-term effects of exposure to dioxin has been studied and can serve as an example of this issue. Jennings et al. (1988) investigated immunological abnormalities 17 years after workers had been accidentally exposed to dioxin. They found a change in the immune system that may reflect prior tissue damage and cellular destruction in the exposed population. The number of natural killer cells identified was higher. These cells are believed to contribute to the body's defense against viruses and tumors. If exposure to dioxin is associated with an increased risk of neoplastic disease, the number and function of natural killer cells may be important in its pathogenesis. Conversely, changes in the number of these cells may show activation of the body's defenses.

The residents of Quail Run Mobile Home Park in Missouri were accidentally exposed to dioxin. Follow-up studies suggest alterations in immune function, but these were not consistently found (Hoffman, 1986; Knutsen et al., 1987; Stehr-Green et al., 1987, 1988). Immunologic tests showed that the exposed groups had an increased inability to react to specific allergens. According to Clapp et al. (1990), these findings suggest an association between long-term exposure to dioxin and depressed cell-mediated immunity, although the effects had not resulted in an excess of clinical illness in the exposed group.

Clapp et al. (1990) reported a study by Morarelli Clinical Laboratory (1985) in which immune function was evaluated. Between 1976 and 1979, 48 children from Seveso, Italy who were heavily exposed to dioxin were studied. Their lymphocyte responses to select allergens were significantly higher than those of an experimental control group.

The term environmental illness is used to describe an acquired disease characterized by series of symptoms caused and/or exacerbated by exposure to environmental agents. The triggering agents include industrial and domestic chemicals, cigarette smoke, diesel fumes, and alcoholic beverages. The symptoms involve multiple organs in the neuralgic, endocrine, genitourinary, and immunologic systems. A large body of information documents symptoms seen in individuals subjected to known acute or chronic chemical exposure; the only novel aspect of environmental illness is the realization that similar symptom complexes frequently are seen in individuals without known "massive" exposure and the diagnosis can be made on the basis of these complexes.

Are Alterations in Immune Functions a Teratologic Effect?

A growing number of agents are known to perturb one or more of the interconnected processes involved in human reproduction. Because effects on any one of these processes may interfere with normal reproduction and development, the entire spectrum of processes may be targets for the action of toxic agents. Teratologic effects can act specifically on the developing reproductive system of the fetus (Shepard, 1980) to produce dysfunctions that are later observed at reproductive maturity. Teratological effects are not solely female-mediated reproductive effects, although by definition they involve prenatal exposures that occur to the offspring while in utero. Paternally-mediated exposures may also pose teratogenic risks through the secretion of chemicals into seminal fluid and uptake across the uterine mucosa. The latter has been demonstrated with persistent lipophilic toxicants such as organochlorine (Upton & Goldstein, 1984).

... Because we are now exposed to much higher concentrations of natural chemicals as well as massive amounts of synthetic chemicals to which our ancestors were never exposed, it is easy to see that, with regard to chemical exposures, our protective resources are taxed to a much greater extent than were theirs.

Are these dysfunctions developmental disabilities by themselves, as opposed to conditions occurring concurrently with a developmental disability?

The term developmental disability is defined by Public Law 98-527 (1984) to mean a severe, chronic disability of a person which --

> A) is attributable to a mental or physical impairment or combination of mental and physical impairments;

B) is manifested before the person attains age twenty-two;
C) is likely to continue indefinitely;
D) results in substantial functional limitations in three or more of the following areas of major life activity: (i) self-care, (ii) receptive and expressive language, (iii) learning, (iv) mobility, (v) self-direction, (vi) capacity for independent living, and (vii) economic self-sufficiency; and
E) reflects the person's need for a combination and sequence of special, interdisciplinary, or generic care, treatment, or other services which are of lifelong or extended duration and are individually planned and co-coordinated (Public Law 98-517, 1984).

While it appears that severe immune dysfunction in children meets most of the characteristics of the functional definition for developmental disabilities, the issue of lifelong illness is the most difficult to reconcile.

Allergies, fungal infections, asthma, and chronic fevers are usually considered to be medically solvable, at least symptomatically treatable so as to render the patient capable of self-sufficiency. Yet these conditions seem to persist and seem to be medically untreatable in the affected children of Vietnam veterans.

Are These Immunological Problems Medically Treatable?

Chemically induced immune dysregulation is a recognized medical disorder (Koller, 1985). A wide variety of symptoms referable as immune dysregulation were described to the NIS staff. Skin manifestations such as hives, urticaria and induration are common. The Agent Orange Scientific Force (Clapp et al. 1990) have stated that after their literature review they found there was a significant statistical association between Agent Orange and immune/dermatological disorders of chloracne and porphyria cutanea tarda.

Other symptoms referable to immune dysregulation include an increasing intensity of ordinary type 1 allergies and increasing sensitivity to body molds such as Candida albicans and Trichophyton. Mold allergy can manifest itself clinically as chronic dermatitis, gastroenteritis, and endogenous depression (Crook, 1986; Trowbridge & Walker, 1986).

A casual agent in environmental illness is defined as a substantial contributing factor to the development of illness. If patients were not exposed to this agent, they would not develop the disease at the same time and with the same intensity. The potential causal agent must be one that can realistically initiate an illness. For example, if a patient whose history, physical findings, and laboratory results are consistent with a diagnosis of environmental illness, described himself as completely well until he was exposed to an intensely toxic material that is associated with severe acute symptoms, the toxic material would be a candidate as the causal factor, since this appears to be an etiologic agent that can reasonably cause disease.

Clinicians have recognized the similarity between the symptoms of environmental illness and acute infectious hepatitis patient. Fatigue, intolerance to alcohol and cigarette smoke, and multi-organ symptomatology are shared by those with environmental illness and hepatitis. Of importance is the fact that hepatitis does not become symptomatic until the patient has circulating immune complexes. Since immune dysregulation leads to immune complex disease, there is a possibility that an immune-complex-mediated, complement-consuming process could be partially responsible for the symptoms of environmental illness. Upon evaluation a population of symptomatic patient, Levin and Byers (1987) discovered a significant number with elevated prostaglandin, suggesting that part of their symptomatology was associated with an immune-complex-mediated inflammatory process (Straus et al., 1984).

Medical treatment for the immune dysfunction varies based on the clinical orientation of the physician. From the literature it appears that clinical improvement can often be accelerated by reducing the overall load on the immune system. This can be accomplished in most people with allergen reduction or elimination efforts. For example, with a hypersensitive patient a diet may be structured to remove the more common potential allergic offenders in the diet. These include milk and milk products, cereal grains (wheat and corn), and refined carbohydrates (white sugar and white flour). A very common offender in individuals whose biological regulatory system has been damaged by environmental agents is the Candida albicans organism. This ubiquitous fungus is widely recognized as an allergen responsible for multi-organ symptomatology (Rippon, 1982). Oral administration of Nystatin (Nilstat) in large doses or careful administration of ketoconazole (Nizoral) can be very helpful. This treatment course has been described elsewhere (Crook, 1986).

Specific antigen immunotherapy with ordinary allergy treatment for dust, grass pollens, molds, tree pollens, and weed pollens can be instituted to take the pressure off the damaged immune system. In some cases, non-specific immunotherapy and intravenous gamma globulin provides the damaged immune system with antibodies against various pathogens like virus, bacterium and fungus, that reduce some reactions (Carson, Seto, & Wasson, 1986).

REFERENCES

Asher, I.M. (ed.) Inadvertent Modification of the Immune Response: The Effects of Foods, Drugs and Environmental Contaminants. Proceeding of The Fourth FDW Science Symposium, August 28-30, 1978. Superintendent of Documents, U.S. Government Printing Office, Washington, D.C. 20402.

Clapp, R.W., Commoner, B., Constable, J.D., Epstein, S.S., Kahn, P.C., Olson, J.R., and Ozonoff, D.M. Human Health Effects Associated with Exposure to Herbicides and/or their Associated Contaminants - Chlorinated Dioxins, Agent Orange and the Vietnam Veteran: A Review of the Scientific Literature. April, 1990.

Crook, W.G. The Yeast Connection, 3rd ed. New York, Random House Books, 1986.

Dean, J.H., Padarathsing M. (eds.) Biological Relevance of Immune Suppression as Induced by Genetic, Therapeutic and Environmental Factors. San Francisco, Van Nostrand Reinhold Co., 1981.

Hoffman, R. Health Effects of Long-Term Exposure to 2,3,7,8-tetrachlorodibenzo-p-dioxin. Jour Am Med Assoc 256(15):2031-2038, 1986.

Jennings, A.M., Wild, G., Ward, J.D., Ward, A.M. Immunological Abnormalities 17 Years After Accidental Exposure to 2,3,7,8-tetrachlorodibenzo-p-dioxin. Br J Ind Med 45:701-704, 1988.

Koller, L.D. Effect of Chemical Sensitivity on the Immune System: Immunology and Allergy Practice 7(10):405-417, 1985.

Knutsen, A.P., Roodman, S.T., Evans, R.G., Mueller, K.R., Webb, K.B., Stehr-Green, P., Hoffman, R.E., and Schramm, W.F. Immune Studies in Dioxin-exposed Missouri Residents: Quail Run. Bull Environ Contam Toxicol. 39:481-489, 1987.

LaDou, J. (ed.) Occupational Medicine: State of the Art Reviews. The Microelectronics Industry. Philadelphia, Hansley & Belfus, Inc., January, 1985.

Levin A.S. Transfer Factory Therapy in Food Allergies. Brostoff, J., and Challacombe, L. (eds.) Food Allergies. London, Tindall-Saunders Books, 1987, pp 995-1004.

Levin A.S., and Byers, V.S. Environmental Illness: A Disorder of Immune Regulation. Occup Med 2:669-681, 1987.

Morarelli Clinical Laboratory Manifestations of Exposures to Dioxin in Children: A Six Year Study of the Effects of an Environmental Disaster Near Seveso, Italy. Jour Am Med Assoc 256:2687-2695, 1986.

Sharma, R.P. Immunologic Considerations in Toxicology, I & II. Boca Raton, FL, CRC Press, 1986.

Staake, J., Gibson, B., Steinberg, K., Strauss, S.E., et al. Persisting Illness and Fatigue in Adults With Evidence of Epstein-Barr Virus Infection. Clin Exp Immunol 58:7, 1984.

Stampf, J.L., Castognoli, N., Epstein, W.L., and Byers, V.S. Transfer of Tolerance to Mice by IgG From Humans Desensitized to Poison Oak. Ms. submitted, 1987.

Stehr-Green, P., Hoffman, R., Webb, K., Evans, R.G., Knutsen, A., Schramm, W., Staake, J., Gibson, B., and Steinberg, K. Health Effects of Long-Term Exposure to 2378-TCDD. Chemosphere 16:2089-2094, 1987.

Stehr-Green, P., Andrews, J.S., Hoffman, R., Webbs, K., and Schramm, W. An Overview of the Missouri Dioxin Study. Arch Environ Heal 43:174-177, 1988.

Trowbridge, J.P., and Walker, M. The Yeast Syndrome. New York, Bantam Books, 1986.

Upton, A.C., and Goldstein, B.D. Human Health and the Environment: Some Research Needs. Report of the Third Task Force for Research Planning in Environmental Health Science. NIH Publication No. 86-1277, 1984.

IV

ARE THE LOCAL VIOLATIONS REAL?

Chapter Outline

The People You Know

As a consultant, I find myself spending considerable time out in the field. I enjoy working on location, observing and learning while experiencing the up-to-date, "hands-on" techniques. Theory is necessary, because it provides direction for our research; however, knowing and understanding the people and their exposure to chemical hazards in the workplace on a first hand basis is essential. This chapter contains examples from my own experience of work-related exposures to chemical patches.

Ruben Was Afraid

Recently, I had the privilege of working with a meat packing plant. Management expressed repeatedly that their main interest was to save immediate cash. They had hired a fine young comptroller who was to count and save pennies. He was less than cooperative when I made several inquiries about chemical products being used and their insurance coverage. Rumor had it that five partners each owned approximately 20% of the company. Their salaries and extra benefits were not discussed specifically, but it was inferred that they were more than comfortable. In addition, in the previous year each partner enjoyed *a bonus* of between $250,000 and $300,000. They had watched their "pennies" well.

Ruben, the clean-up supervisor at the meat packing plant, and his five helpers were exceptionally hard working men and appeared to be very conscientious. The cleaning program began with the scrape-up of the meat and fat scraps. Next, equipment and the floors were washed with hot water and steam. The stainless steel equipment and floors then were sprayed with a mixture of chemicals from containers that specifically stated: DO NOT MIX WITH ANY OTHER CHEMICAL MATERIAL. The chemical components used are quite common in the meat processing industry. Those chemicals consist of a potassium hydroxide solution (lye) and a pesticide that included a sodium hypochlorite solution. This material was sprayed on all of the equipment, including the flexible conveyor belts, and allowed to stand while the men took an evening dinner break. Following the break, the area was rinsed down again with hot water and steam. The animal fat and the multiple chemical mixture were not totally water soluble, however, and a problem appeared. Once dry, the stainless steel equipment had a heavy whitish-gray, water spotted film on it. It was obvious that it was not clean. Later, the clean-up crew wiped down all of the equipment with oil-covered rags. This gave the equipment a shiny wet look so the dirty-looking film was less noticeable.

The truth is, in no way could another coat of oil make that equipment cleaner, but when people walk in, everything looks shiny, clean to them! When I asked about the oil treatment and the EPA or USDA inspectors, I was told "They know all processing plants have this problem, so they look the other way." This residue found on the equipment was not only unclean, it was the residue from deadly chemicals found in the mixture that had been sprayed on the equipment daily.

Later that evening, Ruben used a nontoxic, nonhazardous, USDA-approved cleaner that I suggested he try. Not only did it clean the difficult areas, but it also removed the "impossible film." The new cleaner was 100% water soluble and rinsed off very quickly, leaving those pieces of stainless steel equipment that had been cleaned, bright and as shining as new. No oil was needed as a cover-up. We were all excited and happy!

While on break, Ruben told me about the new home he and his wife had purchased. They had worked hard and long and they had finally qualified for a mortgage. The children were so happy, his mother was so proud, and he and his wife were pleased. During the conversation, I asked Ruben if he liked the new product and he strongly affirmed that he did. "Most of all," he said, "it is so safe." He then asked, "Is it expensive?" I replied "No, especially if you take everything into consideration." Ruben said he would like to tell his boss about it, but if it was too expensive, he would be afraid to suggest it.

Several days later, I spoke to the plant superintendent who was a 20% partner and responsible for employee supervision and the acquisition of the plant chemicals. We discussed the option of a safer cleaning method and the fact that it cleaned even better than the old system, to which he agreed. Then we discussed cost. He calculated the immediate increase of dollars and replied: "That would cost me personally $1,400 per year from my bonus!" In that greed-filled moment, I recalled my first and second grade Dick and Jane reading books. The following "story" went through my head:

See Dick pound his proud chest! Oh, how strong.
See Jane count big money, then go shopping! Oh, how fun.
See daughter Sally leave in her BMW convertible! Oh, wow.
See spots appear! Oh, how sad.
See Ruben wear the CHEMICAL PATCH! Oh, poor Ruben.

Aloud, I said, "I know you are kidding my friend, let's look at the labels on the chemicals used in the mixture of your cleaning system. We need to inspect the hazardous warnings." The following cautions were listed:

DANGER

1. Causes irreversible eye damage;

2. Harmful or fatal if swallowed;

3. Causes chemical burns to the skin and body;

4. If spilled on clothing or shoes, wash clothing before reuse and throw leather shoes away;

5. Use chemical-proof protective gear:

   A. Chemical-proof rubber gloves;
   B. Chemical-proof protective splash-proof goggles;
   C. Wear chemical-proof protective clothing;
   D. Do not inhale these hazardous fumes.

6. When diluting, add to warm water slowly with continuous stirring to avoid splattering;

7. Do not allow to contaminate food, feed or water;

8. May be reactive to metal and ceramic surfaces by causing corrosion or embrittlement;

9. Respiratory / Ventilation Requirements: Use NIOSH approved self-contained breathing apparatus if product is subject to decomposition conditions.

After reading the label together, the plant managing partner said to me, "It still costs too much; I don't want to discuss it. But, maybe I can get

Ruben and the boys some safety glasses. That would cost less; besides, they have never complained. After all, I did post the MSDS (Material Safety Data Sheet) in the work area, and the labels are on the chemical containers."

My immediate mental questions were:

- CAN RUBEN READ AND COMPREHEND TECHNICAL, SCIENTIFIC DATA?

- DOES RUBEN HAVE A THOROUGH UNDERSTANDING OF SCIENCE AND CHEMISTRY?

- DOES RUBEN KNOW THE POSSIBLE CONSEQUENCES OF THE "CHEMICAL PATCH" TO HIMSELF AND HIS CHILDREN (see Chapter 3)?

- IF RUBEN CAN READ AND CAN UNDERSTAND ALL OF THE INFORMATION, CAN HE TAKE THE CHANCE OF LOSING HIS JOB BY COMPLAINING ABOUT THE HAZARDS OF THE PRODUCTS HE MUST USE DAILY IN HIS WORK?

As I slowly walked out to my car, I felt that I had really created a mess. I thought, "How can I go back to the basics of this issue?" As I sat there in the car for a few reflective moments, I recalled several nights before when we had all worked together cleaning. Then I became more concerned.

1. If the men on the clean-up crew had been in the FEDERALLY REQUIRED protective gear, they would have probably been able to work 15 minutes, then had to take a 45 minute break, work another 15 minutes then another 45 minute break, throughout the evening. If this were the case and they were in compliance with the law, the supervising partner would have spent much more than the extra $1,400 per year he was worried about, relative to the increase in labor costs.

2. The "dirty film" on the equipment which had to be hidden with a hand rubbed coat of oil was actually an accumulation of deadly chemical residue on the food processing equipment, day after day, month after month.

3. The processing rooms were so steam-filled that it was very difficult to see or

breath with ease. To wear protective goggles or any breathing equipment would only complicate the men's work task.

4. The chemical mixture that was airborne via the sprayers is the same material that causes irreversible eye damage, is harmful or fatal if swallowed, causes chemical burns to the skin and internal tissues, and requires respiratory ventilation.

5. All evening, my clothes were wet from the airborne, chemical-filled, spray and steam.

6. Then I recalled that none of us had the proper safety gear that night. There were no approved, self-contained breathing apparatuses, no goggles, etc. What a fool I was, tired, soaking wet, and contaminated. We all had on a wet, full body CHEMICAL PATCH.

As I drove down the highway toward home that night, many thoughts continued to cycle through my mind. I tried not to become too personally involved, to keep the happenings in proper perspective. I rationalized:

I AM NOT THE OWNER.
I AM NOT AN INSPECTOR.
I AM NOT AN ENFORCEMENT OFFICER.
I AM NOT THE CHEMICAL SALESMAN.

I AM A CONSULTANT.
I GIVE ADVICE.
TODAY MY ADVICE WAS NOT ACCEPTED, AND YET, I FEEL SOMEWHAT RESPONSIBLE.

SHARE MY HAUNTING QUESTIONS WITH ME:

THE PREMISE: **It is a violation of Federal law to use these products in a manner inconsistent with the printed labels.**

1. Who is ultimately responsible to enforce the proper use of these hazardous chemical materials?

2. Who actually breaks the law?
   The government agents?
   The general employer?
   The company?
   All of the individual owners of the company?
   The plant supervisor?
   The comptroller?
   Ruben?

3. Would Ruben give his life to keep his job?

4. Can anyone help Ruben?

5. How many "Rubens" do you know?

6. Are you afraid to admit that you know someone like Ruben?

7. Are you a "Ruben" yourself?

8. Would you help Ruben if you could?

9. Is this chain of questions disturbing to you? I hope so.

We must learn to help each other and live together so we are not silently forced to die together.

Sometimes we wear a harmful CHEMICAL PATCH because we are afraid to speak up.

* * * * *

Self-Gratification and the Decision Makers

A few months ago, we were asked to evaluate the safety practices of a chain of ice cream stores. One of their specific problems involved the cleaning of a build-up of protein on the stainless steel vats in which the ice cream mix was processed. A second issue included problems with the drain system. The animal fat, protein, and some of the other ingredients found in the ice cream product have a tendency to clog the plumbing system. Consequently, every two to three days, strong acid or alkaline based drain cleaners had to be used to break loose the animal fat, protein, and ice cream mix to allow the congested disposal drains to function properly. Two or three days later, the same process would have to be repeated. The concern of the company leaders was two-fold: 1) the specific chemicals they were using were hazardous and were especially risky when used around food products; and 2) they were being fined by the local waste water treatment plant for the disposal of chemically hazardous waste water into the local sewer system. An additional problem was the effect of the strong chemicals on the plumbing: drain lines would have to be replaced once, or as often as twice a year. Needless to say, the local plumbers were not very happy about working on such a deadly and contaminated project.

A new USDA-approved, nontoxic, nonhazardous, biodegradable product that was more efficient and safe was offered, but it did not include in its price structure season tickets for management to attend the local professional football games. The hazardous CHEMICAL PATCH may be worn at the expense of the employees, and for the sake of the self-gratification of the decision makers.

* * * * *

The Chemical Patch and the Innocent

Last year, the local newspapers published information stating that a large dairy corporation had agreed to pay over a quarter of a million dollars to settle water pollution charges, according to the U.S. Environmental Protection Agency. The dairy also agreed to a series of environmental audits at all of its plants located throughout several states.

Another dairy processing plant inquired about a safe product for cleaning their processing equipment. They were using strong chemical solutions consisting of potassium hydroxide, sodium hypochlorite, phosphoric acid, and sodium hydroxide. First, a strong acid solution was used in an attempt to clean the vats and tanks, to break down the protein build-up on the stainless steel equipment. Second, a strong alkaline solution was used on the vats and tanks in an attempt to neutralize the first treatment process. Because chemical residues from these treatments often give a distasteful, tainted flavor to the milk products, milk is used as a final rinse, to absorb and help overcome the chemically tainted taste.

Then a better cleaning system was tried. The better cleaning system worked very well, without any chemical taste problems! A considerable problem was then introduced. The dairy processing plant did not own the equipment; it was procured on a long-term lease. The company that held the long-term lease on the equipment also brokered the harsh cleaning chemicals that were being used. The long-term lease stated that no other company could provide cleaners to be used on the leased equipment.

My advice as a consultant: The leasing, chemical brokering company should spend some research dollars and come up with their own safe cleaning material. It is possible. There are safer and better cleaners available on the market as illustrated in our brief trial. Whether the milk products are being used for infants, through public school lunch programs, or by adults who like milk in their coffee, we all have a right to safe food. Both the consumer and the employees need protection from the direct or indirect hazardous CHEMICAL PATCH.

* * * * *

The Hazards of Ignorance and Carelessness

This past year a friend of mine, Elmer Neff, President of Green Hope, Inc., shared an article with me. Published in the DENVER POST, the large bold headline read: FUMES FELL 11 WORKERS CLEANING HOTEL KITCHEN. The eleven workers were cleaning a kitchen in an Aurora, Colorado hotel. When they mixed bleach and ammonia, they were overcome by fumes from cleaning chemicals and rushed to the hospital, according to the local fire department.

Upon arrival at the medical center, they were treated with oxygen. The hazardous CHEMICAL PATCH can be worn due to ignorance or carelessness.

* * * * *

Sandy and the Fatal Patch

A tragic story was relayed to me a few months ago by Lorettann Keith, President of Enviro Balance International and a relative of the victim. In the state of Kansas, a number of restaurants, senior citizen homes, and nonprofit organizations were using a very strong cleaning solution. It contained buloxyethanol, sodium hydroxide, sodium lauryl ether sulfate, and sodium xylene sulfonate. The cleaning solution worked fast and well, but its label very clearly included the following:

WARNING

- For industrial use only
- Do not mix with anything but water
- Use only with adequate ventilation
- This material will etch aluminum
- Do not use on painted surfaces
- Avoid contamination of food

The label clearly stated these DANGERS:

- Causes severe chemical burns
- Eye contact may cause blindness
- Harmful contact may not cause immediate pain
- Harmful or fatal if swallowed
- Harmful if inhaled
- Protect mucus membranes, eyes and skin from contact with this product and its use solutions
- Wear chemical-proof rubber gloves
- Wear chemical-proof, splash-proof goggles/full face shield
- If exposed, call a poison control center and physician immediately

According to Ms. Keith, Sandy was a young newly-wed who was working as a waitress at one of the local restaurants that used this product. It was being used for general clean-up including kitchen, stoves, and floors. Sandy was given the cleaning materials to use for her cleaning tasks, day after day.

One day, Sandy became seriously ill and was examined by a doctor, only to discover she was in the process of a miscarriage. The doctor discovered a strange irregularity. The egg had been fertilized but there was no specifically defined fetus, and the activity had abnormally located on the outer side of the uterus. The placenta had begun to grow very rapidly, and the fertilized egg, non-fetus placenta matter was malignant. The couple and their families were heart broken. Sandy was required to go through chemotherapy. The couple did not know how long she might live, and if she lived, if they would ever be able to have children.

The same spontaneous aborting happened to at least three other young ladies in this same general area of the country, leading the doctors to speculate about a common cause. Did the ingredients in this product cause cancer and possible miscarriage? Sandy's response later was, "I had no idea what I was given to use, nor how dangerous it was. None of us was ever warned to take precautions or to use protective gear. I just knew it smelled very strong." It was assumed that the hazardous CHEMICAL PATCH was fatal to the unborn baby.

Please be observant of those around you. There are "Rubens" in your life who are afraid to speak up for their safety. Be aware of those who naively justify their "ignorance" at the risk of others, and those who take payment or favors "under the table" and thus intentionally benefit themselves at the risk of others and our environment. Try to assist those who simply find themselves in a position with no training; help them know that they need not wear the FATAL PATCH.

V

ENVIRONMENTAL CRIME AND PUNISHMENT

Chapter Outline

Definitions and Warnings

The terms "hazardous" waste and "toxic" materials are identified broadly as petroleum products, paints and solvents, lead, cyanide, DDT, printing inks, acids, pesticides, ammonium compounds, PCB, and other chemical products. Today, for example, you could walk into any hotel or commercial building and legitimately be concerned about all of the "hazardous" or "toxic" compounds that had just been used for cleaning purposes. For example, the tub in your hotel room could actually become a CHEMICAL BATH PATCH.

Following Chapter VII, the gray edged pages display some of the harmful and hazardous chemicals listed by OSHA, EPA, and California Proposition 65. From now on, you may use this list to check the ingredients in products you use at home or at work. Read all labels and warnings and abide by the advice. Doing so may save your life. This chapter contains information to help you understand how some individuals have violated the environmental warnings and laws, have been found guilty of a crime, and have been punished.

Violating the Law

The task of developing environmental protection rules, trends, and laws has expanded dramatically over the past few years. The 1980s included an increase in environmental laws, rules, and regulations. Incidents during the 1990s demonstrate the expanded and sometimes harsh enforcement of those laws, rules, and regulations.

These same environmental laws, rules, and regulations that many businesses once ignored are now being implemented to pound away at violators. From small family-owned businesses to major corporations, all are feeling the blows. Compared to a decade ago, the high dollar fines and penalties are almost unbelievable and represent the major pressure. Chief executives and responsible employees are being held personally accountable as their companies break the law.

Each year as the federal legislature and various state governing bodies meet, the penalizing amount of potential fines continues to increase. One big change is that the violations that were once dealt with solely through administrative actions, are now SUBJECT TO CRIMINAL PUNISHMENT.

What does it take to get the message across? The district attorneys and governing bodies are trying to demonstrate that environmental laws are not to be ignored, nor treated as just a cost of doing business. We are now witnessing the criminal prosecution of many high-level corporate officers and many of their responsible employees. The following represents specific examples of consequences of environmental crime:

- Polluting the water: up to 30 years in jail and fines of $1 million.

- Unsuitable hazardous waste handling, storage, transportation, or disposal: up to 3 years in prison and fines of up to $250,000 per day, per violation.

- Failure to report a leaking underground tank: up to 1 year in jail and $10,000 per day for failure to take corrective action.

- Polluting the air: up to 1 year in jail and a fine of $25,000 per day, per violation.

- Failure to prepare a specific pro forma or business plan for handling hazardous waste and/or not reporting a release: up to 1 year in jail and fines of $25,000 per day.

For most of these federal or state laws, persons may be charged individually for crimes committed by their company. If an individual person or persons have corporate responsibility or authority to correct or prevent a violation and they fail to do so, they can be held personally liable.

Based upon experience and knowledge concerning criminal law, we might assume that an act is criminal only if it demonstrates wrong or evil intent. One is presumed innocent until proven guilty. The guilt must include the intent to commit that crime. For the prosecution of an environmental crime however, proving such intent is not necessary for conviction. PROSECUTORS ARE DECLARING ENVIRONMENTAL OFFENSES AS PUBLIC WELFARE CRIMES, AND THESE CRIMES ARE PUNISHABLE WITHOUT PROOF OF CRIMINAL INTENT OR NEGLIGENCE.

It should be noted here that these crimes may also be considered as strict liability issues for which no defense is possible even if the act was an accident. For example, it has been declared that an illegal disposal of a hazardous chemical may be punishable without proof of any degree of fault or wrongful intent.

How do you feel about the following legal leverage? The declaration of "aiding and abetting" is another powerful avenue to reach corporate officers and employees who are not directly involved in illegal acts. Incorporated in this legal principle is the assumption: If you have knowledge of any illegal conduct and give substantial assistance or any encouragement to the person committing the act, you may be held liable. Failure to abide by environmental laws can result in serious and costly consequences for individual businesses as well as the persons conducting the businesses. The following list includes the various rules and agencies to which your business or corporation may be accountable on a federal level:

Federal Statutes and Executive Orders

1. Asbestos Hazard Emergency Response Act 15 U.S.C. § 2641, et seq.
2. Atomic Energy Act of 1954, 42 U.S.C. § 2014
3. Clean Air Act, 42 U.S.C. § 7041, et seq.
4. Clean Water Act, 33 U.S.C. §§ 1251-1387
5. Coastal Barrier Resources Act of 1982, 16 U.S.C. § 3501, et seq.
6. Coastal Zone Management Act, 16 U.S.C. §§ 1451-1464
7. Comprehensive Environmental Response, Compensation and Liability Act (CERCLA), 42 U.S.C. § 9601, et seq.
8. Emergency Planning and Community Right-to-Know Act (SARA), 42 U.S.C. § 11001, et seq.
9. Endangered Species Act, 16 U.S.C. 1531, § 7
10. Farmland Protection Policy Act of 1961, 7 U.S.C. § 4201, et seq.

11. Federal Insecticide, Fungicide and Rodenticide Act (FIFRA), 7 U.S.C. § 136, et seq.
12. Federal Land Policy and Management Act of 1976 (FLPMA) 43 U.S.C.A. §§ 1701-1784
13. Fishery Conservation and Management Act, 16 U.S.C. § 1811-1862
14. Forest and Rangeland Renewable Resources Planning Act of 1974 (FRRRPA) 16 U.S.C.A. §§ 1600-1614
15. Forest and Rangeland Renewable Resources Research Act of 1978 (FRRRPA) 16 U.S.C.A. §§ 1641-1647
16. Hazard Communication Act (HAZCOM), (OSHA) 29 C.F.R. 1910.1200 et seq.
17. Hazardous Materials Transportation Act, 49 U.S.C. § 1801 et seq.
18. Low Level Radioactive Waste Act, 42 U.S.C. § 2021 et seq.
19. Marine Protection, Research, and Sanctuaries Act of 1972 (MPRSA) 33 U.S.C.A. §§ 1401-1445
20. Medical Waste Tracking Act, 42 U.S.C. § 6992
21. Mining and Mineral Resources Research Institute Act of 1984 (MMRRIA) 30 U.S.C.A. §§ 1221-1230

22. Multiple-Use Sustained-Yield Act of 1960 (MUSYA), Renewable Surface Resources of National Forests, 16 U.S.C.A. §§ 528-531
23. National Environmental Policy Act (NEPA), 42 U.S.C. § 4321, et seq.
24. National Historic Preservation Act, 16 U.S.C. 470(f), § 106
25. Nuclear Waste Policy Act of 1982, 42 U.S.C. §§ 10101-10270
26. Pollution Prevention Act of 1990, 42 U.S.C.A. §§ 13101-13109
27. Radiation Control Act, 42 U.S.C. 201, 236b, et seq.
28. Radon Abatement Act of 1988, 15 U.S.C. § 2601
29. Railroad Accident Reports 45 U.S.C. § 438
30. Railroad Safety Act of 1970 45 U.S.C. § 421, et seq.
31. Refuse Act, 33 U.S.C. § 401, et seq.
32. Renewable Resources Extension Act of 1978 (RREA) 16 U.S.C.A. §§ 1671-1676
33. Safety of Public Water Systems, Public Health Service Act (Title XIV) 42 U.S.C.A. §§ 300f-300j-26
34. Solid Waste Disposal Act 42 U.S.C.A. §§ 6901-6987

35. Surface Mining Control and Reclamation Act of 1977 (SMCRA) 30 U.S.C.A. §§ 1201-1211, 1231-1328
36. Threatened Fish and Wildlife Act, 50 C.F.R. § 227 et seq.
37. Toxic Substances Control Act (TSAC), 15 U.S.C. § 2601, et seq.
38. Wild and Scenic Rivers Act, 16 U.S.C. §§ 1271-1257
39. Wood Residue Utilization Act of 1980 (WRUA) 16 U.S.C.A. §§ 1681-1687

Federal Agencies Issuing Regulations

1. Agriculture Department
2. Army Corps of Engineers
3. Environmental Protection Agency (EPA)
4. Fish and Wildlife Service
5. Health and Human Services (HHS)
6. Interior Department
7. Interstate Commerce Commission (ICC)
8. Mine Safety and Health Review Commission
9. National Marine Fisheries Service/NOAA, (Dept. of Commerce)
10. Nuclear Regulatory Commission
11. Occupational Safety and Health Administration (OSHA)
12. Public Utilities Commission (PUC)
13. Transportation Department (DOT)
14. U.S. Forest Service (Dept. of Agriculture)

Remember, in addition to the Federal Statutes, Executive Orders, and the list of Federal Agencies issuing regulations, there are also individual state, county, and local agencies ready to enforce their specific areas of concern.

For many unknowing persons, good faith and the best of innocent intentions cannot be used as a defense or a shield from criminal prosecution. As public and political pressures for environmental preservation continue, criminal prosecution will grow.

It is true that environmental law enforcement involves both civil as well as criminal efforts. However, because more and more emphasis is being placed on the seriousness of environmental law, the balance of this chapter focuses on recent developments in environmental criminal law enforcement.

Expanding Prosecution

Enforcement staffs at all levels of state and federal government agencies are growing. The pace of aggressive prosecution is accelerating. The collapse of a company and the serving of prison time by corporate officers and responsible staff members are actual possibilities. It is important that the shareholders of every company, the owners of every family business, and the operators of all commercial entities take expeditious and affirmative measures to prevent criminal violations of environmental laws.

During the early 1980s, environmental statutes contained weak criminal provisions and the federal government seldom prosecuted violators.

Government records indicate that the Department of Justice originally established the ENVIRONMENTAL CRIMES UNIT in 1982, with only three attorneys on the staff. By 1987, the unit had employed 28 full-time attorneys. Since 1987, the unit has continued to grow, doubling its size again and again. Today, the task of the ENVIRONMENTAL CRIMES SECTION (ECS) is to pursue actively and prosecute the criminal infringements of environmental law.

As expected, during the 1980s, the criminal provisions of the law were expanded and strengthened for four major legislative pieces:

RESOURCE CONSERVATION AND RECOVERY ACT (RCRA)[1]

CLEAN WATER ACT[2]

COMPREHENSIVE ENVIRONMENTAL RESPONSE AND LIABILITY ACT (CERCLA)[3] and

---

1 See 42 U.S.C. § 6928(d).

2 See 33 U.S.C. § 1319(d).

3 See 42 U.S.C. § 9603(b).

CLEAN AIR ACT (1990 felony provisions were added).[4]

Thus, it is generally assumed that the severity of penalties will continue to increase beyond the 1990s.

Environmental Protection Agency (EPA)

Not only has the severity of penalties increased during the 1990s, but the number of criminal investigations has also increased. From this we can speculate that prosecution will be encouraged and will heighten during the next decade. It has been reported that the ENVIRONMENTAL PROTECTION AGENCY (EPA) has greatly expanded the size of its force and their capabilities relative to its Criminal Enforcement Division. Government reports indicate that in 1991, the ENVIRONMENTAL PROTECTION AGENCY increased its staff of criminal investigators from 50 to 65. This was followed by a plan to increase the number to over 200 investigators under the Pollution

---

4 See 42 U.S.C. § 7413(c).

Prosecution Act.[5] During this same general period of time, the EPA developed an extensive computer network which enabled the Agency to follow the status of any criminal investigation, involving any business or company nationwide. This computer system allows the ENVIRONMENTAL PROTECTION AGENCY to monitor all enforcement activity proceedings in any given city, county, or state.

Originally, all major environmental criminal probes pursued by the EPA were handled out of Washington, DC. Today, many individual United States Attorneys' Offices (USAO's) located all across the country, actively prosecute environmental criminal cases. In addition to the Federal EPA prosecutions, states have initiated active programs of legal proceedings against environmental law violations. The leading state prosecutions are conducted in California, New York, New Jersey[6] and

---

[5] 42 U.S.C. § 4321. The Pollution Prosecution Act also increases the number of civil investigators and establishes the National Training Institute to train federal, state, and local lawyers, inspectors, and technical experts in the enforcement of federal environmental laws.

[6] See "Toxic Waste SWAT Teams: Enforcement's Front Lines," Environment Today (May 1991), pp. 3, 19, 21.

Pennsylvania.[7] Various criminal task forces exchange investigation information, assist in criminal enforcement and cooperate in sponsoring training for state and local prosecutors of these crimes. Obviously, the federal level of enforcement has been successful at obtaining help for their task from both the local and the state enforcement divisions.[8]

Are All Businesses Liable?

The diversity of businesses in the United States which have been criminally prosecuted is sweeping and very extensive. The scope ranges from meat packing plants to oil companies, dairies to chemical manufacturers, and from custodial companies to food producers and processors. Some of the well-known corporations that have been found

---

7 See address by former EPA Assistant Administrator for Enforcement of Environmental Laws, Washington, D.C. (April 19, 1990) at 14.

8 Supra, Note 7 at 7. State officials are also more likely initially to discover criminal offenses.

guilty of criminal behavior relative to environmental laws include:[9]

Exxon
International Paper
Keebler
Marathon Oil
Nabisco
Ocean Spray
Orkin Exterminating
Pennwalt
Pillsbury
United Technologies

---

[9] See United States v. Exxon Corporation and Exxon Shipping Co., No. A90-15-CR (D. Alaska 1991) (guilty plea); United States v. International Paper, CR-91-00051-B (D. Me. 1991) (guilty plea); United States v. Keebler, No. 86-0401 (D. Colo. 1986) (guilty plea); United States v. Marathon Oil Co., RT 91-68 Cr. (S.D. Ind. 1991) (guilty plea); United States v. Nabisco, CR-86-41T (W.D. Wash. 1986) (guilty plea); United States v. Ocean Spray, No. 85-909 (D. Mass. 1986) (guilty plea); United States v. Orkin Exterminating Co., Inc., 688 F. Supp. 223 (W.D. Va. 1988) (denying defendant's motion to dismiss indictment); United States v. Pennwalt, CR-88-55T (W.D. Wash. 1988) (guilty plea); United States v. The Pillsbury Company No. 90-05020-01-CR-SW-4. (W.D. Mo. 1990) (guilty plea); United States v. United Technologies, No. 2:91 Cr. 00028, (D. Conn. 1991) (guilty plea); United States v. Weyerhaeuser, CR-90-00019 (W.D. Wash 1991) (guilty plea); United States v. W.R. Grace, No. 88-2412K (D. Mass. 1987) (consent decree).

Weyerhaeuser
W.R. Grace

How do corporations and individuals fare in this criminal nightmare? The previous pages have emphasized the fact that environmental prosecutions have focused on corporate offenders. That focus reflects only one part of the story. In cases involving various businesses and corporations, it is the policy of the Department of Justice to target the highest level corporate personnel and the decision-making employees. The record reflects that the Department of Justice has pursued the individual offenders two out of every three cases, while the corporations are prosecuted in one out of three situations. The reason for this policy was stated very bluntly by Joseph G. Block, former Chief of the Department of Justice, Environmental Crimes Section: "...Jail is one cost of business you cannot pass on to the consumer."[10] There are two issues here. First, often the fines are just added in as a cost of business to the consumer by way of the increased cost of product. Second, though corporate fines may be a business write-off, personal jail time is not.

---

[10] Remarks of Joseph G. Block, former Chief, D.O.J. Environmental Crimes Section, Criminal Enforcement of Environmental Laws, Washington, D.C. (April 19, 1990).

Major Increases of Penalty

During the past few years, the fines for RESOURCE CONSERVATION AND RECOVERY (RCRA) violations have escalated rapidly. The fines may now exceed one million dollars. For example, United Technologies paid $3 million under a plea bargain agreement, as payment for unlawful disposal of hazardous waste.[11]

The federal sentencing standards, which became effective on November 1, 1987, are contained in the United States Sentencing Commission Guidelines Manual[12] and have had a strong impact on punishment for environmental criminal violations. The purpose of the Guidelines Manual was to remove differences and uncertainty in criminal sentencing for federal violations. It was an attempt to have a fair balance or consistent impact from the

---

[11] See United States v. United Technologies Corp., No. 2:91 CR 00028 (TEC) (D. Conn. 1991).

[12] These rules, which became effective on November 1, 1987, are contained in the U.S. Sentencing Commission Guidelines Manual published by an eight-member commission established by the Comprehensive Crime Control Act of 1984, 18 U.S.C. § 3551 et seq. and 28 U.S.C. §991 et seq. The guidelines are reprinted at 18 U.S.C.A. app. at 62 (West Supp. 1989).

punishment assigned to similarly situated criminal defendants. The sentencing standard contained specific provisions relative to environmental offenses and established minimum sentences which all judges must impose for such crimes. The Guidelines Manual ABOLISHES PAROLE and limits the instances for which a suspended sentence can be imposed. Therefore, individuals convicted of environmental crimes will now usually serve the entire length of their sentence. For example, in 1983, the average individual penalized for environmental crimes was sentenced to a total of 11 years in prison, but only served five years of imprisonment. By 1991 however, persons guilty of the same kinds of violations were sentenced to an average total of approximately 25 years in prison and the time served averaged 23 years.[13]

THE PROPORTIONAL LENGTH OF SENTENCES HAS ALSO INCREASED RELATIVE TO THE 1987 UNITED STATES SENTENCING COMMISSION GUIDELINES MANUAL. BEFORE 1987, FOR EXAMPLE, THE LONGEST PERIOD OF PUNISHMENT IMPOSED FOR A WETLANDS VIOLATION UNDER THE CLEAN WATER ACT, WAS *7 DAYS IN JAIL.*

---

13 See Memorandum from Peggy Hutchins to Neil Cartusciello, Chief, Environmental Crimes Section, <u>Statistics FY 83 Through FY 91</u> (October 10, 1991).

NOW THAT GUIDELINES MANUAL PRISON TERM IS *27 MONTHS.*[14]

Must the Court Prove Me Wrong?

Generally speaking, the felony provisions of the major federal environmental statutes all require the government to prove the defendant's criminal knowledge. This burden of proof is much more simply accomplished than the standard system relative to the burden of proof with traditional crimes. Remember, environmental criminal laws are considered to be health and welfare statutes, designed to protect the general public. Prosecutors of environmental crimes, therefore, are required only to prove the declared violator's intent to commit the act charged, versus his specific intent to violate the law. Simply stated: "Did you do it?" It puts no weight on questions such as the following: Did you mean to break the law? Did you even know you did it? Did you know you might be breaking the law when you did it? Did you do it purposefully to break the law? Think about this example. Your car has a slight drip of oil or even antifreeze. In some states such a drip may be against the law. Now ask all of

---

[14] 897 F.2d 524 (3d Cir. 1990).

the above questions of yourself. If this illustration were a true fact, all we need to prove is that you knew that the car you were driving actually did have a small drip. YES. The law has been broken. This is very different from proving the specific intent to violate the law. Keep in mind, where the violation prohibits "knowing" conduct (relative to health and welfare laws), the government prosecution may prove the defendant's (your) knowledge simply by demonstrating that your conduct was not done by accident or mistake.

Consider this example: Under RCRA, the ENVIRONMENTAL PROSECUTOR NEED NOT SHOW: (1) that the defendant knew that the disposed material was "hazardous waste"; or (2) that the defendant knew he lacked the necessary permits for such disposal; or (3) that the defendant consciously intended to violate the law.[15]

Here are three common problems. How would you handle them? Even though household waste is still exempt under RCRA, suppose for a moment your home is a business. What are the chances you might be breaking the law?

1. You have a case of old toilet bowl cleaner that is very caustic. You are

---

[15] See e.q., United States v. Baytank Houston, Inc., 934 F.2d 608 (5th Cir. 1991).

cleaning out the garage and you need to dispose of it today. Since it was designed to use in a toilet bowl, why not dump it all down the stool and flush it? Is there any potential problem with the city water system? Is there any chance of breaking the law?

2. You have an old battery and you need to dump the acid out so you can put the old case in the dumpster. Where do you put the acid? Down the sewer? On the ground behind the garage? How about the law? What if you do not know of any legal restrictions?

3. You just overhauled the boat motor, and you have a gallon and a half of very dirty solvent. You need to get rid of it because it is a fire hazard. Do you become a "midnight dumper"? Can you put it down the floor drain? Are you tempted to break a health and welfare law? What might the consequences be if you were caught? Do you know who to call or how to dispose of unwanted hazardous waste?

Difficult Legal Doctrines

In conjunction with the reduced burden of proof, there are several powerful, developing legal doctrines. These are applicable to:

1. Individuals: corporate officers and responsible corporate employees;

2. Organizations: organized businesses, partnerships, and corporations;

3. Subsidiary company liability.

Each of these specific doctrines facilitate the government's ability to prove environmental crimes.

Under the RESPONSIBLE CORPORATE OFFICER DOCTRINE responsible persons may be held criminally liable for the conduct of their subordinates. Responsible persons include: (A) any corporate officers, or in many cases responsible decision-making employees who are directly responsible in the corporate management scheme, and those persons who are responsible for specific conduct that may be in question; and/or (B) any corporate officer or responsible, decision-making employee who knew of an improper activity or knew that a questionable event was occurring.[16] While the definition of a "person" subject to criminal penalties under RCRA does not include "responsible corporate officers," both the Clean Water Act and the Clean Air Act definitions of "persons" include these terms.[17]

The 1991 case of United States v. Brittain[18] clearly demonstrates the potential expanse of the RESPONSIBLE CORPORATE OFFICER DOCTRINE. In Brittain, the court noted that relative to the authoritative pronouncement under the Clean Water Act definition of person, "a 'responsible corporate officer' would not have to 'willfully or negligently' cause a violation. Rather, the willfulness or negligence of the actor would be imputed to him by virtue of his position of responsibility."[19] This is very broad language which indicates that some courts interpret the RESPONSIBLE CORPORATE OFFICER DOCTRINE to be one of imputed or "at fault"

---

16 This doctrine originated in two U.S. Supreme Court cases; Unites States v. Park, 421 U.S. 658 (1975) and United States v. Dotterweich, 320 U.S. 277 (1943).

17 33 U.S.C. § 1319(a)(6); 42 U.S.C. § 7413(c)(6).

18 931 F.2d 1413 (10th Cir.1991).

19 Id. at 1419.

knowledge, which relieves the government from the burden of proving the officer's or responsible employee's actual knowledge.

The second doctrine, which applies to corporations, is called the COLLECTIVE KNOWLEDGE DOCTRINE. Incorporated within this doctrine, the government may simply establish corporate criminal liability by demonstrating that (1) certain employees are engaged in the required and/or necessary conduct, while at the same time, (2) other employees may have possessed the required knowledge, even though no one employee, (3) both acted in a criminal manner and (4) had sufficient criminal intent to commit the violation.[20] To complicate the problem for the defendants, (responsible employees, officers, etc.), add to the above facts the traditional rule that a corporation may be held criminally liable for the acts of an employee, regardless of his position. This is specifically true if the employee was acting within the scope of his duties and for the benefit of the corporation. Under all of these circumstances, the DOCTRINE OF COLLECTIVE KNOWLEDGE significantly enhances the environmental prosecutor's ability to prove environmental crimes.

---

[20] See United States v. Bank of New England, N.A., 821 F.2d 844 (1st Cir. 1987).

Consider now the third developing doctrine of law. An increasing number of cases indicate that the environmental prosecutor's burden of proving corporate knowledge is becoming even simpler. In certain circumstances, under SUBSIDIARY COMPANY DOCTRINE, criminal liability may be imputed and the corporate parent found at fault. This trend was initiated through a line of civil cases which determined that the conduct of a subsidiary could be attributed to its parent corporation. For example, the parent company,[21] Exxon Corporation, was recently declared criminally liable under the agency theory for the oil spill in Prince William's Sound, even though the act was committed by Exxon Shipping Company, a separate corporation, but Exxon Corporation's subsidiary.

---

[21] See United States v. Kayser-Roth Corp., 724 F. Supp. 15 (D.R.I. 1989), aff'd, 910 F.2d 24 (1st Cir. 1990), United States v. Nicolet, 712 F. Supp. 1193 (E.D. Pa. 1989); Rockwell Int'l Corp. v. IU Int'l Corp., 702 F. Supp. 1384 (N.D. Ill. 1988); Idaho v. Bunker Hill Co., 635 F. Supp. 665 (D. Idaho 1986); but see, Joslyn Manufacturing Co. v. T.L. James Co., 696 F. Supp. 222 (W.D. La. 1988), aff'd, 893 F.2d 80 (5th Cir. 1990).

Paid to Squeal

Obviously, not all changes and developments can be anticipated. There are, however, several trends that are being accentuated during the 1990s. One is the increased use of citizens' awards to encourage the reporting of environmental crimes. Today the SARA Citizens Award Program serves as an example of a motivational tool by providing for payments of up to $10,000, for information leading to the successful prosecution of any person violating the criminal provisions of the Superfund law.[22] It has also been suggested that the lower burden of proof required for prosecuting health and welfare violations will encourage prosecutors to use environmental statutes to punish conduct not traditionally associated with the environment, hazardous chemical use, or pollution violations. One rumor suggests this trend and strategy of a health and welfare crime be used relative to the drug industry.

---

[22] 42 U.S.C. § 9609(d).

What if I Say, "I'm Sorry"?

The United States Sentencing Commission Guidelines Manual[23] provides examples of contributing elements that prosecutors should consider in determining whether to proceed with an environmental criminal case. When a corporation finds itself potentially the target of a criminal prosecution, it would be wise if it: (1) makes a voluntary, timely, and complete disclosure to pertinent government authorities, (2) cooperates fully with the investigators, and (3) has an extensive environmentally conforming program in place, preferably prior to the alleged violation.

Under the above ideal circumstances, the environmental prosecutors may, in certain instances, cease to pursue actively certain criminal charges, or in unusual instances, decline to prosecute altogether. It is also suggested by the Guidelines Manual that, in determining whether or not to prosecute, the prosecuting attorneys should study the (1)

---

[23] These rules, which became effective on November 1, 1987, are contained in the U.S. Sentencing Commission Guidelines Manual published by an eight-member commission established by the Comprehensive Crime Control Act of 1984, 18 U.S.C. § 3551 et seq. and 28 U.S.C. § 991 et seq. The guidelines are reprinted at 18 U.S.C.A. app. at 62 (West Supp. 1989).

pervasiveness or far-reaching effects of the criminal behavior involved, (2) any internal disciplinary action that may have followed the violation, and (3) the extent of any follow-up compliance effort.

Beware of another element. The ENVIRONMENTAL PROTECTION AGENCY (EPA) has enormous discretion to define the "condition of compliance." This is a powerful enforcement weapon. By case law, the EPA has already determined that a condition of non-compliance justifying a continued negative or punishable listing may include not only regulatory violations, but also a company's "bad corporate attitude."[24]

---

[24] In the Matter of Valmont Industries, Inc., Valley Nebraska Facility, EPA Contractor Listing Docket No. 07-89-2068 (January 12, 1990).

For additional information and assistance, consider the following: THE CAMBRIDGE INSTITUTE: Thomas J. Kelley, Nancy Venable of Venable, Baeter, Howard & Civiletti: 1201 New York Ave., N.W., Suite 1000, Washington, D.C. 20005; and ENVIRONMENTAL ISSUES FOR BUSINESS OPPORTUNITIES BROKERS: Reed, Elliott Creech & Roth: 99 Alamaden Blvd., San Jose, CA 95113, as helpful examples.

So, my dear friends, I admonish you:

Keep a good attitude,
Love everybody you know,
Follow all directions carefully,
Live by the letter of the law,
Stay chemically safe, and
"Don't drink your hotel bath
water!"

VI

ARE THE CHEMICAL COMPANIES AT FAULT?

Chapter Outline

The Critics and What They Say
Examples of Label Warnings
How to Read the Manufacturing Company's Material Safety Data Sheet (MSDS)
Terms and Abbreviations Used With MSDS
Examples of MSDS Forms For Every Day Use
Dairies and Food Processing Plants
Concrete Cleaner and Degreaser
Degreaser for Restaurants and Hotels, Auto Mechanic Shops, etc.
Steam Cleaning and Car & Truck Wash

Are most chemical manufacturing companies bad? Are they at fault for all of our hazardous chemical problems? The answer is NO! This opinion of "badness" or "at fault" is very common among most people, however.

The Critics and What They Say

Some critics report that the use of various poisonous chemical components damage people's health, contaminate water resources, and injure the environmental balance in general. It has been argued that pesticides (herbicides, insecticides, fungicides, etc.), for example, cause a multitude of health problems and complications. These health conditions may include stomach and liver malfunctions, metabolic irregularities due to abnormal sugar and protein reactions, learning disabilities, the breakdown of sex hormones, deformations, cancerous growths, skin ulcerations, leukemia, abnormal blood pressure, the deterioration of memory, and various irregular psychological reactions. This list of health conditions only provides examples of maladies that may be caused by harmful, out-of-balance, or excessive use of chemicals.

Many activists point out that, in some way, we are all exposed when chemicals are applied. People may be exposed through the food they eat. Some people have pointed out that pesticides, again for example, are often applied to public buildings, homes, hospitals, school playing fields, lunch rooms and restrooms, stores, and even for food processing plant wash-downs. There are also a variety of chemical products sprayed on lawns, parks, golf courses, road right-of-ways, and on utility easements.

Have you observed various chemicals being applied to crops by aerial spraying? Have you known anyone who was chemically sensitive? What would be their recourse if, while driving or walking near a sprayed area, the chemical being sprayed triggered a reaction? This reaction, which could be mild or severe, would depend upon the sensitivity of the individual and upon the level of exposure. Then there are those persons who might not notice a problem immediately. The materials might accumulate over time. The immune system may be weakened and the negative results become apparent five to ten years later.

Other individuals will point out that use of taxpayers' dollars contributes to the use and accumulation of harmful and hazardous chemicals. For example, if toxic chemicals are being applied to road right-of-ways, public grounds, or trees on a municipal parkway, the critics would say it is being done at the expense of taxpayers' funds. Interestingly, the complaints arise from a number of interested groups ranging from the conservatives who just do not want "their money" spent that way, to persons who actually fear for a personal potential medical problem, to individuals who more generally want to preserve the perfection of the world's environmental balance.

There also has been some criticism of the government agencies to which complaints are made. Often pointed out is the frustration with how problems are handled. When objections are filed, it may take weeks or even months before a regulatory agency can test the area in question. By then it is too late to accumulate accurate data. In many instances the citizens are required to carry the burden of proof as to health, crop, water, environmental abuse, or other categories of damage.

Now, let us return to the original question: Are the chemical companies at fault? Again, NO. Chemical companies only manufacture and distribute chemical products. Then who makes the choices as to which, when, and how these "harmful" chemicals will be used? THE PUBLIC. Would the public, "WE THE PEOPLE," be willing to substitute less toxic substances even if additional research was required? What if a slightly more expensive, but safer product was available? How do you evaluate and justify long-range medical expenses? How do you adjust to human suffering? Are most companies and most people often "penny wise and pound foolish?"

What drives the chemical companies and their markets? Is it true that "WE THE PEOPLE" get what we pay for? Do you know any major companies that would continue to manufacture millions and millions of dollars worth of any inventory if there was no market for that inventory? A class in Economics 101 could discuss several principles: Supply and Demand and/or the Ever Growing Demand for an Unlimited Supply. The lesson to be learned? It is

OK to tell the manufacturers what you want. Safe, nonhazardous products are available, or with additional research could be made available. Yankee ingenuity is not dead, but hard choices must be made!

Do we have any evidence that today the chemical companies specifically comply with legal requirements? YES. But you be the judge for your own satisfaction. Study the following examples and instructions. These illustrations will serve to demonstrate how well chemical companies conform, as required by the law. Remember, "WE THE PEOPLE" do not have the luxury of avoiding responsibility by blaming the chemical companies. We make choices for which WE are responsible!

Notice, FIRST, the chemical companies are required to provide adequate warnings on each of their product labels. SECOND, they are to deliver Material Safety Data Sheets (MSDS) with each hazardous or harmful product delivered. This information is well prepared, forthright, and adequately defined according to the law. The following headings and exhibits will give us a better understanding of these specific categories. NOTICE how strong the warnings are, how methodically the Material Safety Data Sheet (MSDS) is organized, and the completeness of the safety information. We as consumers have the responsibility of reading and understanding this information about products we use. Then we can make informed, responsible decisions about continuing to use those products.

Examples of Label Warnings

I

SODIUM HYPOCHLORITE SOLUTION is a pesticide used for many applications. It is commonly used in meat packing plants, dairies, and other food processing areas to keep the bacteria count down. Here is the specific information from the label:

PRECAUTIONARY STATEMENTS

HAZARDS TO HUMANS AND DOMESTIC ANIMALS
DANGER: Corrosive, may cause severe skin and eye irritation or chemical burns to broken skin. Causes eye damage. Wear safety glasses or goggles and rubber gloves when handling this product. Wash after handling. Avoid breathing vapors. Vacate poorly ventilated areas as soon as possible. Do not return until strong odors have dissipated.

ENVIRONMENTAL HAZARDS

This pesticide is toxic to fish and aquatic organisms. Do not discharge effluent containing this product into lakes, streams, ponds, estuaries, oceans or public waters unless this product is specifically identified and addressed in an NPDES permit. Do not discharge effluent containing this product to sewer systems without previously notifying the sewage treatment plant authority. For guidance contact your State Water Board or Regional Office of the EPA.

PHYSICAL OR CHEMICAL HAZARDS

STRONG OXIDIZING AGENT: Mix only with water according to label directions. Mixing this product with chemicals (e.g. ammonia, acids, detergents, etc.) or organic matter (e.g. urine, feces, etc.) will release chlorine gas which is irritating to eyes, lungs and mucous membranes.

STORAGE AND DISPOSAL

Store this product in a cool, dry area, away from direct sunlight and heat to avoid deterioration. In case of spill, flood areas with large quantities of water. Product or rinsates that cannot be used should be diluted with water before disposal in a sanitary sewer. Do not contaminate food or feed by storage, disposal or cleaning of equipment.

CONTAINER DISPOSAL

Triple rinse (or equivalent). Then offer for recycling or reconditioning, or puncture and dispose of in a sanitary landfill, or incineration, or, if allowed by state and local authorities, by burning. If burned stay out of smoke.

KEEP OUT OF REACH OF CHILDREN

DANGER

STATEMENT OF PRACTICAL TREATMENT
(FIRST AID)

IF CONTACT WITH EYES OCCURS, flush with water for at least 15 minutes. Get prompt medical attention.
IF CONTACT WITH SKIN OCCURS, wash with plenty of soap and water.
IF SWALLOWED, drink large amounts of water. DO NOT induce vomiting. Call a physician or Poison Control Center immediately.

II

POTASSIUM HYDROXIDE SOLUTION has many uses and is very often used in packing plants, dairies, and other food processing concessions. With characteristics including alkalinity, it is used as a cleaner/degreaser and is added to solvents and surfactants. The label includes the reminder: **It is a violation of federal law to use this product in a manner inconsistent with its labeling.** The following is taken directly from a label that was found on a specific job site:

DANGER: CORROSIVE MATERIAL
HANDLE WITH CARE

Causes irreversible eye damage. Harmful or fatal if swallowed. Causes burns. Do not get in eyes or on clothing. Use rubber gloves, protective splash-proof goggles, and protective clothing. Do not get on skin or in eyes. When diluting, add slowly to warm water with continuous stirring to avoid violent spattering. Causes burns. In case of contact, immediately flush area with water for at least 15 minutes. Remove contaminated clothing and wash before reuse. Avoid inhalation of fumes.

STATEMENT OF PRACTICAL TREATMENT (FIRST AID)
If on skin or in eyes, flush with water for at least 15 minutes. Seek immediate medical attention. If swallowed, do not induce vomiting. Seek immediate medical attention.

STORAGE AND DISPOSAL
Do not contaminate food, feed, or water. Keep container closed when not in use. Store in a cool, dry location. Supplier is not responsible for disposition of this product. Dispose according to

local, state and Federal regulations. Do not reuse container.

IMPORTANT
Read the Material Safety Data Sheet and Product Information Report carefully. May be reactive with metal and ceramic surfaces by causing corrosion or embrittlement. Consult your equipment manufacturer. May be harmful to the environment.

III

The third example is a heavy duty degreaser, that contains: SODIUM EXYLENE SULFONATE; SODIUM LAURYL ETHER SULFATE; SODIUM HYDROXIDE; and BUTOXYETHANOL. Its label plainly states:

> For Industrial Use Only.
> Do NOT mix with anything but water.
> Use only with Adequate Ventilation.
> This Product will Etch Aluminum.
> Do NOT use on Painted Surfaces.
> Avoid use Around Food.

This product is being used in places such as restaurants, schools, vocational-technology training centers, nursing homes, and auto shops.

WARNINGS FOR THIS PRODUCT

DANGER:

CAUSES SEVERE CHEMICAL BURNS.
CONTAINS SODIUM HYDROXIDE and BUTOXYETHANOL.
EYE CONTACT MAY CAUSE BLINDNESS.
HARMFUL CONTACT MAY NOT CAUSE IMMEDIATE PAIN.
HARMFUL OR FATAL IF SWALLOWED.
HARMFUL IF INHALED.
PROTECT SKIN, EYES AND MUCOUS MEMBRANES FROM CONTACT WITH THIS PRODUCT AND ITS SOLUTIONS.
WEAR RUBBER GLOVES, LONG-SLEEVED GARMENTS & SAFETY GOGGLES and/or FACE SHIELD.
KEEP OUT OF REACH OF CHILDREN.
FOR ADDITIONAL INFORMATION, SEE MATERIAL SAFETY DATA SHEET (MSDS).

FIRST AID:

EXTERNAL: Immediately flush skin with plenty of cool running water for at least 15 minutes. Immediately remove contaminated clothing and shoes and wash before reuse.

EYES: Immediately flush with plenty of cool running water. Remove contacts if applicable. Continue flushing for at least 15 minutes, holding eyelids apart.

INTERNAL: If swallowed, do not induce vomiting. Rinse mouth, then immediately drink one to two large glasses of water or milk. Never give anything by mouth to an unconscious person.

INHALATION: Immediately move to fresh air.

CALL A POISON CONTROL CENTER OR PHYSICIAN IMMEDIATELY.

How to Read the Manufacturing Company's Material Safety Data Sheet (MSDS)

"The manufacturing company supplies this Material Safety Data Sheet to you for your files. The company is concerned for your health and safety. These products can be used safely with proper protective equipment and proper handling practices consistent with label instruction and the MSDS. Before using this product, be sure to read the complete label and the Material Safety Data Sheet."

The Material Safety Data Sheet may be used to comply with OSHA's Hazard Communication Standard, 29 CFR 1910.1200. The Standard must be consulted for specific requirements. The general categories or SECTIONS of information will usually be as follows:

SECTION I - IDENTIFICATION. This section identifies the product according to the label name, the manufacturer, the preparer of the form, and the telephone number where additional information can be obtained in the event of an emergency. It also includes information on the general family or class of chemicals of which the product is composed (i.e., acids, bases, hydrocarbons, etc.)

SECTION II - HAZARDOUS INGREDIENTS. If the product is a mixture, or if any of its ingredients are evaluated as hazardous, the chemical and common names of these ingredients must be listed with associated percentages and Threshold Limit Values (TLVs) or Permissible Exposure Limits (PELs). The TLVs and PELs are the concentrations in air to which most workers can be exposed repeatedly day after day without adverse health effects. These levels have been established from industrial experience and toxicological tests and have been incorporated into many of the OSHA standards. The levels of contaminants in the work place can be measured and compared with these values to determine if a health hazard exists.

SECTION III - PHYSICAL DATA. The physical properties of a material are helpful in evaluating hazards. These are discussed below with interpretive comments.

Boiling Point - Refers to the temperature at which a liquid boils. Water boils at 212° F. Materials with low boiling points tend to evaporate quickly and may give off appreciable quantities of toxic or flammable gases. Materials with higher boiling points are less apt to do this unless heated. Low boiling point materials in closed containers will build up pressure when exposed to heat and can explode.

Vapor Pressure - Refers to the pressure exerted by the escaping gas or vapor from the surface of a liquid. The vapor pressure of a liquid varies with temperature. At the boiling point, the vapor pressure equals atmospheric pressure (760 mm, or 14.7 psi). Materials with low vapor pressures tend to evaporate slowly, while those with high vapor pressures evaporate rapidly and have greater potential to give off toxic or flammable gases.

Vapor Density - Refers to the weight of a vapor or gas relative to the weight of air. Materials with vapor densities greater than one (1) will tend to accumulate on the floor, while those less than one (1) will rise toward the ceiling.

Percent Volatile Material - Refers to the amount of material that will evaporate from the product, over time, at room temperature.

Evaporation Rate - Refers to the time it takes for a liquid to be converted into its vapor at a given temperature. Materials with low rates evaporate quickly, while those with higher rates take more time.

Summary - From a hazardous and toxic properties standpoint, liquids with high vapor pressures, low evaporation rates, and low boiling points are of greatest concern. Unless properly handled, these types of materials tend to vaporize rapidly and can produce high concentrations of potentially toxic or flammable gases.

SECTION IV - FIRE AND EXPLOSION DATA

Flash Point - Refers to the temperature at which liquid will give off enough flammable vapor to produce a flame when a source of ignition (spark or flame) is present. Liquids with flash points below 80° F are especially hazardous, because such liquids can give off vapors at room temperature that can be ignited by sparks or static electricity. Smoking, open flames, or high heat sources should never be permitted near flammable or combustible liquids.

<u>Extinguishing Media</u> - Describes the type of fire fighting media suitable for use on the burning material (e.g., water, CO_2, foam, etc.)

<u>Special Fire Fighting Procedures</u> - Describes any special precautions that are required for fire fighting such as personal protection equipment, how close to approach the fire, explosion hazards, etc. Under certain conditions, some materials can be unstable or can be incompatible when they come in contact with chemicals. At elevated temperatures, for example, some materials can decompose and give off toxic gases. When two incompatible materials come in contact, the reaction may release large amounts of energy, possibly causing a fire or explosion. (This section describes the conditions and materials to avoid to prevent such occurrences.)

Effects of Overexposure - Describes the common health effects a person would experience due to chronic (long-term) or acute (short-term) over-exposures to the material.

Emergency and First Aid Procedures - This describes the emergency and first aid procedures to follow until professional medical help is available.

There are two basic types of respiratory protection devices:

Air Purifying - These respirators prevent air contaminants from entering the body by using different types of filters. "Mechanical filters" are used to eliminate particulate air contaminants such as dust, mists, sprays, and fumes.

Chemical Cartridge - These respirators are equipped with special cartridges that "trap" gases and vapors before inhalation.

If the oxygen level falls below 16%, a person's life is in immediate danger. Mechanical ventilation or air supply equipment is required once the oxygen level falls below 19%.

In the event the material is accidentally spilled or released, this section describes the precautionary measures to be taken and the appropriate clean up and disposal procedures.

V - SPECIAL PROTECTION & CONTROL MEASURES. Any special precautionary information concerning handling, storage, or other matters not mentioned in previous sections would be covered here. This information might include such things as medical conditions which could be aggravated by exposure to the product.

When engineering or administrative controls are not practical, personal protective equipment (PPE) will be required. When selecting PPE, make sure it meets with appropriate American National Standards Institute (ANSI) approval.

Workers can protect themselves in a variety of ways such as gloves, hard hats, respirators, and safety glasses. PPE is only acceptable when engineering controls are not feasible.

When PPE is used, it must be evaluated to ensure proper protection. The following PPE represents some of the equipment now available for use.

Eye & Face Protection

Eye and face protection is required whenever danger exists from:

- Flying particles
- Liquid splashes
- Arcs, radiation, or glare

Simple safety glasses are not acceptable for grinding and splashes. Careful selection of PPE must be done to ensure adequate protection.

Hand Protection

Gloves are used to provide protection against corrosive liquids, shock, heat, sharp surfaces, etc. Again, proper selection is essential.

Respiratory Protection

Respiratory protection must be used when:

- The air contaminant is highly toxic;
- When other controls are not feasible.

Terms and Abbreviations Used With MSDS (Alphabetized Within MSDS Sections)

SECTION I - GENERAL. The following are general abbreviations used within the MSDS document:

C - Ceiling
MP - Maximum Peak
N/A - Not Applicable
N/K - Not Known
P - Potential
PEL - Permissible Exposure Limit
PM - Pensky Martens
S - Skin
ST - Short-Term
TLV - Threshold Limit Value
TWA - Time Weight Average

SECTION II - HAZARDOUS INGREDIENTS. This section includes the physical and chemical characteristics of those ingredients. Only items that are hazardous relative to CFR 1910.1200 are listed.

CAR: Carcinogen - A chemical listed by the National Toxicology Program (NTP), the International Agency for Research on Cancer (IARC) or OSHA as a definite or possible human cancer causing agent.

CAS #: Chemical Abstract Services Registry Number - A universally accepted numbering system for chemical substances.

CBL: Combustible - At temperatures between 100° F and 200° F, chemicals give off enough vapor to ignite if a source of ignition is present as tested with a closed cup tester.

CNS: Central Nervous System depressant reduces the activity of the brain and spinal cord.

COR: Corrosive - Causes irreversible alterations in living tissue (e.g. burns).

DESIGNATIONS: Chemical and common names of hazardous ingredients.

EIR: Eye Irritant Only - Causes reversible reddening and/or inflammation of eye tissues.

EXPOSURE LIMITS: The time weighted average (TWA) airborne concentration at which most workers can be exposed without any expected adverse effects. Primary sources include ACGIH, TLVs, and OSHA PELs (TWA, STEL and ceiling limits.)

> ACGIH: American Conference of Governmental Industrial Hygienists.
>
> CEILING: The concentration that should not be exceeded in the work

place during any part of the working exposure.

OSHA: Occupational Safety and Health Administration.

PEL: Permissible Exposure Limit - A set of time weighted average exposure values, established by OSHA, for a normal 8-hour day and a 40-hour week.

PPM: Parts Per Million - Unit of measure for exposure limits.

(S) SKIN: Skin contact with substance can contribute to overall exposure.

STEL: Short-Term Exposure Limit - Maximum concentration for a continuous 15-minute exposure period.

TLV: Threshold Limit Value - A set of time weighted average exposure limits, established by ACGIH, for a normal 8-hour day and a 40-hour work week.

FBL: Flammable - At temperatures under 100° F, chemical gives off enough vapor to ignite if a source of ignition is present as tested with a closed cup tester.

HAZARDOUS INGREDIENTS: Chemical substances determined to be potential health or physical hazards by the criteria established in the OSHA Hazardous Communication Standard - 29 CFR 1910.1200.

HTX: Highly Toxic - The probable dose causing death for a 150 pound person; may be approximated as less than six teaspoons or two tablespoons.

IRR: Irritant - Causes reversible effects in living tissues (e.g. inflammation) - primarily skin and eyes.

N/A: Not Applicable - Category is not appropriate for this product.

N/D: Not Determined - Insufficient information for a determination for this item.

RTECS #: Registry of Toxic Effects of Chemical Substances - An unreviewed listing of published toxicology data on chemical substances.

SARA: Superfund Amendments and Reauthorization Act - Section 313 designates chemicals for possible reporting for the Toxics Release Inventory.

SEN: Sensitizer - Causes allergic reaction after repeated exposure.

TOX: Toxic - The probable deadly dose for a 150 pound person is one ounce (two tablespoons) or more.

HEALTH HAZARD DATA are of extreme interest to most employers as well as their employees. These explanations inform users of potential health concerns related to the product.

ACUTE EFFECT: An adverse effect on the human body from a single exposure with symptoms developing almost immediately after exposure or within a relatively short time.

CHRONIC EFFECT: Adverse effects that are most likely to occur from repeated exposure over a long period of time.

EST'D PEL, TLV: This estimated, time-weighted average, exposure limit, developed by using a formula provided by the ACGIH, pertains to airborne concentrations from the product as a whole. This value should serve as a guide for providing safe workplace conditions for nearly all workers.

HMIS CODES: Hazardous Material Identification System - A rating system developed by the National Paint and Coating Association for estimating the hazard potential of a chemical under normal workplace conditions. These risk estimates are indicated by a numerical rating given in each of three hazard areas (Health / Flammability / Reactivity), ranging from a low of zero to a high of 4. A chronic hazard is indicated with a Yes. Consult HMIS training guides for Personal Protection letter codes which indicate necessary protective equipment.

PRIMARY ROUTE OF ENTRY: The way one or more hazardous ingredients may enter the body and cause a generalized-systemic or specific-organ toxic effect.

> ING: Ingestion - A primary route of exposure through swallowing of material.

INH: Inhalation - A primary route of exposure through breathing of vapors.

SKIN: A primary route of exposure through contact with the skin.

REACTIVITY DATA.

HAZARDOUS DECOMPOSITION: The breakdown of products expected to be produced upon those products' decomposition or combustion.

INCOMPATIBILITY: Material contact and conditions to avoid to prevent hazardous reactions.

POLYMERIZATION: Indicates the tendency of the product's molecules to combine in a chemical reaction releasing excess pressure and heat.

STABILITY: Indicates the susceptibility of the product to decompose spontaneously and dangerously.

SPILL AND DISPOSAL PROCEDURES.

RCRA WASTE NOS: RCRA (Resource Conservation and Recovery Act) waste codes

(40 CFR 261) applicable to the disposal of spilled or unusable product from the original container.

PROTECTION INFORMATION: Where respiratory protection is recommended, use only MSHA and NIOSH approved respirators and dust masks.

MSHA: Mine Safety and Health Administration.

NIOSH: National Institute for Occupational Safety and Health.

REGULATORY INFORMATION is as follows:

CWA: Clean Water Act.

RQ: Reportable Quantity - The amount of the specific ingredient that, when spilled to the ground and can enter a storm sewer or natural watershed, must be reported to the National Response Center and other regulatory agencies.

TSCA: Toxic Substances Control Act - A federal law requiring all commercial chemical substances to appear on an inventory maintained by the EPA.

All statements, technical information and recommendations contained herein are based on available scientific tests or data which are believed to be reliable. The accuracy and completeness of such data are not under warranty or guaranteed.

SECTION III - PHYSICAL DATA.

EVAPORATION RATE: The rate of change from the liquid state to the vapor state at ambient temperature and pressure in comparison to a given substance (e.g. water).

PH: A value representing the acidity or alkalinity of an aqueous solution (Acidic pH = 6.9 - 1; Neutral pH = 7; Alkaline pH = 7.1 - 14).

PERCENT VOLATILE: The percentage of the product (liquid or solid) that will evaporate at 212° F and ambient pressure.

SOLUBILITY IN WATER: A description of the ability of the product to dissolve in water.

Examples of MSDS Forms for Everyday Use

The general MSDS information described above, helps you better understand the chemical company communication thus enabling you to make better and safer choices. The information can be organized in somewhat different forms, but all applicable information must be included to meet OSHA standards. The text includes upper case and screened or shadowed areas which were added for emphasis.

The following examples include directly quoted information from MSDS forms found most often on the job sites visited by this author. Examples 1 through 6 came from materials used in dairies and/or food processing plants. Examples 7 through 12 are cleaners and degreasers commonly found in restaurants, hotels, auto mechanic shops, and truck and car wash facilities. Each of these categories and specific examples are from everyday use. Note the full disclosure frankness of the chemical manufacturing company.

Dairies and Food Processing Plants

Example 1 - Dairies and Food Processing Plants

Principal Hazardous Components:

(liquid chlorinated cleaner)

Potassium Hydroxide	17%
Sodium Hypochlorite	3%
Sodium Metasilicate	

Physical Data:

Chlorine odor; Fire fighting procedure: Wear full protective gear and self-contained breathing apparatus (SCBA) in fire area. Liquid corrosive material.

Physical Hazards:

Incompatible with: Flammable liquids, acids, organic halogens, chlorine, active metals, and nitrogen containing chemicals such as ammonia.

Health Hazards:

Medical conditions aggravated by exposure: Sensitive skin, dust or mist, aggravates respiratory disease. <u>Primary routes of entry</u>: Inhalation, skin and ingestion.

Acute: Causes burns to EYES and SKIN. Inhalation of mists or dust irritates or causes burns to RESPIRATORY SYSTEM and LUNG TISSUE. Harmful if swallowed.

Emergency and First Aid Procedures:

Inhalation: Remove to fresh air. Get MEDICAL ATTENTION.

Eyes: Immediately flush thoroughly with fresh water for at least 15 minutes. Get MEDICAL ATTENTION if eyes are injured or irritation persists.

Skin: Immediately flush with fresh water. Remove contaminated clothes and shoes.

Ingestion: Give several glasses of water. DO NOT INDUCE VOMITING. Get MEDICAL ATTENTION. Never give fluids by mouth to an unconscious person.

Special Protection Information:

Respiratory Protection: Wear approved cartridge respirator to maintain PEL/TLV, in mist, spray, or dusty conditions.

Ventilation Mechanical: Maintain PEL/TLV.

Protective Gloves: Wear Neoprene, Nitrile, or Natural Rubber Gloves or Gloves with proven resistance to the ingredients listed.

Eye Protection: Wear splash-proof safety goggles especially if contact lenses are worn.
Other Protective Clothing/Equipment: Wear apron, protective clothing and footwear. Launder clothes before reuse. Have safety shower and eye wash available.

Regulatory Information:

All Chemical Ingredients on this MSDS form are listed on the Toxic Substance Control Act (TSCA) Inventory, which is maintained by the Environmental Protection Agency (EPA).

Example 2 - Dairies and Food Processing Plants

Principal Hazardous Components:

(an acid sanitizer)
Phosphoric Acid 30%
Propylene Glycol
Dodecylbenzene Sulfonic Acid
Polyalkoxy Glycol

Physical Data:

Acidic odor. Fire fighting procedure: Wear a self-contained breathing apparatus (SCBA) and protective gear to prevent skin contact with acidic solution.

Physical Hazards:

Incompatible with: Concentrated alkalis, soft metals, or chlorinated compounds.

Health Hazards:

Medical conditions aggravated by exposure: Sensitive skin and eyes, aggravates RESPIRATORY DISEASE.

Primary routes of entry: Inhalation, skin and ingestion.

Acute: Causes BURNS to SKIN AND EYES. Mists cause SEVERE IRRITATION to SKIN, EYES, and RESPIRATORY TRACT. PULMONARY EDEMA. Causes BURNS to DIGESTIVE TRACT. DANGER -- CORROSIVE. Harmful if SWALLOWED.

Emergency and First Aid Procedures:

Inhalation: Remove to fresh air. If DIFFICULT BREATHING, give oxygen. Get MEDICAL ATTENTION.

Eyes: Flush thoroughly with fresh water for at least 15 minutes. Get MEDICAL ATTENTION.

Skin: Flush with fresh water, wash with soap and water. Remove contaminated clothes and shoes.

Ingestion: Give water. DO NOT INDUCE VOMITING. Get MEDICAL ATTENTION. Never give fluids by mouth to an unconscious person.

Special Protection Information:

Respiratory Protection: Use approved Cartridge Respirator to maintain PEL/TLV.

Protective Gloves: Wear acid resistant gloves.

Eye Protection: Wear splash-proof safety goggles, especially when pouring or splash hazard exists.

Other Protective Clothing/ Equipment: This product is a DISINFECTANT CORROSIVE liquid. Wear an Acid Resistant chemical apron when handling. Have safety shower and eye wash available.

Regulatory Information:

All Chemical Ingredients on this MSDS form are listed on the Toxic Substance Control Act (TSCA) Inventory, which is maintained by the Environmental Protection Agency (EPA).

Example 3 - Dairies and Food Processing Plants

Principal Hazardous Components:

(an Alkaline cleaner)

Sodium Hydroxide 48%

Sodium Gluconate

Alkyl Glucoside

Physical Data:

Mild detergent odor. Fire fighting procedure: Wear full protective gear and self-contained breathing apparatus (SCBA) in fire area.

Physical Hazards:

Incompatible with: Flammable liquids, acids, organic halogens, aluminum and soft metals.

Health Hazards:

Medical conditions aggravated by exposure: Sensitive skin, dust or mist aggravates RESPIRATORY DISEASE.

Primary routes of entry: Inhalation, skin and ingestion.

Acute: Causes burns to EYES and SKIN. Inhalation of mists or dust irritates or causes BURNS to the RESPIRATORY SYSTEM and LUNG TISSUE. Harmful if SWALLOWED.

Emergency and First Aid Procedures:

Inhalation: Remove to fresh air. Get MEDICAL ATTENTION.

Eyes: Immediately flush thoroughly with fresh water for at least 15 minutes. Get MEDICAL ATTENTION if eyes are injured or irritation persists.

Skin: Immediately flush with fresh water. Remove contaminated clothes and shoes.

Ingestion: Give several glasses of water. DO NOT INDUCE VOMITING. Get MEDICAL ATTENTION. Never give fluids by mouth to an unconscious person.

Special Protection Information:

Respiratory Protection: Wear approved cartridge respirator to maintain PEL/TLV, in mist, spray, or dusty conditions.

Protective Gloves: Wear Neoprene, Nitrile, or Natural Rubber Gloves or Gloves with proven resistance to the ingredients listed.

Eye Protection: Wear splash-proof safety chemical goggles, with side shield safety glasses, or face shield.

Other Protective Clothing/ Equipment: Wear apron, protective clothing and safety footwear. Launder clothes before reuse. Have safety shower and eye wash available.

Regulatory Information:

Corrosive material; RCRA Hazardous. All Chemical Ingredients on this MSDS form are listed on the Toxic Substance Control Act (TSCA) Inventory, which is maintained by the Environmental Protection Agency (EPA).

Example 4 - Dairies and Food Processing Plants

Principal Hazardous Components:

(liquid chlorinated, foamer-cleaner)

Potassium Hydroxide	16%
Sodium Hypochlorite	3%
Sodium Xylene Sulfonate	
Sodium Tripolyphosphate	

Physical Data:

Slight chlorine odor. Fire fighting procedure: Liquid Corrosive Material. Wear full protective gear and self-contained breathing apparatus (SCBA) in fire area.

Physical Hazards:

Incompatible with: Acids, flammable liquids, soft metals (aluminum),

Nitrogen containing compounds, organic halogens.

Health Hazards:

Medical conditions aggravated by exposure: Sensitive skin, dust or mist aggravates RESPIRATORY DISEASE.

Primary routes of entry: Inhalation, skin and ingestion.

Acute: Causes BURNS to EYES and SKIN. Inhalation of mists or dusts irritates or causes BURNS to RESPIRATORY SYSTEM and LUNG TISSUE. HARMFUL or FATAL if SWALLOWED.

Emergency and First Aid Procedures:

Inhalation: Remove to fresh air. Get MEDICAL ATTENTION.

Eyes: Immediately flush thoroughly with fresh water for at least 15 minutes. Get MEDICAL ATTENTION if eyes are injured or irritation persists.

Skin: Immediately flush with fresh water. Remove contaminated clothes and shoes.

Ingestion: Give several glasses of water. DO NOT INDUCE VOMITING. Get MEDICAL ATTENTION. Never give fluids by mouth to an unconscious person.

Special Protection Information:

Respiratory Protection: Wear approved cartridge respirator to maintain PEL/TLV levels when in mist, spray, or dusty conditions.

Protective Gloves: Wear rubber/chemical resistant gloves.

Eye Protection: Wear splash-proof safety chemical resistant goggles, with side shield safety glasses, or face shield.

Other Protective Clothing/ Equipment: Wear apron, protective clothing and safety footwear. Launder clothes before reuse. Have safety shower and eye wash available.

Regulatory Information:

Corrosive material; RCRA Hazardous. All Chemical Ingredients on this MSDS form are listed on the Toxic Substance Control Act (TSCA) Inventory, which is maintained by the Environmental Protection Agency (EPA).

Example 5 - Dairies and Food Processing Plants

Principal Hazardous Components:

(alkaline cleaner)
Sodium Hydroxide 83%
Sodium Carbonate
Sodium Tripolyphosphate

Physical Data:

Slight detergent odor. Fire fighting procedure: Corrosive Material (Powder). Wear full protective gear and self-contained breathing apparatus (SCBA) in fire area.

Physical Hazards:

Incompatible with: Acids, Flammable liquids, organic halogens, soft metals (aluminum), Nitrogen compounds.

Health Hazards:

Medical conditions aggravated by exposure: sensitive skin. Dust or mist aggravates RESPIRATORY DISEASE.

Primary routes of entry: Inhalation and ingestion.

Acute: Causes BURNS to EYES and SKIN. Inhalation of mists or dust irritates or causes BURNS to the RESPIRATORY SYSTEM and LUNG TISSUE. Harmful if SWALLOWED.

Emergency and First Aid Procedures:
Inhalation: Remove to fresh air. Get MEDICAL ATTENTION.
Eyes: Immediately flush thoroughly with fresh water for at least 15 minutes. Get MEDICAL ATTENTION if eyes are injured or irritation persists.
Skin: Immediately flush with fresh water. Remove contaminated clothes and shoes.
Ingestion: Give several glasses of water. DO NOT INDUCE VOMITING. Get MEDICAL ATTENTION. Never give fluids by mouth to an unconscious person.

Special Protection Information:

Respiratory Protection: Wear approved cartridge respirator to maintain PEL/TLV levels in mist, spray, or dusty conditions.
Protective Gloves: Wear rubber/chemical resistant gloves.
Eye Protection: Wear splash-proof safety chemical resistant goggles, with side shield safety glasses, or face shield.
Other Protective Clothing/ Equipment: Wear apron, protective clothing and safety footwear. Launder clothes

before reuse. Have safety shower and eye wash available.

Regulatory Information:

Corrosive material; RCRA Hazardous.

Example 6 - Dairies and Food Processing Plants

Principal Hazardous Components:

(liquid solvent cleaner)

Dipropylene Glycol Methyl Ether	48%
Potassium Hydroxide	6%
Sodium Hydroxide	
Tetrasodium Ethylene Diamine Tetraacetate	
Sodium Decanoate	

Physical Data:

Liquid with a solvent odor. Fire fighting procedure: Wear full protective gear and self-contained breathing apparatus (SCBA) in fire area.

Physical Hazards:

Incompatible with: Flammable liquids, soft metals, acids, nitrogen containing chemicals.

Health Hazards:

Medical conditions aggravated by exposure: Sensitive skin, dust or mist aggravates RESPIRATORY DISEASE.

Primary routes of entry: Inhalation, skin and ingestion.

Acute: Causes BURNS to EYES and SKIN. Inhalation of mists or dusts irritates or causes BURNS to the RESPIRATORY SYSTEM. Harmful if SWALLOWED.

Emergency and First Aid Procedures:

Inhalation: Remove to fresh air. Get MEDICAL ATTENTION.

Eyes: Immediately flush thoroughly with fresh water for at least 15 minutes. Get MEDICAL ATTENTION if eyes are injured or irritation persists.

Skin: Immediately flush with fresh water. Remove contaminated clothes and shoes.

Ingestion: Give several glasses of water. DO NOT INDUCE VOMITING. Get MEDICAL ATTENTION. Never give fluids by mouth to an unconscious person.

Special Protection Information:

This material is a corrosive liquid.

Respiratory Protection: Wear approved cartridge respirator to maintain PEL/TLV levels in mist, spray, or dusty conditions.
Protective Gloves: Wear rubber/chemical resistant gloves.
Eye Protection: Wear splash-proof safety chemical resistant goggles, with side shield safety glasses, or face shield.
Other Protective Clothing/ Equipment: Wear apron, protective clothing and safety footwear. Launder clothes before reuse. Have safety shower and eye wash available.

Concrete Cleaner and Degreaser

Example 7 - Concrete Cleaner and Degreaser

Principal Hazardous Components:

(an Alkaline degreaser)

Sodium Metasilicate	60-70%
Trisodium Orthophosphate	10-20%
Sodium Carbonate	5-15%
Nonyphenoxypoly (Ethyleneoxy) Ethanol Sodium Chloride	5-10%

Physical Hazards:

Incompatible with: Strong acids and oxidizing agents.

Health Hazards:

Primary routes of entry: Inhalation, skin and ingestion.

Acute effects of overexposure: This product is corrosive to the SKIN and EYES, thus experience BURNS. The amount of tissue damage depends on the length of contact. EYE contact can result in CORNEAL DAMAGE or BLINDNESS. SKIN contact can produce INFLAMMATION and BLISTERING. Inhalation of dust will produce irritation to the GASTROINTESTINAL or RESPIRATORY TRACT, characterized by BURNING, SNEEZING and COUGHING. Overexposure can produce LUNG damage, CHOKING, UNCONSCIOUSNESS or DEATH.

Chronic effects of overexposure: Repeated exposure of the EYES to a low level of dust can produce EYE irritation. Repeated SKIN exposure can produce local SKIN DESTRUCTION or DERMATITIS. Repeated inhalation of dust can produce varying degrees of RESPIRATORY IRRITATION or LUNG DAMAGE.

Emergency and First Aid Procedures:
Inhalation: Remove to fresh air. Get MEDICAL ATTENTION.
Eyes: Immediately flush thoroughly with fresh water for at least 15 minutes. Get MEDICAL ATTENTION if eyes are injured or irritation persists.
Skin: Immediately flush with fresh water. Remove contaminated clothes and shoes.
Ingestion: Give several glasses of water. DO NOT INDUCE VOMITING. Get MEDICAL ATTENTION. Never give fluids by mouth to an unconscious person.

Special Precautions:

Keep product away from Skin and Eyes.
Keep away from food and food products.
DO NOT breathe dust.
Clothing and shoes which become contaminated with substance should be removed promptly and not re-worn until thoroughly cleaned.

Degreaser for Restaurants and Hotels, Auto Mechanic Shops, etc.

Example 8 - Restaurants, Hotels, Auto Mechanic Shops, etc.

Principal Hazardous Components:

(flammable, foam degreaser)

Heavy Aromatic Naphth (solvent petro.)	30-40%
Kerosene (fuel oil #1; coal tar)	10-20%
Potassium Dodecylbenzene Sulfonate	5-10%
Tetrapotassium Pyrophosphate	
Ethylene Glycol Monobutyl Ether	
Naphthalene	

Physical Data:

Extremely flammable. Fire fighting procedure: Wear full protective gear and self-contained breathing apparatus (SCBA) in fire area.

Physical Hazards:

Incompatible with: Heat, open flame, spark, and oxidizing agents.

Health Hazards:

Primary routes of entry: Inhalation, skin and ingestion.

Acute effects of overexposure: Exposure by inhalation may produce EYE, NOSE, and THROAT irritation. Inhalation of harmful amounts of VAPOR may produce MILD CENTRAL NERVOUS SYSTEM DEPRESSION, characterized by HEADACHE, NAUSEA, VERTIGO and STUPOR. If VOMITING occurs, aspiration of the solvent into the LUNGS can cause CHEMICAL PNEUMONIA. Existing RESPIRATORY DISORDERS or SKIN DISEASES may be aggravated by exposure. Warning: This product in concentrated form IS A SEVERE EYE IRRITANT. OVER-EXPOSURE CAN LEAD TO EYE TISSUE DAMAGE WHICH CAN RESULT IN PERMANENT BLINDNESS. SKIN CONTACT MAY PRODUCE IRRITATION.

Chronic effects of overexposure: Repeated or prolonged skin contact may produce MILD CENTRAL NERVOUS SYSTEM DEPRESSION, characterized by HEADACHE, NAUSEA, STUPOR, and COMA. SKIN which if DEFATTED by repeated exposure to Hydrocarbon Solvents is more susceptible to irritation, INFECTION, and DERMATITIS. Animal studies of the effects of prolonged inhalation indicated a potential for LUNG DAMAGE and BLOOD PRODUCTION ABNORMALITIES, some of which were FATAL. Relevance of these studies to human health and the levels of exposure which might produce these results has not been established.

Emergency and First Aid Procedures:

Inhalation: Remove to fresh air. Get MEDICAL ATTENTION.

Eyes: Immediately flush thoroughly with fresh water for at least 15 minutes. Get MEDICAL ATTENTION if eyes are injured or irritation persists.

Skin: Immediately flush with fresh water. Remove contaminated clothes and shoes.

Ingestion: Give several glasses of water. DO NOT INDUCE VOMITING. Get MEDICAL ATTENTION. Never give fluids by mouth to an unconscious person.

Special Protection Information:

For protective clothing, eye protection, respiratory protection, and ventilation: Follow the advice listed in all of the above examples.

Example 9 - Restaurants, Hotels, Auto Mechanic Shops, etc.

Principal Hazardous Components:

(solvent degreaser)
Ethylene Glycol Monobutyl Ether 5-10%
Mineral Spirits 5-10%
Potassium Dodecylbenzene Sulfonate
Tridodium orthosphate; Phosphoric Acid and Trisodium Salt.

Physical Hazards:

Incompatible with: Heat, open flame, spark, and oxidizing agents.

Health Hazards:

Primary routes of entry: Inhalation, skin and ingestion.

Acute effects of overexposure: Overexposure to the VAPORS from this product may produce MUCOUS MEMBRANE irritation. Particularly of the EYE and RESPIRATORY TRACT.

Over-exposure to VAPORS may also produce mild CENTRAL NERVOUS SYSTEM DEPRESSION characterized by HEADACHE, DIZZINESS, NAUSEA, and STUPOR, leading to UNCONSCIOUSNESS in extreme cases. Introduction solvents, as in aspiration of VOMITUS FLUID, may produce CHEMICAL PNEUMONIA. Existing RESPIRATORY DISORDERS and LUNG DISEASES may be aggravated by inhalation of VAPORS.

Chronic effects of overexposure: Repeated or prolonged inhalation can produce reversible LUNG DAMAGE. SKIN which is repeatedly defatted by contact with SOLVENTS can be more susceptible to IRRITATION, INFECTION, and DERMATITIS.

Animal studies indicate a potential for LIVER, KIDNEY, or RED BLOOD CELL DAMAGE. Relevance of these studies or exposure levels which might produce these effects in humans has not been established.

Emergency and First Aid Procedures:
Inhalation: Remove to fresh air. Get MEDICAL ATTENTION.
Eyes: Immediately flush thoroughly with fresh water for at least 15 minutes. Get MEDICAL ATTENTION if eyes are injured or irritation persists.
Skin: Immediately flush with fresh water. Remove contaminated clothes and shoes.
Ingestion: Give several glasses of water. DO NOT INDUCE VOMITING. Get MEDICAL ATTENTION. Never give fluids by mouth to an unconscious person.

Special Protection Information:

Respiratory Protection: Wear approved cartridge respirator to maintain PEL/TLV, in mist, spray, or dusty conditions.
Ventilation Mechanical: Maintain PEL/TLV.
Protective Gloves: Wear Neoprene, Nitrile, or Natural Rubber Gloves or Gloves with proven resistance to the ingredients listed.
Eye Protection: Wear splash-proof safety goggles especially if contact lenses are worn.

Other Protective Clothing/ Equipment: Wear apron, protective clothing and footwear. Launder clothes before reuse. Have safety shower and eye wash available.

Regulatory Information:

Chemical Ingredients on this MSDS form are listed on the Toxic Substance Control Act (TSCA) Inventory, which is maintained by the Environmental Protection Agency (EPA).

Example 10 - Restaurants, Hotels, Auto Mechanic Shops, etc.

Principal Hazardous Components:

(orange distillate, degreaser)
D-Limonene; Citrus Terpene cyclohexene 70-80%
Nonylphenoxypoly (Ethyleneoxy) Ethanol 10-20%

Physical Hazards:

Incompatible with: Heat, (EXTREMELY FLAMMABLE), strong acids and/or oxidizers

Health Hazards:

Acute effects of overexposure: This product can be an eye IRRITANT. Inflammation of EYE TISSUE is characterized by redness, watering and/or itching.
One of the ingredients in this product has caused SENSITIZATION REACTIONS in a percentage of the general population.

Chronic effects of overexposure: Contact, especially if prolonged or repeated, can cause redness, itching or blistering of the SKIN.
Emergency and First Aid Procedures:
Inhalation: Remove to fresh air. Get MEDICAL ATTENTION.

Eyes: Immediately flush thoroughly with fresh water for at least 15 minutes. Get MEDICAL ATTENTION if eyes are injured or irritation persists.
Skin: Immediately flush with fresh water. Remove contaminated clothes and shoes.
Ingestion: Give several glasses of water. DO NOT INDUCE VOMITING. Get MEDICAL ATTENTION. Never

give fluids by mouth to an unconscious person.

Special Protection Information:

Keep product away from SKIN and EYES.

DO NOT BREATHE SPRAY MISTS or VAPORS.

For protective clothing, eye protection, respiratory protection, and ventilation, follow the advice listed:

Respiratory Protection: Wear approved cartridge respirator to maintain PEL/TLV, in mist, spray, or dusty conditions.

Ventilation Mechanical: Maintain PEL/TLV.

Protective Gloves: Wear Neoprene, Nitrile, or Natural Rubber Gloves or gloves with proven resistance to the ingredients listed.

Eye Protection: Wear splash-proof safety goggles especially if contact lenses are worn.

Other Protective Clothing/Equipment: Wear apron, protective clothing and footwear. Launder clothes before reuse. Have safety shower and eye wash available.

Regulatory Information:

Extremely flammable. All Chemical Ingredients on this MSDS form are listed on the Toxic Substance Control Act (TSCA) Inventory, which is maintained by the Environmental Protection Agency (EPA).

Steam Cleaning and Car & Truck Wash

Example 11 - Steam Cleaning and Car & Truck Wash

Principal Hazardous Components:

(Steam Cleaning Compound; pH 13.0 liquid)

Nonylphenoxypoly (Ethyleneoxy) Ethanol

Tetrasodium Ethylenediamine Tetraacetate

Physical Data:

Incompatible with: Strong oxidizing agents.

Health Hazards:

Acute effects of overexposure: This product can irritate EYES and SKIN on contact. Inflammation of the EYE is characterized by redness, watering, and itching. SKIN INFLAMMATION is characterized by itching, scaling, reddening or blistering.

Chronic effects of overexposure: Repeated or prolonged SKIN CONTACT can produce CHRONIC INFLAMMATION or DERMATITIS, characterized by redness, scaling, or itching. Repeated EYE exposure can produce CHRONIC INFLAMMATION of the EYE or CORNEAL DAMAGE.

<u>Emergency and First Aid Procedures</u>:

Inhalation: Remove to fresh air. Get MEDICAL ATTENTION.

Eyes: Immediately flush thoroughly with fresh water for at least 15 minutes. Get MEDICAL ATTENTION if eyes are injured or irritation persists.

Skin: Immediately flush with fresh water. Remove contaminated clothes and shoes.

Ingestion: Give several glasses of water. DO NOT INDUCE VOMITING. Get MEDICAL ATTENTION. Never give fluids by mouth to an unconscious person.

Special Protection Information:

Protective Gloves: Wear Neoprene, Nitrile, or Natural Rubber Gloves or Gloves with proven resistance to the ingredients listed.

Eye Protection: Wear splash-proof safety chemical resistant glasses or goggles, especially if contact lenses are worn.

Example 12 - Steam Cleaning and Car & Truck Wash

Principal Hazardous Components:

Sodium Dodecylbenzene Sulfonate
Nonylphenoxypoly (Ethyleneoxy) Ethanol
Sodium Metasilicate
Alpha Olefin Sulfonate
Sodium Lauryl Ether Sulfate, and
Sodium Laureth Sulfate

Physical Data:

Liquid with a mild odor. Fire fighting procedure: Wear full protective gear and self-contained breathing apparatus (SCBA) in fire area.

Health Hazards:

Primary routes of entry: Inhalation, skin and ingestion.

Acute effects of overexposure: This product in concentrated form is a SEVERE EYE IRRITANT. Overexposure can lead to EYE TISSUE DAMAGE which can be PERMANENT. SKIN contact can produce irritation. Ingredients in this product can AGGRAVATE EXISTING SKIN, EYE or RESPIRATORY DISORDERS.

Chronic effects of overexposure: Repeated or prolonged SKIN contact can produce CHRONIC INFLAMMATION of DERMATITIS, characterized by redness, scaling, or itching. Repeated EYE exposure can produce CHRONIC INFLAMMATION of the EYE or CORNEAL DAMAGE.

Emergency and First Aid Procedures:

Inhalation: Remove to fresh air. Get MEDICAL ATTENTION.

Eyes: Immediately flush thoroughly with fresh water for at least 15 minutes. Get MEDICAL ATTENTION if eyes are injured or irritation persists.

Skin: Immediately flush with fresh water. Remove contaminated clothes and shoes.

Ingestion: Give several glasses of water. DO NOT INDUCE VOMITING. Get MEDICAL ATTENTION. Never give fluids by mouth to an unconscious person.

Special Protection Information:

Ventilation: Ventilation should be equivalent to outdoors. Use exhaust fans and open windows in enclosed spaces.

Respiratory Protection: Keep face away from spray mist and do not breath vapors.

Eye Protection: Wear tight-fitting splash-proof safety glasses, especially if contact lenses are worn.

Protective Gloves: Wear Neoprene, Nitrile, or Natural Rubber Gloves or Gloves with proven resistance to the ingredients listed.

Regulatory Information:

All Chemical Ingredients on this MSDS form are listed on the Toxic Substance Control Act (TSCA) Inventory, which is maintained by the Environmental Protection Agency (EPA).

Conclusion

This review of a dozen MSDS forms, representing commonly used chemical products makes it easier to conclude that the chemical manufacturing companies practice full disclosure as required by the law, and do so with frankness.

It is also easier to conclude that the chemical manufacturing companies are NOT AT FAULT in spite of critical public opinion and charges of blame regarding chemical contamination. Who, then, is responsible for chemically damaging the health of the people and the health of the land here on our spaceship earth? Let's put the responsibility where it best fits. "WE THE PEOPLE" sell, and "WE THE PEOPLE" buy, and "WE THE PEOPLE" use, and "WE THE PEOPLE" may choose to misuse and contaminate ourselves. ALTERNATIVELY, we may insist on better research, and better, safer products in the future. Insisting on better research, and choosing to sell and purchase better, safer products would start and continue rebalancing our spaceship ecosystem and preserve healthy life here on earth.

VII

ARE INSURANCE COMPANIES ENVIRONMENTALLY HELPFUL ?

Chapter Outline

"Right to Know" Act
Reflective Thoughts
The "Now What" Conclusions
"Cover Your Actions"

Are You Sure You Are Insured?

Have you ever thought about insurance companies relative to our environment? Have you ever read anything in the newspapers, heard on radio, or ever seen news releases on TV about insurance companies and their participation or interest in encouraging and promoting a better balanced ecosystem? How active are insurers in preventative care? Would the insurance company profit if certain hazards were reduced, thus lowering the claim rate? Would you who care about our health and environment appreciate their additional participation and active development of a safer, more accident free environment? Would you be willing to keep both eyes and ears open and to compliment your insurance agent if you noticed positive efforts and involvement? Might you have a more positive attitude toward insurance companies if we saw ourselves as a team, working together to achieve common goals?

There is a growing awareness that insurance companies can have a positive influence on human environmental safety issues. This is a "people business" that is greatly affected by our health and safety. It is possible for insurers to help motivate and educate us to be safer, especially regarding accidents, toxic and hazardous problems, and general safety.

In collecting information for this chapter, an interview was conducted with an executive of a large insurance company. He was very polite and very open with his explanations. When asked questions about ways his insurance company could promote or motivate environmental and personal safety, he concluded with a generalization that insurance companies have to be very careful not to appear to over-motivate people with the idea of "paying people" to "buy policies." The conclusion was that insurers must stick to the business of giving insurance to individuals who need specific coverage and insure those who have paid specifically for that coverage.

The response of another general insurance broker was most interesting. After showing frustration about a few questions related to pollutants and hazardous or toxic substances, he stated, "Insurance companies, since the early 1980s have been exempt from paying claims related to pollution, hazardous or toxic materials pertaining to bodily injury and personal property loss. They absolutely have been excluded from paying these kinds of claims." My next question was: "Is this a little misleading, covering issues, for example in the Commercial General Liability policy, and then in the fine print of an exclusion, endorsement or a rider, have the coverage taken away?" The broker's response was, "Maybe so," and the inference was that all policyholders can read and are responsible for understanding the fine print, too. Then came the classic statement. The general insurance broker said: "Look at it this way. Maybe the best contribution to the environmental clean-up issue is that we will not cover a policyholder's loss that results from use of harmful chemicals. Therefore they are encouraged not even to consider using polluting, hazardous, and toxic substances. Under Pollution, subheading (f), Section A: Bodily Injury and Property Damage, the document specifically excludes all insurance company responsibility, at least on our policies." The following is a copy of a restrictive endorsement attached to the back of a specific insurance policy. Check the exclusions on your liability and medical insurance policies. Example:

ENDORSEMENT #3
(attached to an actual standard policy)

This endorsement, effective 3-25-93 a.m. and, forms a part of Policy No. __________, issued to _____________.

Absolute Pollution Exclusion

Exclusion (f) is deleted from form ________ and is replaced by the following:

(f) to "bodily injury" or "property damage" (including the loss of the use thereof) caused by, contributed to or arising out of the actual or threatened discharge, dispersal, release or escape of smoke, vapors, soot, fumes, acids, alkalis, toxic chemicals, liquids or gases, waste materials or other irritants into or upon the land the atmosphere or any course or body of water, whether above or below ground.

It is understood and agreed that the intent and effect of this exclusion is to delete from any and all coverage afforded by this policy and claim, action, judgment, liability, settlement, defense or expense (including any loss, cost or expense arising out of any governmental direction or request that the 'insured' test for, monitor, clean-up, remove, contain, treat, detoxify or neutralize pollutants) in any way arising out of such actual or threatened discharge, dispersal, release or escape, whether such results from the 'insured's' activities or the activities of

> others and whether or not such is sudden or gradual and whether or not such is accidental, intended, foreseeable, expected, fortuitous or inevitable and wherever such occurs.

Has your feeling of security under your general liability coverage just been reduced? Under what circumstances are you NOT covered? At the end of this chapter, you will find the list of polluting, hazardous, toxic, or "considered to be harmful to human health" chemicals. The list includes those substances listed by the Environmental Protection Agency (EPA), the Occupational Safety and Health Act (OSHA), and the State of California Proposition 65: the Safe Drinking Water and Toxic Enforcement Act of 1986. Every time you have a question regarding the ingredients on the label of a container, refer to that list and locate any possibly hazardous or toxic pollutants. Ask yourself these questions: DOES MY INSURANCE COVER ME IF I USE OR AUTHORIZE THE USE OF ANY ONE OF THESE CHEMICALS? IS MY FINANCIAL SECURITY AT RISK BECAUSE I AM UNINSURED IN SUCH INSTANCES? IS LIFE, HEALTH, OR THE ENVIRONMENT AT RISK?

What Is This All About Anyhow?

In all fairness to this issue of insurance coverage and environmental risks, we must first look at the basic concepts included in discussions, definitions, and legal terms related to the insurance industry. The following is a very brief outline which will help us as we explore the issue of insurance and liability.

I. TORT LAW AND INSURANCE:

- A. What is a tort?
  1. Definition: wrongdoing or wrongdoer
  2. Largely based on common law -- innocent until proven guilty.
  3. Examples:
     - a. Negligence
     - b. Intentional torts
     - c. Strict liability
     - d. Absolute liability
- B. Negligence:
  1. Basis of most torts and liability insurance claims
  2. Measures
     - a. Prudent Person Doctrine
     - b. Elements of negligence

1. duty owed
2. breach of duty
3. proximate cause
4. damages

C. Intentional Torts:
   1. Definition: malice of forethought (for example, if I choose harmful chemicals for you to use)
   2. Types:
      a. Defamation of character, discrimination
      b. Assault and battery, etc.
   3. Insurance treatment of such exposures

D. Strict Liability
   1. What is it? Each issue speaks for itself
   2. How does it differ from a less culpable tort? One is guilty unless determined innocent

E. Absolute Liability:
   1. What is it? Responsible without fault or negligence
   2. Dangerous Materials or Instrument Doctrine: Anyone who possesses, stores, maintains, or transports a hazardous material or dangerous instrument is absolutely liable

for injury or damage caused by the material or instrument, regardless of the presence of due care

3. Application of absolute liability:
    a. Animals
    b. Firearms
    c. Explosive or highly flammable materials
    d. Hazardous or toxic pollutants

F. Common Law Defenses:
1. Assumption of Risk: the injured party's actions placed him or her at risk
2. Contributory Negligence: what did the injured party do to contribute to the risk
3. Fellow-Servant Rule: another person causes the accident
4. Acts of Nature

II. STATUTORY LAW:

A. Concepts:
1. Definition: a rule or law enacted by a legislative body providing direction or prohibition
2. Statutes supersede common law

3. Comparative negligence: statutory modification of contributory negligence
4. Workers' Compensation Statutes: changed the common law obligations of the employer to the employee from traditional tort law negligence to no-fault - more specific details will be provided in the Workers' Compensation Section
5. Liability of Manufacturers, Retailers and Owners re: Products:
    a. Basis of liability:
        1. strict tort liability
        2. breach of guarantees: expressed or implied
        3. statutes
    b. Defenses:
        1. abnormal use
        2. modification of product
        3. notice of breach

III. DAMAGES:

A. Definition: anything resulting from a harmful or damaging action

B. Types of Damage:

1. Compensatory Damages:
   a. Special: economic or dollar value loss
   b. General: non-economic, for example, pain and suffering
2. Punitive or Exemplary Damages:
   a. Definition: to punish or make an example thus to encourage the non-occurrence of these types of damage
   b. Permissibility: regulated state by state
   c. Insurability: relative to individual states and specific insurance companies
3. Concepts Related to Damages:
   a. DUTY to Mitigate or Press Charges: an attempt to stop the current ongoing damages via court enforcement

b. Collateral Sources: the company, its owners, insurance coverage or possibly government agencies afforded by a special statute: For example, Workers' Compensation Fund

The Insurance Service Office, Inc. (ISO), for example, provides standardized forms for many insurance companies. When you shop from one insurance company to another, therefore, you will recognize a basic similarity (if not exactness) in the forms of each company using an ISO COMMERCIAL GENERAL LIABILITY COVERAGE FORM as a standard.

Bodily Injury and Property Damage Liability Coverage

The Commercial General Liability (CGL) coverage forms provide for bodily injury and property damage liability insurance. These include (1) an insuring agreement as well as (2) a section of exclusions that shape the broad scope of the insuring document.

The opening sentence of the insuring agreement reads as follows: "We will pay those sums that the insured becomes legally obligated to pay as damages because of bodily injury or property damage to which this insurance applies." The instructions regarding Public Liability state that the purpose for this statement is to avoid creating unreasonable expectations among insureds that the coverage literally might extend to all sums, regardless of policy exclusions and conditions.

This sentence should cause alarm to some insurance buyers and their advisors. First, it does not retain the promise of the earlier insuring agreement of Comprehensive General Liability policy to pay "all sums which the insured shall become legally obligated to pay." Second, it does not promise to pay these sums "on behalf" of the insured. These coverage limitations raise the possibility that the insurance company is covering on an "indemnity" basis; that is, an insurer might not be required to pay until after you have paid the person making the claim against you. In earlier cases, the insurance company would have defended itself and you, but now you must defend yourself against the insurance company. How would this affect you and your insurance assurances? Are you protected if exclusions are involved? Do you know in which cases you actually are covered and in which cases you are not covered?

General Exclusion (f): Hazardous, Toxic, Pollution

The 1973 general liability policy, as originally worded, excluded bodily injury or property damage resulting from pollution or contamination; but excepted from the exclusion, and therefore insured, were pollution incidents that were sudden and accidental. This exclusion has been interpreted by some courts to include a wide range of accidents, wider apparently than the scope of coverage that the insurance companies ever intended to provide for a hazardous, toxic pollution liability. As a result of these interpretations, as well as the expanded potential for pollution liability under the Comprehensive Environmental Response Compensation and Liability Act of 1980, the ISO has issued an absolute pollution exclusion to the standard Commercial General Liability coverage forms. It has been concluded that additional insurance may be purchased to cover hazardous and toxic pollution situations, however, you should check for low limits of coverage. For example, you might buy additional coverage in the amount of not more than $25,000 to cover your pollution risk at your local service station. Then you could find out that $25,000 might not even cover the testing for a problem, to say nothing of $500,000 or more for a problem with a leaking tank.

Now look at the sample found in the standard insurance form under LIABILITY COVERAGE

POLICY as outlined to discover how to read your liability policy and learn how to understand better your protection, or lack thereof. The following is taken from information provided on an actual ISO standard COMMERCIAL GENERAL LIABILITY COVERAGE form. Sections not applicable to this discussion were omitted and are indicated in this chapter by the use of three dots (...). The shading was added for emphasis in this chapter.

COMMERCIAL GENERAL LIABILITY COVERAGE FORM

"Various provisions in this policy restrict coverage. Read the entire policy carefully to determine rights, duties and what is and is not covered." ...

SECTION I - COVERAGES

COVERAGE A. BODILY INJURY AND PROPERTY DAMAGE LIABILITY

1. Insuring Agreement.

   a. We will pay those sums that the insured becomes legally obligated to pay as damages because of "bodily injury" or "property damage" to which this insurance applies. We will have the right and duty to defend any "suit" seeking those damages. We may at our discretion investigate any "occurrence" and settle any claim or "suit" that may result. But:

      (1) The amount we will pay for damages is limited as described in LIMITS OF

INSURANCE (SECTION III); and

(2) Our right and duty to defend end when we have used up the applicable limit of insurance in the payment of judgments or settlements under Coverages A or B or medical expenses under Coverage C.

No other obligation or liability to pay sums or perform acts or services is covered unless explicitly provided for under SUPPLEMENTARY PAYMENTS - COVERAGES A AND B.

b. This insurance applies to "bodily injury" and "property damage" only if:

(1) The "bodily injury" or "property damage" is caused by an "occurrence" that takes place in the "coverage territory"; and

(2) The "bodily injury" or "property damage" occurs during the policy period.

c. Damages because of "bodily injury" include damages claimed by any person or organization for care, loss of services or death resulting at any time from the "bodily injury."

2. Exclusions.

This insurance does not apply to:

a. Expected or Intended Injury

"Bodily injury" or "property damage" expected or intended from the standpoint of the insured. This exclusion does not apply to "bodily injury" resulting from the use of reasonable force to protect persons or property.

b. Contractual Liability ...

c. Liquor Liability ...

d. Workers' Compensation and Similar Laws

Any obligation of the insured under a workers' compensation, disability benefits or unemployment compensation law or any similar law.

e. Employer's Liability

"Bodily injury" to:

(1) An "employee" of the insured arising out of and in the course of:
   (a) Employment by the insured; or
   (b) Performing duties related to the conduct of the insured's business; or

(2) The spouse, child, parent, brother or sister of that "employee" as a consequence of paragraph (1) above.

This exclusion applies:

(1) Whether the insured may be liable as an employer or in any other capacity; and

(2) To any obligation to share damages with or repay someone else who must pay damages because of the injury.

This exclusion does not apply to liability assumed by the insured under an "insured contract."

f. Pollution (This insurance does not apply to:)

(1) "Bodily injury" or "property damage" arising out of the actual, alleged or threatened discharge, dispersal, seepage, migration, release or escape of pollutants:

(a) At or from any premises, site or location which is or was at any time owned or occupied by, or rented or loaned to, any insured;

(b) At or from any premises, site or location which is or was at any time used by or for any insured or others for the handling, storage, disposal, processing or treatment of waste;

(c) Which are or were at any time transported, handled, stored, treated, disposed of, or processed as waste by or for any insured or any person or organization for whom you may be legally responsible; or

(d) At or from any premises, site or location on which any insured or any contractors or subcontractors working directly or indirectly on any insured's behalf are performing operations:

(i) If the pollutants are brought on or to the premises, site or location in connection with such operations by such insured, contractor or subcontractor; or

(ii) If the operations are to test for, monitor, clean up, remove, contain, treat, detoxify or neutralize, or in any way respond to, or assess the effects of pollutants.

Subparagraphs (a) and (d)(i) do not apply to "bodily injury" or "property damage" arising out of heat, smoke or fumes from a hostile fire.

As used in this exclusion, a hostile fire means one which becomes uncontrollable or breaks out from where it was intended to be.

(2) Any loss, cost or expense arising out of any:

(a) Request, demand or order that any insured or others test for, monitor, clean up, remove, contain, treat, detoxify or neutralize, or in any way respond to, or assess the effects of pollutants; or

(b) Claim or suit by or on behalf of a governmental authority for damages because of testing for, monitoring, cleaning up, removing, containing, treating, detoxifying or neutralizing, or in any way responding to, or assessing the effects of pollutants.

Pollutants means any solid, liquid, gaseous or thermal irritant or contaminant, including smoke, vapor, soot, fumes, acids, alkalis, chemicals and waste. Waste includes materials to be recycled, reconditioned or reclaimed.

g. Aircraft, Auto or Watercraft ...

COVERAGE B. PERSONAL AND ADVERTISING INJURY LIABILITY ...

COVERAGE C. MEDICAL PAYMENTS

1. Insuring Agreement.

   a. We will pay medical expenses as described below for "bodily injury" caused by an accident:

      (1) On premises you own or rent;

      (2) On ways next to premises you own or rent; or

(3) Because of your operations; provided that:

(1) The accident takes place in the "coverage territory" and during the policy period;
(2) The expenses are incurred and reported to us within one year of the date of the accident; and
(3) The injured person submits to examination, at our expense, by physicians of our choice as often as we reasonably require.

b. We will make these payments regardless of fault. These payments will not exceed the applicable limit of insurance. We will pay reasonable expenses for:

(1) First aid administered at the time of an accident;

(2) Necessary medical, surgical, x-ray and dental services,

including prosthetic devices; and

(3) Necessary ambulance, hospital, professional nursing and funeral services.

2. Exclusions.

We will not pay expenses for "bodily injury:"

a. To any insured.

b. To a person hired to do work for or on behalf of any insured or a tenant of any insured.

c. To a person injured on that part of premises you own or rent that the person normally occupies.

d. To a person, whether or not an "employee" of any insured, if benefits for the "bodily injury" are payable or must be provided under a workers' compensation or disability benefits law or a similar law.

e. To a person injured while taking part in athletics.

f. Included within the "products-completed operations hazard".

g. Excluded under Coverage A.

h. Due to war, whether or not declared, or any act or condition incident to war. War includes civil war, insurrection, rebellion or revolution.

SUPPLEMENTARY PAYMENTS - COVERAGES A AND B...

SECTION V - DEFINITIONS

1. ...

2. ...

3. "Bodily injury" means bodily injury, sickness or disease sustained by a person, including death resulting from any of these at any time. ...

Looking, Looking, Looking

We are still looking for the responsible parties who can and will assist in environmental clean-up and the design and implementation of environmental safety strategies. Could the giant corporations assist? Employees? Employers? Government agencies? Insurance companies? The government working with various insurance companies?

Who will dare to help?
Who can afford to help?
Who knows what to do to help?

Where might the motivation be found within this massive social machine actually to change the course of our spaceship earth's environmental pressures? Are you concerned about your health? The health of your children? The health of your grandchildren? The health of yet unborn children? Are hazardous, toxic polluting accidents really accidents after all? The answers to these questions greatly affect the inhabitants of our spaceship earth. Let's take a look at one attempt by the government to work with various insurance carriers.

The Workers' Compensation Experiment

The Workers' Compensation protection plan is an example of government, employers, and various insurance carriers working together in an attempt to provide protection for employees while also attempting to motivate the employees to exercise safer working habits. The cost of the program continues to grow, the number of accidents is increasing, and privileges have been abused.

Workers' Compensation Insurance covers work-related injuries and diseases. Coverage includes medical and death benefits, and compensation for lost time. The full cost of this insurance is paid by the employer and cannot be deducted from employees' wages. Coverage may be purchased through private insurance carriers or the various State Compensation Insurance Authorities. Benefits may be set by state legislation, and if so, the rates will be the same for all carriers underwriting the coverage in that particular state.

All employers who have at least one employee must carry workers' compensation insurance. As a general rule, the insurance coverage begins with the first day of work for the employee.

In cases of life-or-limb threatening injuries, employees are instructed to seek medical attention immediately at the nearest emergency room and then notify the company supervisors of the incident in writing. For all other injuries, employees are instructed to notify their employer or supervisor in writing that they have received an injury prior to obtaining any medical care.

There may be times when an injury or illness is not diagnosed, when symptoms do not appear until after employment has been terminated, or when there was no apparent injury from an "accident" (for example, exposure to hazardous chemicals or diagnosis of a repetitive motion disease.) Employees have two years from the date of injury to file a claim for compensation. If a person is still working for the same employer where the injury or accident occurred, the employee may report the injury to the employer and have him file the injury form. If the employee is not working for the same employer, the former employee may file a claim with the Division of Workers' Compensation.

The Colorado guide to Workers' Compensation states that Workers' Compensation Benefits may be reduced for a variety of reasons. For example, benefits can be reduced by 50% under the following conditions:

1. The injury is caused by the willful failure of the employee to use employer provided safety devices.

2. The injury results from the employee's willful failure to obey a reasonable

safety rule adopted and enforced by the employer for the safety of the employees.

3. The injury results from employee intoxication or drug use. Legitimate medical benefits will continue to be paid until the worker has reached maximum medical improvement.

A quote from the California Workers' Compensation folder states, "If you believe a person other than your employer is responsible for your injury, you may be able to seek payment from that party in a civic court." The folder goes on to ask and answer the following question: What if my employer discriminates against me because of my industrial injury or illness? Workers' Compensation and labor laws prohibit discrimination against:

1. Workers who are injured because of their employment;

2. Workers who testify or intend to testify before the Workers' Compensation appeals board regarding another employee's case.

The insurance companies that underwrite the coverage in California report that an injury or illness may result from a single incident or from repeated or prolonged exposure to activities or substances at work. In California, more than four out of five workers who receive Workers' Compensation benefits do so from insurance carriers who cover their employers' liability. The remainder receive benefits directly from employers who are self-insured. Because the California law requires all employers to carry workers' compensation insurance, it is important that California workers contact an information and assistance officer immediately if they suspect that their employer is illegally uninsured. On the other hand, consider this quote regarding the Rights To Workers' Compensation Benefits in California: "Any person who makes or causes to be made, any knowingly false or fraudulent material statement, or material representation for the purpose of obtaining or denying Workers' Compensation benefits or payments, is guilty of a felony."

There are many other items which relate to Workers' Compensation and injury information. Most of these items are simple to follow and can be found in an employer's corporate handbook which should be made available to each employee. Please note that an employer's liability exclusion extends to all employees including leased workers, but not to temporary workers. It is important to note that an occupational disease is a disease that results directly from the employment or work conditions. It cannot come from a hazard outside the workplace to which the worker has been equally exposed. Occupational diseases include cumulative trauma, such as diseases or illnesses that may result from constant exposure to chemicals, dust, noise, or other work place hazards.

QUESTION: Regarding hazardous and toxic pollutants, when and how are we going to be motivated to CARE and demonstrate CONCERN for our employees, as well as for ourselves? The above information is aimed at taking care of employees after an accident. Why not emphasize more preventative measures?

Please Give Us a Motivational Model

The first state legislature to pass a motivational Workers' Compensation Loss Prevention and Loss Control Program was the State of Colorado. The program allows a participating business to save up to 25% on its insurance premiums, and the state legislature has approved another automatic 5% savings on premiums after a business has qualified and been registered in the safety program for one year. Larry Kehn, the Cost Containment Advisor for the Colorado Department of Labor and Employment, Division of Workers' Compensation, pointed out that the motivation and cooperation has begun to pay off with accident frequency reduced by 22%, a total of 3,188 fewer accidents, and accident costs reduced by

61%, a cash savings of $26,193,843 as of April 27, 1994!

The cost containment schedule for workplace safety and loss control included procedures which were presented with overall goals of helping prevent accidents and increase safety awareness. The following are adopted from Colorado's legislative cost containment guidelines.

Purpose

In addition to using every safeguard and precaution available to protect employees from on-the-job injuries, there are a number of significant economic benefits available as a result of an organized accident prevention program.

An accident or unexpected hazardous exposure includes any unforeseen interruption to the work schedule. Bearing this in mind, risk assessment must be made an important part of every operation to maximize production efficiency while eliminating injuries. Consider the following COSTS of accidents:

1. Direct costs:
   - (a) Cost of medical and indemnity payments on behalf of the injured worker;
   - (b) Cost regarding loss of life.

2. Indirect costs:
   (a) Cost of business interruption;
   (b) Public and employee relations.

The cost(s) associated with Workers' Compensation impacts the EMPLOYER in two ways:

1. For the most part, rates are calculated on the loss experience (costs) associated with a specific class of employment. There are approximately 600 different classifications of employment in the rate-making system. Rates are determined by the National Council on Compensation Insurance (N.C.C.I.) on a state-by-state basis.

   N.C.C.I. determines rates with respect to adequate funding to pay claims and administrative expenses and to ensure economic survival of the insurer.

   According to the 1989 Colorado rate schedule, rates for each $100 of payroll ranged from $.06 for board members to $112 for steel erectors, based upon the past and expected future costs within these classifications.

2. Through experience modifications, each individual employer's historical, actual incurred losses are compared with N.C.C.I. expected losses for the employer's given classifications and payroll. If accidents are prevented, there are no costs to drive up the premiums.

Production Interference

Relative to business interruption, the costs become difficult to measure and are usually overlooked entirely. In an industrial accident, indirect costs may be many times the direct costs mentioned above. All or some of the indirect cost items mentioned below are found in every accident:

1. Loss of production due to shut down of the work area or processes under the control of the injured employee(s);

2. Time lost by fellow employees in assisting the injured employee(s), discussing the accident, and returning to normal production schedules;

3. Loss of future business or goodwill because of failure to meet production schedules;

4. Time spent by the supervisor in preparing the accident report, investigating the accident, assisting the injured employee, and training a replacement;

5. Possible decreased efficiency of the injured employee for the period immediately following his or her return to work;

6. Decreased efficiency of the replacement; and

7. Wages paid to the employee for the time lost on the date of the accident.

Employee Morale

A low accident rate can be an important factor in establishing a reputation as a good employer. An accident prevention program, which is effective in maintaining low injury rates, may be viewed by employees as evidence that management is interested in employee welfare.

Public Relations

Poor safety records, particularly those involving catastrophes such as exposures to hazardous or toxic chemicals, explosions and major fires, and all other items receiving wide publicity, have an unfavorable effect on public opinion and may be reflected in decreased consumer acceptance of products. In recognition of this situation, an outstanding safety record can be used as a means of improving public relations. At a local level, a poor safety record can be instrumental in giving the employer a bad reputation, which will make maintaining good community relations difficult, and also hinder recruitment of a satisfactory labor force during periods of high employment.

Loss Prevention

The loss prevention program must begin with a declaration from top management of a prevention and loss control policy. A good policy makes it easier to enforce safe practices and conditions, to implement company goals, to follow safety rules and instructions, and to acquire and maintain equipment and safe chemical substitutes. Basic to a policy declaration are these statements:

1. Safety of employees, the public, and company operations is paramount;

2. Safety will take precedence over expediency or short cuts;

3. Every attempt will be made to reduce the possibility of accident occurrence.

Choose Your Company Philosophy

The following examples of policy statements are offered by the National Safety Council:

1. It is a basic responsibility of all executives to make the safety of human beings a part of their daily, hourly concern. This responsibility must be accepted by all who have a part in the affairs of the business, no matter in what capacity they may function.

2. Management considers no phase of operation or administration as being of greater importance than accident prevention. It is the policy of the company, therefore, to provide and maintain safe and healthful working conditions and to follow operating practices that will safeguard all employees and result in safe working conditions and efficient operation.

3. We believe in the dignity and importance of the individual employees and in their rights to derive personal satisfaction from their employment. Also spelled out in this creed is our belief that the safety of employees continues to be first consideration in the operation of the business.

4. Safety is our responsibility in management. Without question it is our number one responsibility, taking precedence over everything else.

5. The supervisor is the key in the safety program because he or she is in constant contact with employees. No foreman, supervisor, or operating head may ever be relieved of any part of his

or her responsibility for safety. Safety is an operating function and cannot be transferred to a staff organization.

6. Safe practices on the part of employees must be part of all operations. No job shall be considered efficiently completed unless workers have followed every precaution and safety rule to protect themselves and their fellow workers. The ideals of production and safety are inseparable.

7. When workers enter the employ of this company, they have a right to expect to be provided with a proper place in which to work and proper supplies and equipment with which to do their jobs so that they will be able to devote their energies to their work without fear of possible harm to their life and health.

Personal Protective Environment

Personal protective environment becomes necessary when there is a hazardous exposure that is impractical or impossible to eliminate as a cause of accidents by engineering revision, by safeguarding, or by limiting exposure time.

Two important considerations need to be made when it is determined that personal protective environment is necessary:

1. Selection is made of the proper type of supplies and equipment. For example, a mask designed to protect against particulates is worthless against vapor, gases, or fumes. If there is doubt, the supplier should be able to assure that the application conforms to standards as set forth by:
   American National Standards Institute
   American Society for Testing and Materials
   The National Institute for Occupational Safety and Health
   Mining Enforcement and Safety Administration

2. The supervisor needs to make sure that the equipment is used correctly and maintained. Using personal protective equipment requires awareness and training on the part of the user. Employees must be aware that the equipment does not eliminate the hazard. If the equipment fails,

exposure will occur. To reduce possibility of failure, equipment must be properly fitted and maintained in a clean, serviceable condition. Fit is extremely important in assuring employees' acceptance and safety.

Loss Prevention Guide

In order to prevent losses effectively, there must be clearly defined rules. Again, in the training phase, employees must be made aware of the rules, and, when possible, rules should be posted in appropriate and conspicuous areas. A worker who willfully violates a work place safety rule, and in so doing injures him or herself, may sustain a 50% reduction in Workers' Compensation disability benefits (motivation).

Hazard Communication Program "RIGHT TO KNOW" Act

This federally mandated program REQUIRES THAT EMPLOYEES BE TOTALLY INFORMED ABOUT THE HAZARDS OF CHEMICAL COMPOUNDS with which they are working, and how to protect themselves. All manufacturers and importers of chemicals must evaluate the hazards of their products and provide all such information to the users. (See Chapter VI, Are The Chemical Companies At Fault?) The employers' responsibilities are summarized as follows:

1. The material safety data sheet (MSDS), furnished by the manufacturer, describing chemical, physical, and hazardous properties of industrial chemicals, must be made available to all employees in the work area and updated as necessary.

2. All containers must be labeled in a manner that discloses health and physical hazards.

3. All personnel in contact with any compound(s) included under this program must be specifically trained in proper handling, storage, transfer, and application as well as appropriate personal protective equipment, leak and spill procedures, and first aid.

4. In all areas where there is exposure to chemical hazards, engineering controls and/or ventilation should be facilitated.

Personal protective equipment is, of course, the last resort, when all other procedures prove inadequate.

The following outlined suggestions pertain to engineering control methods:

1. SUBSTITUTION:
   (a) Substitution of a less toxic material is an effective control method.
   (b) Make sure that if you substitute, you do not introduce a new hazard.
2. PROCESS CHANGE:
   Process operations, materials, or equipment can be modified to reduce the generation of contaminants.

The following four pages are copies of the Colorado Workers' Compensation -- Premium Cost Containment Program, REQUEST FOR CERTIFICATION, followed by a copy of the PREMIUM COST CONTAINMENT CERTIFICATE.

COLORADO WORKERS' COMPENSATION
--- PREMIUM COST CONTAINMENT PROGRAM ---
REQUEST FOR CERTIFICATION

COMPANY NAME: ____________________

COMPANY MAILING ADDRESS: ____________________

____

____

NAME OF INSURANCE CARRIER: ____________________

EMPLOYEE CLASSIFICATION TITLE(S): ____________________

DATE PROGRAM WAS IMPLEMENTED: ____________________

In order to obtain/maintain certification status in the Colorado Workers' Compensation Premium Cost Containment Program, it must be confirmed that an approved loss prevention and loss control program has been actively followed in this company for a period of at least one year. Loss prevention documentation which clearly shows that compliance with each of the following requirements has been in effect for at least one year must accompany this Request For Certification.

COST CONTAINMENT PROGRAM REQUIREMENTS

1. FORMAL DECLARATION OF A COMPANY-WIDE LOSS PREVENTION AND LOSS CONTROL POLICY (COPY ENCLOSED).

   (a) The policy reflects the philosophy of top management.
   (b) The safety and health of all employees is a top priority.

2. FORMAL CREATION OF A SAFETY COMMITTEE OR COORDINATOR (COPY ENCLOSED).

   (a) Committee or coordinator has clearly defined tasks and objectives.
   (b) Discuss/recommend safety policies and objectives.
   (c) Identify unsafe conditions and practices.
   (d) Investigate all accidents.
   (e) Conduct safety meetings and promote safety awareness.
   (f) Establish and update safety rules.

COLORADO WORKERS' COMPENSATION
PREMIUM COST CONTAINMENT PROGRAM
REQUEST FOR CERTIFICATION
Page Two

3. CLEARLY DEFINED AND CONSPICUOUSLY POSTED SAFETY/LOSS PREVENTION RULES (COPY ENCLOSED).

   (a) Hazards are identified and accident prevention rules are clearly communicated.
   (b) All employees are made aware of the safety rules.
   (c) Safety rules are applicable and updated as needed.

4. ALL EMPLOYEES UNDERGO SAFETY AWARENESS AND LOSS PREVENTION TRAINING (VERIFICATION OF EMPLOYEE TRAINING PROGRAM ENCLOSED).

   (a) The supervisor has provided and documented individual job/task safety training.
   (b) Loss prevention training meetings are held and attendance (employee sign-off) recorded.

5. WRITTEN DESIGNATION OF A MEDICAL PROVIDER (COPY ENCLOSED).

   (a) Provider is knowledgeable of fee schedules and agrees to honor designated provider agreements.
   (b) Provider communicates with the employer on issues such as case management and modified duty.
   (c) Employer will keep in contact with the injured worker and will inform employees on matters concerning the designated medical provider.

6. WRITTEN POLICIES AND PROCEDURES ON CLAIMS MANAGEMENT (COPY ENCLOSED).

   (a) Employer has investigated all incidents with third party ramifications.
   (b) Employer ensures the insurance carrier is contacted in a timely manner and confirms that the employee was working at the time of the accident.
   (c) Employer coordinates with the insurance carrier (at least annually) on issues such as loss runs review, outstanding reserves, and employee classification.
   (d) Employer, when practicable, institutes a modified duty program in conformance with the attending physician's restrictions.

COLORADO WORKERS' COMPENSATION
PREMIUM COST CONTAINMENT PROGRAM
REQUEST FOR CERTIFICATION
Page Three

7. A COPY OF YOUR INSURANCE CARRIER'S LOSS REPORT FOR THE FIRST YEAR OF THIS PROGRAM TOGETHER WITH THE TOTAL NUMBER OF PEOPLE EMPLOYED DURING THAT YEAR, AND COPIES OF THE LOSS REPORTS FOR THE TWO YEARS PRIOR TO IMPLEMENTATION OF THIS PROGRAM WITH THE TOTAL NUMBER OF PEOPLE EMPLOYED DURING THOSE YEARS MUST BE INCLUDED WITH THIS REQUEST FOR CERTIFICATION.

TODAY'S DATE: ______________________________

SIGNATURE OF CONTACT PERSON:* ______________________________

CONTACT PERSON'S TELEPHONE NUMBER: ______________________________

PLEASE RETURN THIS COMPLETED FORM AND DOCUMENTATION TO:

Premium Cost Containment Program Board
The Colorado Division of Workers' Compensation
1120 Lincoln Street, Room 1200
Denver, CO 80203

* By signing this request, the contact person affirms that the above requirements have been met.

(Revised 01/04/93)

STATE OF COLORADO

DEPARTMENT OF LABOR AND EMPLOYMENT
DIVISION OF WORKERS' COMPENSATION

PREMIUM COST CONTAINMENT CERTIFICATE

In consideration that ______________________________
has met all of the Workers' Compensation Cost Containment Program requirements, the employer is hereby granted certified status beginning ______________
for a period of one year.

This certificate is granted subject to the provisions of the Workers' Compensation Act, as it now exists or as it may from time to time be amended, and also subject to the rules and regulations of the Cost Containment Board, as they now exist or may from time to time be made, altered, or amended.

By ______________________________
Director, Division of Workers' Compensation

By ______________________________
Workers' Compensation Cost Containment Board

Reflective Thoughts

As inhabitants of spaceship earth, we must realize the importance of determining why and how accidents happen so we can prevent reoccurrences. Another important labyrinth of issues lies in IMPLEMENTING the changes! We can study, review and discuss what changes are needed until "the cows come home," but we must actually MAKE THE CHANGES to MAKE THE DIFFERENCE! Individuals as well as committees may participate to promote loss prevention and to review accidents as an integral part of the evaluation and inspection process. This must include both the actual inspections as well as the hazard abatement process. Establishing a local committee composed of management and employees who represent a broad cross-section of the workplace and have comprehensive knowledge of environmental impacts and their local operations, is strongly suggested. These committees will improve safety by the following means:

1. Preventing fiscal losses, while allowing the employees the freedom to express openly their health and safety concerns.

2. Allowing management to maintain an active and responsive interest, rather than simply delegating its responsibility to the committee.

Are we making progress in developing environmental safety awareness? Recent studies by the Colorado Workers' Compensation project revealed that companies actively involved in limited duty cost and loss control programs were able to reduce:

1. Workers' Compensation costs by 28%;

2. Lost work days by 25%; and

3. Lost time case settlement by four months.

Without the cost and loss controls, consider this information: According to the Colorado Workers' Compensation data, the 1988 Workers' Compensation benefits nationwide totaled over 30 billion dollars; between 1973 and 1987, lost work days per 100 full-time workers went from 52 to 70; and since 1980, the average claims loss has increased from $6,000 to $10,000. It seems evident that our system needs strong environmental health and safety motivation.

The "NOW WHAT" Conclusions

Are insurance companies environmentally helpful? They could be, being such a giant of an industry! Think of it, these companies affect almost every person in America. The assurance these companies give us adds stability to our insecurities and lets us sleep better at night. What a tremendous influence insurers are in the investment world! Consider their holdings, their stocks, bonds, and real property. These companies have influence over an extensive army of workers, executives, investors, underwriters, office staff, brokers, agents, as well as the masses of the insured. Insurance-related mail saturates every state of our union, and insurance cash flow circulates through every bank in our great land and in most countries around the world. It is only reasonable that we ask, "Are the insurance companies environmentally helpful?"

How about Workers' Compensation coverage? Yes, the government enacted the law to create it, the employees are protected by it, the employers pay for it, and the various insurance carriers underwrite it -- for a profit. This entire process is reasonable, and no one is at fault. We all live in America, and this process is the American way. But is it the best way? We are just now seeing the beginnings of change, of real safety, and cost and loss controls being motivated through several Workers' Compensation programs. Are more motivations needed?

We need to talk about helping preserve our ecological balance, our environment, health, and safety. Please understand, we are not suggesting that insurance companies give up their profit, nor do they need to spend tax deductible dollars on our behalf. If those in this powerful financial sector would just lend their influence to addressing environmental concerns and facing these issues head-on, greater strides might be made. Imagine this for a moment: What if your local insurance broker or your personal insurance agent, were to take the time to explain in detail the exclusions on your various policies? For example, what does the standard form "bodily injury" and "property damage" exclusion (f), hazardous and toxic pollutants mean to you? Has your agent explained to you the circumstances under which you have no insurance, even if you paid for it and thought you had adequate coverage? Have your insurers helped educate you, for example, about certain possible substitutes that would not be classified as hazardous, toxic pollutants and would allow your insurance to remain in full effect? Who is to say how a giant company or industry is to run its affairs? "We the people" may not all be voting stockholders, but we would appreciate any help we could get for the common cause of survival. If we could count on the encouragement and influence of insurance companies, on permission and encouragement for insurance agents to be open and helpful to "we the people," it would make a big difference. We can do better, we need to do better, and we would appreciate the help of our insurers.

"Cover Your Actions"

A concluding word of caution to our brave employers and their key decision-making employees. Understand your liability exposure. Understand your insurance coverage. Understand the law. Understand that there are government agencies who "pay to squeal." Our best advice, CYA, cover your actions. Consider the following brief example:

> You own a local motel or hotel. Housekeeping personnel have just pushed their cleaning cart down to Room 234. There are four cleaning spray bottles hanging by handles from each end of the cart. An inquisitive guest of your hotel, a 10 year old lad, bounds up the hallway. He knows that if you squeeze the handle of a squirt bottle, it will emit a spray. The bottle is hanging by the handle with the nozzle pointed at him. One good squeeze and the liquid is dispensed.

> The bottle was full of toxic toilet bowl cleaner which is now on his face and in his eyes. Will your insurance cover you? Are hazardous, toxic polluting substances excluded from the coverage on your insurance policy? Did you knowingly and willfully maintain a hazard, a blinding trap? Were other, safer substitute or alternative cleaning materials available?

You have a potential liability risk for anyone who is involved with you and your property, everyone except your employees (due to Workers' Compensation legislation.) Workers' Compensation relieves you from the possibility of a tort or common law risk with your employees. Now it is a government passed statute which makes you immune or considered at "no-fault" regarding risk with the employees. Keep in mind, however, that while you have relief on one hand, you still have responsibility to the insurance carrier, the labor boards, department of Workers' Compensation, and various government regulatory agencies as listed in Chapter II. Is it possible you just moved from a civil matter between you and your employees to a potential felony charge as described in Chapter V, Environmental Crime and Punishment? Also study the earlier portions of this chapter regarding the law as related to insurance. Have your choices, or your decision-making employees' choices involved negligence? Is a duty owed? Any breach of duty? Any measurable damages? How about intentional torts: Malice of forethought -- "the chemical materials or the faulty equipment is not safe, but it costs less?" Do you wish to consider strict liability -- "because of your responsibility, you are now guilty until proven innocent?" Might we have to live with absolute liability? ... Being responsible without negligence?"... Dangerous Materials or Instrument Doctrine: Anyone who possesses, stores, maintains, or transports a hazardous material or dangerous instrument is absolutely liable for injury or damage caused by the material or instrument, regardless of the presence of due care."

Out of this collage of opportunities, responsibilities, problems, and diversified parties, we must face reality, develop a cooperative plan, and pursue safe and sound solutions. We must do better.

United States Environmental Protection Agency | Pesticides And Toxic Substances (TS-779) | Solid Waste And Emergency Response (OS-120)
EPA 560/4-92-011 | 500-B-92-002 | January 1992

EPA

Title III List Of Lists

Consolidated List Of Chemicals Subject To Reporting Under The Emergency Planning And Community Right-To-Know Act

(Title III Of The Superfund Amendments And Reauthorization Act Of 1986)

- SARA Section 302 Extremely Hazardous Substances
- CERCLA Hazardous Substances
- SARA Section 313 Toxic Chemicals

ERRATA SHEET TO 1992 LIST OF LISTS
February 1993

I. ADDITIONS

RCRA Waste Streams and Unlisted Hazardous Wastes. Add the following:

RCRA Code	Description	RQ (lbs)
F039	Leachate resulting from disposal of more than 1 restricted waste class. hazard.	1
K149	Distillation bottoms from the production of chlorinated toluenes	10
K150	Organic residuals of Cl gas and HCl from production of chlorinated toluenes	10
K151	Wastewater treatment sludge from production of chlorinated toluenes	10

SARA Title III Consolidated List

1. Add the following CERCLA chemical:

CAS Number	Chemical Name	Sec. 302(EHS) TPQ	EHS RQ	CERCLA RQ	Sec 313	RCRA Code
26952-23-8	Dichloropropene			100		

2. Add the following CERCLA chemical category:

Chemical Category	Sec. 302(EHS) TPQ	EHS RQ	CERCLA RQ	Sec 313	RCRA Code
Hexachlorocyclohexane (all isomers) CAS 608-73-1			***		

II. CORRECTIONS

SARA Title III Consolidated List. Correct RCRA codes for four chemicals and add 'X' to Sec. 313 for one chemical as follows:

CAS Number	Chemical Name	Sec. 302(EHS) TPQ	EHS RQ	CERCLA RQ	Sec 313	RCRA Code
88-06-2	2,4,6-Trichlorophenol			10	313	U231
496-72-0	Diaminotoluene			10		U221
823-40-5	Diaminotoluene			10		U221
8001-58-9	Creosote			1	313	U051
534-52-1	Dinitrocresol	10/10,000		10	X	P047

SARA TITLE III
CONSOLIDATED CHEMICAL LIST

This consolidated chemical list includes chemicals subject to reporting requirements under Title III of the Superfund Amendments and Reauthorization Act of 1986 (SARA)[1], also known as the Emergency Planning and Community Right-to-Know Act (EPCRA). It has been prepared to help firms handling chemicals determine whether they need to submit reports under sections 302, 304, or 313 of Title III and, for a specific chemical, what reports may need to be submitted. Separate lists are also provided of RCRA waste streams and unlisted hazardous wastes, and of radionuclides reportable under CERCLA. These lists should be used as a reference tool, not as a definitive source of compliance information. Compliance information is published in the Code of Federal Regulations, 40 CFR Parts 302, 355, and 372.

The chemicals on the consolidated list are ordered by Chemical Abstract Service (CAS) registry number. Categories of chemicals, which do not have CAS registry numbers, but which are cited under CERCLA and section 313, are placed at the end of the list. For reference purposes, the chemicals (with their CAS numbers) are ordered alphabetically following the CAS-order list. Long chemical names may have been truncated to facilitate printing of this list.

The list includes chemicals referenced under four federal statutory provisions, discussed below. More than one chemical name may be listed for one CAS number because the same chemical may appear on different lists under different names. For example, for CAS number 8001-35-2, the names toxaphene (from the section 313 list), camphechlor (from the section 302 list), and camphene, octachloro- (from the CERCLA list) all appear on this consolidated list. However, the chemicals listed under SARA Title III have many more synonyms than appear on this list.

(1) SARA Section 302 Extremely Hazardous Substances (EHSs)

The presence of EHSs in quantities in excess of the Threshold Planning Quantity (TPQ), requires certain emergency planning activities to be conducted. The extremely hazardous substances and their TPQs are listed in 40 CFR Part 355, Appendices A and B.

TPQ. The consolidated list presents the TPQ (in pounds) for section 302 chemicals in the column following the chemical name. For chemicals that are solids, there may be two TPQs given (e.g., 500/10,000). In these cases, the lower quantity applies for solids in powder form with particle size less than 100 microns, or if the substance is in solution or in molten form. Otherwise, the 10,000 pound TPQ applies.

EHS RQ. Releases of reportable quantities (RQ) of EHSs are subject to state and local reporting under section 304 of Title III. If a chemical listed under section 302 does not have a CERCLA RQ, a statutory RQ of one pound applies for section 304 reporting. The EHS RQ column lists the one-pound statutory RQ for EHSs not listed under CERCLA.

---

[1] **This consolidated list does not include all chemicals subject to the reporting requirements in sections 311 and 312 of SARA Title III. These hazardous chemicals, for which material safety data sheets (MSDS) must be developed under Occupational Safety and Health Act Hazard Communication Standards, are identified by broad criteria, rather than by enumeration. There are over 500,000 products that satisfy the criteria. See 40 CFR Part 370 for more information.**

(2) CERCLA Hazardous Substances ("RQ chemicals")

Releases of CERCLA hazardous substances, in quantities equal to or greater than their reportable quantity (RQ), are subject to reporting to the National Response Center under the Comprehensive Environmental Response, Compensation, and Liability Act of 1980 (CERCLA, or "Superfund"). Such releases are also subject to state and local reporting under section 304 of Title III. CERCLA hazardous substances, and their reportable quantities, are listed in 40 CFR Part 302, Table 302.4. On January 23, 1989, all section 302 chemicals not already listed under CERCLA were proposed for listing, and on August 30, 1989, adjusted RQs (not included in this document) were proposed for these chemicals. This document includes chemicals added to the CERCLA list because they are listed as hazardous air pollutants under section 112(b) of the Clean Air Act (CAA) of 1990. Radionuclides listed under CERCLA are provided in a separate list, with RQs in Curies.

RQ. The CERCLA RQ column in the consolidated list shows the RQs (in pounds) for chemicals that are CERCLA hazardous substances. An asterisk ("*") following the RQ indicates that no reporting of releases is required if the diameter of the pieces of the solid metal released is 100 micrometers (0.004 inches) or greater. Substances listed under CAA section 112(b) that have been added to the CERCLA list with statutory one-pound RQs are indicated by a plus sign ("+") following the RQ.

Note that the consolidated list does not include all CERCLA regulatory synonyms. See 40 CFR Part 302, Table 302.4 for a complete list.

(3) SARA Section 313 Toxic Chemicals

Emissions or releases of chemicals listed under section 313 must be reported annually as part of SARA Title III's community right-to-know provisions. The rule containing these chemicals was published on February 16, 1988 (53 FR 4500) (40 CFR Part 372).

Section 313. The notation "313" in the column for section 313 indicates that the chemical is subject to reporting under section 313 under the name listed. An "X" in this column indicates that the same chemical with the same CAS number appears on another list with a different chemical name.

Be aware that using or processing dissociable ammonium salts may produce ammonia in solution. Ammonia is reportable under section 313.

(4) Chemical Categories

The CERCLA and SARA section 313 lists include a number of chemical categories as well as specific chemicals. The chemicals on this consolidated list have not been systematiclly evaluated to determine whether they fall into any listed categories.

Some chemicals not specifically listed under CERCLA may be subject to CERCLA reporting as part of a category. For example, strychnine, sulfate (CAS number 60-41-3), listed under SARA section 302, is not on the CERCLA list, but may be subject to CERCLA reporting under the listing for strychnine and salts (CAS number 57-24-9), with an RQ of 10 pounds. Similarly, nicotine sulfate (CAS number 65-30-5) may be subject to CERCLA reporting under the listing for nicotine and salts (CAS number 54-11-5, RQ 100 pounds), and warfarin sodium (CAS number 129-06-6) may be subject to CERCLA reporting under the listing for warfarin and salts, concentration >0.3% (CAS number 81-88-9, RQ 100 pounds). The CERCLA list also includes a number of generic categories that have not been assigned RQs; chemicals falling into listed categories are considered CERCLA hazardous substances, but are not required to be reported under CERCLA unless an RQ has been assigned.

A number of chemical categories are subject to section 313 reporting. They appear at the end of the CAS number listing. Be aware that certain chemicals reportable under section 302 or CERCLA may belong to section 313 categories. For example, mercuric acetate (CAS number 1600-27-7), listed under section 302, is not specifically listed under section 313, but could be reported under section 313 as "Mercury Compounds" (no CAS number).

(5) RCRA Hazardous Wastes

The consolidated list includes specific chemicals from the P and U lists only (40 CFR 261.33). This listing is provided as an indicator that companies may already have data on a specific chemical that may be useful for Title III reporting. It is not intended to be a comprehensive list of RCRA P and U chemicals. RCRA hazardous wastes consisting of waste streams on the F and K lists, and wastes exhibiting the characteristics of ignitibility, corrosivity, reactivity, and EP toxicity, are provided in a separate list. The descriptions of the F and K waste streams have been abbreviated; see 40 CFR Part 302, Table 302.4 for complete descriptions.

RCRA Code. The letter-and-digit code in the RCRA Code column is the chemical's RCRA hazardous waste code.

Information Sources

For additional copies of this or other Title III documents, send requests to:

Section 313 Document Distribution Center
P.O. Box 12505
Cincinnati, OH 45212

Refer to document number EPA 560/4-92-012 for additional copies of this document.

A dBase version of this consolidated list is available on disk from:

National Technical Information Service (NTIS)
5285 Port Royal Road
Springfield, VA 22161
(703) 487-4600

Refer to PB89 158653.

Questions concerning changes to the list or other aspects of Title III may be submitted in writing to:

Emergency Planning and Community Right-to-Know Information Hotline
U.S. Environmental Protection Agency (OS-120)
401 M Street, SW
Washington, DC 20460

Alternatively, you may call the hotline at (800) 535-0202 between the hours of 8:30 AM and 7:30 PM Eastern Time.

CAS Number	Chemical Name	Sec. 302(EHS) TPQ	Section 304 EHS RQ	Section 304 CERCLA RQ	Sec 313	RCRA Code
50-00-0	Formaldehyde	500		100	313	U122
50-07-7	Mitomycin C	500/10,000		10		U010
50-14-6	Ergocalciferol	1,000/10,000	1			
50-18-0	Cyclophosphamide			10		U058
50-29-3	DDT			1		U061
50-32-8	Benzo[a]pyrene			1		U022
50-55-5	Reserpine			5,000		U200
51-21-8	Fluorouracil	500/10,000	1			
51-28-5	2,4-Dinitrophenol			10	313	P048
51-43-4	Epinephrine			1,000		P042
51-75-2	Nitrogen mustard	10	1		313	
51-75-2	Mechlorethamine	10	1		X	
51-79-6	Urethane			100	313	U238
51-79-6	Carbamic acid, ethyl ester			100	X	U238
51-79-6	Ethyl carbamate			100	X	U238
51-83-2	Carbachol chloride	500/10,000	1			
52-68-6	Trichlorfon			100	313	
52-85-7	Famphur			1,000		P097
53-70-3	Dibenz[a,h]anthracene			1		U063
53-96-3	2-Acetylaminofluorene			1	313	U005
54-11-5	Nicotine	100		100		P075
54-11-5	Pyridine, 3-(1-methyl-2-pyrrolidinyl)-,(S)	100		100		P075
54-11-5	Nicotine and salts			100		P075
54-62-6	Aminopterin	500/10,000	1			
55-18-5	N-Nitrosodiethylamine			1	313	U174
55-21-0	Benzamide				313	
55-63-0	Nitroglycerin			10	313	P081
55-91-4	Isofluorphate	100		100		P043
55-91-4	Diisopropylfluorophosphate	100		100		P043
56-04-2	Methylthiouracil			10		U164
56-23-5	Carbon tetrachloride			10	313	U211
56-25-7	Cantharidin	100/10,000	1			
56-38-2	Parathion	100		10	313	P089
56-49-5	3-Methylcholanthrene			10		U157
56-53-1	Diethylstilbestrol			1		U089
56-55-3	Benz[a]anthracene			10		U018
56-72-4	Coumaphos	100/10,000		10		
57-12-5	Cyanides (soluble salts and complexes)			10		P030
57-14-7	1,1-Dimethyl hydrazine	1,000		10	313	U098
57-14-7	Dimethylhydrazine	1,000		10	X	U098

CAS Number	Chemical Name	Sec. 302(EHS) TPQ	Section 304 EHS RQ	Section 304 CERCLA RQ	Sec 313	RCRA Code
57-14-7	Hydrazine, 1,1-dimethyl-	1,000		10	X	U098
57-24-9	Strychnine	100/10,000		10		P108
57-24-9	Strychnine, and salts			10		P108
57-47-6	Physostigmine	100/10,000	1			
57-57-8	beta-Propiolactone	500		1+	313	
57-64-7	Physostigmine, salicylate (1:1)	100/10,000	1			
57-74-9	Chlordane	1,000		1	313	U036
57-97-6	7,12-Dimethylbenz[a]anthracene			1		U094
58-36-6	Phenoxarsine, 10,10'-oxydi-	500/10,000	1			
58-89-9	Lindane	1,000/10,000		1	313	U129
58-89-9	Hexachlorocyclohexane (gamma isomer)	1,000/10,000		1	X	U129
58-90-2	2,3,4,6-Tetrachlorophenol			10		U212
59-50-7	p-Chloro-m-cresol			5,000		U039
59-88-1	Phenylhydrazine hydrochloride	1,000/10,000	1			
59-89-2	N-Nitrosomorpholine			1+	313	
60-00-4	Ethylenediamine-tetraacetic acid (EDTA)			5,000		
60-09-3	4-Aminoazobenzene				313	
60-11-7	4-Dimethylaminoazobenzene			10	313	U093
60-11-7	Dimethylaminoazobenzene			10	X	U093
60-29-7	Ethyl ether			100		U117
60-34-4	Methyl hydrazine	500		10	313	P068
60-35-5	Acetamide			1+	313	
60-41-3	Strychnine, sulfate	100/10,000	1			
60-51-5	Dimethoate	500/10,000		10		P044
60-57-1	Dieldrin			1		P037
61-82-5	Amitrole			10		U011
62-38-4	Phenylmercury acetate	500/10,000		100		P092
62-38-4	Phenylmercuric acetate	500/10,000		100		P092
62-44-2	Phenacetin			100		U187
62-50-0	Ethyl methanesulfonate			1		U119
62-53-3	Aniline	1,000		5,000	313	U012
62-55-5	Thioacetamide			10	313	U218
62-56-6	Thiourea			10	313	U219
62-73-7	Dichlorvos	1,000		10	313	
62-74-8	Sodium fluoroacetate	10/10,000		10		P058
62-74-8	Fluoroacetic acid, sodium salt	10/10,000		10		P058
62-75-9	N-Nitrosodimethylamine	1,000		10	313	P082
62-75-9	Nitrosodimethylamine	1,000		10	X	P082
62-75-9	Methanamine, N-methyl-N-nitroso-	1,000		10	X	P082
63-25-2	Carbaryl			100	313	

+ Listed as hazardous air pollutant under section 112(b) of the Clean Air Act; statutory RQ of one pound applies until RQs are adjusted.

CAS Number	Chemical Name	Sec. 302(EHS) TPQ	Section 304 EHS RQ	Section 304 CERCLA RQ	Sec 313	RCRA Code
64-00-6	Phenol, 3-(1-methylethyl)-, methylcarbamat	500/10,000	1			
64-18-6	Formic acid			5,000		U123
64-19-7	Acetic acid			5,000		
64-67-5	Diethyl sulfate			1+	313	
64-86-8	Colchicine	10/10,000	1			
65-30-5	Nicotine sulfate	100/10,000	1			
65-85-0	Benzoic acid			5,000		
66-75-1	Uracil mustard			10		U237
66-81-9	Cycloheximide	100/10,000	1			
67-56-1	Methanol			5,000	313	U154
67-63-0	Isopropyl alcohol (mfg-strong acid process				313	
67-64-1	Acetone			5,000	313	U002
67-66-3	Chloroform	10,000		10	313	U044
67-72-1	Hexachloroethane			100	313	U131
68-12-2	Dimethylformamide			1+		
68-76-8	Triaziquone				313	
70-25-7	Guanidine, N-methyl-N'-nitro-N-nitroso-			10		U163
70-30-4	Hexachlorophene			100		U132
70-69-9	Propiophenone, 4'-amino	100/10,000	1			
71-36-3	n-Butyl alcohol			5,000	313	U031
71-43-2	Benzene			10	313	U019
71-55-6	1,1,1-Trichloroethane			1,000	313	U226
71-55-6	Methyl chloroform			1,000	X	U226
71-63-6	Digitoxin	100/10,000	1			
72-20-8	Endrin	500/10,000		1		P051
72-43-5	Methoxychlor			1	313	U247
72-54-8	DDD			1		U060
72-55-9	DDE			1		
72-57-1	Trypan blue			10		U236
74-83-9	Bromomethane	1,000		1,000	313	U029
74-83-9	Methyl bromide	1,000		1,000	X	U029
74-85-1	Ethylene				313	
74-87-3	Chloromethane			100	313	U045
74-87-3	Methyl chloride			100	X	U045
74-88-4	Methyl iodide			100	313	U138
74-89-5	Monomethylamine			100		
74-90-8	Hydrogen cyanide	100		10	313	P063
74-90-8	Hydrocyanic acid	100		10	X	P063
74-93-1	Methyl mercaptan	500		100		U153
74-93-1	Thiomethanol	500		100		U153

+ Listed as hazardous air pollutant under section 112(b) of the Clean Air Act; statutory RQ of one pound applies until RQs are adjusted.

CAS Number	Chemical Name	Sec. 302(EHS) TPQ	Section 304 EHS RQ	Section 304 CERCLA RQ	Sec 313	RCRA Code
74-95-3	Methylene bromide			1,000	313	U068
75-00-3	Chloroethane			100	313	
75-00-3	Ethyl chloride			100	X	
75-01-4	Vinyl chloride			1	313	U043
75-04-7	Monoethylamine			100		
75-05-8	Acetonitrile			5,000	313	U003
75-07-0	Acetaldehyde			1,000	313	U001
75-09-2	Dichloromethane			1,000	313	U080
75-09-2	Methylene chloride			1,000	X	UC80
75-15-0	Carbon disulfide	10,000		100	313	P022
75-20-7	Calcium carbide			10		
75-21-8	Ethylene oxide	1,000		10	313	U115
75-21-8	Oxirane	1,000		10	X	U115
75-25-2	Bromoform			100	313	U225
75-25-2	Tribromomethane			100	X	U225
75-27-4	Dichlorobromomethane			5,000	313	
75-34-3	1,1-Dichloroethane			1,000		U076
75-35-4	Vinylidene chloride			100	313	U078
75-35-4	1,1-Dichloroethylene			100	X	U078
75-36-5	Acetyl chloride			5,000		U006
75-44-5	Phosgene	10		10	313	P095
75-50-3	Trimethylamine			100		
75-55-8	Propyleneimine	10,000		1	313	P067
75-55-8	Aziridine, 2-methyl	10,000		1	X	P067
75-56-9	Propylene oxide	10,000		100	313	
75-60-5	Cacodylic acid			1		U136
75-63-8	Bromotrifluoromethane [Halon 1301]				313	
75-63-8	Halon 1301				X	
75-64-9	tert-Butylamine			1,000		
75-65-0	tert-Butyl alcohol				313	
75-69-4	Trichlorofluoromethane [CFC-11]			5,000	313	U121
75-69-4	CFC-11			5,000	X	U121
75-69-4	Trichloromonofluoromethane			5,000	X	U121
75-71-8	Dichlorodifluoromethane [CFC-12]			5,000	313	U075
75-71-8	CFC-12			5,000	X	U075
75-74-1	Tetramethyllead	100	1			
75-77-4	Trimethylchlorosilane	1,000	1			
75-78-5	Dimethyldichlorosilane	500	1			
75-79-6	Methyltrichlorosilane	500	1			
75-86-5	Acetone cyanohydrin	1,000		10		P069

CAS Number	Chemical Name	Sec. 302(EHS) TPQ	Section 304 EHS RQ	Section 304 CERCLA RQ	Sec 313	RCRA Code
75-87-6	Acetaldehyde, trichloro-			5,000		U034
75-99-0	2,2-Dichloropropionic acid			5,000		
76-01-7	Pentachloroethane			10		U184
76-02-8	Trichloroacetyl chloride	500	1			
76-13-1	Freon 113				313	
76-14-2	Dichlorotetrafluoroethane [CFC-114]				313	
76-14-2	CFC-114				X	
76-15-3	Monochloropentafluoroethane [CFC-115]				313	
76-15-3	CFC-115				X	
76-44-8	Heptachlor			1	313	P059
77-47-4	Hexachlorocyclopentadiene	100		10	313	U130
77-78-1	Dimethyl sulfate	500		100	313	U103
77-81-6	Tabun	10	1			
78-00-2	Tetraethyl lead	100		10		P110
78-34-2	Dioxathion	500	1			
78-53-5	Amiton	500	1			
78-59-1	Isophorone			5,000		
78-71-7	Oxetane, 3,3-bis(chloromethyl)-	500	1			
78-79-5	Isoprene			100		
78-81-9	iso-Butylamine			1,000		
78-82-0	Isobutyronitrile	1,000	1			
78-83-1	Isobutyl alcohol			5,000		U140
78-84-2	Isobutyraldehyde				313	
78-87-5	1,2-Dichloropropane			1,000	313	U083
78-87-5	Propane 1,2-dichloro-			1,000	X	U083
78-88-6	2,3-Dichloropropene			100	313	
78-92-2	sec-Butyl alcohol				313	
78-93-3	Methyl ethyl ketone			5,000	313	U159
78-93-3	Methyl ethyl ketone (MEK)			5,000	X	U159
78-94-4	Methyl vinyl ketone	10	1			
78-97-7	Lactonitrile	1,000	1			
78-99-9	1,1-Dichloropropane			1,000		
79-00-5	1,1,2-Trichloroethane			100	313	U227
79-01-6	Trichloroethylene			100	313	U228
79-06-1	Acrylamide	1,000/10,000		5,000	313	U007
79-09-4	Propionic acid			5,000		
79-10-7	Acrylic acid			5,000	313	U008
79-11-8	Chloroacetic acid	100/10,000		1+	313	
79-19-6	Thiosemicarbazide	100/10,000		100		P116
79-21-0	Peracetic acid	500	1		313	

+ Listed as hazardous air pollutant under section 112(b) of the Clear Air Act; statutory RQ of one pound applies until RQs are adjusted.

CAS Number	Chemical Name	Sec. 302(EHS) TPQ	Section 304 EHS RQ	Section 304 CERCLA RQ	Sec 313	RCRA Code
79-22-1	Methyl chloroformate	500		1,000		U156
79-31-2	iso-Butyric acid			5,000		
79-34-5	1,1,2,2-Tetrachloroethane			100	313	U209
79-44-7	Dimethylcarbamyl chloride			1	313	U097
79-46-9	2-Nitropropane			10	313	U171
80-05-7	4,4'-Isopropylidenediphenol				313	
80-15-9	Cumene hydroperoxide			10	313	U096
80-15-9	Hydroperoxide, 1-methyl-1-phenylethyl-			10	X	U096
80-62-6	Methyl methacrylate			1,000	313	U162
80-63-7	Methyl 2-chloroacrylate	500	1			
81-07-2	Saccharin (manufacturing)			100	313	U202
81-07-2	Saccharin and salts			100		U202
81-81-2	Warfarin	500/10,000		100		P001
81-81-2	Warfarin, & salts, conc.>0.3%			100		P001
81-88-9	C.I. Food Red 15				313	
82-28-0	1-Amino-2-methylanthraquinone				313	
82-66-6	Diphacinone	10/10,000	1			
82-68-8	Quintozene			100	313	U185
82-68-8	Pentachloronitrobenzene			100	X	U185
82-68-8	PCNB			100	X	U185
83-32-9	Acenaphthene			100		
84-66-2	Diethyl phthalate			1,000	313	U088
84-74-2	Dibutyl phthalate			10	313	U069
84-74-2	n-Butyl phthalate			10	X	U069
85-00-7	Diquat			1,000		
85-01-8	Phenanthrene			5,000		
85-44-9	Phthalic anhydride			5,000	313	U190
85-68-7	Butyl benzyl phthalate			100	313	
86-30-6	N-Nitrosodiphenylamine			100	313	
86-50-0	Azinphos-methyl	10/10,000		1		
86-50-0	Guthion	10/10,000		1		
86-73-7	Fluorene			5,000		
86-88-4	Antu	500/10,000		100		P072
86-88-4	Thiourea, 1-naphthalenyl-	500/10,000		100		P072
87-62-7	2,6-Xylidine				313	
87-65-0	2,6-Dichlorophenol			100		U082
87-68-3	Hexachloro-1,3-butadiene			1	313	U128
87-68-3	Hexachlorobutadiene			1	X	U128
87-86-5	Pentachlorophenol			10	313	U242
87-86-5	PCP			10	X	U242

CAS Number	Chemical Name	Sec. 302(EHS) TPQ	Section 304 EHS RQ	Section 304 CERCLA RQ	Sec 313	RCRA Code
88-05-1	Aniline, 2,4,6-trimethyl-	500	1			
88-06-2	2,4,6-Trichlorophenol			10	313	U230
88-72-2	o-Nitrotoluene			1,000		
88-75-5	2-Nitrophenol			100	313	
88-85-7	Dinoseb	100/10,000		1,000		P020
88-89-1	Picric acid				313	
90-04-0	o-Anisidine			1+	313	
90-43-7	2-Phenylphenol				313	
90-94-8	Michler's ketone				313	
91-08-7	Toluene-2,6-diisocyanate	100		100	313	
91-20-3	Naphthalene			100	313	U165
91-22-5	Quinoline			5,000	313	
91-58-7	2-Chloronaphthalene			5,000		U047
91-59-8	beta-Naphthylamine			10	313	U168
91-80-5	Methapyrilene			5,000		U155
91-94-1	3,3'-Dichlorobenzidine			1	313	U073
92-52-4	Biphenyl			1+	313	
92-67-1	4-Aminobiphenyl			1+	313	
92-87-5	Benzidine			1	313	U021
92-93-3	4-Nitrobiphenyl			1+	313	
93-72-1	Silvex (2,4,5-TP)			100		U233
93-76-5	2,4,5-T acid			1,000		U232
93-79-8	2,4,5-T esters			1,000		
94-11-1	2,4-D Esters			100		
94-36-0	Benzoyl peroxide				313	
94-58-6	Dihydrosafrole			10		U090
94-59-7	Safrole			100	313	U203
94-75-7	2,4-D			100	313	U240
94-75-7	2,4-D Acid			100	X	U240
94-75-7	2,4-D, salts and esters			100		U240
94-79-1	2,4-D Esters			100		
94-80-4	2,4-D Esters			100		
95-47-6	o-Xylene			1,000	313	U239
95-47-6	Benzene, o-dimethyl-			1,000	X	U239
95-48-7	o-Cresol	1,000/10,000		1,000	313	U052
95-50-1	1,2-Dichlorobenzene			100	313	U070
95-50-1	o-Dichlorobenzene			100	X	U070
95-53-4	o-Toluidine			100	313	U328
95-57-8	2-Chlorophenol			100		U048
95-63-6	1,2,4-Trimethylbenzene				313	

+ Listed as hazardous air pollutant under section 112(b) of the Clear Air Act; statutory RQ of one pound applies until RQs are adjusted.

CAS Number	Chemical Name	Sec. 302(EHS) TPQ	Section 304 EHS RQ	Section 304 CERCLA RQ	Sec 313	RCRA Code
95-80-7	2,4-Diaminotoluene			10	313	
95-94-3	1,2,4,5-Tetrachlorobenzene			5,000		U207
95-95-4	2,4,5-Trichlorophenol			10	313	U230
96-09-3	Styrene oxide			1+	313	
96-12-8	1,2-Dibromo-3-chloropropane			1	313	U066
96-12-8	DBCP			1	X	U066
96-33-3	Methyl acrylate				313	
96-45-7	Ethylene thiourea			10	313	U116
97-56-3	C.I. Solvent Yellow 3				313	
97-63-2	Ethyl methacrylate			1,000		U118
98-01-1	Furfural			5,000		U125
98-05-5	Benzenearsonic acid	10/10,000	1			
98-07-7	Benzoic trichloride	100		10	313	U023
98-07-7	Benzotrichloride	100		10	X	U023
98-09-9	Benzenesulfonyl chloride			100		U020
98-13-5	Trichlorophenylsilane	500	1			
98-16-8	Benzenamine, 3-(trifluoromethyl)-	500	1			
98-82-8	Cumene			5,000	313	U055
98-86-2	Acetophenone			5,000		U004
98-87-3	Benzal chloride	500		5,000	313	U017
98-88-4	Benzoyl chloride			1,000	313	
98-95-3	Nitrobenzene	10,000		1,000	313	U169
99-08-1	m-Nitrotoluene			1,000		
99-35-4	1,3,5-Trinitrobenzene			10		U234
99-55-8	5-Nitro-o-toluidine			100		U181
99-59-2	5-Nitro-o-anisidine				313	
99-65-0	m-Dinitrobenzene			100	313	
99-98-9	Dimethyl-p-phenylenediamine	10/10,000	1			
99-99-0	p-Nitrotoluene			1,000		
100-01-6	p-Nitroaniline			5,000		P077
100-02-7	4-Nitrophenol			100	313	U170
100-02-7	p-Nitrophenol			100	X	U170
100-14-1	Benzene, 1-(chloromethyl)-4-nitro-	500/10,000	1			
100-25-4	p-Dinitrobenzene			100	313	
100-41-4	Ethylbenzene			1,000	313	
100-42-5	Styrene			1,000	313	
100-44-7	Benzyl chloride	500		100	313	P028
100-47-0	Benzonitrile			5,000		
100-75-4	N-Nitrosopiperidine			10	313	U179
101-14-4	4,4'-Methylenebis(2-chloroaniline)			10	313	U158

+ Listed as hazardous air pollutant under section 112(b) of the Clean Air Act; statutory RQ of one pound applies until RQs are adjusted.

CAS Number	Chemical Name	Sec. 302(EHS) TPQ	Section 304 EHS RQ	Section 304 CERCLA RQ	Sec 313	RCRA Code
101-14-4	MBOCA			10	X	U158
101-55-3	4-Bromophenyl phenyl ether			100		U030
101-61-1	4,4'-Methylenebis(N,N-dimethyl)benzenamine				313	
101-68-8	Methylenebis(phenylisocyanate)			1+	313	
101-68-8	MBI			1+	X	
101-77-9	4,4'-Methylenedianiline			1+	313	
101-80-4	4,4'-Diaminodiphenyl ether				313	
102-36-3	Isocyanic acid, 3,4-dichlorophenyl ester	500/10,000	1			
103-23-1	Bis(2-ethylhexyl) adipate				313	
103-85-5	Phenylthiourea	100/10,000		100		P093
104-94-9	p-Anisidine				313	
105-46-4	sec-Butyl acetate			5,000		
105-60-2	Caprolactam			1+		
105-67-9	2,4-Dimethylphenol			100	313	U101
106-42-3	p-Xylene			1,000	313	U239
106-42-3	Benzene, p-dimethyl-			1,000	X	U239
106-44-5	p-Cresol			1,000	313	U052
106-46-7	1,4-Dichlorobenzene			100	313	U072
106-47-8	p-Chloroaniline			1,000		P024
106-49-0	p-Toluidine			100		U353
106-50-3	p-Phenylenediamine			1+	313	
106-51-4	Quinone			10	313	U197
106-51-4	p-Benzoquinone			10	X	U197
106-88-7	1,2-Butylene oxide			1+	313	
106-89-8	Epichlorohydrin	1,000		100	313	U041
106-93-4	1,2-Dibromoethane			1	313	U067
106-93-4	Ethylene dibromide			1	X	U067
106-96-7	Propargyl bromide	10	1			
106-99-0	1,3-Butadiene			1+	313	
107-02-8	Acrolein	500		1	313	P003
107-05-1	Allyl chloride			1,000	313	
107-06-2	1,2-Dichloroethane			100	313	U077
107-06-2	Ethylene dichloride			100	X	U077
107-07-3	Chloroethanol	500	1			
107-10-8	n-Propylamine			5,000		U194
107-11-9	Allylamine	500	1			
107-12-0	Propionitrile	500		10		P101
107-12-0	Ethyl cyanide	500		10		P101
107-13-1	Acrylonitrile	10,000		100	313	U009
107-15-3	Ethylenediamine	10,000		5,000		

+ Listed as hazardous air pollutant under section 112(b) of the Clear Air Act; statutory RQ of one pound applies until RQs are adjusted.

CAS Number	Chemical Name	Sec. 302(EHS) TPQ	Section 304 EHS RQ	Section 304 CERCLA RQ	Sec 313	RCRA Code
107-16-4	Formaldehyde cyanohydrin	1,000	1			
107-18-6	Allyl alcohol	1,000		100	313	P005
107-19-7	Propargyl alcohol			1,000		P102
107-20-0	Chloroacetaldehyde			1,000		P023
107-21-1	Ethylene glycol			1+	313	
107-30-2	Chloromethyl methyl ether	100		10	313	U046
107-44-8	Sarin	10	1			
107-49-3	Tepp	100		10		P111
107-49-3	Tetraethyl pyrophosphate	100		10		P111
107-92-6	Butyric acid			5,000		
108-05-4	Vinyl acetate	1,000		5,000	313	
108-05-4	Vinyl acetate monomer	1,000		5,000	X	
108-10-1	Methyl isobutyl ketone			5,000	313	U161
108-23-6	Isopropyl chloroformate	1,000	1			
108-24-7	Acetic anhydride			5,000		
108-31-6	Maleic anhydride			5,000	313	U147
108-38-3	m-Xylene			1,000	313	U239
108-38-3	Benzene, m-dimethyl-			1,000	X	U239
108-39-4	m-Cresol			1,000	313	U052
108-46-3	Resorcinol			5,000		U201
108-60-1	Bis(2-chloro-1-methylethyl)ether			1,000	313	U027
108-60-1	Dichloroisopropyl ether			1,000	X	U027
108-88-3	Toluene			1,000	313	U220
108-90-7	Chlorobenzene			100	313	U037
108-91-8	Cyclohexylamine	10,000	1			
108-94-1	Cyclohexanone			5,000		U057
108-95-2	Phenol	500/10,000		1,000	313	U188
108-98-5	Thiophenol	500		100		P014
108-98-5	Benzenethiol	500		100		P014
109-06-8	2-Picoline			5,000		U191
109-61-5	Propyl chloroformate	500	1			
109-73-9	Butylamine			1,000		
109-77-3	Malononitrile	500/10,000		1,000		U149
109-86-4	2-Methoxyethanol				313	
109-89-7	Diethylamine			1,000		
109-99-9	Furan, tetrahydro-			1,000		U213
110-00-9	Furan	500		100		U124
110-16-7	Maleic acid			5,000		
110-17-8	Fumaric acid			5,000		
110-19-0	iso-Butyl acetate			5,000		

+ Listed as hazardous air pollutant under section 112(b) of the Clear Air Act; statutory RQ of one pound applies until RQs are adjusted.

CAS Number	Chemical Name	Sec. 302(EHS) TPQ	Section 304 EHS RQ	Section 304 CERCLA RQ	Sec 313	RCRA Code
110-54-3	Hexane			1+		
110-57-6	Trans-1,4-dichlorobutene	500	1			
110-75-8	2-Chloroethyl vinyl ether			1,000		U042
110-80-5	2-Ethoxyethanol			1,000	313	U359
110-80-5	Ethanol, 2-ethoxy-			1,000	X	U359
110-82-7	Cyclohexane			1,000	313	U056
110-86-1	Pyridine			1,000	313	U196
110-89-4	Piperidine	1,000	1			
111-42-2	Diethanolamine			1+	313	
111-44-4	Bis(2-chloroethyl) ether	10,000		10	313	U025
111-44-4	Dichloroethyl ether	10,000		10	X	U025
111-54-6	Ethylenebisdithiocarbamic acid, salts & es			5,000		U114
111-69-3	Adiponitrile	1,000	1			
111-91-1	Bis(2-chloroethoxy) methane			1,000		U024
114-26-1	Propoxur			1+	313	
115-02-6	Azaserine			1		U015
115-07-1	Propylene (Propene)				313	
115-21-9	Trichloroethylsilane	500	1			
115-26-4	Dimefox	500	1			
115-29-7	Endosulfan	10/10,000		1		P050
115-32-2	Dicofol			10	313	
115-90-2	Fensulfothion	500	1			
116-06-3	Aldicarb	100/10,000		1		P070
117-79-3	2-Aminoanthraquinone				313	
117-80-6	Dichlone			1		
117-81-7	Di(2-ethylhexyl) phthalate			100	313	U028
117-81-7	Bis(2-ethylhexyl)phthalate			100	X	U028
117-81-7	DEHP			100	X	U028
117-84-0	n-Dioctylphthalate			5,000	313	U107
117-84-0	Di-n-octyl phthalate			5,000	X	U107
118-74-1	Hexachlorobenzene			10	313	U127
119-38-0	Isopropylmethylpyrazolyl dimethylcarbamate	500	1			
119-90-4	3,3'-Dimethoxybenzidine			100	313	U091
119-93-7	3,3'-Dimethylbenzidine			10	313	U095
119-93-7	o-Tolidine			10	X	U095
120-12-7	Anthracene			5,000	313	
120-58-1	Isosafrole			100	313	U141
120-71-8	p-Cresidine				313	
120-80-9	Catechol			1+	313	
120-82-1	1,2,4-Trichlorobenzene			100	313	

+ Listed as hazardous air pollutant under section 112(b) of the Clear Air Act; statutory RQ of one pound applies until RQs are adjusted.

CAS Number	Chemical Name	Sec. 302(EHS) TPQ	Section 304 EHS RQ	Section 304 CERCLA RQ	Sec 313	RCRA Code
120-83-2	2,4-Dichlorophenol			100	313	U081
121-14-2	2,4-Dinitrotoluene			10	313	U105
121-21-1	Pyrethrins			1		
121-29-9	Pyrethrins			1		
121-44-8	Triethylamine			5,000		
121-69-7	N,N-Dimethylaniline			1+	313	
121-75-5	Malathion			100		
122-09-8	Benzeneethanamine, alpha,alpha-dimethyl-			5,000		P046
122-14-5	Fenitrothion	500	1			
122-66-7	1,2-Diphenylhydrazine			10	313	U109
122-66-7	Hydrazine, 1,2-diphenyl-			10	X	U109
122-66-7	Hydrazobenzene			10	X	U109
123-31-9	Hydroquinone	500/10,000		1+	313	
123-33-1	Maleic hydrazide			5,000		U148
123-38-6	Propionaldehyde			1+	313	
123-62-6	Propionic anhydride			5,000		
123-63-7	Paraldehyde			1,000		U182
123-72-8	Butyraldehyde				313	
123-73-9	Crotonaldehyde, (E)-	1,000		100		U053
123-86-4	Butyl acetate			5,000		
123-91-1	1,4-Dioxane			100	313	U108
123-92-2	iso-Amyl acetate			5,000		
124-04-9	Adipic acid			5,000		
124-40-3	Dimethylamine			1,000		U092
124-41-4	Sodium methylate			1,000		
124-48-1	Chlorodibromomethane			100		
124-65-2	Sodium cacodylate	100/10,000	1			
124-73-2	Dibromotetrafluoroethane [Halon 2402]				313	
124-73-2	Halon 2402				X	
124-87-8	Picrotoxin	500/10,000	1			
126-72-7	Tris(2,3-dibromopropyl) phosphate			10	313	U235
126-98-7	Methacrylonitrile	500		1,000		U152
126-99-8	Chloroprene			1+	313	
127-18-4	Tetrachloroethylene			100	313	U210
127-18-4	Perchloroethylene			100	X	U210
127-82-2	Zinc phenolsulfonate			5,000		
128-66-5	C.I. Vat Yellow 4				313	
129-00-0	Pyrene	1,000/10,000		5,000		
129-06-6	Warfarin sodium	100/10,000	1			
130-15-4	1,4-Naphthoquinone			5,000		U166

+ Listed as hazardous air pollutant under section 112(b) of the Clear Air Act; statutory RQ of one pound applies until RQs are adjusted.

CAS Number	Chemical Name	Sec. 302(EHS) TPQ	Section 304 EHS RQ	Section 304 CERCLA RQ	Sec 313	RCRA Code
131-11-3	Dimethyl phthalate			5,000	313	U102
131-74-8	Ammonium picrate			10		P009
131-89-5	2-Cyclohexyl-4,6-Dinitrophenol			100		P034
132-64-9	Dibenzofuran			1+	313	
133-06-2	Captan			10	313	
133-90-4	Chloramben			1+	313	
134-29-2	o-Anisidine hydrochloride				313	
134-32-7	alpha-Naphthylamine			100	313	U167
135-20-6	Cupferron				313	
137-26-8	Thiram			10		U244
139-13-9	Nitrilotriacetic acid				313	
139-65-1	4,4'-Thiodianiline				313	
140-29-4	Benzyl cyanide	500	1			
140-76-1	Pyridine, 2-methyl-5-vinyl-	500	1			
140-88-5	Ethyl acrylate			1,000	313	U113
141-32-2	Butyl acrylate				313	
141-66-2	Dicrotophos	100	1			
141-78-6	Ethyl acetate			5,000		U112
142-28-9	1,3-Dichloropropane			5,000		
142-71-2	Cupric acetate			100		
142-84-7	Dipropylamine			5,000		U110
143-33-9	Sodium cyanide (Na(CN))	100		10		P106
143-50-0	Kepone			1		U142
144-49-0	Fluoroacetic acid	10/10,000	1			
145-73-3	Endothall			1,000		P088
148-82-3	Melphalan			1		U150
149-74-6	Dichloromethylphenylsilane	1,000	1			
151-38-2	Methoxyethylmercuric acetate	500/10,000	1			
151-50-8	Potassium cyanide	100		10		P098
151-56-4	Ethyleneimine	500		1	313	P054
151-56-4	Aziridine	500		1	X	P054
152-16-9	Diphosphoramide, octamethyl-	100		100		P085
156-10-5	p-Nitrosodiphenylamine				313	
156-60-5	1,2-Dichloroethylene			1,000		U079
156-62-7	Calcium cyanamide			1+	313	
189-55-9	Dibenz[a,i]pyrene			10		U064
191-24-2	Benzo[ghi]perylene			5,000		
193-39-5	Indeno(1,2,3-cd)pyrene			100		U137
205-99-2	Benzo[b]fluoranthene			1		
206-44-0	Fluoranthene			100		U120

+ Listed as hazardous air pollutant under section 112(b) of the Clear Air Act; statutory RQ of one pound applies until RQs are adjusted.

CAS Number	Chemical Name	Sec. 302(EHS) TPQ	Section 304 EHS RQ	Section 304 CERCLA RQ	Sec 313	RCRA Code
207-08-9	Benzo(k)fluoranthene			5,000		
208-96-8	Acenaphthylene			5,000		
218-01-9	Chrysene			100		U050
225-51-4	Benz[c]acridine			100		U016
297-78-9	Isobenzan	100/10,000	1			
297-97-2	Thionazin	500		100		P040
297-97-2	O,O-Diethyl O-pyrazinyl phosphorothioate	500		100		P040
298-00-0	Parathion-methyl	100/10,000		100		P071
298-00-0	Methyl parathion	100/10,000		100		P071
298-02-2	Phorate	10		10		P094
298-04-4	Disulfoton	500		1		P039
300-62-9	Amphetamine	1,000	1			
300-76-5	Naled			10		
301-04-2	Lead acetate			5,000		U144
302-01-2	Hydrazine	1,000		1	313	U133
303-34-4	Lasiocarpine			10		U143
305-03-3	Chlorambucil			10		U035
309-00-2	Aldrin	500/10,000		1	313	P004
311-45-5	Diethyl-p-nitrophenyl phosphate			100		P041
315-18-4	Mexacarbate	500/10,000		1,000		
316-42-7	Emetine, dihydrochloride	1/10,000	1			
319-84-6	alpha-BHC			10		
319-85-7	beta-BHC			1		
319-86-8	delta-BHC			1		
327-98-0	Trichloronate	500	1			
329-71-5	2,5-Dinitrophenol			10		
330-54-1	Diuron			100		
333-41-5	Diazinon			1		
334-88-3	Diazomethane			1+	313	
353-42-4	Boron trifluoride compound with methyl eth	1,000	1			
353-50-4	Carbonic difluoride			1,000		U033
353-59-3	Bromochlorodifluoromethane [Halon 1211]				313	
353-59-3	Halon 1211				X	
357-57-3	Brucine			100		P018
359-06-8	Fluoroacetyl chloride	10	1			
371-62-0	Ethylene fluorohydrin	10	1			
379-79-3	Ergotamine tartrate	500/10,000	1			
460-19-5	Cyanogen			100		P031
463-58-1	Carbonyl sulfide			1+	313	
465-73-6	Isodrin	100/10,000		1		P060

+ Listed as hazardous air pollutant under section 112(b) of the Clear Air Act; statutory RQ of one pound applies until RQs are adjusted.

CAS Number	Chemical Name	Sec. 302(EHS) TPQ	Section 304 EHS RQ	Section 304 CERCLA RQ	Sec 313	RCRA Code
470-90-6	Chlorfenvinfos	500	1			
492-80-8	C.I. Solvent Yellow 34			100	313	U014
492-80-8	Auramine			100	X	U014
494-03-1	Chlornaphazine			100		U026
496-72-0	Diaminotoluene			10		
502-39-6	Methylmercuric dicyanamide	500/10,000	1			
504-24-5	Pyridine, 4-amino-	500/10,000		1,000		P008
504-24-5	4-Aminopyridine	500/10,000		1,000		P008
504-60-9	1,3-Pentadiene			100		U186
505-60-2	Mustard gas	500	1		313	
506-61-6	Potassium silver cyanide	500		1		P099
506-64-9	Silver cyanide			1		P104
506-68-3	Cyanogen bromide	500/10,000		1,000		U246
506-77-4	Cyanogen chloride			10		P033
506-78-5	Cyanogen iodide	1,000/10,000	1			
506-87-6	Ammonium carbonate			5,000		
506-96-7	Acetyl bromide			5,000		
509-14-8	Tetranitromethane	500		10		P112
510-15-6	Chlorobenzilate			10	313	U038
513-49-5	sec-Butylamine			1,000		
514-73-8	Dithiazanine iodide	500/10,000	1			
528-29-0	o-Dinitrobenzene			100	313	
532-27-4	2-Chloroacetophenone			1+	313	
534-07-6	Bis(chloromethyl) ketone	10/10,000	1			
534-52-1	Dinitrocresol	10/10,000		10		P047
534-52-1	4,6-Dinitro-o-cresol	10/10,000		10	313	P047
534-52-1	4,6-Dinitro-o-cresol and salts			10		P047
535-89-7	Crimidine	100/10,000	1			
538-07-8	Ethylbis(2-chloroethyl)amine	500	1			
540-59-0	1,2-Dichloroethylene				313	
540-73-8	Hydrazine, 1,2-dimethyl-			1		U099
540-84-1	2,2,4-Trimethylpentane			1+		
540-88-5	tert-Butyl acetate			5,000		
541-09-3	Uranyl acetate			100		
541-25-3	Lewisite	10	1			
541-41-3	Ethyl chloroformate				313	
541-53-7	Dithiobiuret	100/10,000		100		P049
541-73-1	1,3-Dichlorobenzene			100	313	U071
542-62-1	Barium cyanide			10		P013
542-75-6	1,3-Dichloropropylene			100	313	U084

+ Listed as hazardous air pollutant under section 112(b) of the Clear Air Act; statutory RQ of one pound applies until RQs are adjusted.

CAS Number	Chemical Name	Sec. 302(EHS) TPQ	Section 304 EHS RQ	Section 304 CERCLA RQ	Sec 313	RCRA Code
542-75-6	1,3-Dichloropropene			100	X	U084
542-76-7	Propionitrile, 3-chloro-	1,000		1,000		P027
542-76-7	3-Chloropropionitrile	1,000		1,000		P027
542-88-1	Bis(chloromethyl) ether	100		10	313	P016
542-88-1	Chloromethyl ether	100		10	X	P016
542-88-1	Dichloromethyl ether	100		10	X	P016
542-90-5	Ethylthiocyanate	10,000	1			
543-90-8	Cadmium acetate			10		
544-18-3	Cobaltous formate			1,000		
544-92-3	Copper cyanide			10		P029
554-84-7	m-Nitrophenol			100		
555-77-1	Tris(2-chloroethyl)amine	100	1			
556-61-6	Methyl isothiocyanate	500	1			
556-64-9	Methyl thiocyanate	10,000	1			
557-19-7	Nickel cyanide			10		P074
557-21-1	Zinc cyanide			10		P121
557-34-6	Zinc acetate			1,000		
557-41-5	Zinc formate			1,000		
558-25-8	Methanesulfonyl fluoride	1,000	1			
563-12-2	Ethion	1,000		10		
563-41-7	Semicarbazide hydrochloride	1,000/10,000	1			
563-68-8	Thallium(I) acetate			100		U214
569-64-2	C.I. Basic Green 4				313	
573-56-8	2,6-Dinitrophenol			10		
584-84-9	Toluene-2,4-diisocyanate	500		100	313	
591-08-2	1-Acetyl-2-thiourea			1,000		P002
592-01-8	Calcium cyanide			10		P021
592-04-1	Mercuric cyanide			1		
592-85-8	Mercuric thiocyanate			10		
592-87-0	Lead thiocyanate			100		
593-60-2	Vinyl bromide			1+	313	
594-42-3	Perchloromethylmercaptan	500		100		
594-42-3	Trichloromethanesulfenyl chloride	500		100		
597-64-8	Tetraethyltin	100	1			
598-31-2	Bromoacetone			1,000		P017
606-20-2	2,6-Dinitrotoluene			100	313	U106
608-93-5	Pentachlorobenzene			10		U183
609-19-8	3,4,5-Trichlorophenol			10		
610-39-9	3,4-Dinitrotoluene			10		
614-78-8	Thiourea, (2-methylphenyl)-	500/10,000	1			

+ Listed as hazardous air pollutant under section 112(b) of the Clean Air Act; statutory RQ of one pound applies until RQs are adjusted.

CAS Number	Chemical Name	Sec. 302(EHS) TPQ	Section 304 EHS RQ	Section 304 CERCLA RQ	Sec 313	RCRA Code
615-05-4	2,4-Diaminoanisole				313	
615-53-2	N-Nitroso-N-methylurethane			1		U178
621-64-7	N-Nitrosodi-n-propylamine			10	313	U111
621-64-7	Di-n-propylnitrosamine			10	X	U111
624-83-9	Methyl isocyanate	500		1	313	P064
625-16-1	tert-Amyl acetate			5,000		
626-38-0	sec-Amyl acetate			5,000		
627-11-2	Chloroethyl chloroformate	1,000	1			
628-63-7	Amyl acetate			5,000		
628-86-4	Mercury fulminate			10		P065
630-10-4	Selenourea			1,000		P103
630-20-6	Ethane, 1,1,1,2-tetrachloro-			100		U208
630-60-4	Ouabain	100/10,000	1			
631-61-8	Ammonium acetate			5,000		
636-21-5	o-Toluidine hydrochloride			100	313	U222
639-58-7	Triphenyltin chloride	500/10,000	1			
640-19-7	Fluoroacetamide	100/10,000		100		P057
644-64-4	Dimetilan	500/10,000	1			
675-14-9	Cyanuric fluoride	100	1			
676-97-1	Methyl phosphonic dichloride	100	1			
680-31-9	Hexamethylphosphoramide			1+	313	
684-93-5	N-Nitroso-N-methylurea			1	313	U177
692-42-2	Diethylarsine			1		P038
696-28-6	Phenyl dichloroarsine	500		1		P036
696-28-6	Dichlorophenylarsine	500		1		P036
732-11-6	Phosmet	10/10,000	1			
757-58-4	Hexaethyl tetraphosphate			100		P062
759-73-9	N-Nitroso-N-ethylurea			1	313	U176
760-93-0	Methacrylic anhydride	500	1			
764-41-0	2-Butene, 1,4-dichloro-			1		U074
765-34-4	Glycidylaldehyde			10		U126
786-19-6	Carbophenothion	500	1			
814-49-3	Diethyl chlorophosphate	500	1			
814-68-6	Acrylyl chloride	100	1			
815-82-7	Cupric tartrate			100		
822-06-0	Hexamethylene-1,6-diisocyanate			1+		
823-40-5	Diaminotoluene			10		
824-11-3	Trimethylolpropane phosphite	100/10,000	1			
842-07-9	C.I. Solvent Yellow 14				313	
900-95-8	Stannane, acetoxytriphenyl-	500/10,000	1			

+ Listed as hazardous air pollutant under section 112(b) of the Clear Air Act; statutory RQ of one pound applies until RQs are adjusted.

CAS Number	Chemical Name	Sec. 302(EHS) TPQ	Section 304 EHS RQ	Section 304 CERCLA RQ	Sec 313	RCRA Code
919-86-8	Demeton-S-methyl	500	1			
920-46-7	Methacryloyl chloride	100	1			
924-16-3	N-Nitrosodi-n-butylamine			10	313	U172
930-55-2	N-Nitrosopyrrolidine			1		U180
933-75-5	2,3,6-Trichlorophenol			10		
933-78-8	2,3,5-Trichlorophenol			10		
944-22-9	Fonofos	500	1			
947-02-4	Phosfolan	100/10,000	1			
950-10-7	Mephosfolan	500	1			
950-37-8	Methidathion	500/10,000	1			
959-98-8	alpha - Endosulfan			1		
961-11-5	Tetrachlorvinphos				313	
989-38-8	C.I. Basic Red 1				313	
991-42-4	Norbormide	100/10,000	1			
998-30-1	Triethoxysilane	500	1			
999-81-5	Chlormequat chloride	100/10,000	1			
1024-57-3	Heptachlor epoxide			1		
1031-07-8	Endosulfan sulfate			1		
1031-47-6	Triamiphos	500/10,000	1			
1066-30-4	Chromic acetate			1,000		
1066-33-7	Ammonium bicarbonate			5,000		
1066-45-1	Trimethyltin chloride	500/10,000	1			
1072-35-1	Lead stearate			5,000		
1111-78-0	Ammonium carbamate			5,000		
1116-54-7	N-Nitrosodiethanolamine			1		U173
1120-71-4	Propane sultone			10	313	U193
1120-71-4	1,3-Propane sultone			10	X	U193
1122-60-7	Nitrocyclohexane	500	1			
1124-33-0	Pyridine, 4-nitro-, 1-oxide	500/10,000	1			
1129-41-5	Metolcarb	100/10,000	1			
1163-19-5	Decabromodiphenyl oxide				313	
1185-57-5	Ferric ammonium citrate			1,000		
1194-65-6	Dichlobenil			100		
1300-71-6	Xylenol			1,000		
1303-28-2	Arsenic pentoxide	100/10,000		1		P011
1303-32-8	Arsenic disulfide			1		
1303-33-9	Arsenic trisulfide			1		
1306-19-0	Cadmium oxide	100/10,000	1			
1309-64-4	Antimony trioxide			1,000		
1310-58-3	Potassium hydroxide			1,000		

CAS Number	Chemical Name	Sec. 302(EHS) TPQ	Section 304 EHS RQ	Section 304 CERCLA RQ	Sec 313	RCRA Code
1310-73-2	Sodium hydroxide			1,000		
1313-27-5	Molybdenum trioxide				313	
1314-20-1	Thorium dioxide				313	
1314-32-5	Thallic oxide			100		P113
1314-56-3	Phosphorus pentoxide	10	1			
1314-62-1	Vanadium pentoxide	100/10,000		1,000		P120
1314-80-3	Sulfur phosphide			100		U189
1314-84-7	Zinc phosphide	500		100		P122
1314-84-7	Zinc phosphide (conc. <= 10%)	500		100		U249
1314-84-7	Zinc phosphide (conc. > 10%)	500		100		P122
1314-87-0	Lead sulfide			5,000		
1319-72-8	2,4,5-T amines			5,000		
1319-77-3	Cresol (mixed isomers)			1,000	313	U052
1320-18-9	2,4-D Esters			100		
1321-12-6	Nitrotoluene			1,000		
1327-52-2	Arsenic acid			1		P010
1327-53-3	Arsenous oxide	100/10,000		1		P012
1327-53-3	Arsenic trioxide	100/10,000		1		P012
1330-20-7	Xylene (mixed isomers)			1,000	313	U239
1332-07-6	Zinc borate			1,000		
1332-21-4	Asbestos (friable)			1	313	
1333-83-1	Sodium bifluoride			100		
1335-32-6	Lead subacetate			100		U146
1335-87-1	Hexachloronaphthalene				313	
1336-21-6	Ammonium hydroxide			1,000		
1336-36-3	Polychlorinated biphenyls			1	313	
1336-36-3	PCBs			1	X	
1338-23-4	Methyl ethyl ketone peroxide			10		U160
1338-24-5	Naphthenic acid			100		
1341-49-7	Ammonium bifluoride			100		
1344-28-1	Aluminum oxide (fibrous forms)				313	
1397-94-0	Antimycin A	1,000/10,000	1			
1420-07-1	Dinoterb	500/10,000	1			
1464-53-5	Diepoxybutane	500		10	313	U085
1464-53-5	2,2'-Bioxirane	500		10	X	U085
1558-25-4	Trichloro(chloromethyl)silane	100	1			
1563-66-2	Carbofuran	10/10,000		10		
1582-09-8	Trifluralin			1+	313	
1600-27-7	Mercuric acetate	500/10,000	1			
1615-80-1	Hydrazine, 1,2-diethyl-			10		U086

+ Listed as hazardous air pollutant under section 112(b) of the Clear Air Act; statutory RQ of one pound applies until RQs are adjusted.

CAS Number	Chemical Name	Sec. 302(EHS) TPQ	Section 304 EHS RQ	Section 304 CERCLA RQ	Sec 313	RCRA Code
1622-32-8	Ethanesulfonyl chloride, 2-chloro-	500	1			
1634-04-4	Methyl tert-butyl ether			1+	313	
1642-54-2	Diethylcarbamazine citrate	100/10,000	1			
1746-01-6	2,3,7,8-Tetrachlorodibenzo-p-dioxin (TCDD)			1		
1752-30-3	Acetone thiosemicarbazide	1,000/10,000	1			
1762-95-4	Ammonium thiocyanate			5,000		
1836-75-5	Nitrofen				313	
1863-63-4	Ammonium benzoate			5,000		
1888-71-7	Hexachloropropene			1,000		U243
1897-45-6	Chlorothalonil				313	
1910-42-5	Paraquat	10/10,000	1			
1918-00-9	Dicamba			1,000		
1928-38-7	2,4-D Esters			100		
1928-47-8	2,4,5-T esters			1,000		
1928-61-6	2,4-D Esters			100		
1929-73-3	2,4-D Esters			100		
1937-37-7	C.I. Direct Black 38				313	
1982-47-4	Chloroxuron	500/10,000	1			
2001-95-8	Valinomycin	1,000/10,000	1			
2008-46-0	2,4,5-T amines			5,000		
2032-65-7	Methiocarb	500/10,000		10		
2032-65-7	Mercaptodimethur	500/10,000		10		
2074-50-2	Paraquat methosulfate	10/10,000	1			
2097-19-0	Phenylsilatrane	100/10,000	1			
2104-64-5	EPN	100/10,000	1			
2164-17-2	Fluometuron				313	
2223-93-0	Cadmium stearate	1,000/10,000	1			
2231-57-4	Thiocarbazide	1,000/10,000	1			
2234-13-1	Octachloronaphthalene				313	
2238-07-5	Diglycidyl ether	1,000	1			
2275-18-5	Prothoate	100/10,000	1			
2303-16-4	Diallate			100	313	U062
2312-35-8	Propargite			10		
2497-07-6	Oxydisulfoton	500	1			
2524-03-0	Dimethyl phosphorochloridothioate	500	1			
2540-82-1	Formothion	100	1			
2545-59-7	2,4,5-T esters			1,000		
2570-26-5	Pentadecylamine	100/10,000	1			
2587-90-8	Phosphorothioic acid, O,O-dimethyl-5-(2-(m	500	1			
2602-46-2	C.I. Direct Blue 6				313	

+ Listed as hazardous air pollutant under section 112(b) of the Clear Air Act; statutory RQ of one pound applies until RQs are adjusted.

CAS Number	Chemical Name	Sec. 302(EHS) TPQ	Section 304 EHS RQ	Section 304 CERCLA RQ	Sec 313	RCRA Code
2631-37-0	Promecarb	500/10,000	1			
2636-26-2	Cyanophos	1,000	1			
2642-71-9	Azinphos-ethyl	100/10,000	1			
2665-30-7	Phosphonothioic acid, methyl-, O-(4-nitrop	500	1			
2703-13-1	Phosphonothioic acid, methyl-, O-ethyl O-(	500	1			
2757-18-8	Thallous malonate	100/10,000	1			
2763-96-4	Muscimol	500/10,000		1,000		P007
2763-96-4	5-(Aminomethyl)-3-isoxazolol	500/10,000		1,000		P007
2764-72-9	Diquat			1,000		
2778-04-3	Endothion	500/10,000	1			
2832-40-8	C.I. Disperse Yellow 3				313	
2921-88-2	Chlorpyrifos			1		
2944-67-4	Ferric ammonium oxalate			1,000		
2971-38-2	2,4-D Esters			100		
3012-65-5	Ammonium citrate, dibasic			5,000		
3037-72-7	Silane, (4-aminobutyl)diethoxymethyl-	1,000	1			
3118-97-6	C.I. Solvent Orange 7				313	
3164-29-2	Ammonium tartrate			5,000		
3165-93-3	4-Chloro-o-toluidine, hydrochloride			100		U049
3251-23-8	Cupric nitrate			100		
3254-63-5	Phosphoric acid, dimethyl 4-(methylthio) p	500	1			
3288-58-2	O,O-Diethyl S-methyl dithiophosphate			5,000		U087
3486-35-9	Zinc carbonate			1,000		
3547-04-4	DDE			1+		
3569-57-1	Sulfoxide, 3-chloropropyl octyl	500	1			
3615-21-2	Benzimidazole, 4,5-dichloro-2-(trifluorome	500/10,000	1			
3689-24-5	Sulfotep	500		100		P109
3689-24-5	Tetraethyldithiopyrophosphate	500		100		P109
3691-35-8	Chlorophacinone	100/10,000	1			
3734-97-2	Amiton oxalate	100/10,000	1			
3735-23-7	Methyl phenkapton	500	1			
3761-53-3	C.I. Food Red 5				313	
3813-14-7	2,4,5-T amines			5,000		
3878-19-1	Fuberidazole	100/10,000	1			
4044-65-9	Bitoscanate	500/10,000	1			
4098-71-9	Isophorone diisocyanate	100	1			
4104-14-7	Phosacetim	100/10,000	1			
4170-30-3	Crotonaldehyde	1,000		100		U053
4301-50-2	Fluenetil	100/10,000	1			
4418-66-0	Phenol, 2,2'-thiobis(4-chloro-6-methyl-	100/10,000	1			

+ Listed as hazardous air pollutant under section 112(b) of the Clear Air Act; statutory RQ of one pound applies until RQs are adjusted.

CAS Number	Chemical Name	Sec. 302(EHS) TPQ	Section 304 EHS RQ	Section 304 CERCLA RQ	Sec 313	RCRA Code
4549-40-0	N-Nitrosomethylvinylamine			10	313	P084
4680-78-8	C.I. Acid Green 3				313	
4835-11-4	Hexamethylenediamine, N,N'-dibutyl-	500	1			
5344-82-1	Thiourea, (2-chlorophenyl)-	100/10,000		100		P026
5836-29-3	Coumatetralyl	500/10,000	1			
5893-66-3	Cupric oxalate			100		
5972-73-6	Ammonium oxalate			5,000		
6009-70-7	Ammonium oxalate			5,000		
6369-96-6	2,4,5-T amines			5,000		
6369-97-7	2,4,5-T amines			5,000		
6484-52-2	Ammonium nitrate (solution)				313	
6533-73-9	Thallous carbonate	100/10,000		100		U215
6533-73-9	Thallium(I) carbonate	100/10,000		100		U215
6923-22-4	Monocrotophos	10/10,000	1			
7005-72-3	4-Chlorophenyl phenyl ether			5,000		
7421-93-4	Endrin aldehyde			1		
7428-48-0	Lead stearate			5,000		
7429-90-5	Aluminum (fume or dust)				313	
7439-92-1	Lead			1*	313	
7439-96-5	Manganese				313	
7439-97-6	Mercury			1	313	U151
7440-02-0	Nickel			100*	313	
7440-22-4	Silver			1,000*	313	
7440-23-5	Sodium			10		
7440-28-0	Thallium			1,000*	313	
7440-36-0	Antimony			5,000*	313	
7440-38-2	Arsenic			1*	313	
7440-39-3	Barium				313	
7440-41-7	Beryllium			10*	313	P015
7440-43-9	Cadmium			10*	313	
7440-47-3	Chromium			5,000*	313	
7440-48-4	Cobalt				313	
7440-50-8	Copper			5,000*	313	
7440-62-2	Vanadium (fume or dust)				313	
7440-66-6	Zinc (fume or dust)			1,000*	313	
7440-66-6	Zinc			1,000*		
7446-08-4	Selenium dioxide			10		
7446-09-5	Sulfur dioxide	500	1			
7446-11-9	Sulfur trioxide	100	1			
7446-14-2	Lead sulfate			100		

* No reporting of releases is required if the diameter of the pieces of the solid metal released is equal to or exceeds 100 micrometers (0.004 inches).

CAS Number	Chemical Name	Sec. 302(EHS) TPQ	Section 304 EHS RQ	Section 304 CERCLA RQ	Sec 313	RCRA Code
7446-18-6	Thallous sulfate	100/10,000		100		P115
7446-18-6	Thallium(I) sulfate	100/10,000		100		P115
7446-27-7	Lead phosphate			1		U145
7447-39-4	Cupric chloride			10		
7487-94-7	Mercuric chloride	500/10,000	1			
7488-56-4	Selenium sulfide			10		U205
7550-45-0	Titanium tetrachloride	100		1+	313	
7558-79-4	Sodium phosphate, dibasic			5,000		
7580-67-8	Lithium hydride	100	1			
7601-54-9	Sodium phosphate, tribasic			5,000		
7631-89-2	Sodium arsenate	1,000/10,000		1		
7631-90-5	Sodium bisulfite			5,000		
7632-00-0	Sodium nitrite			100		
7637-07-2	Boron trifluoride	500	1			
7645-25-2	Lead arsenate			1		
7646-85-7	Zinc chloride			1,000		
7647-01-0	Hydrochloric acid			5,000	313	
7647-01-0	Hydrogen chloride (gas only)	500		5,000	X	
7647-18-9	Antimony pentachloride			1,000		
7664-38-2	Phosphoric acid			5,000	313	
7664-39-3	Hydrogen fluoride	100		100	313	U134
7664-39-3	Hydrofluoric acid	100		100	X	U134
7664-41-7	Ammonia	500		100	313	
7664-93-9	Sulfuric acid	1,000		1,000	313	
7681-49-4	Sodium fluoride			1,000		
7681-52-9	Sodium hypochlorite			100		
7697-37-2	Nitric acid	1,000		1,000	313	
7699-45-8	Zinc bromide			1,000		
7705-08-0	Ferric chloride			1,000		
7718-54-9	Nickel chloride			100		
7719-12-2	Phosphorus trichloride	1,000		1,000		
7720-78-7	Ferrous sulfate			1,000		
7722-64-7	Potassium permanganate			100		
7722-84-1	Hydrogen peroxide (Conc.> 52%)	1,000	1			
7723-14-0	Phosphorus (yellow or white)	100		1	313	
7723-14-0	Phosphorus	100		1		
7726-95-6	Bromine	500	1			
7733-02-0	Zinc sulfate			1,000		
7738-94-5	Chromic acid			10		
7758-29-4	Sodium phosphate, tribasic			5,000		

+ Listed as hazardous air pollutant under section 112(b) of the Clear Air Act; statutory RQ of one pound applies until RQs are adjusted.

CAS Number	Chemical Name	Sec. 302(EHS) TPQ	Section 304 EHS RQ	Section 304 CERCLA RQ	Sec 313	RCRA Code
7758-94-3	Ferrous chloride			100		
7758-95-4	Lead chloride			100		
7758-98-7	Cupric sulfate			10		
7761-88-8	Silver nitrate			1		
7773-06-0	Ammonium sulfamate			5,000		
7775-11-3	Sodium chromate			10		
7778-39-4	Arsenic acid			1		P010
7778-44-1	Calcium arsenate	500/10,000		1		
7778-50-9	Potassium bichromate			10		
7778-54-3	Calcium hypochlorite			10		
7779-86-4	Zinc hydrosulfite			1,000		
7779-88-6	Zinc nitrate			1,000		
7782-41-4	Fluorine	500		10		P056
7782-49-2	Selenium			100*	313	
7782-50-5	Chlorine	100		10	313	
7782-63-0	Ferrous sulfate			1,000		
7782-82-3	Sodium selenite			100		
7782-86-7	Mercurous nitrate			10		
7783-00-8	Selenious acid	1,000/10,000		10		U204
7783-06-4	Hydrogen sulfide	500		100		U135
7783-07-5	Hydrogen selenide	10	1			
7783-20-2	Ammonium sulfate (solution)				313	
7783-35-9	Mercuric sulfate			10		
7783-46-2	Lead fluoride			100		
7783-49-5	Zinc fluoride			1,000		
7783-50-8	Ferric fluoride			100		
7783-56-4	Antimony trifluoride			1,000		
7783-60-0	Sulfur tetrafluoride	100	1			
7783-70-2	Antimony pentafluoride	500	1			
7783-80-4	Tellurium hexafluoride	100	1			
7784-34-1	Arsenous trichloride	500		1		
7784-40-9	Lead arsenate			1		
7784-41-0	Potassium arsenate			1		
7784-42-1	Arsine	100	1			
7784-46-5	Sodium arsenite	500/10,000		1		
7785-84-4	Sodium phosphate, tribasic			5,000		
7786-34-7	Mevinphos	500		10		
7786-81-4	Nickel sulfate			100		
7787-47-5	Beryllium chloride			1		
7787-49-7	Beryllium fluoride			1		

* No reporting of releases is required if the diameter of the pieces of the solid metal released is equal to or exceeds 100 micrometers (0.004 inches).

CAS Number	Chemical Name	Sec. 302(EHS) TPQ	Section 304 EHS RQ	Section 304 CERCLA RQ	Sec 313	RCRA Code
7787-55-5	Beryllium nitrate			1		
7788-98-9	Ammonium chromate			10		
7789-00-6	Potassium chromate			10		
7789-06-2	Strontium chromate			10		
7789-09-5	Ammonium bichromate			10		
7789-42-6	Cadmium bromide			10		
7789-43-7	Cobaltous bromide			1,000		
7789-61-9	Antimony tribromide			1,000		
7790-94-5	Chlorosulfonic acid			1,000		
7791-12-0	Thallous chloride	100/10,000		100		U216
7791-12-0	Thallium chloride TlCl	100/10,000		100		U216
7791-23-3	Selenium oxychloride	500	1			
7803-51-2	Phosphine	500		100		P096
7803-55-6	Ammonium vanadate			1,000		P119
8001-35-2	Toxaphene	500/10,000		1	313	P123
8001-35-2	Camphechlor	500/10,000		1	X	P123
8001-35-2	Camphene, octachloro-	500/10,000		1	X	P123
8001-58-9	Creosote			1	313	
8003-19-8	Dichloropropane - Dichloropropene (mixture			100		
8003-34-7	Pyrethrins			1		
8014-95-7	Sulfuric acid (fuming)			1,000		
8065-48-3	Demeton	500	1			
10022-70-5	Sodium hypochlorite			100		
10025-73-7	Chromic chloride	1/10,000	1			
10025-87-3	Phosphorus oxychloride	500		1,000		
10025-91-9	Antimony trichloride			1,000		
10026-11-6	Zirconium tetrachloride			5,000		
10026-13-8	Phosphorus pentachloride	500	1			
10028-15-6	Ozone	100	1			
10028-22-5	Ferric sulfate			1,000		
10031-59-1	Thallium sulfate	100/10,000		100		
10034-93-2	Hydrazine sulfate				313	
10039-32-4	Sodium phosphate, dibasic			5,000		
10043-01-3	Aluminum sulfate			5,000		
10045-89-3	Ferrous ammonium sulfate			1,000		
10045-94-0	Mercuric nitrate			10		
10049-04-4	Chlorine dioxide				313	
10049-05-5	Chromous chloride			1,000		
10099-74-8	Lead nitrate			100		
10101-53-8	Chromic sulfate			1,000		

CAS Number	Chemical Name	Sec. 302(EHS) TPQ	Section 304 EHS RQ	Section 304 CERCLA RQ	Sec 313	RCRA Code
10101-63-0	Lead iodide			100		
10101-89-0	Sodium phosphate, tribasic			5,000		
10102-06-4	Uranyl nitrate			100		
10102-18-8	Sodium selenite	100/10,000		100		
10102-20-2	Sodium tellurite	500/10,000	1			
10102-43-9	Nitric oxide	100		10		P076
10102-44-0	Nitrogen dioxide	100		10		P078
10102-45-1	Thallium(I) nitrate			100		U217
10102-48-4	Lead arsenate			1		
10108-64-2	Cadmium chloride			10		
10124-50-2	Potassium arsenite	500/10,000		1		
10124-56-8	Sodium phosphate, tribasic			5,000		
10140-65-5	Sodium phosphate, dibasic			5,000		
10140-87-1	Ethanol, 1,2-dichloro-, acetate	1,000	1			
10192-30-0	Ammonium bisulfite			5,000		
10196-04-0	Ammonium sulfite			5,000		
10210-68-1	Cobalt carbonyl	10/10,000	1			
10265-92-6	Methamidophos	100/10,000	1			
10294-34-5	Boron trichloride	500	1			
10311-84-9	Dialifor	100/10,000	1			
10361-89-4	Sodium phosphate, tribasic			5,000		
10380-29-7	Cupric sulfate, ammoniated			100		
10415-75-5	Mercurous nitrate			10		
10421-48-4	Ferric nitrate			1,000		
10476-95-6	Methacrolein diacetate	1,000	1			
10544-72-6	Nitrogen dioxide			10		
10588-01-9	Sodium bichromate			10		
11096-82-5	Aroclor 1260			1		
11097-69-1	Aroclor 1254			1		
11104-28-2	Aroclor 1221			1		
11115-74-5	Chromic acid			10		
11141-16-5	Aroclor 1232			1		
12002-03-8	Paris green	500/10,000		1		
12002-03-8	Cupric acetoarsenite	500/10,000		1		
12039-52-0	Selenious acid, dithallium(1+) salt			1,000		P114
12054-48-7	Nickel hydroxide			10		
12108-13-3	Manganese, tricarbonyl methylcyclopentadie	100	1			
12122-67-7	Zineb				313	
12125-01-8	Ammonium fluoride			100		
12125-02-9	Ammonium chloride			5,000		

CAS Number	Chemical Name	Sec. 302(EHS) TPQ	Section 304 EHS RQ	Section 304 CERCLA RQ	Sec 313	RCRA Code
12135-76-1	Ammonium sulfide			100		
12427-38-2	Maneb				313	
12672-29-6	Aroclor 1248			1		
12674-11-2	Aroclor 1016			1		
12771-08-3	Sulfur monochloride			1,000		
13071-79-9	Terbufos	100	1			
13171-21-6	Phosphamidon	100	1			
13194-48-4	Ethoprophos	1,000	1			
13410-01-0	Sodium selenate	100/10,000	1			
13450-90-3	Gallium trichloride	500/10,000	1			
13463-39-3	Nickel carbonyl	1		10		P073
13463-40-6	Iron, pentacarbonyl-	100	1			
13494-80-9	Tellurium	500/10,000	1			
13560-99-1	2,4,5-T salts			1,000		
13597-99-4	Beryllium nitrate			1		
13746-89-9	Zirconium nitrate			5,000		
13765-19-0	Calcium chromate			10		U032
13814-96-5	Lead fluoborate			100		
13826-83-0	Ammonium fluoborate			5,000		
13952-84-6	sec-Butylamine			1,000		
14017-41-5	Cobaltous sulfamate			1,000		
14167-18-1	Salcomine	500/10,000	1			
14216-75-2	Nickel nitrate			100		
14258-49-2	Ammonium oxalate			5,000		
14307-35-8	Lithium chromate			10		
14307-43-8	Ammonium tartrate			5,000		
14639-97-5	Zinc ammonium chloride			1,000		
14639-98-6	Zinc ammonium chloride			1,000		
14644-61-2	Zirconium sulfate			5,000		
15271-41-7	Bicyclo[2.2.1]heptane-2-carbonitrile, 5-ch	500/10,000	1			
15699-18-0	Nickel ammonium sulfate			100		
15739-80-7	Lead sulfate			100		
15950-66-0	2,3,4-Trichlorophenol			10		
16071-86-6	C.I. Direct Brown 95				313	
16543-55-8	N-Nitrosonornicotine				313	
16721-80-5	Sodium hydrosulfide			5,000		
16752-77-5	Methomyl	500/10,000		100		P066
16752-77-5	Ethanimidothioic acid, N-[[methylamino)car	500/10,000		100		P066
16871-71-9	Zinc silicofluoride			5,000		
16919-19-0	Ammonium silicofluoride			1,000		

CAS Number	Chemical Name	Sec. 302(EHS) TPQ	Section 304 EHS RQ	Section 304 CERCLA RQ	Sec 313	RCRA Code
16923-95-8	Zirconium potassium fluoride			1,000		
17702-41-9	Decaborane(14)	500/10,000	1			
17702-57-7	Formparanate	100/10,000	1			
18883-66-4	D-Glucose, 2-deoxy-2-[[(methylnitrosoamino			1		U206
19287-45-7	Diborane	100	1			
19624-22-7	Pentaborane	500	1			
20816-12-0	Osmium tetroxide			1,000	313	P087
20816-12-0	Osmium oxide OsO4 (T-4)-			1,000	X	P087
20830-75-5	Digoxin	10/10,000	1			
20830-81-3	Daunomycin			10		U059
20859-73-8	Aluminum phosphide	500		100		P006
21548-32-3	Fosthietan	500	1			
21609-90-5	Leptophos	500/10,000	1			
21908-53-2	Mercuric oxide	500/10,000	1			
21923-23-9	Chlorthiophos	500	1			
22224-92-6	Fenamiphos	10/10,000	1			
23135-22-0	Oxamyl	100/10,000	1			
23422-53-9	Formetanate hydrochloride	500/10,000	1			
23505-41-1	Pirimifos-ethyl	1,000	1			
23950-58-5	Benzamide,3,5-dichloro-N-(1,1-dimethyl-2-p			5,000		U192
24017-47-8	Triazofos	500	1			
24934-91-6	Chlormephos	500	1			
25154-54-5	Dinitrobenzene (mixed isomers)			100		
25154-55-6	Nitrophenol (mixed isomers)			100		
25155-30-0	Sodium dodecylbenzenesulfonate			1,000		
25167-82-2	Trichlorophenol			10		
25168-15-4	2,4,5-T esters			1,000		
25168-26-7	2,4-D Esters			100		
25321-14-6	Dinitrotoluene (mixed isomers)			10	313	
25321-22-6	Dichlorobenzene (mixed isomers)			100	313	
25321-22-6	Dichlorobenzene			100	X	
25376-45-8	Diaminotoluene (mixed isomers)			10	313	U221
25376-45-8	Toluenediamine			10	X	
25550-58-7	Dinitrophenol			10		
26264-06-2	Calcium dodecylbenzenesulfonate			1,000		
26419-73-8	Carbamic acid, methyl-, O-(((2,4-dimethyl-	100/10,000	1			
26471-62-5	Toluenediisocyanate (mixed isomers)			100	313	U223
26628-22-8	Sodium azide (Na(N3))	500		1,000		P105
26638-19-7	Dichloropropane			1,000		
27137-85-5	Trichloro(dichlorophenyl)silane	500	1			

CAS Number	Chemical Name	Sec. 302(EHS) TPQ	Section 304 EHS RQ	Section 304 CERCLA RQ	Sec 313	RCRA Code
27176-87-0	Dodecylbenzenesulfonic acid			1,000		
27323-41-7	Triethanolamine dodecylbenzene sulfonate			1,000		
27774-13-6	Vanadyl sulfate			1,000		
28300-74-5	Antimony potassium tartrate			100		
28347-13-9	Xylylene dichloride	100/10,000	1			
28772-56-7	Bromadiolone	100/10,000	1			
30525-89-4	Paraformaldehyde			1,000		
30674-80-7	Methacryloyloxyethyl isocyanate	100	1			
32534-95-5	2,4,5-TP esters			100		
33213-65-9	beta - Endosulfan			1		
36478-76-9	Uranyl nitrate			100		
37211-05-5	Nickel chloride			100		
39156-41-7	2,4-Diaminoanisole sulfate				313	
39196-18-4	Thiofanox	100/10,000		100		P045
42504-46-1	Isopropanolamine dodecylbenzene sulfonate			1,000		
50782-69-9	Phosphonothioic acid, methyl-, S-(2-(bis(1	100	1			
52628-25-8	Zinc ammonium chloride			1,000		
52652-59-2	Lead stearate			5,000		
52740-16-6	Calcium arsenite			1		
53467-11-1	2,4-D Esters			100		
53469-21-9	Aroclor 1242			1		
53558-25-1	Pyriminil	100/10,000	1			
55488-87-4	Ferric ammonium oxalate			1,000		
56189-09-4	Lead stearate			5,000		
58270-08-9	Zinc, dichloro(4,4-dimethyl-5((((methylami	100/10,000	1			
61792-07-2	2,4,5-T esters			1,000		
62207-76-5	Cobalt, ((2,2'-(1,2-ethanediylbis(nitrilom	100/10,000	1			
**	Organorhodium Complex (PMN-82-147)	10/10,000	1			

** This chemical was identified from a Premanufacture Review Notice (PMN) submitted to EPA. The submitter has claimed certain information on the submission to be confidential, including specific chemical identity.

Chemical Category	Sec. 302(EHS) TPQ	Section 304 EHS RQ	Section 304 CERCLA RQ	Sec 313	RCRA Code
Antimony Compounds			***	313	
Arsenic Compounds			***	313	
Barium Compounds				313	
Beryllium Compounds			***	313	
Cadmium Compounds			***	313	
Chlordane (Technical Mixture and Metabolites)			***		
Chlorinated Benzenes			***		
Chlorinated Ethanes			***		
Chlorinated Naphthalene			***		
Chlorophenols			***	313	
Chlorinated Phenols			***	X	
Chloroalkyl Ethers			***		
Chromium Compounds			***	313	
Cobalt Compounds			1+	313	
Coke Oven Emissions			1		
Copper Compounds			***	313	
Cyanide Compounds			***	313	
DDT and Metabolites			***		
Dichlorobenzidine			***		
Diphenylhydrazine			***		
Endosulfan and Metabolites			***		
Endrin and Metabolites			***		
Glycol Ethers			1+	313	
Haloethers			***		
Halomethanes			***		
heptachlor and Metabolites			***		
Lead Compounds			***	313	
Manganese Compounds			1+	313	
Mercury Compounds			***	313	
Fine mineral fibers			1+		
Nickel Compounds			***	313	
Nitrophenols			***		
Nitrosamines			***		
Phthalate Esters			***		
Polybrominated Biphenyls (PBBs)				313	
Polycyclic organic matter			1+		
Polynuclear Aromatic Hydrocarbons			***		
Selenium Compounds			***	313	
Silver Compounds			***	313	
Thallium Compounds			***	313	
Zinc Compounds			***	313	

*** Indicates that no RQ is assigned to this generic or broad class, although the class is a CERCLA hazardous substance. See 50 Federal Register 13456 (April 4, 1985).

+ Listed as hazardous air pollutant under section 112(b) of the Clear Air Act; statutory RQ of one pound applies until RQs are adjusted.

ALPHABETICAL LISTING OF CHEMICAL NAME AND CAS NUMBER

CAS Number	Chemical Name
83-32-9	Acenaphthene
208-96-8	Acenaphthylene
75-07-0	Acetaldehyde
75-87-6	Acetaldehyde, trichloro-
60-35-5	Acetamide
64-19-7	Acetic acid
108-24-7	Acetic anhydride
67-64-1	Acetone
75-86-5	Acetone cyanohydrin
1752-30-3	Acetone thiosemicarbazide
75-05-8	Acetonitrile
98-86-2	Acetophenone
53-96-3	2-Acetylaminofluorene
506-96-7	Acetyl bromide
75-36-5	Acetyl chloride
591-08-2	1-Acetyl-2-thiourea
107-02-8	Acrolein
79-06-1	Acrylamide
79-10-7	Acrylic acid
107-13-1	Acrylonitrile
814-68-6	Acrylyl chloride
124-04-9	Adipic acid
111-69-3	Adiponitrile
116-06-3	Aldicarb
309-00-2	Aldrin
107-18-6	Allyl alcohol
107-11-9	Allylamine
107-05-1	Allyl chloride
7429-90-5	Aluminum (fume or dust)
1344-28-1	Aluminum oxide (fibrous forms)
20859-73-8	Aluminum phosphide
10043-01-3	Aluminum sulfate
117-79-3	2-Aminoanthraquinone
60-09-3	4-Aminoazobenzene
92-67-1	4-Aminobiphenyl
82-28-0	1-Amino-2-methylanthraquinone
54-62-6	Aminopterin
504-24-5	4-Aminopyridine
78-53-5	Amiton
3734-97-2	Amiton oxalate
61-82-5	Amitrole
7664-41-7	Ammonia
631-61-8	Ammonium acetate
1863-63-4	Ammonium benzoate
1066-33-7	Ammonium bicarbonate
7789-09-5	Ammonium bichromate
1341-49-7	Ammonium bifluoride
10192-30-0	Ammonium bisulfite
1111-78-0	Ammonium carbamate
506-87-6	Ammonium carbonate
12125-02-9	Ammonium chloride
7788-98-9	Ammonium chromate
3012-65-5	Ammonium citrate, dibasic
13826-83-0	Ammonium fluoborate
12125-01-8	Ammonium fluoride
1336-21-6	Ammonium hydroxide
6484-52-2	Ammonium nitrate (solution)
6009-70-7	Ammonium oxalate
5972-73-6	Ammonium oxalate
14258-49-2	Ammonium oxalate
131-74-8	Ammonium picrate
16919-19-0	Ammonium silicofluoride
7773-06-0	Ammonium sulfamate
7783-20-2	Ammonium sulfate (solution)
12135-76-1	Ammonium sulfide
10196-04-0	Ammonium sulfite
14307-43-8	Ammonium tartrate
3164-29-2	Ammonium tartrate
1762-95-4	Ammonium thiocyanate
7803-55-6	Ammonium vanadate
300-62-9	Amphetamine
628-63-7	Amyl acetate
123-92-2	iso-Amyl acetate
626-38-0	sec-Amyl acetate
625-16-1	tert-Amyl acetate
62-53-3	Aniline
88-05-1	Aniline, 2,4,6-trimethyl-
90-04-0	o-Anisidine
104-94-9	p-Anisidine
134-29-2	o-Anisidine hydrochloride
120-12-7	Anthracene
7440-36-0	Antimony
	Antimony Compounds
7647-18-9	Antimony pentachloride
7783-70-2	Antimony pentafluoride
28300-74-5	Antimony potassium tartrate
7789-61-9	Antimony tribromide
10025-91-9	Antimony trichloride
7783-56-4	Antimony trifluoride
1309-64-4	Antimony trioxide
1397-94-0	Antimycin A
86-88-4	Antu
12674-11-2	Aroclor 1016
11104-28-2	Aroclor 1221
11141-16-5	Aroclor 1232
53469-21-9	Aroclor 1242
12672-29-6	Aroclor 1248
11097-69-1	Aroclor 1254
11096-82-5	Aroclor 1260
7440-38-2	Arsenic

CAS Number	Chemical Name	CAS Number	Chemical Name
1327-52-2	Arsenic acid	7440-41-7	Beryllium
7778-39-4	Arsenic acid	7787-47-5	Beryllium chloride
	Arsenic Compounds		Beryllium Compounds
1303-32-8	Arsenic disulfide	7787-49-7	Beryllium fluoride
1303-28-2	Arsenic pentoxide	13597-99-4	Beryllium nitrate
1327-53-3	Arsenic trioxide	7787-55-5	Beryllium nitrate
1303-33-9	Arsenic trisulfide	319-84-6	alpha-BHC
1327-53-3	Arsenous oxide	319-85-7	beta-BHC
7784-34-1	Arsenous trichloride	319-86-8	delta-BHC
7784-42-1	Arsine	15271-41-7	Bicyclo[2.2.1]heptane-2-carbonitrile, 5-ch
1332-21-4	Asbestos (friable)	1464-53-5	2,2'-Bioxirane
492-80-8	Auramine	92-52-4	Biphenyl
115-02-6	Azaserine	111-91-1	Bis(2-chloroethoxy) methane
2642-71-9	Azinphos-ethyl	111-44-4	Bis(2-chloroethyl) ether
86-50-0	Azinphos-methyl	542-88-1	Bis(chloromethyl) ether
151-56-4	Aziridine	108-60-1	Bis(2-chloro-1-methylethyl)ether
75-55-8	Aziridine, 2-methyl	534-07-6	Bis(chloromethyl) ketone
7440-39-3	Barium	103-23-1	Bis(2-ethylhexyl) adipate
	Barium Compounds	117-81-7	Bis(2-ethylhexyl)phthalate
542-62-1	Barium cyanide	4044-65-9	Bitoscanate
225-51-4	Benz[c]acridine	10294-34-5	Boron trichloride
98-87-3	Benzal chloride	7637-07-2	Boron trifluoride
55-21-0	Benzamide	353-42-4	Boron trifluoride compound with methyl eth
23950-58-5	Benzamide,3,5-dichloro-N-(1,1-dimethyl-2-p	28772-56-7	Bromadiolone
56-55-3	Benz[a]anthracene	7726-95-6	Bromine
98-16-8	Benzenamine, 3-(trifluoromethyl)-	598-31-2	Bromoacetone
71-43-2	Benzene	353-59-3	Bromochlorodifluoromethane [Halon 1211]
98-05-5	Benzenearsonic acid	75-25-2	Bromoform
100-14-1	Benzene, 1-(chloromethyl)-4-nitro-	74-83-9	Bromomethane
108-38-3	Benzene, m-dimethyl-	101-55-3	4-Bromophenyl phenyl ether
95-47-6	Benzene, o-dimethyl-	75-63-8	Bromotrifluoromethane [Halon 1301]
106-42-3	Benzene, p-dimethyl-	357-57-3	Brucine
122-09-8	Benzeneethanamine, alpha,alpha-dimethyl-	106-99-0	1,3-Butadiene
98-09-9	Benzenesulfonyl chloride	764-41-0	2-Butene, 1,4-dichloro-
108-98-5	Benzenethiol	123-86-4	Butyl acetate
92-87-5	Benzidine	110-19-0	iso-Butyl acetate
3615-21-2	Benzimidazole, 4,5-dichloro-2-(trifluorome	105-46-4	sec-Butyl acetate
205-99-2	Benzo[b]fluoranthene	540-88-5	tert-Butyl acetate
207-08-9	Benzo(k)fluoranthene	141-32-2	Butyl acrylate
65-85-0	Benzoic acid	71-36-3	n-Butyl alcohol
98-07-7	Benzoic trichloride	78-92-2	sec-Butyl alcohol
100-47-0	Benzonitrile	75-65-0	tert-Butyl alcohol
191-24-2	Benzo[ghi]perylene	109-73-9	Butylamine
50-32-8	Benzo[a]pyrene	78-81-9	iso-Butylamine
106-51-4	p-Benzoquinone	513-49-5	sec-Butylamine
98-07-7	Benzotrichloride	13952-84-6	sec-Butylamine
98-88-4	Benzoyl chloride	75-64-9	tert-Butylamine
94-36-0	Benzoyl peroxide	85-68-7	Butyl benzyl phthalate
100-44-7	Benzyl chloride	106-88-7	1,2-Butylene oxide
140-29-4	Benzyl cyanide	84-74-2	n-Butyl phthalate

ALPHABETICAL LISTING OF CHEMICAL NAME AND CAS NUMBER

CAS Number	Chemical Name
123-72-8	Butyraldehyde
107-92-6	Butyric acid
79-31-2	iso-Butyric acid
75-60-5	Cacodylic acid
7440-43-9	Cadmium
543-90-8	Cadmium acetate
7789-42-6	Cadmium bromide
10108-64-2	Cadmium chloride
	Cadmium Compounds
1306-19-0	Cadmium oxide
2223-93-0	Cadmium stearate
7778-44-1	Calcium arsenate
52740-16-6	Calcium arsenite
75-20-7	Calcium carbide
13765-19-0	Calcium chromate
156-62-7	Calcium cyanamide
592-01-8	Calcium cyanide
26264-06-2	Calcium dodecylbenzenesulfonate
7778-54-3	Calcium hypochlorite
8001-35-2	Camphechlor
8C01-35-2	Camphene, octachloro-
56-25-7	Cantharidin
105-60-2	Caprolactam
133-06-2	Captan
51-83-2	Carbachol chloride
51-79-6	Carbamic acid, ethyl ester
26419-73-8	Carbamic acid, methyl-, O-(((2,4-dimethyl-
63-25-2	Carbaryl
1563-66-2	Carbofuran
75-15-0	Carbon disulfide
353-50-4	Carbonic difluoride
56-23-5	Carbon tetrachloride
463-58-1	Carbonyl sulfide
786-19-6	Carbophenothion
120-80-9	Catechol
75-69-4	CFC-11
75-71-8	CFC-12
76-14-2	CFC-114
76-15-3	CFC-115
133-90-4	Chloramben
305-03-3	Chlorambucil
57-74-9	Chlordane
	Chlordane (Technical Mixture and Metabolit
470-90-6	Chlorfenvinfos
	Chlorinated Benzenes
	Chlorinated Ethanes
	Chlorinated Naphthalene
	Chlorinated Phenols
7782-50-5	Chlorine
10049-04-4	Chlorine dioxide
24934-91-6	Chlormephos
999-81-5	Chlormequat chloride
494-03-1	Chlornaphazine
107-20-0	Chloroacetaldehyde
79-11-8	Chloroacetic acid
532-27-4	2-Chloroacetophenone
	Chloroalkyl Ethers
106-47-8	p-Chloroaniline
108-90-7	Chlorobenzene
510-15-6	Chlorobenzilate
59-50-7	p-Chloro-m-cresol
124-48-1	Chlorodibromomethane
75-00-3	Chloroethane
107-07-3	Chloroethanol
627-11-2	Chloroethyl chloroformate
110-75-8	2-Chloroethyl vinyl ether
67-66-3	Chloroform
74-87-3	Chloromethane
107-30-2	Chloromethyl methyl ether
542-88-1	Chloromethyl ether
91-58-7	2-Chloronaphthalene
3691-35-8	Chlorophacinone
95-57-8	2-Chlorophenol
	Chlorophenols
7005-72-3	4-Chlorophenyl phenyl ether
126-99-8	Chloroprene
542-76-7	3-Chloropropionitrile
7790-94-5	Chlorosulfonic acid
1897-45-6	Chlorothalonil
3165-93-3	4-Chloro-o-toluidine, hydrochloride
1982-47-4	Chloroxuron
2921-88-2	Chlorpyrifos
21923-23-9	Chlorthiophos
1066-30-4	Chromic acetate
11115-74-5	Chromic acid
7738-94-5	Chromic acid
10025-73-7	Chromic chloride
10101-53-8	Chromic sulfate
7440-47-3	Chromium
	Chromium Compounds
10049-05-5	Chromous chloride
218-01-9	Chrysene
4680-78-8	C.I. Acid Green 3
569-64-2	C.I. Basic Green 4
989-38-8	C.I. Basic Red 1
1937-37-7	C.I. Direct Black 38
2602-46-2	C.I. Direct Blue 6
16071-86-6	C.I. Direct Brown 95
2832-40-8	C.I. Disperse Yellow 3
3761-53-3	C.I. Food Red 5

CAS Number	Chemical Name	CAS Number	Chemical Name
81-88-9	C.I. Food Red 15	66-81-9	Cycloheximide
3118-97-6	C.I. Solvent Orange 7	108-91-8	Cyclohexylamine
97-56-3	C.I. Solvent Yellow 3	131-89-5	2-Cyclohexyl-4,6-Dinitrophenol
842-07-9	C.I. Solvent Yellow 14	50-18-0	Cyclophosphamide
492-80-8	C.I. Solvent Yellow 34	94-75-7	2,4-D
128-66-5	C.I. Vat Yellow 4	94-75-7	2,4-D Acid
7440-48-4	Cobalt	94-11-1	2,4-D Esters
10210-68-1	Cobalt carbonyl	94-79-1	2,4-D Esters
	Cobalt Compounds	94-80-4	2,4-D Esters
62207-76-5	Cobalt, ((2,2'-(1,2-ethanediylbis(nitrilom	1320-18-9	2,4-D Esters
7789-43-7	Cobaltous bromide	1928-38-7	2,4-D Esters
544-18-3	Cobaltous formate	1928-61-6	2,4-D Esters
14017-41-5	Cobaltous sulfamate	1929-73-3	2,4-D Esters
	Coke Oven Emissions	2971-38-2	2,4-D Esters
64-86-8	Colchicine	25168-26-7	2,4-D Esters
7440-50-8	Copper	53467-11-1	2,4-D Esters
	Copper Compounds	94-75-7	2,4-D, salts and esters
544-92-3	Copper cyanide	20830-81-3	Daunomycin
56-72-4	Coumaphos	96-12-8	DBCP
5836-29-3	Coumatetralyl	72-54-8	DDD
8001-58-9	Creosote	72-55-9	DDE
120-71-8	p-Cresidine	3547-04-4	DDE
108-39-4	m-Cresol	50-29-3	DDT
95-48-7	o-Cresol		DDT and Metabolites
106-44-5	p-Cresol	17702-41-9	Decaborane(14)
1319-77-3	Cresol (mixed isomers)	1163-19-5	Decabromodiphenyl oxide
535-89-7	Crimidine	117-81-7	DEHP
4170-30-3	Crotonaldehyde	8065-48-3	Demeton
123-73-9	Crotonaldehyde, (E)-	919-86-8	Demeton-S-methyl
98-82-8	Cumene	10311-84-9	Dialifor
80-15-9	Cumene hydroperoxide	2303-16-4	Diallate
135-20-6	Cupferron	615-05-4	2,4-Diaminoanisole
142-71-2	Cupric acetate	39156-41-7	2,4-Diaminoanisole sulfate
12002-03-8	Cupric acetoarsenite	101-80-4	4,4'-Diaminodiphenyl ether
7447-39-4	Cupric chloride	496-72-0	Diaminotoluene
3251-23-8	Cupric nitrate	823-40-5	Diaminotoluene
5893-66-3	Cupric oxalate	95-80-7	2,4-Diaminotoluene
7758-98-7	Cupric sulfate	25376-45-8	Diaminotoluene (mixed isomers)
10380-29-7	Cupric sulfate, ammoniated	333-41-5	Diazinon
815-82-7	Cupric tartrate	334-88-3	Diazomethane
	Cyanide Compounds	53-70-3	Dibenz[a,h]anthracene
57-12-5	Cyanides (soluble salts and complexes)	132-64-9	Dibenzofuran
460-19-5	Cyanogen	189-55-9	Dibenz[a,i]pyrene
506-68-3	Cyanogen bromide	19287-45-7	Diborane
506-77-4	Cyanogen chloride	96-12-8	1,2-Dibromo-3-chloropropane
506-78-5	Cyanogen iodide	106-93-4	1,2-Dibromoethane
2636-26-2	Cyanophos	124-73-2	Dibromotetrafluoroethane [Halon 2402]
675-14-9	Cyanuric fluoride	84-74-2	Dibutyl phthalate
110-82-7	Cyclohexane	1918-00-9	Dicamba
108-94-1	Cyclohexanone	1194-65-6	Dichlobenil

CAS Number	Chemical Name	CAS Number	Chemical Name
117-80-6	Dichlone	64-67-5	Diethyl sulfate
25321-22-6	Dichlorobenzene	71-63-6	Digitoxin
95-50-1	o-Dichlorobenzene	2238-07-5	Diglycidyl ether
95-50-1	1,2-Dichlorobenzene	20830-75-5	Digoxin
541-73-1	1,3-Dichlorobenzene	94-58-6	Dihydrosafrole
106-46-7	1,4-Dichlorobenzene	55-91-4	Diisopropylfluorophosphate
25321-22-6	Dichlorobenzene (mixed isomers)	115-26-4	Dimefox
91-94-1	3,3'-Dichlorobenzidine	60-51-5	Dimethoate
	Dichlorobenzidine	119-90-4	3,3'-Dimethoxybenzidine
75-27-4	Dichlorobromomethane	124-40-3	Dimethylamine
110-57-6	Trans-1,4-dichlorobutene	60-11-7	4-Dimethylaminoazobenzene
75-71-8	Dichlorodifluoromethane [CFC-12]	60-11-7	Dimethylaminoazobenzene
107-06-2	1,2-Dichloroethane	121-69-7	N,N-Dimethylaniline
75-34-3	1,1-Dichloroethane	57-97-6	7,12-Dimethylbenz[a]anthracene
540-59-0	1,2-Dichloroethylene	119-93-7	3,3'-Dimethylbenzidine
75-35-4	1,1-Dichloroethylene	79-44-7	Dimethylcarbamyl chloride
156-60-5	1,2-Dichloroethylene	75-78-5	Dimethyldichlorosilane
111-44-4	Dichloroethyl ether	68-12-2	Dimethylformamide
108-60-1	Dichloroisopropyl ether	57-14-7	1,1-Dimethyl hydrazine
75-09-2	Dichloromethane	57-14-7	Dimethylhydrazine
542-88-1	Dichloromethyl ether	105-67-9	2,4-Dimethylphenol
149-74-6	Dichloromethylphenylsilane	99-98-9	Dimethyl-p-phenylenediamine
120-83-2	2,4-Dichlorophenol	2524-03-0	Dimethyl phosphorochloridothioate
87-65-0	2,6-Dichlorophenol	131-11-3	Dimethyl phthalate
696-28-6	Dichlorophenylarsine	77-78-1	Dimethyl sulfate
78-87-5	1,2-Dichloropropane	644-64-4	Dimetilan
26638-19-7	Dichloropropane	25154-54-5	Dinitrobenzene (mixed isomers)
8003-19-8	Dichloropropane - Dichloropropene (mixture	99-65-0	m-Dinitrobenzene
78-99-9	1,1-Dichloropropane	528-29-0	o-Dinitrobenzene
142-28-9	1,3-Dichloropropane	100-25-4	p-Dinitrobenzene
542-75-6	1,3-Dichloropropene	534-52-1	Dinitrocresol
78-88-6	2,3-Dichloropropene	534-52-1	4,6-Dinitro-o-cresol
75-99-0	2,2-Dichloropropionic acid	534-52-1	4,6-Dinitro-o-cresol and salts
542-75-6	1,3-Dichloropropylene	25550-58-7	Dinitrophenol
76-14-2	Dichlorotetrafluoroethane [CFC-114]	51-28-5	2,4-Dinitrophenol
62-73-7	Dichlorvos	329-71-5	2,5-Dinitrophenol
115-32-2	Dicofol	573-56-8	2,6-Dinitrophenol
141-66-2	Dicrotophos	25321-14-6	Dinitrotoluene (mixed isomers)
60-57-1	Dieldrin	121-14-2	2,4-Dinitrotoluene
1464-53-5	Diepoxybutane	606-20-2	2,6-Dinitrotoluene
111-42-2	Diethanolamine	610-39-9	3,4-Dinitrotoluene
109-89-7	Diethylamine	88-85-7	Dinoseb
692-42-2	Diethylarsine	1420-07-1	Dinoterb
1642-54-2	Diethylcarbamazine citrate	117-84-0	n-Dioctylphthalate
814-49-3	Diethyl chlorophosphate	117-84-0	Di-n-octyl phthalate
117-81-7	Di(2-ethylhexyl) phthalate	123-91-1	1,4-Dioxane
311-45-5	Diethyl-p-nitrophenyl phosphate	78-34-2	Dioxathion
84-66-2	Diethyl phthalate	82-66-6	Diphacinone
297-97-2	O,O-Diethyl O-pyrazinyl phosphorothioate	122-66-7	1,2-Diphenylhydrazine
56-53-1	Diethylstilbestrol		Diphenylhydrazine

CAS Number	Chemical Name
152-16-9	Diphosphoramide, octamethyl-
142-84-7	Dipropylamine
85-00-7	Diquat
2764-72-9	Diquat
298-04-4	Disulfoton
514-73-8	Dithiazanine iodide
541-53-7	Dithiobiuret
3288-58-2	O,O-Diethyl S-methyl dithiophosphate
330-54-1	Diuron
27176-87-0	Dodecylbenzenesulfonic acid
316-42-7	Emetine, dihydrochloride
115-29-7	Endosulfan
959-98-8	alpha - Endosulfan
33213-65-9	beta - Endosulfan
	Endosulfan and Metabolites
1031-07-8	Endosulfan sulfate
145-73-3	Endothall
2778-04-3	Endothion
72-20-8	Endrin
7421-93-4	Endrin aldehyde
	Endrin and Metabolites
106-89-8	Epichlorohydrin
51-43-4	Epinephrine
2104-64-5	EPN
50-14-6	Ergocalciferol
379-79-3	Ergotamine tartrate
1622-32-8	Ethanesulfonyl chloride, 2-chloro-
630-20-6	Ethane, 1,1,1,2-tetrachloro-
16752-77-5	Ethanimidothioic acid, N-[[methylamino)car
10140-87-1	Ethanol, 1,2-dichloro-, acetate
110-80-5	Ethanol, 2-ethoxy-
563-12-2	Ethion
13194-48-4	Ethoprophos
110-80-5	2-Ethoxyethanol
141-78-6	Ethyl acetate
140-88-5	Ethyl acrylate
100-41-4	Ethylbenzene
538-07-8	Ethylbis(2-chloroethyl)amine
51-79-6	Ethyl carbamate
75-00-3	Ethyl chloride
541-41-3	Ethyl chloroformate
107-12-0	Ethyl cyanide
74-85-1	Ethylene
111-54-6	Ethylenebisdithiocarbamic acid, salts & es
107-15-3	Ethylenediamine
60-00-4	Ethylenediamine-tetraacetic acid (EDTA)
106-93-4	Ethylene dibromide
107-06-2	Ethylene dichloride
371-62-0	Ethylene fluorohydrin
107-21-1	Ethylene glycol
151-56-4	Ethyleneimine
75-21-8	Ethylene oxide
96-45-7	Ethylene thiourea
60-29-7	Ethyl ether
97-63-2	Ethyl methacrylate
62-50-0	Ethyl methanesulfonate
542-90-5	Ethylthiocyanate
52-85-7	Famphur
22224-92-6	Fenamiphos
122-14-5	Fenitrothion
115-90-2	Fensulfothion
1185-57-5	Ferric ammonium citrate
2944-67-4	Ferric ammonium oxalate
55488-87-4	Ferric ammonium oxalate
7705-08-0	Ferric chloride
7783-50-8	Ferric fluoride
10421-48-4	Ferric nitrate
10028-22-5	Ferric sulfate
10045-89-3	Ferrous ammonium sulfate
7758-94-3	Ferrous chloride
7720-78-7	Ferrous sulfate
7782-63-0	Ferrous sulfate
4301-50-2	Fluenetil
2164-17-2	Fluometuron
206-44-0	Fluoranthene
86-73-7	Fluorene
7782-41-4	Fluorine
640-19-7	Fluoroacetamide
144-49-0	Fluoroacetic acid
62-74-8	Fluoroacetic acid, sodium salt
359-06-8	Fluoroacetyl chloride
51-21-8	Fluorouracil
944-22-9	Fonofos
50-00-0	Formaldehyde
107-16-4	Formaldehyde cyanohydrin
23422-53-9	Formetanate hydrochloride
64-18-6	Formic acid
2540-82-1	Formothion
17702-57-7	Formparanate
21548-32-3	Fosthietan
76-13-1	Freon 113
3878-19-1	Fuberidazole
110-17-8	Fumaric acid
110-00-9	Furan
109-99-9	Furan, tetrahydro-
98-01-1	Furfural
13450-90-3	Gallium trichloride
18883-66-4	D-Glucose, 2-deoxy-2-[[(methylnitrosoamino
765-34-4	Glycidylaldehyde
	Glycol Ethers

ALPHABETICAL LISTING OF CHEMICAL NAME AND CAS NUMBER

CAS Number	Chemical Name
70-25-7	Guanidine, N-methyl-N'-nitro-N-nitroso-
86-50-0	Guthion
	Haloethers
	Halomethanes
353-59-3	Halon 1211
75-63-8	Halon 1301
124-73-2	Halon 2402
76-44-8	Heptachlor
	Heptachlor and Metabolites
1024-57-3	Heptachlor epoxide
118-74-1	Hexachlorobenzene
87-68-3	Hexachloro-1,3-butadiene
87-68-3	Hexachlorobutadiene
77-47-4	Hexachlorocyclopentadiene
58-89-9	Hexachlorocyclohexane (gamma isomer)
67-72-1	Hexachloroethane
1335-87-1	Hexachloronaphthalene
70-30-4	Hexachlorophene
1888-71-7	Hexachloropropene
757-58-4	Hexaethyl tetraphosphate
822-06-0	Hexamethylene-1,6-diisocyanate
4835-11-4	Hexamethylenediamine, N,N'-dibutyl-
680-31-9	Hexamethylphosphoramide
110-54-3	Hexane
302-01-2	Hydrazine
1615-80-1	Hydrazine, 1,2-diethyl-
57-14-7	Hydrazine, 1,1-dimethyl-
540-73-8	Hydrazine, 1,2-dimethyl-
122-66-7	Hydrazine, 1,2-diphenyl-
10034-93-2	Hydrazine sulfate
122-66-7	Hydrazobenzene
7647-01-0	Hydrochloric acid
74-90-8	Hydrocyanic acid
7664-39-3	Hydrofluoric acid
7647-01-0	Hydrogen chloride (gas only)
74-90-8	Hydrogen cyanide
7664-39-3	Hydrogen fluoride
7722-84-1	Hydrogen peroxide (Conc.> 52%)
7783-07-5	Hydrogen selenide
7783-06-4	Hydrogen sulfide
80-15-9	Hydroperoxide, 1-methyl-1-phenylethyl-
123-31-9	Hydroquinone
193-39-5	Indeno(1,2,3-cd)pyrene
13463-40-6	Iron, pentacarbonyl-
297-78-9	Isobenzan
78-83-1	Isobutyl alcohol
78-84-2	Isobutyraldehyde
78-82-0	Isobutyronitrile
102-36-3	Isocyanic acid, 3,4-dichlorophenyl ester
465-73-6	Isodrin
55-91-4	Isofluorphate
78-59-1	Isophorone
4098-71-9	Isophorone diisocyanate
78-79-5	Isoprene
42504-46-1	Isopropanolamine dodecylbenzene sulfonate
67-63-0	Isopropyl alcohol (mfg-strong acid process
108-23-6	Isopropyl chloroformate
80-05-7	4,4'-Isopropylidenediphenol
119-38-0	Isopropylmethylpyrazolyl dimethylcarbamate
120-58-1	Isosafrole
2763-96-4	5-(Aminomethyl)-3-isoxazolol
143-50-0	Kepone
78-97-7	Lactonitrile
303-34-4	Lasiocarpine
7439-92-1	Lead
	Lead Compounds
301-04-2	Lead acetate
7784-40-9	Lead arsenate
7645-25-2	Lead arsenate
10102-48-4	Lead arsenate
7758-95-4	Lead chloride
13814-96-5	Lead fluoborate
7783-46-2	Lead fluoride
10101-63-0	Lead iodide
10099-74-8	Lead nitrate
7446-27-7	Lead phosphate
7428-48-0	Lead stearate
1072-35-1	Lead stearate
52652-59-2	Lead stearate
56189-09-4	Lead stearate
1335-32-6	Lead subacetate
15739-80-7	Lead sulfate
7446-14-2	Lead sulfate
1314-87-0	Lead sulfide
592-87-0	Lead thiocyanate
21609-90-5	Leptophos
541-25-3	Lewisite
58-89-9	Lindane
14307-35-8	Lithium chromate
7580-67-8	Lithium hydride
121-75-5	Malathion
110-16-7	Maleic acid
108-31-6	Maleic anhydride
123-33-1	Maleic hydrazide
109-77-3	Malononitrile
12427-38-2	Maneb
7439-96-5	Manganese
	Manganese Compounds
12108-13-3	Manganese, tricarbonyl methylcyclopentadie
101-68-8	MBI

CAS Number	Chemical Name
101-14-4	MBOCA
51-75-2	Mechlorethamine
148-82-3	Melphalan
950-10-7	Mephosfolan
2032-65-7	Mercaptodimethur
1600-27-7	Mercuric acetate
7487-94-7	Mercuric chloride
592-04-1	Mercuric cyanide
10045-94-0	Mercuric nitrate
21908-53-2	Mercuric oxide
7783-35-9	Mercuric sulfate
592-85-8	Mercuric thiocyanate
10415-75-5	Mercurous nitrate
7782-86-7	Mercurous nitrate
7439-97-6	Mercury
	Mercury Compounds
628-86-4	Mercury fulminate
10476-95-6	Methacrolein diacetate
760-93-0	Methacrylic anhydride
126-98-7	Methacrylonitrile
920-46-7	Methacryloyl chloride
30674-80-7	Methacryloyloxyethyl isocyanate
10265-92-6	Methamidophos
62-75-9	Methanamine, N-methyl-N-nitroso-
558-25-8	Methanesulfonyl fluoride
67-56-1	Methanol
91-80-5	Methapyrilene
950-37-8	Methidathion
2032-65-7	Methiocarb
16752-77-5	Methomyl
72-43-5	Methoxychlor
109-86-4	2-Methoxyethanol
151-38-2	Methoxyethylmercuric acetate
96-33-3	Methyl acrylate
74-83-9	Methyl bromide
74-87-3	Methyl chloride
80-63-7	Methyl 2-chloroacrylate
71-55-6	Methyl chloroform
79-22-1	Methyl chloroformate
56-49-5	3-Methylcholanthrene
101-14-4	4,4'-Methylenebis(2-chloroaniline)
101-61-1	4,4'-Methylenebis(N,N-dimethyl)benzenamine
101-68-8	Methylenebis(phenylisocyanate)
74-95-3	Methylene bromide
75-09-2	Methylene chloride
101-77-9	4,4'-Methylenedianiline
78-93-3	Methyl ethyl ketone
78-93-3	Methyl ethyl ketone (MEK)
1338-23-4	Methyl ethyl ketone peroxide
60-34-4	Methyl hydrazine
74-88-4	Methyl iodide
108-10-1	Methyl isobutyl ketone
624-83-9	Methyl isocyanate
556-61-6	Methyl isothiocyanate
74-93-1	Methyl mercaptan
502-39-6	Methylmercuric dicyanamide
80-62-6	Methyl methacrylate
298-00-0	Methyl parathion
3735-23-7	Methyl phenkapton
676-97-1	Methyl phosphonic dichloride
1634-04-4	Methyl tert-butyl ether
556-64-9	Methyl thiocyanate
56-04-2	Methylthiouracil
75-79-6	Methyltrichlorosilane
78-94-4	Methyl vinyl ketone
1129-41-5	Metolcarb
7786-34-7	Mevinphos
315-18-4	Mexacarbate
90-94-8	Michler's ketone
	Fine mineral fibers
50-07-7	Mitomycin C
1313-27-5	Molybdenum trioxide
76-15-3	Monochloropentafluoroethane [CFC-115]
6923-22-4	Monocrotophos
75-04-7	Monoethylamine
74-89-5	Monomethylamine
2763-96-4	Muscimol
505-60-2	Mustard gas
300-76-5	Naled
91-20-3	Naphthalene
1338-24-5	Naphthenic acid
130-15-4	1,4-Naphthoquinone
134-32-7	alpha-Naphthylamine
91-59-8	beta-Naphthylamine
7440-02-0	Nickel
	Nickel Compounds
15699-18-0	Nickel ammonium sulfate
13463-39-3	Nickel carbonyl
7718-54-9	Nickel chloride
37211-05-5	Nickel chloride
557-19-7	Nickel cyanide
12054-48-7	Nickel hydroxide
14216-75-2	Nickel nitrate
7786-81-4	Nickel sulfate
54-11-5	Nicotine
54-11-5	Nicotine and salts
65-30-5	Nicotine sulfate
7697-37-2	Nitric acid
10102-43-9	Nitric oxide
139-13-9	Nitrilotriacetic acid

CAS Number	Chemical Name	CAS Number	Chemical Name
100-01-6	p-Nitroaniline	30525-89-4	Paraformaldehyde
99-59-2	5-Nitro-o-anisidine	123-63-7	Paraldehyde
98-95-3	Nitrobenzene	1910-42-5	Paraquat
92-93-3	4-Nitrobiphenyl	2074-50-2	Paraquat methosulfate
1122-60-7	Nitrocyclohexane	56-38-2	Parathion
1836-75-5	Nitrofen	298-00-0	Parathion-methyl
10102-44-0	Nitrogen dioxide	12002-03-8	Paris green
10544-72-6	Nitrogen dioxide	1336-36-3	PCBs
51-75-2	Nitrogen mustard	82-68-8	PCNB
55-63-0	Nitroglycerin	19624-22-7	Pentaborane
25154-55-6	Nitrophenol (mixed isomers)	608-93-5	Pentachlorobenzene
554-84-7	m-Nitrophenol	76-01-7	Pentachloroethane
100-02-7	p-Nitrophenol	82-68-8	Pentachloronitrobenzene
88-75-5	2-Nitrophenol	87-86-5	PCP
100-02-7	4-Nitrophenol	87-86-5	Pentachlorophenol
	Nitrophenols	2570-26-5	Pentadecylamine
79-46-9	2-Nitropropane	504-60-9	1,3-Pentadiene
	Nitrosamines	79-21-0	Peracetic acid
924-16-3	N-Nitrosodi-n-butylamine	127-18-4	Perchloroethylene
1116-54-7	N-Nitrosodiethanolamine	594-42-3	Perchloromethylmercaptan
55-18-5	N-Nitrosodiethylamine	62-44-2	Phenacetin
62-75-9	N-Nitrosodimethylamine	85-01-8	Phenanthrene
62-75-9	Nitrosodimethylamine	108-95-2	Phenol
86-30-6	N-Nitrosodiphenylamine	64-00-6	Phenol, 3-(1-methylethyl)-, methylcarbamat
156-10-5	p-Nitrosodiphenylamine	4418-66-0	Phenol, 2,2'-thiobis(4-chloro-6-methyl-
621-64-7	N-Nitrosodi-n-propylamine	58-36-6	Phenoxarsine, 10,10'-oxydi-
759-73-9	N-Nitroso-N-ethylurea	696-28-6	Phenyl dichloroarsine
684-93-5	N-Nitroso-N-methylurea	106-50-3	p-Phenylenediamine
4549-40-0	N-Nitrosomethylvinylamine	59-88-1	Phenylhydrazine hydrochloride
59-89-2	N-Nitrosomorpholine	62-38-4	Phenylmercuric acetate
615-53-2	N-Nitroso-N-methylurethane	62-38-4	Phenylmercury acetate
16543-55-8	N-Nitrosonornicotine	90-43-7	2-Phenylphenol
100-75-4	N-Nitrosopiperidine	2097-19-0	Phenylsilatrane
930-55-2	N-Nitrosopyrrolidine	103-85-5	Phenylthiourea
1321-12-6	Nitrotoluene	298-02-2	Phorate
99-08-1	m-Nitrotoluene	4104-14-7	Phosacetim
88-72-2	o-Nitrotoluene	947-02-4	Phosfolan
99-99-0	p-Nitrotoluene	75-44-5	Phosgene
99-55-8	5-Nitro-o-toluidine	732-11-6	Phosmet
991-42-4	Norbormide	13171-21-6	Phosphamidon
2234-13-1	Octachloronaphthalene	7803-51-2	Phosphine
	Organorhodium Complex (PMN-82-147)	2703-13-1	Phosphonothioic acid, methyl-, O-ethyl O-(
20816-12-0	Osmium oxide OsO4 (T-4)-	50782-69-9	Phosphonothioic acid, methyl-, S-(2-(bis(1
20816-12-0	Osmium tetroxide	2665-30-7	Phosphonothioic acid, methyl-, O-(4-nitrop
630-60-4	Ouabain	7664-38-2	Phosphoric acid
23135-22-0	Oxamyl	3254-63-5	Phosphoric acid, dimethyl 4-(methylthio) p
78-71-7	Oxetane, 3,3-bis(chloromethyl)-	2587-90-8	Phosphorothioic acid, O,O-dimethyl-5-(2-(m
75-21-8	Oxirane	7723-14-0	Phosphorus (yellow or white)
2497-07-6	Oxydisulfoton	7723-14-0	Phosphorus
10028-15-6	Ozone	10025-87-3	Phosphorus oxychloride

CAS Number	Chemical Name
10026-13-8	Phosphorus pentachloride
1314-56-3	Phosphorus pentoxide
7719-12-2	Phosphorus trichloride
	Phthalate Esters
85-44-9	Phthalic anhydride
57-47-6	Physostigmine
57-64-7	Physostigmine, salicylate (1:1)
109-06-8	2-Picoline
88-89-1	Picric acid
124-87-8	Picrotoxin
110-89-4	Piperidine
23505-41-1	Pirimifos-ethyl
	Polybrominated Biphenyls (PBBs)
1336-36-3	Polychlorinated biphenyls
	Polycyclic organic matter
	Polynuclear Aromatic Hydrocarbons
7784-41-0	Potassium arsenate
10124-50-2	Potassium arsenite
7778-50-9	Potassium bichromate
7789-00-6	Potassium chromate
151-50-8	Potassium cyanide
1310-58-3	Potassium hydroxide
7722-64-7	Potassium permanganate
506-61-6	Potassium silver cyanide
2631-37-0	Promecarb
78-87-5	Propane 1,2-dichloro-
1120-71-4	1,3-Propane sultone
1120-71-4	Propane sultone
2312-35-8	Propargite
107-19-7	Propargyl alcohol
106-96-7	Propargyl bromide
57-57-8	beta-Propiolactone
123-38-6	Propionaldehyde
79-09-4	Propionic acid
123-62-6	Propionic anhydride
107-12-0	Propionitrile
542-76-7	Propionitrile, 3-chloro-
70-69-9	Propiophenone, 4'-amino
114-26-1	Propoxur
109-61-5	Propyl chloroformate
107-10-8	n-Propylamine
115-07-1	Propylene (Propene)
75-55-8	Propyleneimine
75-56-9	Propylene oxide
621-64-7	Di-n-propylnitrosamine
2275-18-5	Prothoate
129-00-0	Pyrene
121-29-9	Pyrethrins
121-21-1	Pyrethrins
8003-34-7	Pyrethrins
110-86-1	Pyridine
504-24-5	Pyridine, 4-amino-
54-11-5	Pyridine, 3-(1-methyl-2-pyrrolidinyl)-,(S)
140-76-1	Pyridine, 2-methyl-5-vinyl-
1124-33-0	Pyridine, 4-nitro-, 1-oxide
53558-25-1	Pyriminil
91-22-5	Quinoline
106-51-4	Quinone
82-68-8	Quintozene
50-55-5	Reserpine
108-46-3	Resorcinol
81-07-2	Saccharin (manufacturing)
81-07-2	Saccharin and salts
94-59-7	Safrole
14167-18-1	Salcomine
107-44-8	Sarin
7783-00-8	Selenious acid
12039-52-0	Selenious acid, dithallium(1+) salt
7782-49-2	Selenium
	Selenium Compounds
7446-08-4	Selenium dioxide
7791-23-3	Selenium oxychloride
7488-56-4	Selenium sulfide
630-10-4	Selenourea
563-41-7	Semicarbazide hydrochloride
3037-72-7	Silane, (4-aminobutyl)diethoxymethyl-
7440-22-4	Silver
	Silver Compounds
506-64-9	Silver cyanide
7761-88-8	Silver nitrate
93-72-1	Silvex (2,4,5-TP)
7440-23-5	Sodium
7631-89-2	Sodium arsenate
7784-46-5	Sodium arsenite
26628-22-8	Sodium azide (Na(N3))
10588-01-9	Sodium bichromate
1333-83-1	Sodium bifluoride
7631-90-5	Sodium bisulfite
124-65-2	Sodium cacodylate
7775-11-3	Sodium chromate
143-33-9	Sodium cyanide (Na(CN))
25155-30-0	Sodium dodecylbenzenesulfonate
7681-49-4	Sodium fluoride
62-74-8	Sodium fluoroacetate
16721-80-5	Sodium hydrosulfide
1310-73-2	Sodium hydroxide
7681-52-9	Sodium hypochlorite
10022-70-5	Sodium hypochlorite
124-41-4	Sodium methylate
7632-00-0	Sodium nitrite

CAS Number	Chemical Name
7558-79-4	Sodium phosphate, dibasic
10039-32-4	Sodium phosphate, dibasic
10140-65-5	Sodium phosphate, dibasic
7601-54-9	Sodium phosphate, tribasic
7758-29-4	Sodium phosphate, tribasic
7785-84-4	Sodium phosphate, tribasic
10101-89-0	Sodium phosphate, tribasic
10124-56-8	Sodium phosphate, tribasic
10361-89-4	Sodium phosphate, tribasic
13410-01-0	Sodium selenate
10102-18-8	Sodium selenite
7782-82-3	Sodium selenite
10102-20-2	Sodium tellurite
900-95-8	Stannane, acetoxytriphenyl-
7789-06-2	Strontium chromate
57-24-9	Strychnine
57-24-9	Strycnnine, and salts
60-41-3	Strychnine, sulfate
100-42-5	Styrene
96-09-3	Styrene oxide
3689-24-5	Sulfotep
3569-57-1	Sulfoxide, 3-chloropropyl octyl
7446-09-5	Sulfur dioxide
7664-93-9	Sulfuric acid
8014-95-7	Sulfuric acid (fuming)
12771-08-3	Sulfur monochloride
1314-80-3	Sulfur phosphide
7783-60-0	Sulfur tetrafluoride
7446-11-9	Sulfur trioxide
93-76-5	2,4,5-T acid
2008-46-0	2,4,5-T amines
1319-72-8	2,4,5-T amines
3813-14-7	2,4,5-T amines
6369-96-6	2,4,5-T amines
6369-97-7	2,4,5-T amines
93-79-8	2,4,5-T esters
1928-47-8	2,4,5-T esters
2545-59-7	2,4,5-T esters
25168-15-4	2,4,5-T esters
61792-07-2	2,4,5-T esters
13560-99-1	2,4,5-T salts
77-81-6	Tabun
13494-80-9	Tellurium
7783-80-4	Tellurium hexafluoride
107-49-3	Tepp
13071-79-9	Terbufos
95-94-3	1,2,4,5-Tetrachlorobenzene
1746-01-6	2,3,7,8-Tetrachlorodibenzo-p-dioxin (TCDD)
79-34-5	1,1,2,2-Tetrachloroethane
127-18-4	Tetrachloroethylene
58-90-2	2,3,4,6-Tetrachlorophenol
961-11-5	Tetrachlorvinphos
3689-24-5	Tetraethyldithiopyrophosphate
78-00-2	Tetraethyl lead
107-49-3	Tetraethyl pyrophosphate
597-64-8	Tetraethyltin
75-74-1	Tetramethyllead
509-14-8	Tetranitromethane
1314-32-5	Thallic oxide
7440-28-0	Thallium
	Thallium Compounds
563-68-8	Thallium(I) acetate
6533-73-9	Thallium(I) carbonate
7791-12-0	Thallium chloride TlCl
10102-45-1	Thallium(I) nitrate
10031-59-1	Thallium sulfate
7446-18-6	Thallium(I) sulfate
6533-73-9	Thallous carbonate
7791-12-0	Thallous chloride
2757-18-8	Thallous malonate
7446-18-6	Thallous sulfate
62-55-5	Thioacetamide
2231-57-4	Thiocarbazide
139-65-1	4,4'-Thiodianiline
39196-18-4	Thiofanox
74-93-1	Thiomethanol
297-97-2	Thionazin
108-98-5	Thiophenol
79-19-6	Thiosemicarbazide
62-56-6	Thiourea
5344-82-1	Thiourea, (2-chlorophenyl)-
614-78-8	Thiourea, (2-methylphenyl)-
86-88-4	Thiourea, 1-naphthalenyl-
137-26-8	Thiram
1314-20-1	Thorium dioxide
7550-45-0	Titanium tetrachloride
119-93-7	o-Tolidine
108-88-3	Toluene
25376-45-8	Toluenediamine
91-08-7	Toluene-2,6-diisocyanate
584-84-9	Toluene-2,4-diisocyanate
26471-62-5	Toluenediisocyanate (mixed isomers)
95-53-4	o-Toluidine
106-49-0	p-Toluidine
636-21-5	o-Toluidine hydrochloride
8001-35-2	Toxaphene
32534-95-5	2,4,5-TP esters
1031-47-6	Triamiphos
68-76-8	Triaziquone
24017-47-8	Triazofos

CAS Number	Chemical Name
75-25-2	Tribromomethane
52-68-6	Trichlorfon
76-02-8	Trichloroacetyl chloride
120-82-1	1,2,4-Trichlorobenzene
1558-25-4	Trichloro(chloromethyl)silane
27137-85-5	Trichloro(dichlorophenyl)silane
71-55-6	1,1,1-Trichloroethane
79-00-5	1,1,2-Trichloroethane
79-01-6	Trichloroethylene
115-21-9	Trichloroethylsilane
75-69-4	Trichlorofluoromethane [CFC-11]
594-42-3	Trichloromethanesulfenyl chloride
75-69-4	Trichloromonofluoromethane
327-98-0	Trichloronate
25167-82-2	Trichlorophenol
15950-66-0	2,3,4-Trichlorophenol
933-78-8	2,3,5-Trichlorophenol
933-75-5	2,3,6-Trichlorophenol
95-95-4	2,4,5-Trichlorophenol
88-06-2	2,4,6-Trichlorophenol
609-19-8	3,4,5-Trichlorophenol
98-13-5	Trichlorophenylsilane
27323-41-7	Triethanolamine dodecylbenzene sulfonate
998-30-1	Triethoxysilane
121-44-8	Triethylamine
1582-09-8	Trifluralin
75-50-3	Trimethylamine
95-63-6	1,2,4-Trimethylbenzene
75-77-4	Trimethylchlorosilane
824-11-3	Trimethylolpropane phosphite
540-84-1	2,2,4-Trimethylpentane
1066-45-1	Trimethyltin chloride
99-35-4	1,3,5-Trinitrobenzene
639-58-7	Triphenyltin chloride
555-77-1	Tris(2-chloroethyl)amine
126-72-7	Tris(2,3-dibromopropyl) phosphate
72-57-1	Trypan blue
66-75-1	Uracil mustard
541-09-3	Uranyl acetate
10102-06-4	Uranyl nitrate
36478-76-9	Uranyl nitrate
51-79-6	Urethane
2001-95-8	Valinomycin
7440-62-2	Vanadium (fume or dust)
1314-62-1	Vanadium pentoxide
27774-13-6	Vanadyl sulfate
108-05-4	Vinyl acetate monomer
108-05-4	Vinyl acetate
593-60-2	Vinyl bromide
75-01-4	Vinyl chloride
75-35-4	Vinylidene chloride
81-81-2	Warfarin
81-81-2	Warfarin, & salts, conc.>0.3%
129-06-6	Warfarin sodium
108-38-3	m-Xylene
95-47-6	o-Xylene
106-42-3	p-Xylene
1330-20-7	Xylene (mixed isomers)
1300-71-6	Xylenol
87-62-7	2,6-Xylidine
28347-13-9	Xylylene dichloride
7440-66-6	Zinc (fume or dust)
7440-66-6	Zinc
	Zinc Compounds
557-34-6	Zinc acetate
52628-25-8	Zinc ammonium chloride
14639-97-5	Zinc ammonium chloride
14639-98-6	Zinc ammonium chloride
1332-07-6	Zinc borate
7699-45-8	Zinc bromide
3486-35-9	Zinc carbonate
7646-85-7	Zinc chloride
557-21-1	Zinc cyanide
58270-08-9	Zinc, dichloro(4,4-dimethyl-5((((methylami
7783-49-5	Zinc fluoride
557-41-5	Zinc formate
7779-86-4	Zinc hydrosulfite
7779-88-6	Zinc nitrate
127-82-2	Zinc phenolsulfonate
1314-84-7	Zinc phosphide
1314-84-7	Zinc phosphide (conc. <= 10%)
1314-84-7	Zinc phosphide (conc. > 10%)
16871-71-9	Zinc silicofluoride
7733-02-0	Zinc sulfate
12122-67-7	Zineb
13746-89-9	Zirconium nitrate
16923-95-8	Zirconium potassium fluoride
14644-61-2	Zirconium sulfate
10026-11-6	Zirconium tetrachloride

FOR REFERENCE ONLY, NOT FOR REGULATORY COMPLIANCE
SEE 40 CFR PART 302, TABLE 302.4, APPENDIX B, FOR MORE INFORMATION

Radionuclide Name	Atomic Number	RQ (curies)	Radionuclide Name	Atomic Number	RQ (curies)
Radionuclides (unlisted)		1	Arsenic-077	33	1000
Actinium-224	89	100	Arsenic-078	33	100
Actinium-225	89	1	Astatine-207	85	100
Actinium-225	89	1	Astatine-211	85	100
Actinium-226	89	10	Barium-126	56	1000
Actinium-227	89	0.001	Barium-128	56	10
Actinium-228	89	10	Barium-131	56	10
Aluminum-026	13	10	Barium-131m	56	1000
Americium-237	95	1000	Barium-133	56	10
Americium-238	95	100	Barium-133m	56	100
Americium-239	95	100	Barium-135m	56	1000
Americium-240	95	10	Barium-139	56	1000
Americium-241	95	0.01	Barium-140	56	10
Americium-242	95	100	Barium-141	56	1000
Americium-242m	95	0.01	Barium-142	56	1000
Americium-243	95	0.01	Berkelium-245	97	100
Americium-244	95	10	Berkelium-246	97	10
Americium-244m	95	1000	Berkelium-247	97	0.01
Americium-245	95	1000	Berkelium-249	97	1
Americium-246	95	1000	Berkelium-250	97	100
Americium-246m	95	1000	Beryllium-007	4	100
Antimony-115	51	1000	Beryllium-010	4	1
Antimony-116	51	1000	Bismuth-200	83	100
Antimony-116m	51	100	Bismuth-201	83	100
Antimony-117	51	1000	Bismuth-202	83	1000
Antimony-118m	51	10	Bismuth-203	83	10
Antimony-119	51	1000	Bismuth-205	83	10
Antimony-120 (16 min)	51	1000	Bismuth-206	83	10
Antimony-120 (5.76 day)	51	10	Bismuth-207	83	10
Antimony-122	51	10	Bismuth-210	83	10
Antimony-124	51	10	Bismuth-210m	83	0.1
Antimony-124m	51	1000	Bismuth-212	83	100
Antimony-125	51	10	Bismuth-213	83	100
Antimony-126	51	10	Bismuth-214	83	100
Antimony-126m	51	1000	Bromine-074	35	100
Antimony-127	51	10	Bromine-074m	35	100
Antimony-128 (10.4 min)	51	1000	Bromine-075	35	100
Antimony-128 (9.01 hours)	51	10	Bromine-076	35	10
Antimony-129	51	100	Bromine-077	35	100
Antimony-130	51	100	Bromine-080	35	1000
Antimony-131	51	1000	Bromine-080m	35	1000
Argon-039	18	1000	Bromine-082	35	10
Argon-041	18	10	Bromine-083	35	1000
Arsenic-069	33	1000	Bromine-084	35	100
Arsenic-070	33	100	Cadmium-104	48	1000
Arsenic-071	33	100	Cadmium-107	48	1000
Arsenic-072	33	10	Cadmium-109	48	1
Arsenic-073	33	100	Cadmium-113	48	0.1
Arsenic-074	33	10	Cadmium-113m	48	0.1
Arsenic-076	33	100	Cadmium-115	48	100

Radionuclide Name	Atomic Number	RQ (curies)	Radionuclide Name	Atomic Number	RQ (curies)
Cadmium-115m	48	10	Cobalt-060m	27	1000
Cadmium-117	48	100	Cobalt-061	27	1000
Cadmium-117m	48	10	Cobalt-062m	27	1000
Calcium-041	20	10	Copper-060	29	100
Calcium-045	20	10	Copper-061	29	100
Calcium-047	20	10	Copper-064	29	1000
Californium-244	98	1000	Copper-067	29	100
Californium-246	98	10	Curium-238	96	1000
Californium-248	98	0.1	Curium-240	96	1
Californium-249	98	0.01	Curium-241	96	10
Californium-250	98	0.01	Curium-242	96	1
Californium-251	98	0.01	Curium-243	96	0.01
Californium-252	98	0.1	Curium-244	96	0.01
Californium-253	98	10	Curium-245	96	0.01
Californium-254	98	0.1	Curium-246	96	0.01
Carbon-011	6	1000	Curium-247	96	0.01
Carbon-014	6	10	Curium-248	96	0.001
Cerium-134	58	10	Curium-249	96	1000
Cerium-135	58	10	Dysprosium-155	66	100
Cerium-137	58	1000	Dysprosium-157	66	100
Cerium-137m	58	100	Dysprosium-159	66	100
Cerium-139	58	100	Dysprosium-165	66	1000
Cerium-141	58	10	Dysprosium-166	66	10
Cerium-143	58	100	Einsteinium-250	99	10
Cerium-144	58	1	Einsteinium-251	99	1000
Cesium-125	55	1000	Einsteinium-253	99	10
Cesium-127	55	100	Einsteinium-254	99	0.1
Cesium-129	55	100	Einsteinium-254m	99	1
Cesium-130	55	1000	Erbium-161	68	100
Cesium-131	55	1000	Erbium-165	68	1000
Cesium-132	55	10	Erbium-169	68	100
Cesium-134	55	1	Erbium-171	68	100
Cesium-134m	55	1000	Erbium-172	68	10
Cesium-135	55	10	Europium-145	63	10
Cesium-135m	55	100	Europium-146	63	10
Cesium-136	55	10	Europium-147	63	10
Cesium-137	55	1	Europium-148	63	10
Cesium-138	55	100	Europium-149	63	100
Chlorine-036	17	10	Europium-150	63	1000
Chlorine-038	17	100	Europium-150	63	10
Chlorine-039	17	100	Europium-152	63	10
Chromium-048	24	100	Europium-152m	63	100
Chromium-049	24	1000	Europium-154	63	10
Chromium-051	24	1000	Europium-155	63	10
Cobalt-055	27	10	Europium-156	63	10
Cobalt-056	27	10	Europium-157	63	10
Cobalt-057	27	100	Europium-158	63	1000
Cobalt-058	27	10	Fermium-252	100	10
Cobalt-058m	27	1000	Fermium-253	100	10
Cobalt-060	27	10	Fermium-254	100	100

FOR REFERENCE ONLY, NOT FOR REGULATORY COMPLIANCE

SEE 40 CFR PART 302, TABLE 302.4, APPENDIX B, FOR MORE INFORMATION

Radionuclide Name	Atomic Number	RQ (curies)
Fermium-255	100	100
Fermium-257	100	100
Fluorine-018	9	1000
Francium-222	87	100
Francium-223	87	100
Gadolinium-145	64	100
Gadolinium-146	64	10
Gadolinium-147	64	10
Gadolinium-148	64	0.001
Gadolinium-149	64	100
Gadolinium-151	64	100
Gadolinium-152	64	0.001
Gadolinium-153	64	10
Gadolinium-159	64	1000
Gallium-065	31	1000
Gallium-066	31	10
Gallium-067	31	100
Gallium-068	31	1000
Gallium-070	31	1000
Gallium-072	31	10
Gallium-073	31	100
Germanium-066	32	100
Germanium-067	32	1000
Germanium-068	32	10
Germanium-069	32	10
Germanium-071	32	1000
Germanium-075	32	1000
Germanium-077	32	10
Germanium-078	32	1000
Gold-193	79	100
Gold-194	79	10
Gold-195	79	100
Gold-198	79	100
Gold-198m	79	10
Gold-199	79	100
Gold-200	79	1000
Gold-200m	79	10
Gold-201	79	1000
Hafnium-170	72	100
Hafnium-172	72	1
Hafnium-173	72	100
Hafnium-175	72	100
Hafnium-177m	72	1000
Hafnium-178m	72	0.1
Hafnium-179m	72	100
Hafnium-180m	72	100
Hafnium-181	72	10
Hafnium-182	72	0.1
Hafnium-182m	72	100
Hafnium-183	72	100
Hafnium-184	72	100
Holmium-155	67	1000
Holmium-157	67	1000
Holmium-159	67	1000
Holmium-161	67	1000
Holmium-162	67	1000
Holmium-162m	67	1000
Holmium-164	67	1000
Holmium-164m	67	1000
Holmium-166	67	100
Holmium-166m	67	1
Holmium-167	67	100
Hydrogen-003	1	100
Indium-109	49	100
Indium-110 (4.9 hours)	49	10
Indium-110 (69.1 min)	49	100
Indium-111	49	100
Indium-112	49	1000
Indium-113m	49	1000
Indium-114m	49	10
Indium-115	49	0.1
Indium-115m	49	100
Indium-116m	49	100
Indium-117	49	1000
Indium-117m	49	100
Iodine-119m	53	1000
Iodine-120	53	10
Iodine-120m	53	100
Iodine-121	53	100
Iodine-123	53	10
Iodine-124	53	0.1
Iodine-125	53	0.01
Iodine-126	53	0.01
Iodine-128	53	1000
Iodine-129	53	0.001
Iodine-130	53	1
Iodine-131	53	0.01
Iodine-132	53	10
Iodine-132m	53	10
Iodine-133	53	0.1
Iodine-134	53	100
Iodine-135	53	10
Iridium-182	77	1000
Iridium-184	77	100
Iridium-185	77	100
Iridium-186	77	10
Iridium-187	77	100
Iridium-188	77	10
Iridium-189	77	100
Iridium-190	77	10

RADIONUCLIDES LISTED UNDER CERCLA
FOR REFERENCE ONLY, NOT FOR REGULATORY COMPLIANCE
SEE 40 CFR PART 302, TABLE 302.4, APPENDIX B, FOR MORE INFORMATION

Radionuclide Name	Atomic Number	RQ (curies)
Iridium-190m	77	1000
Iridium-192	77	10
Iridium-192m	77	100
Iridium-194	77	100
Iridium-194m	77	10
Iridium-195	77	1000
Iridium-195m	77	100
Iron-052	26	100
Iron-055	26	100
Iron-059	26	10
Iron-060	26	0.1
Krypton-074	36	10
Krypton-076	36	10
Krypton-077	36	10
Krypton-079	36	100
Krypton-081	36	1000
Krypton-083m	36	1000
Krypton-085	36	1000
Krypton-085m	36	100
Krypton-087	36	10
Krypton-088	36	10
Lanthanum-131	57	1000
Lanthanum-132	57	100
Lanthanum-135	57	1000
Lanthanum-137	57	10
Lanthanum-138	57	1
Lanthanum-140	57	10
Lanthanum-141	57	1000
Lanthanum-142	57	100
Lanthanum-143	57	1000
Lead-195m	82	1000
Lead-198	82	100
Lead-199	82	100
Lead-200	82	100
Lead-201	82	100
Lead-202	82	1
Lead-202m	82	10
Lead-203	82	100
Lead-205	82	100
Lead-209	82	1000
Lead-210	82	0.01
Lead-211	82	100
Lead-212	82	10
Lead-214	82	100
Lutetium-169	71	10
Lutetium-170	71	10
Lutetium-171	71	10
Lutetium-172	71	10
Lutetium-173	71	100
Lutetium-174	71	10
Lutetium-174m	71	10
Lutetium-176	71	1
Lutetium-176m	71	1000
Lutetium-177	71	100
Lutetium-177m	71	10
Lutetium-178	71	1000
Lutetium-178m	71	1000
Lutetium-179	71	1000
Magnesium-028	12	10
Manganese-051	25	1000
Manganese-052	25	10
Manganese-053	25	1000
Manganese-054	25	10
Manganese-056	25	100
Manganese-052m	25	1000
Mendelevium-257	101	100
Mendelevium-258	101	1
Mercury-193	80	100
Mercury-193m	80	10
Mercury-194	80	0.1
Mercury-195	80	100
Mercury-195m	80	100
Mercury-197	80	1000
Mercury-197m	80	1000
Mercury-199m	80	1000
Mercury-203	80	10
Molybdenum-090	42	100
Molybdenum-093	42	100
Molybdenum-093m	42	10
Molybdenum-099	42	100
Molybdenum-101	42	1000
Neodymium-136	60	1000
Neodymium-138	60	1000
Neodymium-139	60	1000
Neodymium-139m	60	100
Neodymium-141	60	1000
Neodymium-147	60	10
Neodymium-149	60	100
Neodymium-151	60	1000
Neptunium-232	93	1000
Neptunium-233	93	1000
Neptunium-234	93	10
Neptunium-235	93	1000
Neptunium-236 (1.2 e 5 yr)	93	0.1
Neptunium-236 (22.5 hours)	93	100
Neptunium-237	93	0.01
Neptunium-238	93	10
Neptunium-239	93	100
Neptunium-240	93	100
Nickel-056	28	10

Radionuclide Name	Atomic Number	RQ (curies)	Radionuclide Name	Atomic Number	RQ (curies)
Nickel-057	28	10	Plutonium-241	94	1
Nickel-059	28	100	Plutonium-242	94	0.01
Nickel-063	28	100	Plutonium-243	94	1000
Nickel-065	28	100	Plutonium-244	94	0.01
Nickel-066	28	10	Plutonium-245	94	100
Niobium-088	41	100	Polonium-203	84	100
Niobium-089 (122 minutes)	41	100	Polonium-205	84	100
Niobium-089 (66 minutes)	41	100	Polonium-207	84	10
Niobium-090	41	10	Polonium-210	84	0.01
Niobium-093m	41	100	Potassium-040	19	1
Niobium-094	41	10	Potassium-042	19	100
Niobium-095	41	10	Potassium-043	19	10
Niobium-095m	41	100	Potassium-044	19	100
Niobium-096	41	10	Potassium-045	19	1000
Niobium-097	41	100	Praseodymium-136	59	1000
Niobium-098	41	1000	Praseodymium-137	59	1000
Osmium-180	76	1000	Praseodymium-138m	59	100
Osmium-181	76	100	Praseodymium-139	59	1000
Osmium-182	76	100	Praseodymium-142	59	100
Osmium-185	76	10	Praseodymium-142m	59	1000
Osmium-189m	76	1000	Praseodymium-143	59	10
Osmium-191	76	100	Praseodymium-144	59	1000
Osmium-191m	76	1000	Praseodymium-145	59	1000
Osmium-193	76	100	Praseodymium-147	59	1000
Osmium-194	76	1	Promethium-141	61	1000
Palladium-100	46	100	Promethium-143	61	100
Palladium-101	46	100	Promethium-144	61	10
Palladium-103	46	100	Promethium-145	61	100
Palladium-107	46	100	Promethium-146	61	10
Palladium-109	46	1000	Promethium-147	61	10
Phosphorus-032	15	0.1	Promethium-148	61	10
Phosphorus-033	15	1	Promethium-148m	61	10
Platinum-186	78	100	Promethium-149	61	100
Platinum-188	78	100	Promethium-150	61	100
Platinum-189	78	100	Promethium-151	61	100
Platinum-191	78	100	Protactinium-227	91	100
Platinum-193	78	1000	Protactinium-228	91	10
Platinum-193m	78	100	Protactinium-230	91	10
Platinum-195m	78	100	Protactinium-231	91	0.01
Platinum-197	78	1000	Protactinium-232	91	10
Platinum-197m	78	1000	Protactinium-233	91	100
Platinum-199	78	1000	Protactinium-234	91	10
Platinum-200	78	100	Radium-223	88	1
Plutonium-234	94	1000	Radium-224	88	10
Plutonium-235	94	1000	Radium-225	88	1
Plutonium-236	94	0.1	Radium-226	88	0.1
Plutonium-237	94	1000	Radium-227	88	1000
Plutonium-238	94	0.01	Radium-228	88	0.1
Plutonium-239	94	0.01	Radon-220	86	0.1
Plutonium-240	94	0.01	Radon-222	86	0.1

Radionuclide Name	Atomic Number	RQ (curies)
Rhenium-177	75	1000
Rhenium-178	75	1000
Rhenium-181	75	100
Rhenium-182 (12.7 hours)	75	10
Rhenium-182 (64.0 hours)	75	10
Rhenium-184	75	10
Rhenium-184m	75	10
Rhenium-186	75	100
Rhenium-186m	75	10
Rhenium-187	75	1000
Rhenium-188	75	1000
Rhenium-188m	75	1000
Rhenium-189	75	1000
Rhodium-099	45	10
Rhodium-099m	45	100
Rhodium-100	45	10
Rhodium-101	45	10
Rhodium-101m	45	100
Rhodium-102	45	10
Rhodium-102m	45	10
Rhodium-103m	45	1000
Rhodium-105	45	100
Rhodium-106m	45	10
Rhodium-107	45	1000
Rubidium-079	37	1000
Rubidium-081	37	100
Rubidium-081m	37	1000
Rubidium-082m	37	10
Rubidium-083	37	10
Rubidium-084	37	10
Rubidium-086	37	10
Rubidium-087	37	10
Rubidium-088	37	1000
Rubidium-089	37	1000
Ruthenium-094	44	1000
Ruthenium-097	44	100
Ruthenium-103	44	10
Ruthenium-105	44	100
Ruthenium-106	44	1
Samarium-141	62	1000
Samarium-141m	62	1000
Samarium-142	62	1000
Samarium-145	62	100
Samarium-146	62	0.01
Samarium-147	62	0.01
Samarium-151	62	10
Samarium-153	62	100
Samarium-155	62	1000
Samarium-156	62	100
Scandium-043	21	1000
Scandium-044	21	100
Scandium-044m	21	10
Scandium-046	21	10
Scandium-047	21	100
Scandium-048	21	10
Scandium-049	21	1000
Selenium-070	34	1000
Selenium-073	34	10
Selenium-073m	34	100
Selenium-075	34	10
Selenium-079	34	10
Selenium-081	34	1000
Selenium-081m	34	1000
Selenium-083	34	1000
Silicon-031	14	1000
Silicon-032	14	1
Silver-102	47	100
Silver-103	47	1000
Silver-104	47	1000
Silver-104m	47	1000
Silver-105	47	10
Silver-106	47	1000
Silver-106m	47	10
Silver-108m	47	10
Silver-110m	47	10
Silver-111	47	10
Silver-112	47	100
Silver-115	47	1000
Sodium-022	11	10
Sodium-024	11	10
Strontium-080	38	100
Strontium-081	38	1000
Strontium-083	38	100
Strontium-085	38	10
Strontium-085m	38	1000
Strontium-087m	38	100
Strontium-089	38	10
Strontium-090	38	0.1
Strontium-091	38	10
Strontium-092	38	100
Sulfur-035	16	1
Tantalum-172	73	100
Tantalum-173	73	100
Tantalum-174	73	100
Tantalum-175	73	100
Tantalum-176	73	10
Tantalum-177	73	1000
Tantalum-178	73	1000
Tantalum-179	73	1000
Tantalum-180	73	100

Radionuclide Name	Atomic Number	RQ (curies)	Radionuclide Name	Atomic Number	RQ (curies)
Tantalum-180m	73	1000	Thallium-194	81	1000
Tantalum-182	73	10	Thallium-194m	81	100
Tantalum-182m	73	1000	Thallium-195	81	100
Tantalum-183	73	100	Thallium-197	81	100
Tantalum-184	73	10	Thallium-198	81	10
Tantalum-185	73	1000	Thallium-198m	81	100
Tantalum-186	73	1000	Thallium-199	81	100
Technetium-093	43	100	Thallium-200	81	10
Technetium-093m	43	1000	Thallium-201	81	1000
Technetium-094	43	10	Thallium-202	81	10
Technetium-094m	43	100	Thallium-204	81	10
Technetium-096	43	10	Thorium-226	90	100
Technetium-096m	43	1000	Thorium-227	90	1
Technetium-097	43	100	Thorium-228	90	0.01
Technetium-097m	43	100	Thorium-229	90	0.001
Technetium-098	43	10	Thorium-230	90	0.01
Technetium-099	43	10	Thorium-231	90	100
Technetium-099m	43	100	Thorium-232	90	0.001
Technetium-101	43	1000	Thorium-234	90	100
Technetium-104	43	1000	Thulium-162	69	1000
Tellurium-116	52	1000	Thulium-166	69	10
Tellurium-121	52	10	Thulium-167	69	100
Tellurium-121m	52	10	Thulium-170	69	10
Tellurium-123	52	10	Thulium-171	69	100
Tellurium-123m	52	10	Thulium-172	69	100
Tellurium-125m	52	10	Thulium-173	69	100
Tellurium-127	52	1000	Thulium-175	69	1000
Tellurium-127m	52	10	Tin-110	50	100
Tellurium-129	52	1000	Tin-111	50	1000
Tellurium-129m	52	10	Tin-113	50	10
Tellurium-131	52	1000	Tin-117m	50	100
Tellurium-131m	52	10	Tin-119m	50	10
Tellurium-132	52	10	Tin-121	50	1000
Tellurium-133	52	1000	Tin-121m	50	10
Tellurium-133m	52	1000	Tin-123	50	10
Tellurium-134	52	1000	Tin-123m	50	1000
Terbium-147	65	100	Tin-125	50	10
Terbium-149	65	100	Tin-126	50	1
Terbium-150	65	100	Tin-127	50	100
Terbium-151	65	10	Tin-128	50	1000
Terbium-153	65	100	Titanium-044	22	1
Terbium-154	65	10	Titanium-045	22	1000
Terbium-155	65	100	Tungsten-176	74	1000
Terbium-156	65	10	Tungsten-177	74	100
Terbium-156m (24.4 hours)	65	1000	Tungsten-178	74	100
Terbium-156m (5.0 hours)	65	1000	Tungsten-179	74	1000
Terbium-157	65	100	Tungsten-181	74	100
Terbium-158	65	10	Tungsten-185	74	10
Terbium-160	65	10	Tungsten-187	74	100
Terbium-161	65	100	Tungsten-188	74	10

RADIONUCLIDES LISTED UNDER CERCLA
FOR REFERENCE ONLY, NOT FOR REGULATORY COMPLIANCE
SEE 40 CFR PART 302, TABLE 302.4, APPENDIX B, FOR MORE INFORMATION

Radionuclide Name	Atomic Number	RQ (curies)
Uranium-230	92	1
Uranium-231	92	1000
Uranium-232	92	0.01
Uranium-233	92	0.1
Uranium-234	92	0.1
Uranium-235	92	0.1
Uranium-236	92	0.1
Uranium-237	92	100
Uranium-238	92	0.1
Uranium-239	92	1000
Uranium-240	92	1000
Vanadium-047	23	1000
Vanadium-048	23	10
Vanadium-049	23	1000
Xenon-120	54	100
Xenon-121	54	10
Xenon-122	54	100
Xenon-123	54	10
Xenon-125	54	100
Xenon-127	54	100
Xenon-129m	54	1000
Xenon-131m	54	1000
Xenon-133	54	1000
Xenon-133m	54	1000
Xenon-135	54	100
Xenon-135m	54	10
Xenon-138	54	10
Ytterbium-162	70	1000
Ytterbium-166	70	10
Ytterbium-167	70	1000
Ytterbium-169	70	10
Ytterbium-175	70	100
Ytterbium-177	70	1000
Ytterbium-178	70	1000
Yttrium-086	39	10
Yttrium-086m	39	1000
Yttrium-087	39	10
Yttrium-088	39	10
Yttrium-090	39	10
Yttrium-090m	39	100
Yttrium-091	39	10
Yttrium-091m	39	1000
Yttrium-092	39	100
Yttrium-093	39	100
Yttrium-094	39	1000
Yttrium-095	39	1000
Zinc-062	30	100
Zinc-063	30	1000
Zinc-065	30	10
Zinc-069	30	1000
Zinc-069m	30	100
Zinc-071m	30	100
Zinc-072	30	100
Zirconium-086	40	100
Zirconium-088	40	10
Zirconium-089	40	100
Zirconium-093	40	1
Zirconium-095	40	10
Zirconium-097	40	10

NOTES:

m - Signifies a nuclear isomer which is a radionuclide in a higher energy metastable state relative to the parent isotope.

Final RQs for all radionuclides apply to chemical compounds containing the radionuclides and elemental forms regardless of the diameter of pieces of solid material.

An adjusted RQ of one curie applies to all radionuclides not otherwise listed. Whenever the RQs in the SARA Title III Consolidated List and this list are in conflict, the lowest RQ applies.

Notification requirements for releases of mixtures or solutions of radionuclides can be found in 40 CFR section 302.6(b).

ERRATA SHEET TO 1992 LIST OF LISTS
February 1993

I. ADDITIONS

RCRA Waste Streams and Unlisted Hazardous Wastes. Add the following:

RCRA Code	Description	RQ (lbs)
F039	Leachate resulting from disposal of more than 1 restricted waste class. hazard.	1
K149	Distillation bottoms from the production of chlorinated toluenes	10
K150	Organic residuals of Cl gas and HCl from production of chlorinated toluenes	10
K151	Wastewater treatment sludge from production of chlorinated toluenes	10

SARA Title III Consolidated List

1. Add the following CERCLA chemical:

CAS Number	Chemical Name	Sec. 302(EHS) TPQ	EHS RQ	CERCLA RQ	Sec 313	RCRA Code
26952-23-8	Dichloropropene			100		

2. Add the following CERCLA chemical category:

Chemical Category	Sec. 302(EHS) TPQ	EHS RQ	CERCLA RQ	Sec 313	RCRA Code
Hexachlorocyclohexane (all isomers) CAS 608-73-1			***		

II. CORRECTIONS

SARA Title III Consolidated List. Correct RCRA codes for four chemicals and add 'X' to Sec. 313 for one chemical as follows:

CAS Number	Chemical Name	Sec. 302(EHS) TPQ	EHS RQ	CERCLA RQ	Sec 313	RCRA Code
88-06-2	2,4,6-Trichlorophenol			10	313	U231
496-72-0	Diaminotoluene			10		U221
823-40-5	Diaminotoluene			10		U221
8001-58-9	Creosote			1	313	U051
534-52-1	Dinitrocresol	10/10,000		10	X	P047

OSHA

OCCUPATIONAL SAFETY AND HEALTH ADMIN., LABOR

1910.1000 29 CFR XVII (7-1-92 Edition)

TABLE Z-1-A. - Limits for Air Contaminants
TABLE Z-2
TABLE Z-3 - Mineral Dusts

Table Z-1-A. - Limits for Air Contaminants - Cont.

Substance	CAS No. (f)	Transitional limits PEL* ppm (a)	mg/m³ (b)	Skin designation
Bromine pentafluoride	7789-30-2			
Bromoform	75-25-2	0.5	5	X
Butadiene (1,3-Butadiene)	106-99-0	1000	2200	
Butane	106-97-8			
Butanethiol; see Butyl mercaptan				
2-Butanone (Methyl ethyl ketone)	78-93-3	200	590	
2-Butoxyethanol	111-76-2	50	240	X
n-Butyl-acetate	123-86-4	150	710	
sec-Butyl acetate	105-46-4	200	950	
tert-Butyl acetate	540-88-5	200	950	
Butyl acrylate	141-32-2			
n-Butyl alcohol	71-36-3	100	300	
sec-Butyl alcohol	78-92-2	150	450	
tert-Butyl alcohol	75-65-0	100	300	
Butylamine	109-73-9	(C)5	(C)15	X
tert-Butyl chromate (as CrO_3)	1189-85-1		(C)0.1	X
n-Butyl glycidyl ether (BGE)	2426-08-6	50	270	
n-Butyl lactate	138-22-7			
Butyl mercaptan	109-79-5	10	35	
o-sec-Butylphenol	89-72-5			
p-tert-Butyltoluene	98-51-1	10	60	
Cadmium fume (as Cd)	7440-43-9		Tbl. Z-2	
Cadmium dust (as Cd)	7440-43-9		Tbl. Z-2	
Calcium carbonate	1317-65-3			
Total dust			15	
Respirable fraction			5	
Calcium cyanamide	156-62-7			
Calcium hydroxide[i]	1305-62-0			
Calcium oxide[j]	1305-78-8		5	
Calcium silicate	1344-95-2			
Total dust			15	
Respirable fraction			5	
Calcium sulfate	7778-18-9			

Total dust			15	
Respirable fraction			5	
Camphor, synthetic	76-22-2		2	
Caprolactam	105-60-2			
Dust				
Vapor				
Captafol (Difolatan®)	2425-06-1			
Captan	133-06-2			
Carbaryl (Sevin®)	63-25-2		5	
Carbofuran (Furadan®)	1563-66-2			
Carbon black	1333-86-4		3.5	
Carbon dioxide	124-38-9	5000[e]	9000	
Carbon disulfide	75-15-0	Tbl. Z-2		
Carbon monoxide	630-08-0	50	55	
Carbon tetrabromide	558-13-4			
Carbon tetrachloride	56-23-5	Tbl. Z-2		
Carbonyl fluoride	353-50-4			
Catechol (Pyrocatechol)	120-80-9			
Cellulose	9004-34-6			
Total dust			15	
Respirable fraction			5	
Cesium hydroxide	21351-79-1			
Chlordane	57-74-9		0.5	X
Chlorinated camphene	8001-35-2		0.5	X
Chlorinated diphenyl oxide	55720-99-5		0.5	
Chlorine	7782-50-5	(C)1	(C)3	
Chlorine dioxide	10049-04-4	0.1	0.3	
Chlorine trifluoride	7790-91-2	(C)0.1	(C)0.4	
Chloroacetaldehyde	107-20-0	(C)1	(C)3	
a-Chloroacetophenone (Phenacyl chloride)	532-27-4	0.05	0.3	
Chloroacetyl chloride	79-04-9			
Chlorobenzene	108-90-7	75	350	
o-Chlorobenzylidene malononitrile	2698-41-1	0.05	0.4	
Chlorobromomethane	74-97-5	200	1050	
2-Chloro-1,3-butadiene; see b-Chloroprene				
Chlorodifluoromethane	75-45-6			
Chlorodiphenyl (42% Chlorine) (PCB)	53469-21-9		1	X
Chlorodiphenyl (54% Chlorine) (PCB)	11097-69-1		0.5	X
1-Chloro,2,3-epoxypropane; see Epichlorohydrin				
2-Chloroethanol; see Ethylene chlorohydrin				
Chloroethylene; see Vinyl chloride				
Chloroform (Trichloromethane)	67-66-3	(C)50	(C)240	
bis(Chloromethyl) ether; see 1910.1008	542-88-1			

Table Z-1-A. - Limits for Air Contaminants - Cont.

Substance	CAS No. (f)	Transitional limits		
		PEL*		Skin designation
		ppm (a)	mg/m³ (b)	
Chloromethyl methyl ether; see 1910.1006	107-30-2			
1-Chloro-1-nitropropane	600-25-9	20	100	
Chloropentafluoroethane	76-15-3			
Chloropicrin	76-06-2	0.1	0.7	
beta-Chloroprene	126-99-8	25	90	X
o-Chlorostyrene	2039-87-4			
o-Chlorotoluene	95-49-8			
2-Chloro-6-trichloro-methyl pyridine	1929-82-4			
Total dust			15	
Respirable fraction			5	
Chlorpyrifos	2921-88-2			
Chromic acid and chromates (as CrO_3)	7440-47-3		Tbl. Z-2	
Chromium, sol. chromic, chromous salts (as Cr)	7440-47-3		0.5	
Chromium, metal and insoluble salts	7440-47-3		1	
Chrysene; see Coal tar pitch volatiles				
Clopidol	2971-90-6			
Total dust			15	
Respirable fraction			5	
Coal dust (less than 5% SiO_2), Respirable fraction			Tbl. Z-3	
Coal dust (greater than or equal to 5% SiO_2), Respirable quartz fraction.			Tbl. Z-3	
Coal tar pitch volatiles (benzene soluble fraction), anthracene, BaP, phenanthrene, acridine, chrysene, pyrene.	65966-93-2		0.2	
Cobalt metal, dust, and fume (as Co)	7440-48-4		0.1	
Cobalt carbonyl (as Co)	10210-68-1			
Cobalt hydrocarbonyl (as Co)	16842-03-8			
Coke oven emissions; see 1910.1029	-			
Copper	7440-50-8			
Fume (as Cu)			0.1	
Dusts and mists (as Cu)			1	
Cotton dust (raw)			1	
This 8-hour TWA applies to respirable dust as measured by a vertical elutriator cotton dust sampler or equ processing operations of waste recycling (sorting, blending, cleaning and willowing) and garnetting.				
Crag herbicide (Sesone)	136-78-7			

Total dust			15	
Respirable fraction			5	
Cresol, all isomers	1319-77-3	5	22	X
Crotonaldehyde	123-73-9; 4170-30-3	2	6	
Crufomate	299-86-5			
Cumene	98-82-8	50	245	X
Cyanamide	420-04-2			
Cyanides (as CN)	Varies with compound		5	
Cyanogen	460-19-5			
Cyanogen chloride	506-77-4			
Cyclohexane	110-82-7	300	1050	
Cyclohexanol	108-93-0	50	200	
Cyclohexanone	108-94-1	50	200	
Cyclohexene	110-83-8	300	1015	
Cyclohexylamine	108-91-8			
Cyclonite	121-82-4			
Cyclopentadiene	542-92-7	75	200	
Cyclopentane	287-92-3			
Cyhexatin	13121-70-5			
2,4-D (Dichlorophenoxyacetic acid)	94-75-7		10	
Decaborane	17702-41-9	0.05	0.3	X
Demeton (Systox®)	8065-48-3		0.1	X
Dichlorodiphenyltrichloroethane (DDT)	50-29-3		1	X
Dichlorvos (DDVP)	62-73-7		1	X
Diacetone alcohol (4-Hydroxy-4-methyl-2-pentanone)	123-42-2	50	240	
1,2-Diaminoethane, see Ethylenediamine				
Diazinon	333-41-5			
Diazomethane	334-88-3	0.2	0.4	
Diborane	19287-45-7	0.1	0.1	
1,2-Dibromo-3-chloropropane; see 1910.1044	96-12-8			
2-N-Dibutylaminoethanol	102-81-8			
Dibutyl phosphate	107-66-4	1	5	
Dibutyl phthalate	84-74-2		5	
Dichloroacetylene	7572-29-4			
o-Dichlorobenzene	95-50-1	(C)50	(C)300	
p-Dichlorobenzene	106-46-7	75	450	
3,3'-Dichlorobenzidine; see 1910.1007	91-94-1			
Dichlorodifluoromethane	75-71-8	1000	4950	
1,3-Dichloro-5,5-dimethyl hydantoin	118-52-5		0.2	
1,1-Dichloroethane	75-34-3	100	400	

Table Z-1-A. - Limits for Air Contaminants - Cont.

Substance	CAS No. (f)	Transitional limits		
		PEL*		Skin designation
		ppm (a)	mg/m³ (b)	
1,2-Dichloroethylene	540-59-0	200	790	
Dichloroethyl ether	111-44-4	(C)15	(C)90	X
Dichloromethane; see Methylene chloride				
Dichloromonofluoromethane	75-43-4	1000	4200	
1,1-Dichloro-1-nitroethane	594-72-9	(C)10	(C)60	
1,2-Dichloropropane; see Propylenedichloride				
1,3-Dichloropropene	542-75-6			
2,2-Dichloropropionic acid	75-99-0			
Dichlorotetrafluoroethane	76-14-2	1000	7000	
Dicrotophos	141-66-2			
Dicyclopentadiene	77-73-6			
Dicyclopentadienyl iron	102-54-5			
Total dust			15	
Respirable fraction			5	
Dieldrin	60-57-1		0.25	X
Diethanolamine	111-42-2			
Diethylamine	109-89-7	25	75	
2-Diethylaminoethanol	100-37-8	10	50	X
Diethylene triamine	111-40-0			
Diethyl ether; see Ethyl ether				
Diethyl ketone	96-22-0			
Diethyl phthalate	84-66-2			
Difluorodibromomethane	75-61-6	100	860	
Diglycidyl ether (DGE)	2238-07-5	(C)0.5	(C)2.8	
Dihydroxybenzene; see Hydroquinone				
Diisobutyl ketone	108-83-8	50	290	
Diisopropylamine	108-18-9	5	20	X
4-Dimethylaminoazobenzene; see 1910.1015	60-11-7			
Dimethoxymethane; see Methylal				
Dimethyl acetamide	127-19-5	10	35	X
Dimethylamine	124-40-3	10	18	
Dimethylaminobenzene; see Xylidine				
Dimethylaniline (N,N-Dimethylaniline)	121-69-7	5	25	X

Dimethylbenzene; see Xylene				
Dimethyl-1,2-dibromo-2,2-dichloroethyl phosphate	300-76-5		3	
Dimethylformamide	68-12-2	10	30	X
2,6-Dimethyl-4-hepta-none; see Diisobutyl ketone				
1,1-Dimethylhydrazine	57-14-7	0.5	1	X
Dimethylphthalate	131-11-3		5	
Dimethyl sulfate	77-78-1	1	5	X
Dinitolmide (3,5-Dinitro-o-toluamide)	148-01-6			
Dinitrobenzene (all isomers)	(alpha-) 528-29-0 (meta-) 99-65-0 (para-) 100-25-4		1	X
Dinitro-o-cresol	534-52-1		0.2	X
Dinitrotoluene	25321-14-6		1.5	X
Dioxane (Diethylene dioxide)	123-91-1	100	360	X
Dioxathion (Delnav)	78-34-2			
Diphenyl (Biphenyl)	92-52-4	0.2	1	
Diphenylamine	122-39-4			
Diphenylmethane diisocyanate; see Methylene bisphenyl isocyanate				
Dipropylene glycol methyl ether	34590-94-8	100	600	X
Dipropyl ketone	123-19-3			
Diquat	85-00-7			
Di-sec octyl phthalate (Di-2-ethylhexyl-phthalate)	117-81-7		5	
Disulfiram	97-77-8			
Disulfoton	298-04-4			
2,6-Di-tert-butyl-p-cresol	128-37-0			
Diuron	330-54-1			
Divinyl benzene	1321-74-0			
Emery	12415-34-8			
Total dust			15	
Respirable fraction			5	
Endosulfan	115-29-7			
Endrin	72-20-8		0.1	X
Epichlorohydrin	106-89-8	5	19	X
EPN	2104-64-5		0.5	X
1,2-Epoxypropane; see Propylene oxide				
2,3-Epoxy-1-propanol; see Glycidol				
Ethanethiol; see Ethyl mercaptan				
Ethanolamine	141-43-5	3	6	
Ethion	563-12-2			
2-Ethoxyethanol	110-80-5	200	740	X

Table Z-1-A. - Limits for Air Contaminants - Cont.

Substance	CAS No. (f)	Transitional limits		
		PEL*		Skin designation
		ppm (a)	mg/m³ (b)	
2-Ethoxyethyl acetate (Cellosolve acetate)	111-15-9	100	540	X
Ethyl acetate	141-78-6	400	1400	
Ethyl acrylate	140-88-5	25	100	X
Ethyl alcohol (Ethanol)	64-17-5	1000	1900	
Ethylamine	75-04-7	10	18	
Ethyl amyl ketone (5-Methyl-3-heptanone)	541-85-5	25	130	
Ethyl benzene	100-41-4	100	435	
Ethyl bromide	74-96-4	200	890	
Ethyl butyl ketone (3-Heptanone)	106-35-4	50	230	
Ethyl chloride	75-00-3	1000	2600	
Ethyl ether	60-29-7	400	1200	
Ethyl formate	109-94-4	100	300	
Ethyl mercaptan	75-08-1	(C)10	(C)25	
Ethyl silicate	78-10-4	100	850	
Ethylene chlorohydrin	107-07-3	5	16	X
Ethylenediamine	107-15-3	10	25	
Ethylene dibromide	106-93-4	Tbl. Z-2	Tbl. Z-2	Tbl. Z-2
Ethylene dichloride	107-06-2	Tbl. Z-2	Tbl. Z-2	Tbl. Z-2
Ethylene glycol	107-21-1			
Ethylene glycol dinitrate [k]	628-96-6	(C)0.2	(C)1	X
Ethylene glycol methyl acetate; see Methyl cellosolve acetate				
Ethyleneimine; see 1910.1012	151-56-4			
Ethylene oxide; see 1910.1047	75-21-8			
Ethylidene chloride; see 1,1-Dichloroethane				
Ethylidene norbornene	16219-75-3			
N-Ethylmorpholine	100-74-3	20	94	X
Fenamiphos	22224-92-6			
Fensulfothion (Dasanit)	115-90-2			
Fenthion	55-38-9			
Ferbam	14484-64-1			
Total dust			15	
Ferrovanadium dust	12604-58-9		1	

Fluorides (as F)	Varies with compound		2.5	
Fluorine	7782-41-4	0.1	0.2	
Fluorotrichloromethane (Trichlorofluoromethane)	75-69-4	1000	5600	
Fonofos	944-22-9			
Formaldehyde; see 1910.1048	50-00-0			
Formamide	75-12-7			
Formic acid	64-18-6	5	9	
Furfural	98-01-1	5	20	X
Furfuryl alcohol	98-00-0	50	200	
Gasoline	8006-61-9			
Germanium tetrahydride	7782-65-2			
Glutaraldehyde	111-30-8			
Glycerin (mist)	56-81-5			
Total dust			15	
Respirable fraction			5	
Glycidol	556-52-5	50	150	
Glycol monoethyl ether; see 2-Ethoxyethanol				
Grain dust (oat, wheat, barley)				
Graphite, natural respirable dust	7782-42-5		Tbl. Z-3	
Graphite, synthetic				
Total dust			15	
Respirable fraction			5	
Guthion[R]; see Azinphos methyl				
Gypsum	13397-24-5			
Total dust			15	
Respirable fraction			5	
Hafnium	7440-58-6		0.5	
Heptachlor	76-44-8		0.5	X
Heptane (n-Heptane)	142-82-5	500	2000	
Hexachlorobutadiene	87-68-3			
Hexachlorocyclo-pentadiene	77-47-4			
Hexachloroethane	67-72-1	1	10	X
Hexachloronaphthalene	1335-87-1		0.2	X
Hexafluoroacetone	684-16-2			
n-Hexane	110-54-3	500	1800	
Hexane isomers	Varies with compound			
2-Hexanone (Methyl n-butyl ketone)	591-78-6	100	410	
Hexone (Methyl isobutyl ketone)	108-10-1	100	410	
sec-Hexyl acetate	108-84-9	50	300	
Hexylene glycol	107-41-5			
Hydrazine	302-01-2	1	1.3	X
Hydrogenated terphenyls	61788-32-7			

Table Z-1-A. - Limits for Air Contaminants - Cont.

Substance	CAS No. (f)	Transitional limits		
		PEL*		Skin designation
		ppm (a)	mg/m³ (b)	
Hydrogen bromide	10035-10-6	3	10	
Hydrogen chloride	7647-01-0	(C)5	(C)7	
Hydrogen cyanide	74-90-8	10	11	X
Hydrogen fluoride (as F)	7664-39-3	Tbl. Z-2		
Hydrogen peroxide	7722-84-1	1	1.4	
Hydrogen selenide (as Se)	7783-07-5	0.05	0.2	
Hydrogen sulfide	7783-06-4	Tbl. Z-2	Tbl. Z-2	
Hydroquinone	123-31-9		2	
2-Hydroxypropyl acrylate	999-61-1			
Indene	95-13-6			
Indium and compounds (as In)	7440-74-6			
Iodine	7553-56-2	(C)0.1	(C)1	
Iodoform	75-47-8			
Iron oxide fume	1309-37-1		10	
Iron pentacarbonyl (as Fe)	13463-40-6			
Iron salts (soluble) (as Fe)	Varies with compound			
Isoamyl acetate	123-92-2	100	525	
Isoamyl alcohol (primary and secondary)	123-51-3	100	360	
Isobutyl acetate	110-19-0	150	700	
Isobutyl alcohol	78-83-1	100	300	
Isooctyl alcohol	26952-21-6			
Isophorone	78-59-1	25	140	
Isophorone diisocyanate	4098-71-9			
2-Isopropoxyethanol	109-59-1			
Isopropyl acetate	108-21-4	250	950	
Isopropyl alcohol	67-63-0	400	980	
Isopropylamine	75-31-0	5	12	
N-isopropylaniline	768-52-5			
Isopropyl ether	108-20-3	500	2100	
Isopropyl glycidyl ether (IGE)	4016-14-2	50	240	
Kaolin				
Total dust			15	

Respirable fraction			5	
Ketene	463-51-4	0.5	0.9	
Lead inorganic (as Pb); see 1910.1025	7439-92-1			
Limestone	1317-65-3			
Total dust			15	
Respirable fraction			5	
Lindane	58-89-9		0.5	X
Lithium hydride	7580-67-8		0.025	
L.P.G. (liquefied petroleum gas)	68476-85-7	1000	1800	
Magnesite	546-93-0			
Total dust			15	
Respirable fraction			5	
Magnesium oxide fume	1309-48-4			
Total particulate			15	
Malathion	121-75-5			
Total dust			15	X
Maleic anhydride	108-31-6	0.25	1	
Manganese compounds (as Mn)	7439-96-5		(C)5	
Manganese fume (as Mn)	7439-96-5		(C)5	
Manganese cyclopenta-dienyl tricarbonyl (as Mn)	12079-65-1			
Manganese tetroxide (as Mn)	1317-35-7			
Marble	1317-65-3			
Total dust			15	
Respirable fraction			5	
Mercury (aryl and inorganic) (as Hg)	7439-97-6		Tbl. Z-2	
Mercury (organo) alkyl compounds (as Hg)	7439-97-6		Tbl. Z-2	
Mercury (vapor) (as Hg)	7439-97-6		Tbl. Z-2	
Mesityl oxide	141-79-7	25	100	
Methacrylic acid	79-41-4			
Methanethiol; see Methyl mercaptan				
Methomyl (Lannate)	16752-77-5			
Methoxychlor	72-43-5			
Total dust			15	
2-Methoxyethanol; see Methyl cellosolve				
4-Methoxyphenol	150-76-5			
Methyl acetate	79-20-9	200	610	
Methyl acetylene (Propyne)	74-99-7	1000	1650	
Methyl acetylene-propadiene mixture (MAPP)		1000	1800	
Methyl acrylate	96-33-3	10	35	X
Methylacrylonitrile	126-98-7			
Methylal (Dimethoxy-methane)	109-87-5	1000	3100	
Methyl alcohol	67-56-1	200	260	
Methylamine	74-89-5	10	12	

Table Z-1-A. - Limits for Air Contaminants - Cont.

Substance	CAS No. (f)	Transitional limits PEL* ppm (a)	mg/m³ (b)	Skin designation
Methyl amyl alcohol; see Methyl isobutyl carbinol				
Methyl n-amyl ketone	110-43-0	100	465	
Methyl bromide	74-83-9	(C)20	(C)80	X
Methyl butyl ketone; see 2-Hexanone				
Methyl cellosolve (2-Methoxyethanol)	109-86-4	25	80	X
Methyl cellosolve acetate (2-Methoxyethyl acetate)	110-49-6	25	120	X
Methyl chloride	74-87-3	Tbl. Z-2		
Methyl chloroform (1,1,1-Trichloroethane)	71-55-6	350	1900	
Methyl 2-cyanoacrylate	137-05-3			
Methyl cyclohexane	108-87-2	500	2000	
Methylcyclohexanol	25639-42-3	100	470	
o-Methylcyclohexanone	583-60-8	100	460	X
Methylcyclopentadienyl manganese tricarbonyl (as Mn)	12108-13-3			
Methyl demeton	8022-00-2			
4,4'-Methylene bis (2-chloroaniline) (MBOCA)	101-14-4			
Methylene bis(4-cyclohexylisocyanate)	5124-30-1			
Methylene chloride	75-09-2	Tbl. Z-2		
Methyl ethyl ketone peroxide (MEKP)	1338-23-4			
Methyl formate	107-31-3	100	250	
Methyl hydrazine (Monomethyl hydrazine)	60-34-4	(C)0.2	(C)0.35	X
Methyl iodide	74-88-4	5	28	X
Methyl isoamyl ketone	110-12-3			
Methyl isobutyl carbinol	108-11-2	25	100	X
Methyl isobutyl ketone; see Hexone				
Methyl isocyanate	624-83-9	0.02	0.05	X
Methyl isopropyl ketone	563-80-4			
Methyl mercaptan	74-93-1	(C)10	(C)20	
Methyl methacrylate	80-62-6	100	410	
Methyl parathion	298-00-0			
Methyl propyl ketone; see 2-Pentanone				
Methyl silicate	681-84-5			
alpha-Methyl styrene	98-83-9	(C)100	(C)480	
Methylene bisphenyl isocyanate (MDI)	101-68-8	(C)0.02	(C)0.2	

Metribuzin	21087-64-9			
Mica; see Silicates				
Molybdenum (as Mo)	7439-98-7			
Soluble compounds			5	
Insoluble compounds				
Total dust			15	
Monocrotophos (Azodrin[R])	6923-22-4			
Monomethyl aniline	100-61-8	2	9	X
Morpholine	110-91-8	20	70	X
Naphtha (Coal tar)	8030-30-6	100	400	
Naphthalene	91-20-3	10	50	
alpha-Naphthylamine; see 1910.1004	134-32-7			
beta-Naphthylamine; see 1910.1009	91-59-8			
Nickel carbonyl (as Ni)	13463-39-3	0.001	0.007	
Nickel, metal and insoluble compounds (as Ni)	7440-02-0		1	
Nickel, soluble compounds (as Ni)	7440-02-0		1	
Nicotine	54-11-5		0.5	X
Nitric acid	7697-37-2	2	5	
Nitric oxide	10102-43-9	25	30	
p-Nitroaniline	100-01-6	1	6	X
Nitrobenzene	98-95-3	1	5	X
p-Nitrochlorobenzene	100-00-5		1	X
4-Nitrodiphenyl; see 1910.1003	92-93-3			
Nitroethane	79-24-3	100	310	
Nitrogen dioxide	10102-44-0	(C)5	(C)9	
Nitrogen trifluoride	7783-54-2	10	29	
Nitroglycerin [1]	55-63-0	(C)0.2	(C)2	X
Nitromethane	75-52-5	100	250	
1-Nitropropane	108-03-2	25	90	
2-Nitropropane	79-46-9	25	90	
N-Nitrosodimethylamine; see 1910.1016	62-79-9			
Nitrotoluene		5	30	X
o-isomer	88-72-2			
m-isomer	99-08-1			
p-isomer	99-99-0			
Nitrotrichloromethane; see Chloropicrin				
Nonane	111-84-2			
Octachloronaphthalene	2234-13-1		0.1	X
Octane	111-65-9	500	2350	
Oil mist, mineral	8012-95-1		5	
Osmium tetroxide (as Os)	20816-12-0		0.002	
Oxalic acid	144-62-7		1	
Oxygen difluoride	7783-41-7	0.05	0.1	

Table Z-1-A. - Limits for Air Contaminants - Cont.

Substance	CAS No. (f)	Transitional limits PEL* ppm (a)	mg/m³ (b)	Skin designation
Ozone	10028-15-6	0.1	0.2	
Paraffin wax fume	8002-74-2			
Paraquat, respirable dust	1910-42-5 4685-14-7 2074-50-2		0.5	X
Parathion	56-38-2		0.1	X
Particulates not otherwise regulated				
Total dust			15	
Respirable fraction			5	
Pentaborane	19624-22-7	0.005	0.01	
Pentachloronaphthalene	1321-64-8		0.5	X
Pentachlorophenol	87-86-5		0.5	X
Pentaerythritol	115-77-5			
Total dust			15	
Respirable fraction			5	
Pentane	109-66-0	1000	2950	
2-Pentanone (Methyl propyl ketone)	107-87-9	200	700	
Perchloroethylene (Tetrachloroethylene)	127-18-4	Tbl. Z-2		
Perchloromethyl mercaptan	594-42-3	0.1	0.8	
Perchloryl fluoride	7616-94-6	3	13.5	
Perlite				
Total dust			15	
Respirable fraction			5	
Petroleum distillates (Naphtha)(Rubber Solvent)		500	2000	
Phenol	108-95-2	5	19	X
Phenothiazine	92-84-2			
p-Phenylene diamine	106-50-3		0.1	X
Phenyl ether, vapor	101-84-8	1	7	
Phenyl ether-biphenyl mixture, vapor		1	7	
Phenylethylene; see Styrene				
Phenyl glycidyl ether (PGE)	122-60-1	10	60	
Phenylhydrazine	100-63-0	5	22	X
Phenyl mercaptan	108-98-5			
Phenylphosphine	638-21-1			

Phorate	298-02-2			
Phosdrin (Mevinphos[a])	7786-34-7		0.1	X
Phosgene (Carbonyl chloride)	75-44-5	0.1	0.4	
Phosphine	7803-51-2	0.3	0.4	
Phosphoric acid	7664-38-2		1	
Phosphorus (yellow)	7723-14-0		0.1	
Phosphorus oxychloride	10025-87-3			
Phosphorus pentachloride	10026-13-8		1	
Phosphorus pentasulfide	1314-80-3		1	
Phosphorus trichloride	7719-12-2	0.5	3	
Phthalic anhydride	85-44-9	2	12	
m-Phthalodinitrile	626-17-5			
Picloram	1918-02-1			
Total dust			15	
Respirable fraction			5	
Picric acid	88-89-1		0.1	X
Piperazine dihydro-chloride	142-64-3			
Pindone (2-Pivalyl-1,3-indandione)	83-26-1		0.1	
Plaster of Paris	26499-65-0			
Total dust			15	
Respirable fraction			5	
Platinum (as Pt)	7440-06-4			
Metal				
Soluble salts			0.002	
Portland cement	65997-15-1			
Total dust			Tbl. Z-3	
Respirable fraction			Tbl. Z-3	
Potassium hydroxide	1310-58-3			
Propane	74-98-6	1000	1800	
Propargyl alcohol	107-19-7			
beta-Propriolactone; see 1910.1013	57-57-8			
Propionic acid	79-09-4			
Propoxur (Baygon)	114-26-1			
n-Propyl acetate	109-60-4	200	840	
n-Propyl alcohol	71-23-8	200	500	
n-Propyl nitrate	627-13-4	25	110	
Propylene dichloride	78-87-5	75	350	
Propylene glycol dinitrate	6423-43-4			
Propylene glycol monomethyl ether	107-98-2			
Propylene imine	75-55-8	2	5	X
Propylene oxide	75-56-9	100	240	
Propyne; see Methyl acetylene				
Pyrethrum	8003-34-7		5	

Table Z-1-A. - Limits for Air Contaminants - Cont.

Substance	CAS No. (f)	Transitional limits PEL* ppm (a)	mg/m³ (b)	Skin designation
Pyridine	110-86-1	5	15	
Quinone	106-51-4	0.1	0.4	
Resorcinol	108-46-3			
Rhodium (as Rh), metal fume and insoluble compounds	7440-16-6		0.1	
Rhodium (as Rh), soluble compounds	7440-16-6		0.001	
Ronnel	299-84-3		15	
Rosin core solder pyrolysis products, as formaldehyde				
Rotenone	83-79-4		5	
Rouge				
Total dust			15	
Respirable fraction			5	
Selenium compounds (as Se)	7782-49-2		0.2	
Selenium hexafluoride (as Se)	7783-79-1	0.05	0.4	
Silica, amorphous, precipitated and gel	112926-00-8		Tbl. Z-3	
Silica, amorphous, diatomaceous earth, containing less than 1% crystalline silica.	61790-53-2		Tbl. Z-3	
Silica, crystalline cristobalite, respirable dust	14464-46-1		Tbl. Z-3	
Silica, crystalline quartz, respirable dust	14808-60-7		Tbl. Z-3	
Silica, crystalline tripoli (as quartz), respirable dust	1317-95-9		Tbl. Z-3	
Silica, crystalline tridymite, respirable dust	15468-32-3		Tbl. Z-3	
Silica, fused, respirable dust	60676-86-0		Tbl. Z-3	
Silicates (less than 1% crystalline silica)				
Mica (respirable dust)	12001-26-2		Tbl. Z-3	
Soapstone, total dust			Tbl. Z-3	
Soapstone, respirable dust			Tbl. Z-3	
Talc (containing asbestos): use asbestos limit - See 29 CFR 1910.1001			Tbl. Z-3	
Talc (containing no asbestos), respirable dust	14807-96-6		Tbl. Z-3	
Tremolite. See 29 CFR 1910.1101			Tbl. Z-3	
Silicon	7440-21-3			
Total dust			15	
Respirable fraction			5	
Silicon carbide	409-21-2			
Total dust			15	
Respirable fraction			5	

Silicon tetrahydride	7803-62-5			
Silver, metal and soluble compounds (as Ag)	7440-22-4		0.01	
Soapstone; see Silicates				
Sodium azide	26628-22-8			
(as HN_3)				
(as NaN_3)				
Sodium bisulfite	7631-90-5			
Sodium fluoroacetate	62-74-8		0.05	X
Sodium hydroxide	1310-73-2		2	
Sodium metabisulfite	7681-57-4			
Starch	9005-25-8			
Total dust			15	
Respirable fraction			5	
Stibine	7803-52-3	0.1	0.5	
Stoddard solvent	8052-41-3	500	2900	
Strychnine	57-24-9		0.15	
Styrene	100-42-5	Tbl. Z-2		
Subtilisins (Proteolytic enzymes)	9014-01-1			
Sucrose	57-50-1			
Total dust			15	
Respirable fraction			5	
Sulfur dioxide	7446-09-5	5	13	
Sulfur hexafluoride	2551-62-4	1000	6000	
Sulfuric acid	7664-93-9		1	
Sulfur monochloride	10025-67-9	1	6	
Sulfur pentafluoride	5714-22-7	0.025	0.25	
Sulfur tetrafluoride	7783-60-0			
Sulfuryl fluoride	2699-79-8	5	20	
Sulprofos	35400-43-2			
Systox[R], see Demeton				
2,4,5-T	93-76-5		10	
Talc; see Silicates				
Tantalum, metal and oxide dust	7440-25-7		5	
TEDP (Sulfotep)	3689-24-5		0.2	X
Tellurium and compounds (as Te)	13494-80-9		0.1	
Tellurium hexafluoride (as Te)	7783-80-4	0.02	0.2	
Temephos	3383-96-8			
Total dust			15	
Respirable fraction			5	
TEPP	107-49-3		0.05	X
Terphenyls	26140-60-3	(C)1	(C)9	
1,1,1,2-Tetrachloro-2,2-difluoroethane	76-11-9	500	4170	

Table Z-1-A. - Limits for Air Contaminants - Cont.

Substance	CAS No. (f)	Transitional limits		
		PEL*		Skin designation
		ppm (a)	mg/m³ (b)	
1,1,2,2-Tetrachloro-1,2-difluoroethane	76-12-0	500	4170	
1,1,2,2-Tetrachloroethane	79-34-5	5	35	X
Tetrachoroethylene; see Perchloroethylene				
Tetrachloromethane; see Carbon tetrachloride				
Tetrachloronaphthalene	1335-88-2		2	X
Tetraethyl lead (as Pb)	78-00-2		0.075	X
Tetrahydrofuran	109-99-9	200	590	
Tetramethyl lead, (as Pb)	75-74-1		0.075	X
Tetramethyl succinonitrile	3333-52-6	0.5	3	X
Tetranitromethane	509-14-8	1	8	
Tetrasodium pyrophosphate	7722-88-5			
Tetryl (2,4,6-Trinitrophenyl-methyl-nitramine)	479-45-8		1.5	X
Thallium, soluble compounds (as Tl)	7440-28-0		0.1	X
4,4'-Thiobis(6-tert, Butyl-m-cresol)	96-69-5			
Total dust			15	
Respirable fraction			5	
Thioglycolic acid	68-11-1			
Thionyl chloride	7719-09-7			
Thiram	137-26-8		5	
Tin, inorganic compounds (except oxides) (as Sn)	7440-31-5		2	
Tin, organic compounds (as Sn)	7440-31-5		0.1	
Tin oxide (as Sn)	21651-19-4			
Titanium dioxide	13463-67-7			
Total dust			15	
Toluene	108-88-3	Tbl. Z-2		
Toluene-2,4-diisocyanate (TDI)	584-84-9	(C)0.02	(C)0.14	
m-Toluidine	108-44-1			
o-Toluidine	95-53-4	5	22	X
p-Toluidine	106-49-0			
Toxaphene; see Chlorinated camphene				
Tremolite; see Silicates				
Tributyl phosphate	126-73-8		5	
Trichloroacetic acid	76-03-9			
1,2,4-Trichlorobenzene	120-82-1			

1,1,1-Trichloroethane; see Methyl chloroform				
1,1,2-Trichloroethane	79–00–5	10	45	X
Trichloroethylene	79–01–6	Tbl. Z-2	Tbl. Z-2	Tbl. Z-2
Trichloromethane; see Chloroform				
Trichloronaphthalene	1321–65–9		5	X
1,2,3-Trichloropropane	96–18–4	50	300	
1,1,2-Trichloro-1,2,2-trifluoroethane	76–13–1	1000	7600	
Triethylamine	121–44–8	25	100	
Trifluorobromomethane	75–63–8	1000	6100	
Trimellitic anhydride	552–30–7			
Trimethylamine	75–50–3			
Trimethyl benzene	25551–13–7			
Trimethyl phosphite	121–45–9			
2,4,6-Trinitrophenyl; see Picric acid				
2,4,6-Trinitrophenylmethyl nitramine; see Tetryl				
2,4,6-Trinitrotoluene (TNT)	118–96–7		1.5	X
Triorthocresyl phosphate	78–30–8		0.1	
Triphenyl amine	603–34–9			
Triphenyl phosphate	115–86–6		3	
Tungsten (as W)	7440–33–7			
Insoluble compounds				
Soluble compounds				
Turpentine	8006–64–2	100	560	
Uranium (as U)	7440–61–1			
Soluble compounds			0.05	
Insoluble compounds			0.25	
n-Valeraldehyde	110–62–3			
Vanadium	1314–62–1			
Respirable dust (as V_2O_5)			(C)0.5	
Fume (as V_2O_5)			(C)0.1	
Vegetable oil mist				
Total dust			15	
Respirable fraction			5	
Vinyl acetate	108–05–4			
Vinyl benzene; see Styrene				
Vinyl bromide	593–60–2			
Vinyl chloride; see 1910.1017	75–01–4			
Vinyl cyanide; see Acrylonitrile				
Vinyl cyclohexene dioxide	106–87–6			
Vinylidene chloride (1,1-Dichloroethylene)	75–35–4			
Vinyl toluene	25013–15–4	100	480	
VM & P Naphtha	8032–32–4			
Warfarin	81–81–2		0.1	
Welding fumes (total particulate)***				

Table Z-1-A. - Limits for Air Contaminants - Cont.

Substance	CAS No. (f)	Transitional limits PEL* ppm (a)	Transitional limits PEL* mg/m³ (b)	Skin designation
Wood dust, all soft and hard woods, except Western red cedar.				
Wood dust, Western red cedar				
Xylenes (o-, m-, p- isomers)	1330-20-7	100	435	
m-Xylene alpha, alpha'- diamine	1477-55-0			
Xylidine	1300-73-8	5	25	X
Yttrium	7440-65-5		1	
Zinc chloride fume	7646-85-7		1	
Zinc chromate (as CrO_3)	Varies with compound	Tbl. Z-2	Tbl. Z-2	Tbl. Z-2
Zinc oxide fume	1314-13-2		5	
Zinc oxide	1314-13-2			
Total dust			15	
Respirable fraction			5	
Zinc stearate	557-05-1			
Total dust			15	
Respirable fraction			5	
Zirconium compounds (as Zr)	7440-67-7		5	

*The transitional PELs are 8-hour TWAs unless otherwise noted; a (C) designation denotes a

**Unless otherwise noted, employers in General Industry (i.e., those covered by 29 *CFR* 19 until Dec. 31, 1993 as set forth in 29 CFR 1910.1000(f).

***As determined from breathing-zone air samples.

(a) Parts of vapor or gas per million parts of contaminated air by volume at 25°C and 760 tor

(b) Milligrams of substance per cubic meter of air. When a numerical entry for a substanc number in the mg/m³ column is exact. When numerical entries for a substance are in both the p exact and the number in the mg/m³ column may be rounded off.

(c) Duration is for 15 minutes, unless otherwise noted.

(d) The final benzene standard in 1910.1028 applies to all occupational exposures to benz consistently under the action level (i.e., distribution and sale of fuels, sealed containers and pipe gas processing, and the percentage exclusion for liquid mixtures); for the excepted subsegments,

(e) Exposures under 10,000 ppm to be cited de minimus.

(f) The CAS number is for information only. Enforcement is based on the substance name. I as the metal, the CAS number for the metal is given—not the CAS numbers for the individual con

(g) Compliance with the subtilisins PEL is assessed by sampling with a high volume

(h) The acetone STEL does not apply to the cellulose acetate fiber industry. It is in effect for

(i) The Final Rule Limit of 5 mg/m³ is not in effect as a result of reconsideration. Calcium otherwise regulated of 5 mg/m³ respirable dust and 15 mg/m³ total dust.

(j)The Final Rule Limit TWA of 5 mg/m³ is not in effect as a result of reconsideration. The c employee exposures shall be kept below that level pursuant to the methods of compliance specif

(k)The Final Rule Limit STEL of 0.1 mg/m³ is not in effect as a result of reconsideration fo explosives and propellants for civilian use. The Final rule limits skin designation and the Transitic until completion of the reconsideration.

(l)The Final Rule Limit STEL of 0.1 mg/m³ is not in effect as a result of reconsideration fo explosives and propellants for civilian use. The Final rule limits skin designation and the Transitio until completion of the reconsideration.

(m) Sampling for the carbon monoxide ceiling shall be averaged over 5 minutes but an

TABLE Z-2

Material	8-hour time-weighted average	Acceptable ceiling concentration	Acceptable maximum peak above the acceptable ceiling concentration for an 8-hour shift	
			Concentration	Maximum duration
Benzene (Z37.40–1969) [1]	10 ppm	25 ppm	50 ppm	10 minutes.
Beryllium and Beryllium compounds (Z37.29–1970)	2 $\mu g/m^3$	5 $\mu g/m^3$	25 $\mu g/m^3$	30 minutes.
Cadmium fume (Z37.5–1970)	0.1 mg/m^3	0.3 mg/m^3		
Cadmium dust (Z37.5–1970)	0.2 mg/m^3	0.6 mg/m^3		
Carbon disulfide (Z37.3–1968)	20 ppm	30 ppm	100 ppm	30 minutes.
Carbon Tetrachloride (Z37.17–1967)	10 ppm	25 ppm	200 ppm	5 minutes in any 4 hours.
Chromic acid and chromates (Z37.7–1971)		1 $mg/10\ m^3$		
Ethylene dibromide (Z37.31–1970	20 ppm	30 ppm	50 ppm	5 minutes.
Ethylene dichloride (Z37.21–1969)	50 ppm	100 ppm	200 ppm	5 minutes in any 3 hours.
Formaldehyde (Z37.16–1967) [2]	3 ppm	5 ppm	10 ppm	30 minutes.
Hydrogen fluoride (Z37.28–1969)	3 ppm			
Hydrogen sulfide (Z37.2–1966)		20 ppm	50 ppm	10 minutes once only if no other measurable exposure occurs.
Fluoride as dust (Z37.38–1969)	2.5 mg/m^3			
Mercury (Z37.8–1971)		1 $mg/10\ m^3$		
Methyl chloride(Z37.18–1969	100 ppm	200 ppm	300 ppm	5 minutes in any 3 hours.
Methylene chloride (Z37.23–1969)	500 ppm	1,000 ppm	2,000 ppm	5 minutes in any 2 hours.
Organo (alkyl) mercury (Z37.30–1969)	0.01 mg/m^3	0.04 mg/m^3		.
Styrene (Z37.15–1969)	100 ppm	200 ppm	600 ppm	5 minutes in any 3 hours.
Tetrachloroethylene (Z37.22–1967)	100 ppm	200 ppm	300 ppm	5 minutes in any 3 hours.
Toluene (Z37.12–1967)	200 ppm	300 ppm	500 ppm	10 minutes.
Trichloroethylene (Z37.19–1967)	100 ppm	200 ppm	300 ppm	5 minutes in any 2 hours.

[1] This standard applies to the industry segments exempt from the 1 ppm 8-hour TWA and 5 ppm STEL of the benzene standard at 1910.1028. This standard also applies to any industry for which 1910.1028 is stayed or otherwise not in effect.

[2] This standard applies to any industry for which 1910.1048 is stayed or otherwise not in effect.

Table Z-3 - Mineral Dusts

TABLE Z-3–Mineral Dusts

Substance	mppcf[a]	mg/m³
SILICA:		
CRYSTALLINE		
QUARTZ (RESPIRABLE)	250[f]	10 mg/m³[m]
	%SiO₂+5	%SiO₂+2
QUARTZ (TOTAL DUST)		30 mg/m³
		%SiO₂+2
CRISTOBALITE: Use ½ the value calculated from the count or mass formulae for quartz		
TRIDYMITE: Use ½ the value calculated from the formulae for quartz		
AMORPHOUS, including natural diatomaceous earth	20	80 mg/m³
		%SiO₂
SILICATES (less than 1% crystalline silica):		
Mica	20	
Soapstone	20	
Talc (not containing asbestos)	20[m]	
Talc (containing asbestos). Use asbestos limit		
Tremolite (see 29 CFR 1910.1101)		
Portland cement	50	
GRAPHITE (NATURAL)	15	
COAL DUST (respirable fraction less than 5% SiO_2)		2.4 mg/m³ or
For more than 5% SiO_2		10 mg/m³
		%SiO₂+2
INERT OR NUISANCE DUST:[e]		
Respirable fraction	15	5 mg/m³
Total dust	50	15 mg/m³

Note.—Conversion Factors—mppcf × 35.3 = million particles per cubic meter = particles per c.c.
[a] Millions of particles per cubic foot of air, based on impinger samples counted by light-field techniques.
[f] The percentage of crystalline silica in the formula is the amount determined from airborne samples, except in those instances in which other methods have been shown to be applicable.
[e] All inert or nuisance dusts, whether mineral, inorganic, or organic, not listed specifically by substance name, are covered by the Particulates Not Otherwise Regulated (PNOR) limit in Table Z-1-A.
[m] Both concentration and percent quartz for the application of this limit are to be determined from the fraction passing a size-selector with the following characteristics:

Aerodynamic diameter (unit density sphere)	Percent passing selector
2	90
2.5	75
3.5	50
5.0	25
10	0

[m] Containing less than 1% quartz; if 1% quartz, use quartz limit.
The measurements under this note refer to the use of an AEC (now NRC) instrument. The respirable fraction of coal dust is determined with an MRE: the figure corresponding to that of 2.4 mg/m³ in the table for coal dust is 4.5 mg/m³.

State of California, Prop. 65
The Safe Drinking Water and Toxic Enforcement Act, 1986

STATE OF CALIFORNIA
ENVIRONMENTAL PROTECTION AGENCY
OFFICE OF ENVIRONMENTAL HEALTH HAZARD ASSESSMENT
SAFE DRINKING WATER AND TOXIC ENFORCEMENT ACT OF 1986

CHEMICALS KNOWN TO THE STATE TO CAUSE CANCER OR REPRODUCTIVE TOXICITY

The Safe Drinking Water and Toxic Enforcement Act of 1986 requires that the Governor revise and republish at least once per year the list of chemicals known to the State to cause cancer or reproductive toxicity. The identification number indicated in the following list is the Chemical Abstracts Service (CAS) Registry Number. No CAS number is given when several substances are presented as a single listing. The date refers to the initial appearance of the chemical on the list.

CHEMICALS KNOWN TO THE STATE TO CAUSE CANCER

Chemical	CAS Number	Date
A-alpha-C (2-Amino-9H-pyrido[2,3-b]indole)	26148685	January 1, 1990
Acetaldehyde	75070	April 1, 1988
Acetamide	60355	January 1, 1990
Acetochlor	34256821	January 1, 1989
2-Acetylaminofluorene	53963	July 1, 1987
Acifluorfen	62476599	January 1, 1990
Acrylamide	79061	January 1, 1990
Acrylonitrile	107131	July 1, 1987
Actinomycin D	50760	October 1, 1989
Adriamycin (Doxorubicin hydrochloride)	23214928	July 1, 1987
AF-2;[2-(2-furyl)-3-(5-nitro-2-furyl)]acrylamide	3688537	July 1, 1987
Aflatoxins	—	January 1, 1988
Alachlor	15972608	January 1, 1989
Alcoholic beverages, when associated with alcohol abuse	—	July 1, 1988
Aldrin	309002	July 1, 1988
Allyl chloride	107051	January 1, 1990
2-Aminoanthraquinone	117793	October 1, 1989
p-Aminoazobenzene	60093	January 1, 1990
ortho-Aminoazotoluene	97563	July 1, 1987
4-Aminobiphenyl (4-aminodiphenyl)	92671	February 27, 1987
3-Amino-9-ethylcarbazole hydrochloride	6109973	July 1, 1989
1-Amino-2-methylanthraquinone	82280	October 1, 1989
2-Amino-5-(5-nitro-2-furyl)-1,3,4-thiadiazole	712685	July 1, 1987
Amitrole	61825	July 1, 1987
Analgesic mixtures containing phenacetin	—	February 27, 1987
Aniline	62533	January 1, 1990
ortho-Anisidine	90040	July 1, 1987
ortho-Anisidine hydrochloride	134292	July 1, 1987
Antimony oxide (Antimony trioxide)	1309644	October 1, 1990
Aramite	140578	July 1, 1987
Arsenic (inorganic arsenic compounds)	—	February 27, 1987
Asbestos	1332214	February 27, 1987
Auramine	492808	July 1, 1987
Azaserine	115026	July 1, 1987
Azathioprine	446866	February 27, 1987
Azacitidine	320672	January 1, 1992
Azobenzene	103333	January 1, 1990

State of California, Prop. 65 The Safe Drinking Water and Toxic Enforcement Act, 1986

Benz[a]anthracene	56553	July 1, 1987
Benzene	71432	February 27, 1987
Benzidine [and its salts]	92875	February 27, 1987
Benzidine-based dyes	---	October 1, 1992
Benzo[b]fluoranthene	205992	July 1, 1987
Benzo[j]fluoranthene	205823	July 1, 1987
Benzo[k]fluoranthene	207089	July 1, 1987
Benzofuran	271896	October 1, 1990
Benzo[a]pyrene	50328	July 1, 1987
Benzotrichloride	98077	July 1, 1987
Benzyl chloride	100447	January 1, 1990
Benzyl violet 4B	1694093	July 1, 1987
Beryllium and beryllium compounds	---	October 1, 1987
Betel quid with tobacco	---	January 1, 1990
Bis(2-chloroethyl)ether	111444	April 1, 1988
N,N-Bis(2-chloroethyl)-2-naphthylamine (Chlornapazine)	494031	February 27, 1987
Bischloroethyl nitrosourea (BCNU) (Carmustine)	154938	July 1, 1987
Bis(chloromethyl)ether	542881	February 27, 1987
Bitumens, extracts of steam-refined and air refined	---	January 1, 1990
Bracken fern	---	January 1, 1990
Bromodichloromethane	75274	January 1, 1990
Bromoform	75252	April 1, 1991
1,3-Butadiene	106990	April 1, 1988
1,4-Butanediol dimethanesulfonate (Busulfan)	55981	February 27, 1987
Butylated hydroxyanisole	25013165	January 1, 1990
beta-Butyrolactone	3068880	July 1, 1987
Cadmium and cadmium compounds	---	October 1, 1987
Caffeic acid	331395	October 1, 1994
Captafol	2425061	October 1, 1988
Captan	133062	January 1, 1990
Carbon tetrachloride	56235	October 1, 1987
Carbon-black extracts	---	January 1, 1990
Ceramic fibers (airborne particles of respirable size)	---	July 1, 1990
Certain combined chemotherapy for lymphomas	---	February 27, 1987
Chlorambucil	305033	February 27, 1987
Chloramphenicol	56757	October 1, 1989
Chlordane	57749	July 1, 1988
Chlordecone (Kepone)	143500	January 1, 1988
Chlordimeform	6164983	January 1, 1989
Chlorendic acid	115286	July 1, 1989
Chlorinated paraffins (Average chain length, C12; approximately 60 percent chlorine by weight)	108171262	July 1, 1989
p-Chloroaniline	106478	October 1, 1994
Chlorodibromomethane	124481	January 1, 1990
Chloroethane (Ethyl chloride)	75003	July 1, 1990
1-(2-Chloroethyl)-3-cyclohexyl-1-nitrosourea (CCNU) (Lomustine)	13010474	January 1, 1988
1-(2-Chloroethyl)-3-(4-methylcyclohexyl)-1-nitrosourea (Methyl-CCNU)	13909096	October 1, 1988
Chloroform	67663	October 1, 1987
Chloromethyl methyl ether (technical grade)	107302	February 27, 1987
3-Chloro-2-methylpropene	563473	July 1, 1989
4-Chloro-ortho-phenylenediamine	95830	January 1, 1988
p-Chloro-o-toluidine	95692	January 1, 1990

State of California, Prop. 65 The Safe Drinking Water and Toxic Enforcement Act, 1986

Chlorothalonil	1897456	January 1, 1989
Chlorozotocin	54749905	January 1, 1992
Chromium (hexavalent compounds)	---	February 27, 1987
Chrysene	218019	January 1, 1990
C. I. Acid Red 114	6459945	July 1, 1992
C. I. Basic Red 9 monohydrochloride	569619	July 1, 1989
Ciclosporin (Cyclosporin A; Cyclosporine)	59865133 79217600	January 1, 1992
Cinnamyl anthranilate	87296	July 1, 1989
Cisplatin	15663271	October 1, 1988
Citrus Red No. 2	6358538	October 1, 1989
Cobalt metal powder	7440484	July 1, 1992
Cobalt [II] oxide	1307966	July 1, 1992
Coke oven emissions	---	February 27, 1987
Conjugated estrogens	---	February 27, 1987
Creosotes	---	October 1, 1988
para-Cresidine	120718	January 1, 1988
Cupferron	135206	January 1, 1988
Cycasin	14901087	January 1, 1988
Cyclophosphamide (anhydrous)	50180	February 27, 1987
Cyclophosphamide (hydrated)	6055192	February 27, 1987
D&C Orange No. 17	3468631	July 1, 1990
D&C Red No. 8	2092560	October 1, 1990
D&C Red No. 9	5160021	July 1, 1990
D&C Red No. 19	81889	July 1, 1990
Dacarbazine	4342034	January 1, 1988
Daminozide	1596845	January 1, 1990
Dantron (Chrysazin; 1,8-Dihydroxyanthraquinone)	117102	January 1, 1992
Daunomycin	20830813	January 1, 1988
DDD (Dichlorodiphenyldichloroethane)	72548	January 1, 1989
DDE (Dichlorodiphenyldichloroethylene)	72559	January 1, 1989
DDT (Dichlorodiphenyltrichloroethane)	50293	October 1, 1987
DDVP (Dichlorvos)	62737	January 1, 1989
N,N'-Diacetylbenzidine	613354	October 1, 1989
2,4-Diaminoanisole	615054	October 1, 1990
2,4-Diaminoanisole sulfate	39156417	January 1, 1988
4,4'-Diaminodiphenyl ether (4,4'-Oxydianiline)	101804	January 1, 1988
2,4-Diaminotoluene	95807	January 1, 1988
Diaminotoluene (mixed)	---	January 1, 1990
Dibenz[a,h]acridine	226368	January 1, 1988
Dibenz[a,j]acridine	224420	January 1, 1988
Dibenz[a,h]anthracene	53703	January 1, 1988
7H-Dibenzo[c,g]carbazole	194592	January 1, 1988
Dibenzo[a,e]pyrene	192654	January 1, 1988
Dibenzo[a,h]pyrene	189640	January 1, 1988
Dibenzo[a,i]pyrene	189559	January 1, 1988
Dibenzo[a,l]pyrene	191300	January 1, 1988
1,2-Dibromo-3-chloropropane (DBCP)	96128	July 1, 1987
2,3-Dibromo-1-propanol	96139	October 1, 1994
p-Dichlorobenzene	106467	January 1, 1989
3,3'-Dichlorobenzidine	91941	October 1, 1987
1,4-Dichloro-2-butene	764410	January 1, 1990
3,3'-Dichloro-4,4'-diaminodiphenyl ether	28434868	January 1, 1988
1,1-Dichloroethane	75343	January 1, 1990

State of California, Prop. 65 The Safe Drinking Water and Toxic Enforcement Act, 1986

Dichloromethane (Methylene chloride)	75092	April 1, 1988
1,2-Dichloropropane	78875	January 1, 1990
1,3-Dichloropropene	542756	January 1, 1989
Dieldrin	60571	July 1, 1988
Dienestrol	84173	January 1, 1990
Diepoxybutane	1464535	January 1, 1988
Diesel engine exhaust	---	October 1, 1990
Di(2-ethylhexyl)phthalate	117817	January 1, 1988
1,2-Diethylhydrazine	1615801	January 1, 1988
Diethyl sulfate	64675	January 1, 1988
Diethylstilbestrol	56531	February 27, 1987
Diglycidyl resorcinol ether (DGRE)	101906	July 1, 1989
Dihydrosafrole	94586	January 1, 1988
Diisopropyl sulfate	2973106	April 1, 1993
3,3'-Dimethoxybenzidine (ortho-Dianisidine)	119904	January 1, 1988
3,3'-Dimethoxybenzidine dihydrochloride (ortho-Dianisidine dihydrochloride)	20325400	October 1, 1990
Dimethyl sulfate	77781	January 1, 1988
4-Dimethylaminoazobenzene	60117	January 1, 1988
trans-2-[(Dimethylamino)methylimino]-5-[2-(5-nitro-2-furyl)vinyl]-1,3,4-oxadiazole	55738540	January 1, 1988
7,12-Dimethylbenz(a)anthracene	57976	January 1, 1990
3,3'-Dimethylbenzidine (ortho-Tolidine)	119937	January 1, 1988
3,3'-Dimethylbenzidine dihydrochloride	612828	April 1, 1992
Dimethylcarbamoyl chloride	79447	January 1, 1988
1,1-Dimethylhydrazine (UDMH)	57147	October 1, 1989
1,2-Dimethylhydrazine	540738	January 1, 1988
Dimethylvinylchloride	513371	July 1, 1989
1,6-Dinitropyrene	42397648	October 1, 1990
1,8-Dinitropyrene	42397659	October 1, 1990
2,4-Dinitrotoluene	121142	July 1, 1988
1,4-Dioxane	123911	January 1, 1988
Diphenylhydantoin (Phenytoin)	57410	January 1, 1988
Diphenylhydantoin (Phenytoin), sodium salt	630933	January 1, 1988
Direct Black 38 (technical grade)	1937377	January 1, 1988
Direct Blue 6 (technical grade)	2602462	January 1, 1988
Direct Brown 95 (technical grade)	16071866	October 1, 1988
Disperse Blue 1	2475458	October 1, 1990
Epichlorohydrin	106898	October 1, 1987
Erionite	12510428	October 1, 1988
Estradiol 17B	50282	January 1, 1988
Estrone	53167	January 1, 1988
Ethinylestradiol	57636	January 1, 1988
Ethyl acrylate	140885	July 1, 1989
Ethyl methanesulfonate	62500	January 1, 1988
Ethyl-4,4'-dichlorobenzilate	510156	January 1, 1990
Ethylene dibromide	106934	July 1, 1987
Ethylene dichloride (1,2-Dichloroethane)	107062	October 1, 1987
Ethylene oxide	75218	July 1, 1987
Ethylene thiourea	96457	January 1, 1988
Ethyleneimine	151564	January 1, 1988

State of California, Prop. 65
The Safe Drinking Water and Toxic Enforcement Act, 1986

Folpet	133073	January 1, 1989
Formaldehyde (gas)	50000	January 1, 1988
2-(2-Formylhydrazino)-4-(5-nitro-2-furyl)thiazole	3570750	January 1, 1988
Furan	110009	October 1,
1993Furazolidone	67458	January 1, 1990
Furmecyclox	60568050	January 1, 1990
Gasoline engine exhaust (condensates/extracts)	—	October 1, 1990
Glasswool fibers (airborne particles of respirable size)	—	July 1, 1990
Glu-P-1 (2-Amino-6-methyldipyrido[1,2-a:3',2'-d]imidazole)	67730114	January 1, 1990
Glu-P-2 (2-Aminodipyrido[1,2-a:3',2'-d]imidazole)	67730103	January 1, 1990
Glycidaldehyde	765344	January 1, 1988
Glycidol	556525	July 1, 1990
Griseofulvin	126078	January 1, 1990
Gyromitrin (Acetaldehyde methylformylhydrazone)	16568028	January 1, 1988
HC Blue 1	2784943	July 1, 1989
Heptachlor	76448	July 1, 1988
Heptachlor epoxide	1024573	July 1, 1988
Hexachlorobenzene	118741	October 1, 1987
Hexachlorocyclohexane (technical grade)	—	October 1, 1987
Hexachlorodibenzodioxin	34465468	April 1, 1988
Hexachloroethane	67721	July 1, 1990
Hexamethylphosphoramide	680319	January 1, 1988
Hydrazine	302012	January 1, 1988
Hydrazine sulfate	10034932	January 1, 1988
Hydrazobenzene (1,2-Diphenylhydrazine)	122667	January 1, 1988
Indeno [1,2,3-cd]pyrene	193395	January 1, 1988
IQ (2-Amino-3-methylimidazo[4,5-f]quinoline)	76180966	April 1, 1990
Iron dextran complex	9004664	January 1, 1988
Isosafrole	120581	October 1, 1989
Lactofen	77501634	January 1, 1989
Lasiocarpine	303344	April 1, 1988
Lead acetate	301042	January 1, 1988
Lead and lead compounds	—	October 1, 1992
Lead phosphate	7446277	April 1, 1988
Lead subacetate	1335326	October 1, 1989
Lindane and other hexachlorocyclohexane isomers	—	October 1, 1989
Mancozeb	8018017	January 1, 1990
Maneb	12427382	January 1, 1990
Me-A-alpha-C (2-Amino-3-methyl-9H-pyrido[2,3-b]indole)	68006837	January 1, 1990
Medroxyprogesterone acetate	71589	January 1, 1990
MeIQ(2-Amino-3,4-dimethylimidazo[4,5-f]quinoline)	7094112	October 1, 1994
MeIQx(2-Amino-3,8-dimethylimidazo[4,5-f]quinoxaline)	7500040	October 1, 1994
Melphalan	148823	February 27, 1987
Merphalan	531760	April 1, 1988
Mestranol	72333	April 1, 1988
8-Methoxypsoralen with ultraviolet A therapy	298817	February 27, 1987
5-Methoxypsoralen with ultraviolet A therapy	484208	October 1, 1988
2-Methylaziridine (Propyleneimine)	75558	January 1, 1988
Methylazoxymethanol	590965	April 1, 1988

State of California, Prop. 65
The Safe Drinking Water and Toxic Enforcement Act, 1986

Methylazoxymethanol acetate	592621	April 1, 1988
3-Methylcholanthrene	56495	January 1, 1990
5-Methylchrysene	3697243	April 1, 1988
4,4'-Methylene bis(2-chloroaniline)	101144	July 1, 1987
4,4'-Methylene bis(N,N-dimethyl)benzenamine	101611	October 1, 1989
4,4'-Methylene bis(2-methylaniline)	838880	April 1, 1988
4,4'-Methylenedianiline	101779	January 1, 1988
4,4'-Methylenedianiline dihydrochloride	13552448	January 1, 1988
Methylhydrazine and its salts	---	July 1, 1992
Methyl iodide	74884	April 1, 1988
Methyl methanesulfonate	66273	April 1, 1988
2-Methyl-1-nitroanthraquinone (of uncertain purity)	129157	April 1, 1988
N-Methyl-N'-nitro-N-nitrosoguanidine	70257	April 1, 1988
N-Methylolacrylamide	924425	July 1, 1990
Methylthiouracil	56042	October 1, 1989
Metiram	9006422	January 1, 1990
Metronidazole	443481	January 1, 1988
Michler's ketone	90948	January 1, 1988
Mirex	2385855	January 1, 1988
Mitomycin C	50077	April 1, 1988
Monocrotaline	315220	April 1, 1988
5-(Morpholinomethyl)-3-[(5-nitro-furfurylidene)-amino]-2-oxazolidinone	139913	April 1, 1988
Mustard Gas	505602	February 27, 1987
Nafenopin	3771195	April 1, 1988
1-Naphthylamine	134327	October 1, 1989
2-Naphthylamine	91598	February 27, 1987
Nickel and certain nickel compounds	---	October 1, 1989
Nickel carbonyl	13463393	October 1, 1987
Nickel refinery dust from the pyrometallurgical process	---	October 1, 1987
Nickel subsulfide	12035722	October 1, 1987
Niridazole	61574	April 1, 1988
Nitrilotriacetic acid	139139	January 1, 1988
Nitrilotriacetic acid, trisodium salt monohydrate	18662538	April 1, 1989
5-Nitroacenaphthene	602879	April 1, 1988
5-Nitro-o-anisidine	99592	October 1, 1989
o-Nitroanisole	91236	October 1, 1992
4-Nitrobiphenyl	92933	April 1, 1988
6-Nitrochrysene	7496028	October 1, 1990
Nitrofen (technical grade)	1836755	January 1, 1988
2-Nitrofluorene	607578	October 1, 1990
Nitrofurazone	59870	January 1, 1990
1-[(5-Nitrofurfurylidene)-amino]-2-imidazolidinone	555840	April 1, 1988
N-[4-(5-Nitro-2-furyl)-2-thiazolyl]acetamide	531828	April 1, 1988
Nitrogen mustard (Mechlorethamine)	51752	January 1, 1988
Nitrogen mustard hydrochloride (Mechlorethamine hydrochloride)	55867	April 1, 1988
Nitrogen mustard N-oxide	126852	April 1, 1988
Nitrogen mustard N-oxide hydrochloride	302705	April 1, 1988
2-Nitropropane	79469	January 1, 1988
1-Nitropyrene	5522430	October 1, 1990
4-Nitropyrene	57835924	October 1, 1990
N-Nitrosodi-n-butylamine	924163	October 1, 1987
N-Nitrosodiethanolamine	1116547	January 1, 1988

State of California, Prop. 65 The Safe Drinking Water and Toxic Enforcement Act, 1986

N-Nitrosodiethylamine	55185	October 1, 1987
N-Nitrosodimethylamine	62759	October 1, 1987
p-Nitrosodiphenylamine	156105	January 1, 1988
N-Nitrosodiphenylamine	86306	April 1, 1988
N-Nitrosodi-n-propylamine	621647	January 1, 1988
N-Nitroso-N-ethylurea	759739	October 1, 1987
3-(N-Nitrosomethylamino)propionitrile	60153493	April 1, 1990
4-(N-Nitrosomethylamino)-1-(3-pyridyl)1-butanone	64091914	April 1, 1990
N-Nitrosomethylethylamine	10595956	October 1, 1989
N-Nitroso-N-methylurea	684935	October 1, 1987
N-Nitroso-N-methylurethane	615532	April 1, 1988
N-Nitrosomethylvinylamine	4549400	January 1, 1988
N-Nitrosomorpholine	59892	January 1, 1988
N-Nitrosonornicotine	16543558	January 1, 1988
N-Nitrosopiperidine	100754	January 1, 1988
N-Nitrosopyrrolidine	930552	October 1, 1987
N-Nitrososarcosine	13256229	January 1, 1988
Norethisterone (Norethindrone)	68224	October 1, 1989
Ochratoxin A	303479	July 1, 1990
Oil Orange SS	2646175	April 1, 1988
Oral contraceptives, combined	—	October 1, 1989
Oral contraceptives, sequential	—	October 1, 1989
Oxadiazon	19666309	July 1, 1991
Oxymetholone	434071	January 1, 1988
Oxazepam	604751	October 1, 1994
Panfuran S	794934	January 1, 1988
Pentachlorophenol	87865	January 1, 1990
Phenacetin	62442	October 1, 1989
Phenazopyridine	94780	January 1, 1988
Phenazopyridine hydrochloride	136403	January 1, 1988
Phenesterin	3546109	July 1, 1989
Phenobarbital	50066	January 1, 1990
Phenoxybenzamine	59961	April 1, 1988
Phenoxybenzamine hydrochloride	63923	April 1, 1988
Phenyl glycidyl ether	122601	October 1, 1990
Phenylhydrazine and its salts	—	July 1, 1992
o-Phenylphenate, sodium	132274	January 1, 1990
PhiP(2-Amino-1-methyl-6-phenylimidazol[4,5-b]pyridine)	105650235	October 1, 1994
Polybrominated biphenyls	—	January 1, 1988
Polychlorinated biphenyls	—	October 1, 1989
Polychlorinated biphenyls (containing 60 or more percent chlorine by molecular weight)	—	January 1, 1988
Polychlorinated dibenzo-p-dioxins	—	October 1, 1992
Polychlorinated dibenzofurans	—	October 1, 1992
Polygeenan	53973981	January 1, 1988
Ponceau MX	3761533	April 1, 1988
Ponceau 3R	3564098	April 1, 1988
Potassium bromate	7758012	January 1, 1990
Procarbazine	671169	January 1, 1988
Procarbazine hydrochloride	366701	January 1, 1988
Procymidone	32809168	October 1, 1994
Progesterone	57830	January 1, 1988
1,3-Propane sultone	1120714	January 1, 1988

State of California, Prop. 65 The Safe Drinking Water and Toxic Enforcement Act, 1986

Progargite	2312358	October 1, 1994
beta-Propiolactone	57578	January 1, 1988
Propylene oxide	75569	October 1, 1988
Propylthiouracil	51525	January 1, 1988
Radionuclides	---	July 1, 1989
Reserpine	50555	October 1, 1989
Residual (heavy) fuel oils	---	October 1, 1990
Saccharin	81072	October 1, 1989
Saccharin, sodium	128449	January 1, 1988
Safrole	94597	January 1, 1988
Selenium sulfide	7446346	October 1, 1989
Shale-oils	68308349	April 1, 1990
Silica, crystalline (airborne particles of respirable size)	---	October 1, 1988
Soots, tars, and mineral oils (untreated and mildly treated oils and used engine oils)	---	February 27, 1987
Sterigmatocystin	10048132	April 1, 1988
Streptozotocin	18883664	January 1, 1988
Styrene oxide	96093	October 1, 1988
Sulfallate	95067	January 1, 1988
Talc containing asbestiform fibers	---	April 1, 1990
Terrazole	2593159	October 1, 1994
Testosterone and its esters	58220	April 1, 1988
2,3,7,8-Tetrachlorodibenzo-para-dioxin (TCDD)	1746016	January 1, 1988
1,1,2,2-Tetrachloroethane	79345	July 1, 1990
Tetrachloroethylene (Perchloroethylene)	127184	April 1, 1988
p-a,a,a-Tetrachlorotoluene	5216251	January 1, 19906
Tetranitromethane	509148	July 1, 1990
Thioacetamide	62555	January 1, 1988
4,4'-Thiodianiline	139651	April 1, 1988
Thiourea	62566	January 1, 1988
Thorium dioxide	1314201	February 27, 1987
Tobacco, oral use of smokeless products	---	April 1, 1988
Tobacco smoke	---	April 1, 1988
Toluene diisocyanate	26471625	October 1, 1989
ortho-Toluidine	95534	January 1, 1988
ortho-Toluidine hydrochloride	636215	January 1, 1988
para-Toluidine	106490	January 1, 1990
Toxaphene (Polychorinated camphenes)	8001352	January 1, 1988
Treosulfan	299752	February 27, 1987
Trichlormethine (Trimustine hydrochloride)	817094	January 1, 1992
2,4,6-Trichlorophenol	88062	January 1, 1988
1,2,3-Trichloropropane	96184	October 1,1992
Triphenyltin hydroxide	76879	July 1, 1992
Trichloroethylene	79016	April 1, 1988
Tris(aziridinyl)-para-benzoquinone (Triaziquone)	68768	October 1, 1989
Tris(1-aziridinyl)phosphine sulfide (Thiotepa)	52244	January 1, 1988
Tris(2-chloroethyl) phosphate	115968	April 1, 1992
Tris(2,3-dibromopropyl)phosphate	126727	January 1, 1988
Trp-P-1 (Tryptophan-P-1)	62450060	April 1, 1988
Trp-P-2 (Tryptophan-P-2)	62450071	April 1, 1988
Trypan blue (commercial grade)	72571	October 1, 1989

State of California, Prop. 65
The Safe Drinking Water and Toxic Enforcement Act, 1986

Unleaded gasoline (wholly vaporized)	---	April 1, 1988
Uracil mustard	66751	April 1, 1988
Urethane (Ethyl carbamate)	51796	January 1, 1988
Vinyl bromide	593602	October 1, 1988
Vinyl chloride	75014	February 27, 1987
4-Vinyl-1-cyclohexene diepoxide (Vinyl cyclohexenedioxide)	106876	July 1, 1990
Vinyl trichloride (1,1,2-Trichloroethane)	79005	October 1, 1990
2,6-Xylidine (2,6-Dimethylaniline)	87627	January 1, 1991
Zineb	12122677	January 1, 1990

* CHEMICALS KNOWN TO THE STATE TO CAUSE REPRODUCTIVE TOXICITY

<u>Developmental toxicity</u>

Acetohydroxamic acid	546883	April 1, 1990
Actinomycin D	50760	October 1, 1992
All-trans retinoic acid	302794	January 1, 1989
Alprazolam	28981977	July 1, 1990
Amikacin sulfate	39831555	July 1, 1990
Aminoglutethimide	125848	July 1, 1990
Aminoglycosides	---	October 1, 1992
Aminopterin	54626	July 1, 1987
Angiotensin converting enzyme (ACE) inhibitors	---	October 1, 1992
Anisindione	117373	October 1, 1992
Aspirin (NOTE: It is especially important not to use aspirin during the last three months of pregnancy, unless specifically directed to do so by a physician because it may cause problems in the unborn child or complications during delivery.)	50782	July 1, 1990
Barbiturates	---	October 1, 1992
Benomyl	17804352	July 1, 1991
Benzphetamine hydrochloride	5411223	April 1, 1990
Benzodiazepines	---	October 1, 1992
Bischloroethyl nitrosourea (BCNU) (Carmustine)	154938	July 1, 1990
Bromoxynil	1689845	October 1, 1990
Butabarbital sodium	143817	October 1, 1992
1,4-Butanediol dimethylsulfonate (Busulfan)	55981	January 1, 1989
Carbon disulfide	75150	July 1, 1989
Carbon monoxide	630080	July 1, 1989
Carboplatin	41575944	July 1, 1990
Chenodiol	474259	April 1, 1990
Chlorcyclizine hydrochloride	1620219	July 1, 1987
Chlorambucil	305033	January 1, 1989
Chlordecone (Kepone)	143500	January 1, 1989
Chlordiazepoxide	58253	January 1, 1992
Chlordiazepoxide hydrochloride	438415	January 1, 1992
1-(2-Chloroethyl)-3-cyclohexyl-l-nitrosourea (CCNU) (Lomustine)	13010474	July 1, 1990
Clomiphene citrate	50419	April 1, 1990

State of California, Prop. 65 The Safe Drinking Water and Toxic Enforcement Act, 1986

Clorazepate dipotassium	57109907	October 1, 1992
Cocaine	50362	July 1, 1989
Colchicine	64868	October 1, 1992
Conjugated estrogens	---	April 1, 1990
Cyanazine	21725462	April 1, 1990
Cycloheximide	66819	January 1, 1989
Cyclophosphamide (anhydrous)	50180	January 1, 1989
Cyclophosphamide (hydrated)	6055192	January 1, 1989
Cyhexatin	13121705	January 1, 1989
Cytarabine	147944	January 1, 1989
Danazol	17230885	April 1, 1990
Daunorubicin hydrochloride	23541506	July 1, 1990
Demeclocycline hydrochloride (internal use)	64733	January 1, 1992
Diazepam	439145	January 1, 1992
Dicumarol	66762	October 1, 1992
Diethylstilbestrol (DES)	56531	July 1, 1987
Dinocap	39300453	April 1, 1990
Dinoseb	88857	January 1, 1989
Diphenylhydantoin (Phenytoin)	57410	July 1, 1987
Doxycycline (internal use)	564250	July 1, 1990
Doxycycline calcium (internal use)	94088854	January 1, 1992
Doxycycline hyclate (internal use)	24390145	October 1, 1991
Doxycycline monohydrate (internal use)	17086281	October 1, 1991
Ergotamine tartrate	379793	April 1, 1990
Ethyl alcohol in alcoholic beverages	---	October 1, 1987
Ethylene glycol monoethyl ether	110805	January 1, 1989
Ethylene glycol monomethyl ether	109864	January 1, 1989
Ethylene glycol monoethyl ether acetate	111159	January 1, 1993
Ethylene glycol monomethyl ether acetate	110496	Janaury 1, 1993
Ethylene thiourea	96457	January 1, 1993
Etoposide	33419420	July 1, 1990
Etretinate	54350480	July 1, 1987
Fluorouracil	51218	January 1, 1989
Fluoxymesterone	76437	April 1, 1990
Flurazepam hydrochloride	1172185	October 1, 1992
Flutamide	13311847	July 1, 1990
Halazepam	23092173	July 1, 1990
Hexachlorobenzene	118741	January 1, 1989
Ifosfamide	3778732	July 1, 1990
Iodine-131	10043660	January 1, 1989
Isotretinoin	4759482	July 1, 1987
Lead	---	February 27, 1987
Lithium carbonate	554132	January 1, 1991
Lithium citrate	919164	January 1, 1991
Lorazepam	846491	July 1, 1990
Lovastatin	75330755	October 1, 1992

State of California, Prop. 65
The Safe Drinking Water and
Toxic Enforcement Act, 1986

Medroxyprogesterone acetate	71589	April 1, 1990
Megestrol acetate	595335	January 1, 1991
Melphalan	148823	July 1, 1990
Menotropins	9002680	April 1, 1990
Meprobamate	57534	January 1, 1992
Mercaptopurine	6112761	July 1, 1990
Mercury and mercury compounds	---	July 1, 1990
Methacycline hydrochloride	3963959	January 1, 1991
Methimazole	60560	July 1, 1990
Methotrexate	59052	January 1, 1989
Methotrexate sodium	15475566	April 1, 1990
Methyl bromide as a structural fumigant	74839	January 1, 1993
Methyl mercury	---	July 1, 1987
Methyltestosterone	58184	April 1, 1990
Midazolam hydrochloride	59467968	July 1, 1990
Minocycline hydrochloride (internal use)	13614987	January 1, 1992
Misoprostol	59122462	April 1, 1990
Mitoxantrone hydrochloride	70476823	July 1, 1990
Nafarelin acetate	86220420	April 1, 1990
Neomycin sulfate (internal use)	1405103	October 1, 1992
Netilmicin sulfate	56391572	July 1, 1990
Nicotine	54115	April 1, 1990
Nitrogen mustard (Mechlorethamine)	51752	January 1, 1989
Nitrogen mustard hydrochloride (Mechlorethamine hydrochloride)	55867	July 1, 1990
Norethisterone (Norethindrone)	68224	April 1, 1990
Norethisterone acetate (Norethindrone acetate)	51989	October 1, 1991
Norethisterone (Norethindrone)/Ethinyl estradiol	68224/57636	April 1, 1990
Norethisterone (Norethindrone)/Mestranol	68224/72333	April 1, 1990
Norgestrel	6533002	April 1, 1990
Oxazepam	604751	October 1, 1992
Oxytetracycline (internal use)	79572	January 1, 1991
Oxytetracycline hydrochloride (internal use)	2058460	October 1, 1991
Paramethadione	115673	July 1, 1990
Penicillamine	52675	January 1, 1991
Pentobarbital sodium	57330	July 1, 1990
Phenacemide	63989	July 1, 1990
Phenprocoumon	435972	October 1, 1992
Pipobroman	54911	July 1, 1990
Plicamycin	18378897	April 1, 1990
Polybrominated biphenyls	922660	October 1, 1994
Polychlorinated biphenyls	---	January 1, 1991
Procarbazine hydrochloride	366701	July 1, 1990
Propylthiouracil	51525	July 1, 1990
Retinol/retinyl esters, when in daily dosages in excess of 10,000 IU, or 3,000 retinol equivalents. (NOTE: Retinol/retinyl esters are required and essential for maintenance of normal reproductive function. The recommended daily level during pregnancy is 8,000 IU.)	---	July 1, 1989
Ribavirin	36791045	April 1, 1990

State of California, Prop. 65 The Safe Drinking Water and Toxic Enforcement Act, 1986

Secobarbital sodium	309433	October 1, 1992
Streptomycin sulfate	3810740	January 1, 1991
Tamoxifen citrate	54965241	July 1, 1990
Temazepam	846504	April 1, 1990
Testosterone cypionate	58208	October 1, 1991
Testosterone enanthate	315377	April 1, 1990
2,3,7,8-Tetrachlorodibenzo-para-dioxin (TCDD)	1746016	April 1, 1991
Tetracyclines (internal use)	---	October 1, 1992
Tetracycline (internal use)	60548	October 1, 1991
Tetracycline hydrochloride (internal use)	64755	January 1, 1991
Thalidomide	50351	July 1, 1987
Thioguanine	154427	July 1, 1990
Tobacco smoke (primary)	---	April 1, 1988
Tobramycin sulfate	49842071	July 1, 1990
Toluene	108883	January 1, 1991
Triazolam	28911015	April 1, 1990
Trilostane	13647353	April 1, 1990
Trimethadione	127480	January 1, 1991
Uracil mustard	66751	January 1, 1992
Urethane	51796	October 1, 1994
Urofollitropin	26995915	April 1, 1990
Valproate (Valproic acid)	99661	July 1, 1987
Vinblastine sulfate	143679	July 1, 1990
Vincristine sulfate	2068782	July 1, 1990
Warfarin	81812	July 1, 1987

Female reproductive toxicity

Aminopterin	54626	July 1, 1987
Anabolic steroids	---	April 1, 1990
Aspirin (NOTE: It is especially important not to use aspirin during the last three months of pregnancy, unless specifically directed to do so by a physician because it may cause problems in the unborn child or complications during delivery.)	50782	July 1, 1990
Carbon disulfide	75150	July 1, 1989
Cocaine	50362	July 1, 1989
Cyclophosphamide (anhydrous)	50180	January 1, 1989
Cyclophosphamide (hydrated)	6055192	January 1, 1989
Ethylene oxide	75218	February 27, 1987
Lead	---	February 27, 1987
Tobacco smoke (primary)	---	April 1, 1988
Uracil mustard	66751	January 1, 1992

State of California, Prop. 65
The Safe Drinking Water and Toxic Enforcement Act, 1986

Male reproductive toxicity

Anabolic steroids	—	April 1, 1990
Benomyl	17804352	July 1, 1991
Carbon disulfide	75150	July 1, 1989
Colchicine	64868	October 1, 1992
Cyclophosphamide (anhydrous)	50180	January 1, 1989
Cyclophosphamide (hydrated)	6055192	January 1, 1989
1,2-Dibromo-3-chloropropane (DBCP)	96128	February 27, 1987
m-Dinitrobenzene	99650	July 1, 1990
o-Dinitrobenzene	528290	July 1, 1990
p-Dinitrobenzene	100254	July 1, 1990
Dinoseb	88857	January 1, 1989
Ethylene glycol monoethyl ether	110805	January 1, 1989
Ethylene glycol monomethyl ether	109864	January 1, 1989
Ethylene glycol monoethyl ether acetate	111159	January 1, 1993
Ethylene glycol monomethyl ether acetate	110496	Janaury 1, 1993
Hexamethylphosphoramide	680319	October 1, 1994
Lead	—	February 27, 1987
Nitrofurantoin	67209	April 1, 1991
Tobacco smoke (primary)	—	April 1, 1988
Uracil mustard	66751	January 1, 1992

Date: October 1, 1994

VIII

WHERE ARE THE UNIONS?

Chapter Outline

Labor Movement History
Probing Questions

Labor Movement History

Various historians trace the beginnings of labor organizations to different sources. Some authors have compared labor movements with medieval craft guilds. The guilds were associations of skilled workers in Europe during the Middle Ages, which lasted approximately from A.D. 400 to 1500. Other historians have different theories about the origins of the labor movements. Most scholars trace the American labor movement to the early 1800s. Through the 1820s and 1830s, carpenters, printers, bricklayers and other skilled workers established city-wide organizations to obtain better work conditions.

It is reported that during the late 1800s in the United States, entire families worked for pitiful wages sewing garments in the sweatshops in New York City. Out of this era emerged the philosophy which "favored working for bread and butter objectives." This was followed by many advances influenced by the labor movement, including developments sparked by middle-class reformers known as Progressives. Various state legislatures as well as the United States Congress enacted laws regulating the labor of children, and establishing safety and health regulations in factories, mines, and overcrowded slum housing. This movement also included insurance coverage for industrial accidents. Early in the 20th century, legislation was passed limiting the work hours of women, men employed in public works, railroad workers, seagoing laborers, miners, and federal employees. In addition, the use of antitrust laws and injunctions relative to industrial disputes were clarified.

The strength and the local membership of the unions developed rapidly during World War II. By 1945 over one-third of all non-agricultural workers had joined a union. While the U.S. government prohibited general wage increases during the war, the unions won many important fringe benefits. These benefits included employer financed hospital insurance, paid vacations and holidays, and retirement pensions. The combined union membership expanded to about 17 million by 1961, and then to approximately 22.4 million by 1980.

Probing Questions

How does this historical information apply to our subject of environmental health and welfare? Well, where are the unions today? Governmental agencies have declared thousands of chemicals to be hazardous and harmful to our health (review list, end of Chapter VII). Many of these substances that are used every day in the workplace could be replaced with safer materials. New and safer replacements might be researched, developed, and incorporated into the mainstream of our work environments. In the meantime, our working citizens' lives and well-being are threatened by work-related chemicals. The questions are threefold:

1. Why do we tolerate wrongful deaths, disease, illness, birth defects, fatal accidents, etc.? (See Chapter III).

2. Why do we spend excessive dollars on medical expenses, when part of the problematic cause could be prevented?

3. Is there an organization that could champion the cause of worker safety?

This is a worthy and overlooked cause. Historically, the unions have been known for their concern for better working conditions. These organizations may be one of the best sources for helping improve our environmental health and welfare. We can do better.

IX

TRUSTEES' ENVIRONMENTAL RESPONSIBILITIES

Chapter Outline

Locate Yourself
Identify
Classify
Comply
By All Means, Try

Locate Yourself

Today we are beginning to understand that a destructive, degenerative cycle has been thrust into motion. Our mistaken assumptions about how our ecosystem works and our place in it have created negative effects, and the widespread use of out-of-balance chemicals has bankrupted much of our land and has threatened our health. These problems overtly demonstrate the toxic condition of the food we eat and the very lawns upon which our families and our pets play. This abuse and imbalance has left us with significant problems with our air quality, water purity and our land productivity thereby affecting the entire ecosystem of our spaceship earth. The following information is organized around four concepts: identify, classify, comply, and try. IDENTIFY local ecosystem problems within your neighborhood workplace, and your general sphere of influence. CLASSIFY possible problems and probable answers, for example agriculture manufacturing and clean-up practices. Determine to COMPLY with present environmental improvement plans. And TRY to implement a strong personal philosophy and practical process for improving our environment.

Identify

When I was a child, my father told me that Walt Disney said, "If you don't define the problem, you can't solve the problem." Can you identify some of your ecosystem problems? Make a list now so you can begin to do something constructive about the problems you see. Let me stimulate your thinking with several statements and a series of questions.

1. POOR SOIL FERTILITY. Poor soil fertility is usually related to a lack of

organic material and major and minor trace elements. Poor soil causes the production of poor crops, foods deficient in nutrients, and a variety of pathological modifications in the lives and behavior of animals and human beings.

2. TOXICITY. Amerigo Mosca, an Italian scientist who conducted extensive research about environmental issues, went so far as to proclaim the social injustice of environmental deception. He reported that toxic farm chemicals are similar in character to the radiation from atomic fallout. He argued that the annual use of fungicides or the products of organic synthesis causes the same damage to present and future generations as the atomic fallout from 29 H-bombs (a force equal to 14,500 atomic bombs of the size dropped on Hiroshima.) Although evidence for this claim was not confirmed by the author of this book, if Mosca's claim is true to any extent, it is too much!

3. ENERGETIC BIOPOWER. Do you have balanced soil? Have some

necessary elements been depleted, while an over-abundance of toxic elements have been added? You read labels at the grocery store about the food you buy for your body. Do you study and understand the nutrients necessary for our soil? By improving the balance of humic materials and microorganisms, the energetic biopower of your soil will return and undesirable conditions will be remedied. Economically, the investment will return benefits in several different ways.

4. INDUSTRIAL AND COMMERCIAL USE. This concept, as well as the following, Numbers 5 and 6, are covered in more detail in other segments of the book, including Chapter VI, "Are Chemical Companies at Fault?" and Chapter XIII, "EC&S Bio-Stimulant." This concept includes replacing solvents now being used in many of our larger industries. Manufacturing materials known to be hazardous or polluting, the generation of hazardous or toxic waste water byproducts, just to suggest a few.

5. DEADLY SANITIZING CHEMICALS. This area includes the replacement of harmful custodial cleaning compounds used in dairy equipment clean-up, federally inspected meat packing plants, slaughter houses, and egg and poultry processing plants. Most of these industries are using cleaning materials listed on the OSHA and EPA lists as being hazardous or toxic.

6. WASTE DISPOSAL. Mismanagement of hazardous materials such as hydrocarbons, their products and their byproducts. This could also include the hazardous ammonium nitrates found in animal waste which pollutes our water.

This section, "Identify," was written to help you in establishing where you are today in relation to where you would like to be through improving your personal and local environment. **It is one thing to stand on a soapbox and tell others what they should do. It is much more important and practical to change the part of the world right where you live!** So, think it through and make a list. As you consider the above statements and questions, you will better perceive your desired plan.

Classify

Take a moment to look at the problems you have identified on your personal list, and classify them under a system of headings such as industrial, agricultural, personal, or classify the problems as large or small scale issues. Consider which categories are urgent, and which issues you can address directly both alone and with other people.

You can now begin to work on a number of systematized answers to the topics identified above. You can sort out those that are important and useful for you individually. Some are just now considering whether to accept a new challenge. May this section introduce you to an elementary point of beginning. Learn to take these orderly steps so you can experience success with your newly identified goals.

Because of the wonderful yet rampant advancement of technological developments in all aspects of human endeavor, more and more negative situations are surfacing in our environment.

As we consider the full spectrum of "out-of-balance" components here on spaceship earth, we are made aware of many problem areas. For example, industrial waste and its wide variety of chemical complications. First, consider the following:

- The overload of toxic metals including lead, mercury, copper, chromium, and zinc.

- The increased use of fossil fuels by both developed and developing nations, allowing excessive petroleum, petrochemical products, and byproducts into our environmental system, thus affecting nature's balancing ability to keep these environmental infusions from being harmful.

Second, a tremendous volume of synthetic agricultural compounds are manufactured each year. Over 45,000 registered pesticide formulations exist in the United States alone. In addition to pesticides, there are also many herbicides. It has been estimated that hundreds of thousands of tons of these materials are used on our lands every year. There is genuine concern in industrialized countries about the ever-increasing use of these synthetic chemicals and the resulting "out-of-balance" toxicity in our environment. More attention is now being focused on the need for restoration and healing of our greatest agricultural resource, the land.

We have good reason for alarm because many chemical compounds are not only causing toxic deterioration in nature, but they are also functioning as deadly toxins for inhabitants of spaceship earth. These toxic problems have long-term environmental and ecological effects. These consequences reach wildlife, marine life, and human life. In fact, scores and scores of humans die annually, for example, from pesticide poisoning and heavy metal chemical toxicities. Our local and national news include tragic reports of massive losses of fish, birds, and animals in recent years that have been attributed to petroleum spills and the toxic effects of harmful chemical compounds.

There are, however, at least two sides to every issue. It is this fact that causes the debate. Many of the environmental issues that confront spaceship earth today are not the product of greed, nor the result of deliberate or total disregard for human or animal life. In many cases, the activities are undertaken with benefits to humanity as the goal. City officials, state legislators, and national environmental committees approve of the use of chemicals to help erase disease, such as that caused by disease-producing insects. Insecticides and fungicides are employed to increase the yield of crops and feed the hungry inhabitants of spaceship earth. In our philosophy of comfort and convenience, occupations and businesses often are blamed for creating toxic waste while producing new products for the comfort of spaceship earth's inhabitants. So now what do we do if these products foul the environment and pollute our system by forcing an "out-of-balance" ecology? There are several options:

1. Continue to tolerate the existing chemicals and how these substances have been used in the past, and live with the results.

2. Develop harmless or less harmful substitutes.

3. Implement suitable management practices to help minimize the damage instigated by presently "necessary" chemicals.

4. Look for natural methods and materials to counteract those harmful chemicals now deemed necessary.

These alternatives (serving as examples) can be involved in a practical way only if we can begin to understand the natural behavior of these chemical compounds. We must study related geochemical and biochemical reactions, processes, and the actions, forces, and applications functioning in a particular ecosystem.

Industrial waste mismanagement, agricultural over-application of chemicals, and uninformed consumers in general often contribute to toxic pollution in our waters. These effluents carry toxic metals, harmful chemical compounds, and other poisons throughout our spaceship earth.

We may implore, "Heal our lands." What are some of the concepts and activities that the term "healing" infers? Various dictionary definitions of healing suggest that it means to make whole or sound; to restore to an original state of good health. First, this discussion is initiated to find an answer that can counteract damage that already has occurred. If hundreds of thousands of tons of potentially toxic materials have been dumped on our lands, how do we offset the negative influences? Second, how do we survive while preventing it from happening again?

Our recovery concept must include remedy and retrieval of spaceship earth's natural balance. Natural functions must be restored. Unwholesomeness and destruction must be remediated with sound, functional reclamation. Perhaps the problems involve mishaps, mistakes, or general ignorance, but as trustees of spaceship earth, we are compelled to implement means of counteracting or removing the obvious problems to assure reparation and relief. This rescue is urgent. We must begin at once to initiate a recall from the wrong course of action. Salvage is possible with knowledge, a sound philosophy, and strong resolve to see it happen. Our property can be redeemed. Our lands can be healed!

Comply

Many of today's environmental problems are the result of human activities over the past century. However, the worst damage has come to our attention recently. With the recognition of these critical issues, it is one thing to say "you should not" or "you cannot." The hope is that this book will suggest to you safer, better, and more economical ways "you should" and "you could" help! It is hoped that we will accept the challenge to comply with the "correction burns" necessary for the safe salvage of our spaceship earth.

The United States environmental evolution included three major stages. Stage one emphasized conservation. The second stage included pollution control laws and regulations, while the third stage or wave supported a philosophy that environmental emphasis should be solution-oriented. Let's consider the solution oriented, "third stage environmentalists" in actively solving problems. There are answers for our dilemma, and we need not accept compromise. Pollution remediation and prevention is our policy and pledge. Please comply.

Environmental groups are actively engaged in combatting several large scale environmental problems. Below are several examples of environmental problems for which we could help make a difference: The greenhouse effect; animal life and habitats; acid rain; toxic waste; water purity; recycling; ozone depletion; and saving the rain forests.

1. Greenhouse effect: As the greenhouse effect appears to become more prominent, the temperature of the earth may rise, and new deserts may spread across the mid-latitudes, while ocean warming may be coupled with the north pole/south pole ice melting. This could make sea levels rise as much as three feet per century, thus overtaking lowlands. The widespread burning of the tropical rain forests of the Amazon, for example, eliminated much green foliage that may have helped balance the production of carbon dioxide by animals. The smoke from these fires may contribute directly to carbon dioxide accumulation. In general, we need to consider supporting significant international summit meetings like the United Nations World Conference. Through such negotiations, an international agreement to reduce the gases responsible for the greenhouse effect may be reached and cooperative

implementation may be demonstrated. Short-range, personal involvement could include planting more plants, shrubs, and trees. This green life absorbs carbon dioxide, the major greenhouse gas. In addition, the greenery is beautiful!

2. Animal life and habitats: As responsible human beings, we should be aware of the health and safety of our domesticated farm animals, our pets, wildlife, and endangered species. These inhabitants of spaceship earth are affected by toxic lawns, chemically out-of-balance animal feed, toxic waste water, and the loss of wetlands. We need to comply by avoiding known hazards and being supportive of efforts to lessen the effects of major toxic problems, even if they are not in our own backyard.

3. Acid rain: In the past few years, after the acid rain problem was defined, U.S. federal air pollution rules were written in an attempt to protect the health of those people near the polluting plants. The first steps to correct the problem included attempts to clean up plant

smoke emissions. Too often the regulations allowed these polluting plants to build taller and taller smoke stacks. This action shot the smoke skyward. Although the action reduced the smoke locally, it launched pollutants high into the atmosphere. At higher altitudes, the smoke is chemically changed into acids that may travel long distances before falling back to earth as acid snow or acid rain, thus polluting our soil and threatening our lives.

Fortunately, destructive acid has been reduced in the United States due to strictly enforced pollution legislation and a limit on permissible sulfur dioxide emissions. We can help with further reduction for example, by conserving electricity to reduce the sulfur dioxide and greenhouse gases emitted from power plants.

4. Toxic waste: As responsible trustees, we are concerned and active in toxic waste control issues. Influence and enforcement should be exercised to encourage reductions in the manufacturing sources of known toxins,

as well as limiting the creation of new toxic waste. We also must remediate existing toxic waste. Some of this clean-up must begin on our agricultural soils and work sites. We can support the reduction of toxic materials such as lead in gasoline. Today, you and I can choose products with limited hazardous ingredients.

5. Water purity: The inhabitants of spaceship earth must be concerned and work toward a guaranteed, abundant supply of clean water, not only for ourselves, but also for our children, grandchildren, and the many generations to come. Water is our greatest liquid asset, and its existence and purity must be preserved. This aspect of compliance can be met by working toward better, state-level clean water standards, by safe disposal of toxic animal waste, and by encouraging investigation of ground water quality near toxic and hazardous waste sites, and near leaking underground storage tanks. We can help implement incentives to preserve water. Everyday, we can practice the use of only phosphate-free detergents and lead-

free gasoline, for example, and thus avoid using potentially toxic chemicals.

6. Recycling compliance: Recycling is one of the most efficient systems for the disposal of many cumbersome materials. It offers a way to avoid pollution that ultimately affects everyone of us. Recycling saves energy while protecting the further wholesale use of natural resources. The use of incinerators and landfill systems has created additional hazards. The Environmental Defense Fund Organization in a booklet by Robert Taylor, "Ahead of the Curve," has compiled some very dramatic facts:

   a. Every Sunday, more than 500,000 trees are used to produce the 88% of newspapers that are never recycled.

   b. Americans use 2.5 million plastic bottles every hour and only a small percentage of these are now recycled.

   c. We throw away enough iron and steel in the United States to continuously supply all of our nation's auto makers.

d. American consumers and industries throw away enough aluminum to rebuild our entire commercial air fleet every three months.

e. Every year, Americans dispose of 24 million tons of leaves and grass clippings that could be composted to conserve landfill space (and recycled as humic material.) The fly ash from incinerator smoke usually contains potentially toxic heavy metals.

f. These metals are being carried by the wind and then dropped at random on the soil all across our nation to such an extent that it has been classified as airborne hazardous waste.

So, specifically, what can you do to help? We can each be a part of the acceleration of a nationwide effort to make curbside recycling convenient and more widespread. We can support expanding markets for recycled goods. By participating in the use of recycled goods, we can encourage businesses to recycle and then use recycled materials for packaging, for example. You and I can help educate our family members and friends about the cost-effectiveness and environmental safety of recycling versus incineration and land-filling. Perhaps we could donate reusable clothing and other items to charity or recycle through garage sales instead of throwing those items away. We may wish to participate in a local recycling project or help start a recycling program. If we could reach a point where up to 50% of all throw-away items, including our trash, could be recycled, we would benefit both directly and indirectly.

7. Ozone depletion: We can become aware of such efforts as the Montreal Accord, its goal is to assist in the rapid phaseout of ozone-depleting gases. Use your influence to help enforce state-level actions to capture and recycle the gases found in refrigerators and in home and automobile air

conditioners. On a local level, urge your appliance dealer and service or repair department to use equipment that recycles these ozone depleting gases when servicing refrigerators and home and automobile air conditioners. Support research to find gases to accomplish these refrigeration tasks that will not be hazardous to the ozone in our atmosphere or to our health.

8. Work to save our plant life at home, as well as tropical rain forests. Consider the widely publicized destruction of rain forests as a massive example of damaging waste. During the 1970s and early 1980s, a half-million interested people were allowed into the tropical rain forest of Brazil, lured by the promise of free land surrounding well-financed and well-equipped villages. Mass road building and land clearing practices took place. In 1988, NASA used infrared satellite photographs to reveal that up to 6,000 separate man-made fires were burning daily in the Amazon forests. People were clearing the jungle to build 1,100 miles of road and clearing land for the individual farms they hoped to cultivate. Then

they discovered they were hampered by the forests' thin soils that could not sustain their crops and chemical treatments for more than a few years. So, they chose to move on, a little deeper into the forested jungle, to burn and clear more land to provide a fresh start. Again, they experienced the same cycle. The massive loss of green foliage and the additional carbon dioxide from the burning process itself contributed to an excessive carbon dioxide imbalance, perhaps resulting in the greenhouse effect. These problems exist not only in South America, other examples include Indonesia and India.

We often are tempted to follow this same philosophy and practice wherever we are. We may say, "More harmful chemicals please; we will worry about ecosystem balance later." Often we are desperate for production at any cost. We burn out the soil and move on. What is our fiduciary responsibility as trustees of spaceship earth? Is there something you and I can do to help? Yes. Be aware, sensitive, and responsive to what you are learning about caring for your environment. In this endeavor to comply, that will allow us to make a personal contribution to improving the quality of life here on spaceship earth.

By All Means, Try

As the 21st century approaches, we face a tremendous challenge. We must define and pursue fresh, more environmentally safe practices which will maintain, sustain and perpetuate our healthy and happy existence. We have the privilege of choosing to assume affirmatively, a leadership role in transforming our relationship with spaceship earth. We can exercise our influence in environmental law, the protection of our local neighborhood ecosystems, and the implementation of sound family training for respect of our fragile environment. Would you like to go farther? Consider the worldwide scope and complexity of the inter-connected crises of ocean pollution, forest mismanagement, population explosion and the loss of biodiversity. The problems we face are micro and macro and the answers will require our efficient energy. Will you TRY to improve your local environmental situation?

Consider this example: Our land is a wonderful natural resource. This resource is renewable IF properly managed, and maintained. The farm and garden land of spaceship earth need not deteriorate in productiveness and fertility IF proper attention is directed to the task of restoring the essential soil fertility components as rapidly as they are used by each year's production removal. The incorporation of harmful chemicals for use in industry, commerce and household use may be replaced with safe options in many cases. The important condition here is "IF" we act constructively.

Yes, there are alternatives. For example, prior to the contemporary use of excessive chemicals on our soils, growers relied primarily on natural humus and three to four year (or longer) rotations to maintain or build up fertility and productiveness of their land. The status of our productive soils is different. Our soil has degenerated to an extent that we have become dependent on commercial chemicals to achieve the ends of soil management. Economic circumstances of the past 20 to 25 years also have been altered, precipitating changes in the general pattern of farming (for example, continuous row cropping such as corn followed by corn, or corn followed by soybeans. These rotations burn up organic matter rapidly.) Few growers today are maintaining the organic substances necessary for a healthy balance in their soil. In fact, where excessive chemical applications have been made, microbial activity has been significantly reduced.

On one hand, crop yields per acre have been gradually increasing under current methods, and it has been assumed that soil fertility levels are being maintained or perhaps even increased somewhat. On the other hand, perceptive growers are becoming concerned about their overall soil management practices. All across our land, farm and garden soils have become more compacted, which makes plowing and preparing for seeding more difficult. These soils are less easily drained and aerated. Larger and larger dosages of chemical treatment are required today to obtain the same yields per acre as we could produce a few years earlier. The increases in crop yields per acre resulted from better crop genetic strains, more timely crop seeding, cultivation, harvesting, and the increased use of irrigation water. THESE BENEFITS HAVE BEEN COVERING UP WHAT IS APPARENTLY HAPPENING TO NATIVE SOIL FERTILITY. **What would happen if this improved technology were coupled with humic and microbial balance as we returned to organic soil conditioning?**

A few decades ago, a few strong voices were heard regarding today's environmental problems, and many of them seemed overwhelmed for a time. Today, however, they are being heard and their voices are joined by hundreds and thousands of concerned, responsible citizens like you and me. The movement is developing into a respected force that is growing everyday and includes people from all walks of life. This grassroots movement is beginning to influence organized political and industrial communities. It is a movement that was born out of necessity and has grown as naturally as the example of organic agricultural methods themselves. This effort offers practical answers, and we all can contribute to this endeavor in our homes, apartments, gardens, farms, forests, and at our workplaces. We also can contribute in a significant way to the increased awareness that is the base for creating natural, healthy, and economically feasible alternatives that can revamp the general destructive attitudes and careless practices of the past. BY ALL MEANS, TRY.

X

THE CHANGING OF THE GUARD

Chapter Outline

Who Will Join the Guard?

Has the time come in the evolution of our technological growth to experience a changing of the "chemical" guard? Do health and safety require the removal and replacement of harmful and fatal chemical use? Could this "changing of the guard" represent an exchange of toxic chemical exposure for responsible restraint? Might we pass from one phase of problem solving to a progressive, safer strategy of competence? Would the "changing of the guard" protect spaceship earth and its inhabitants from harm while preserving life itself? Are you willing to consider a transformation of practices in the areas where you make decisions about purchasing or using harmful or hazardous substances? Would you be surprised to learn that there are many hazardous, toxic, and polluting chemicals that could be replaced easily and safely today? Would an altered or modified chemical treatment transition be too much trouble for you and your company or you and your family to adopt?

The call goes out for those who will serve as brave examples, who stand tall as sensible and strong sentinels, and who are willing to defend improvement! We can impede danger while serving as faithful and responsible trustees of the safety and security of our spaceship earth.

Who is willing to face change?
Who is the object of the guard?
Who is to be protected?
Who will initiate bravely
the changing of
the "harmful
chemical" guard?

The following are just a few illustrations of those who are joining the ranks of the change.

Biota Corporation

Lynn M. De Vaney, President of Biota Corporation of the San Francisco Bay Area, California, has appropriately chosen "Preserving Nature by Promoting Balance" as the company slogan. Ms. De Vaney states that, "Nature, the essence and order of all living things in our physical world is in itself, an intricately designed system of an unfathomable number of very simple but well balanced environments. At Biota, this concept encompasses much more than rivers, owls, forests, and the natural outdoors. It is where we live and work, where we raise our families, and where we hope to retire in comfort and good health. It is where we are today and where we will be tomorrow. By promoting balance to preserve nature, we ensure that we solve problems without creating new ones and in doing so, we also preserve this most basic and most important element of our existence on our planet -- our living environment."

Biota Corporation initiated research studies for compost odor control, a major problem for most composting facilities. Studies were conducted at both the East Bay Municipal Utility District (MUD) Waste Water Plant in Oakland and Upper Valley Recycling, Inc. in St. Helena, CA. Joe Arrain, Compost Operations Supervisor at East Bay MUD formulated the use of approximately 50 yards of sewage sludge, mixed with 250 yards of green waste for a compost that is in great demand for landscaping, golf courses, and parks. Customers line up to buy the composted materials that previously went to landfills at great expense to the District. James Rockafellow, Wastewater Treatment Superintendent, stated that not only is this a savings for the Utility District; it is also a very environmentally sound method of helping to reduce landfill. The only major problem was complaints by city residents about odor.

Upper Valley Recycling, Inc. has been doing a remarkable job of recycling hundreds of tons of grape residue and vineyard-green waste. Now composted, this product is in high demand, whereas previously it would only have increased the landfill problem. Once again, however, neighbors in downwind locations complained about the odor.

By using a new product marketed by Biota Corporation, the previously acrid, septic, and offensive odors of both the sewer sludge and the grape residue were significantly reduced by the experiment, and what remained was the milder aroma of rich humus soil. At East Bay MUD, a solution was sprayed on the open face of static piles in the process of transfer to windrows, and at Upper Valley Recycling, Inc., it was sprayed directly on the compost windrows while the Scarab turned and mixed the waste product. The research managers are studying data relative to whether a more complete composting of these waste products would provide more effective plant nutrient support.

Biota Corporation Vice President, Anthony Chantri, in conjunction with the California Department of Fish and Game, recently completed an animal waste remediation project. Research data were collected for (1) the reduction of ammonium nitrates; (2) the reduction of BODs (Biological Oxygen Demand); and (3) the decomposing of the organic solids found in animal waste, specifically reducing this waste product. Using two dairies as research sites and a bio-stimulant as the indigenous microorganisms' stimulant, the project was successful (as described in more detail in Chapter XIII) in demonstrating that (1) odors from animal waste can be controlled; (2) toxic ammonium nitrate, which follows flowing water and accounts for the death of water-life and fish, as well as the poisoning of ground water, can be reduced significantly; and (3) that well-composted manures will have greater fertilizing ability and produce greater results.

In its effort to help individuals and businesses reduce the use of toxic and hazardous chemicals, Biota recently started a marketing program for new products which are both a degreaser and a cleaner. Through the encouragement of Lorettann Keith, President of Enviro Balance International, Inc., of Colorado Springs, Colorado, Biota Corporation has started working with ConAgra Fruit and Nut Division's almond and walnut processing plants. In the almond processing plant in Madera, California, it was suggested by an American Institute of Bakers (AIB) inspector that they try to find a new cleaning product that did not have an odor which could be absorbed by the nuts. Biota was able to fill the need with their USDA approved cleaner. ConAgra's efforts to improve production methods are being well rewarded; the almond plant received an AIB "Superior" rating -- the highest audit rating possible; the walnut plant in Stockton was not far behind with an "Excellent" rating.

Also working toward the reduction of the use of unsafe cleaning products are Price-Costco and L & N Printing, both of Martinez, CA, and Katie's Kloset in Walnut Creek, CA. Additional staff members include, Neil Bowman of Washington state, Paulette and Ray Reeves of Northern California, and Karen Johnson, Biota, Minnesota Division.

Browning-Ferris Industries (BFI), one of the largest solid waste remediation companies in the United States is well aware of the immediate need to reduce hazardous and toxic material. Two other needs are sanitation and odor control. BFI's Pleasant Hill-Bayshore facility in Pacheco, CA cleans dumpsters, waste bins and vehicles on a regular basis with pressure washers and a water recycling system. Though chlorine had been used for odor control and sanitation, Dennis Wilson, Maintenance Manager, said that more and more was being needed and mentioned to Mr. Chantri his concern for employee safety and the toxicity of the waste stream. One of the company's goals is to meet the needs and concerns while reducing the frequency of grease trap clean-out, reducing the frequency of system water change, and being left with a wastewater product that is acceptable to the municipal sewer district. If wastewater is acceptable to the sewer district, the water does not have to be treated as hazardous material and the cost of treating the water is reduced. The savings benefits both customers and BFI. Biota is working with Dennis Wilson and BFI to reach that goal by providing human and environmentally safe products for safe and efficient cleaning, sanitation, odor control, and disposal.

Pacific Gas and Electric (PG&E), the largest generator of power in California, is searching continually for ways to eliminate solvents and other hazardous products used in their power plants and maintenance facilities. Mr. Chantri is working with the staff from PG&E's Environmental Services Materials and Fleet Divisions, and has introduced PG&E to a safe cleaning product as an answer to their concerns for personnel safety, environmental issues, and bottom-line cost effectiveness in all areas of cleaning, from pole mounted glass insulators to shop floors.

Congratulations to the team at Biota Corporation for their diligent research efforts, and to the businesses with which they are working to demonstrate that we can and will do better!

Green Hope Corporation

The Green Hope Corporation, established by its President, Elmer Neff, of Northglenn, Colorado, initially organized to find and market organic soil conditioners to help growers who were interested in growing and marketing organic products.

Mr. Neff's organization, including sons, Ted and Terry Neff, the Strayers, Gouldings, and Floyd Beninteni, subscribes to the concept that as trustees here on spaceship earth, we have the privilege of choice. This responsibility involves not only our gardens and fields, but it also includes the trusteeship of our own personal health. There are tremendous values hidden in the treasures of organic humus. Adequate literature from around the world indicates that humic substances, trace minerals, and microbial balance favorably affect the growth of plants.* The good news is that sick and toxic soil can be healed organically. The group also has been very involved in commercial and industrial nonhazardous improvements.

As stated previously, from growers to consumers, scientists to nursery operators, from

---

*Jackson, William R., Ph.D., (1993). *Humic, Fulvic and Microbial Balance: Organic Soil Conditioning.*

apples to zucchini and asters to zinnias, YOU will benefit most from organic practices. The Green Hope Corporation of Colorado is part of the changing of the guard. They encourage you to examine and implement these powerful tools of humic and microbial balance products which are available today for your growing efforts.

Enviro Balance International, Inc.

Born and raised in a farming community in the state of Kansas, Ms. Lorettann Keith developed a strong interest in farming issues. She is now the President of a Colorado corporation, Enviro Balance International, Inc., a supporting sentinel for safety. Her company would like to revolutionize the excessive use of harmful chemicals that can be replaced by safer substitutes.

Some time ago, her company was instrumental in presenting and supplying the ConAgra Sunflower plant of Goodland, Kansas, with a USDA approved nontoxic, nonhazardous, biodegradable cleaner to replace their cleaning solvents. This new cleaning material now cleans the food processing equipment better and more safely. Lorettann Keith also encouraged Lynn De Vaney of the Biota Corporation to supply safe cleaning product to the ConAgra walnut growers processing plant in Stockton,

California, and to the ConAgra almond growers processing plant of Madera, California.

Enviro Balance also has worked with one of the nation's outstanding organically produced egg businesses, operated by the Wubbena family - Phil, Betty Jo, and Rod. The egg production takes place in a Forreston, Illinois facility that can support up to 100,000 laying hens. Their chickens are not caged; instead their birds can move about the "hen house" in total freedom. Ventilators circulate air gently over the area just above the chickens. Rod reports that the temperature varies no more than one degree anywhere in the building, whether in the winter or summer. He went on to state that the chickens defecate principally at night. The waste falls down below the roosts and is later collected by scraper blades pulled the length of the hen house by a winch. The manure is then used to fertilize organically their 425 acres of farmland on which they grow the grain that makes the meal to feed another batch of chickens.

The family engineered their own feed formula. They roast high-moisture corn and whole soybeans, then blend in alfalfa, calcium, and wheat middlings with a specially formulated pre-mix. They report that the roasting makes the feed more digestible and appetizing, and the roast helps reduce various toxins. This operation represents one of the largest producers of organically grown chickens and organically produced eggs. These chickens, and thus the eggs, are not exposed to antibiotic additives in their food. The Wubbena family practices of supplying nest eggs from uncaged chickens, fed an antibiotic-free diet, certainly places the egg laying operation and the Wubbenas among those who are part of the changing of the guard.

All good things and ideas, however, may still present some problems. For example, chicken manure does not smell good! The ammonia from the manure burns your eyes, nose, throat and lungs, and often causes respiratory problems or even death among the chickens. The operation, "Phil's Fresh Egg" farm, is on the edge of town right across the street from a number of homes. Not all neighbors like the smell of chicken manure. Imagine 100,000 laying hens in your front yard!

Last year, Lorettann Keith through Enviro Balance International, Inc. introduced the Wubbenas to a nonhazardous, nontoxic bio-stimulant that quickly removed the odor from the chicken houses and cleaned the roosts while liquefying and composting the manure for safe application on their fields. The neighbors are no longer tormented by the odor, the animal waste problem is simplified, and Mrs. Wubbena stated recently, "We can now have a picnic in the backyard," which is less than 100 feet from thousands of happy hens.

Enviro Balance International, Inc., through the assistance of the Environmental Health Foundation, also is involved in research efforts with Wayne

Farms, a subsidiary of Continental Grain Company. The project involves approximately 15 large broiler farm operations and five hen operations, which furnish the eggs for incubation to supply the broiler farms with baby chicks. The design of the study includes data relative to reduction of ammonia, reduction of chicken respiratory problems, reduced death rate of chickens, and the possible improvement of food conversion in the healthier birds. Now perhaps, the chickens can use more energy for growth, verses energy burned for survival when fighting respiratory problems. The Enviro Balance International, Inc. staff and officers are additional members of the active changing of the guard.

EnviroCare, Inc. of Oklahoma

Through EnviroCare, Inc. of Oklahoma, the corporate President, Ms. E.G. Hall, introduced the slogan, "Nature helping renew our environment." In a meeting with EnviroCare, Inc. and the environmental group, Oklahoma Toxic Campaign, Inc. the question was asked of Kathleen Logan and her staff, "Are we only looking for issues, or are we looking for and finding solutions for our hazardous and toxic waste problems?"

EnviroCare, Inc., including the sales team and Ms. Hall, market environmentally safe products in

Oklahoma. This group represents three generations of individuals who have been raised in an agricultural setting. In addition to their agricultural experience, their individual credentials include one member who is a CPA and several who have experience in the field of public service and general real estate management.

This group is to be congratulated as they follow their goals to assist in the restoration of spaceship earth, helping it to return to its natural, healthy balance.

Solutions 2000, Inc.

"Solving the environmental problems of the future, now" is the mission of a group in southern California, operated by an attorney, David Jackson. He was a school teacher before obtaining his law degree, and for many years he has had a concern for the safety and welfare of the children and youth in our public schools. His investigation of the products being used in our public schools uncovered an alarming problem: Student exposure to toxic and hazardous materials being used in the facilities and on the equipment in the classrooms. He is developing a system of promotional materials to "educate the educators" and to make the school boards, administrators, and the responsible parties aware of the hazardous exposure to the students, and of the legal liability of those individuals in positions of responsibility and control.

His company, Solutions 2000, Inc., distributes free educational materials to the insurance industry. These materials are designed to make it easier for local brokers and their agents to advise their policyholders and potential customers of unsafe chemicals adversely affecting their health and welfare, and to advise of the hazardous and toxic pollutants which may jeopardize the policyholders' personal and medical insurance coverage and cause direct liability. The program is premised on networking between the public and those insurance agents who are commissioned to provide them with protection, giving greater disclosure about insurance coverage or a lack thereof. Use of safe alternatives to hazardous materials is encouraged.

Southern California's defense industries have been "taken a lickin' and seem to keep on tickin'." There are "wars" these companies have not begun to fight. They include battles against the toxic and hazardous pollutants being used by various branches of the government. As a part of Solutions 2000, Inc., Denny and Mistie Shaw, a husband and wife team who have completed many years of civilian and military government service, are pursuing both the clean-up of past problems, and the replacement of hazardous materials with safe, cost-effective solutions by the military and defense industry.

Another person whose services are being enlisted by Solutions 2000, Inc. to fight environmental battles is Harry Monahan and his Monahan Environmental Group. His expertise was developed through years of marketing innovative wastewater technology and equipment. He recognizes that where the capabilities of the equipment stop is where other solutions must take over. The thrust of his efforts run north and south of our national borders, providing solutions for hazardous waste problems including enhancement of existing aeration systems, odor reduction, converting vineyard lagoon residue to a potent soil enhancer, reclamation of alkaline soil, and dissipation and digestion of surface oils on marina harbors.

The environmental future in southern California appears bright because workable solutions are being developed and implemented.

Environmentally Conscious Options, Inc.

In California, another environmentally conscious family is striving to make an environmental difference. Judy and Ivan Strayer, and sons Mark, John, and Jeff, developed a distribution organization know as "ECO," Environmentally Conscious Options, Inc. The success of their endeavors is gaining momentum as reflected by the following examples.

John Strayer reported that Southern California Edison was looking for a degreaser that was low in volatile organic compounds (VOCs), to comply with the rules of the South Coast Air Quality Management District of California. John introduced and sold to Edison a degreaser that was gentle to the skin and contained no hazardous or health threatening chemicals. There was, however, more testing to be done. The Air Quality Control District tested his degreaser two times for VOCs (see results under Comparative Evidence in Chapter XI.) In general, the district personnel were skeptical that this product could be so low in VOCs and yet accomplish the cleaning task which for years had required toxic solvents. The manufacturer was then asked to present data from a certified laboratory showing both the measurement of the VOCs of his degreaser as well as test results of the VOC tests for individual components. District personnel set the maximum VOCs acceptable as tested by the Volatile Organic Compound partial pressure which must be 35.0 mm Hg or less at 20° C. The certified laboratory reports found John Strayer's commercial concentrate to have a VOC of only .0015 and the stronger industrial concentrate to have a VOC of .0031. According to the Air Quality Management District, Southern California, Edison is at liberty to use this degreaser to replace its solvents.

In Anaheim, California, managers at the Pan Pacific Hotel talked to John Strayer about a product that would not leave a strong odor, as do cleaners that contain solvents. They also were concerned about the safety and health of their employees. When John did a quick demonstration in their kitchen with his hands exposed to the cleaner, he indicated that he needed no protective gloves, as verified by the MSDS. Then the management tried the product themselves and reported that they had never seen or used a cleaner that was so effective and yet so gentle to the skin. They joined the ranks of the changing of the guard and purchased the cleaning product on the spot.

The distributors of janitorial supplies are finding chemical safety a major concern today. EPA and OSHA laws and regulations are now in place, and it is becoming increasingly difficult to conduct a safe business without following federal guidelines. The Strayers' safe cleaning products were presented to two distribution companies. Salespersons of both companies now will offer safer alternatives to their clientele.

Mark Strayer reports that the city yard at Laguna Beach, California is now using the safer degreaser in its shop area and for the general cleaning of tram buses used for various annual events. Mark demonstrated the value of his degreaser when mixed with gasoline or diesel fuel. The hydrocarbon chain was broken, making the fuel water soluble. Thus, when water is added to it, the fuel is "non-flammable." The city yard shop personnel found the product beneficial, and they purchased product that day.

The Newport Beach, California, city yard also uses the Strayers' nonhazardous, nontoxic, biodegradable degreaser in the vehicle maintenance area. Managers acted on their concern about the safety and the long-term health conditions of the employees, and these workers are now safer while working with the city's heavy equipment.

In the same general area of California, personnel at Quality Suites began using Mark Strayer's safer cleaning products for some tasks in their kitchen area. After the first shipment, management decided to begin using the product for all of their kitchen cleaning. The staff often thanks Mark for providing them with a safer cleaner.

The facility manager of a Woolley's Petite Suites saw Mark walk in with a spray bottle of cleaner in his hand and was quick to tell him of his various experiences with cleaning agents. After the manager examined the MSDS sheet thoroughly, he was astounded at the fact that Strayer's cleaner had no hazardous components. Mark challenged the manager to use the product on something very dirty. The manager began to clean the back of a greasy clothes dryer and continued to work on various other problem areas for approximately 20 minutes. He asked if he could keep the sample spray bottle, and the next time Mark stopped by, the company was ready to make a complete order for the amazing product.

A Comfort Suites manager in southern California was surprised to read the motel's current cleaning agent's label. He found that it contained harmful chemicals. Mark reported that the manager now uses the nonhazardous, nontoxic and biodegradable cleaners for all of general housekeeping.

From the kitchen of a Radisson Hotel, near Newport Beach, California, the chef selected the Strayers' degreaser as an all purpose cleaner. When the product also was applied to the men's room and to the trash area, problematic odors were neutralized effectively, much to the surprise of the appreciative management.

The Strayers have been very successful with their presentation of safe products to various restaurants throughout Orange County, California. They often approach the head chefs, who make their living preparing tasty foods that require a sensitive ability to smell. The demonstration is usually short and successful: Chefs observe the cleaning ability of the product and are impressed by the minimal odor. They realize that the various fruity, pine, and minty scents common in restaurant cleaners are used to mask the solvent smell. Chefs' comments include: "Now I won't worry about my tasty food picking up the odor of the cleaner." "My nose is now free to be more sensitive to my cooking." "Now the solvent smell will not interfere with my ability to cook great food!" The Strayers find that this group of professionals is very willing to use a cleaner that does not offend them and detract from their goal of producing pleasant tasting foods.

Mark has also been working with the Los Angeles Zoo in general clean-up tasks and odor control among zoo animals.

You can be proud of the Strayer family who have joined the changing of the guard by offering environmentally conscious options to businesses in California!

Agrisol, Inc. and Solutions Technology, Inc.

Agrisol, Inc. and Solutions Technology, Inc. are companies located in Glencoe, Alabama that wave the corporate banner, "Restoring the Environment Naturally." The officers of these companies believe that how we respond to the environmental challenges of today will, in a dynamic way, determine the kind of future we all give to our children. Mike and Marvin Fisher and Sandra Tucker are not strangers to the waste management industry. They take environmental concerns and responsibilities to the future very seriously. They meet the challenge daily with high-tech, yet practical solutions. Through the rapidly expanding field of hazardous waste technology, the Fishers and Ms. Tucker saw an opportunity to serve the community, the environment, and the future. Their long-term vision, a deep sense of responsibility, and unwavering integrity have been key elements in their success in this field. The three of them jointly have over 30 years of experience in the management of hazardous waste.

After their discussions with the Alabama Department of Environmental Management (ADEM), they feel timing is critical for the introduction of safe, effective solutions to a wide range of hazardous problems, including diesel contaminated soil, ground water contamination, and solidified and contaminated agricultural lagoons seeping into state waterways. Agrisol and Solutions Technology are working closely with ADEM on several research projects. The results will be submitted to the State and be made available to the public and to anyone seeking similar solutions.

The Alabama Farmers Federation (ALFA) has taken an active interest in Agrisol's current pilot projects, particularly the remediation of a completely solidified dairy farm lagoon in North Alabama and a chicken layer operation close to the Gulf Coast of Alabama. The support, communication, common interest, and acceptance of innovative solutions to environmental problems by state agencies, industries and companies like Agrisol and Solutions Technology are vital to altering our current course of environmental destruction.

Agrisol, Inc., the sister company of Solutions Technology, Inc., engineers natural solutions for agriculture. Mike Fisher, the president of Agrisol feels a strong sense of responsibility to implement natural solutions to agriculture's pressing environmental issues by utilizing naturally occurring microbial life. Agrisol's USDA approved products are nature's state-of-the-art technologies. This natural, economical technology has been tested and proven through the Environmental Health Foundation in conjunction with various state agencies and universities.

The management staff of Agrisol and Solutions Technology believe firmly in the EPA's program of waste minimization and report that over the last five years they actually have seen a reduction of certain hazardous waste streams. Certainly, the introduction of products such as those being made available by these two companies can enable industry to attack waste minimization at the best point, the point of generation.

Meantime, the reality of contamination already in existence can be addressed by their safe, proven, and economically viable bio-remediation technology. The EPA has cited "in-situ" remediation as the preferred method whenever it can be performed effectively and economically in order to prevent the risk of accidental release in transporting the hazardous material or contaminating another site. The people at Agrisol and Solutions have their sights set on advancing, documenting and verifying these methods in a market place that is desperate for safe, viable solutions.

For example, B.F. Goodrich-Cleveland Pneumatic in Tullahoma, Tennessee is replacing a caustic wash for degreasing with an environmentally safe, nonhazardous degreaser. This will eliminate the need to evaporate and ship off-site for wastewater treatment approximately 6,000 gallons of contaminated wastewater a month. The wastewater from the use of the safe degreaser is now a dischargeable water that can be discharged directly into the sewer.

Solutions Technology, Inc. was conceived with long-term objectives in mind. Those involved with this company are familiar and comfortable with the high-tech processes and often complex policies of modern hazardous and toxic waste management. For these reasons, Solutions Technology, Inc. has adopted the use of safe products, which have been approved by the USDA, as dispersants of hydrocarbons and the remediation of other toxic and hazardous substances. The incorporation of a bio-stimulant assists the digestion of the dispersed molecules of waste products by using the indigenous microorganisms presently in place. The management of Agrisol, Inc. and Solutions Technology, Inc. include a unified family working together with various industries, toxic wastewater generators, state regulatory organizations, and federal enforcement agencies to make our ecosystem more balanced and safe.

We salute the efforts of Agrisol, Inc. and Solutions Technology, Inc., as well as the State of Alabama and ALFA as true participants in the changing of the guard.

XI

THE MISSION OF THIS BOOK

Chapter Outline

WARNING: This book contains material which has been researched, documented and assembled with care. The majority of the data is factual in nature and referenced when possible. As the author, I hope this book will be informative and beneficial to you. However, for the first portion of Chapter XI, I beg the privilege to replace my "research hat" for a "concern hat" that allows me to express my own personal opinions, and do so with strong conviction. The style of writing will be more persuasive and will be spoken with heart-felt emotion, a call to action if you please. At the end of the next 15 pages, we will return to the factual data, COMPARATIVE EVIDENCE, followed by Chapters XII and XIII.

Inspiration and Motivation for Accountability

You are invited to join the company of the changing of the guard. With mental assent, please RSVP as soon as possible! We can do better as we all work together. Please join us as we explore ideas of inspiration and motivation for planning environmental accountability.

Chapter XI reflects affirmative conviction, with an observable confidence and a determination to ACT NOW. The very fact that you are reading this chapter serves as an indication that perhaps you are willing to be environmentally accountable. As we visualize the following thoughts, begin to see yourself as part of the dynamic answer rather than as a part of the problem.

What do inspiration, motivation, and accountability mean? INSPIRATION, or to be inspired, certainly includes being aroused; to advocate or recommend, while at the same time, to incite; evoke; stir up; give new life to; to kindle and perhaps inflame a cause or a situation. MOTIVATION suggests prompting; stimulating, while involving and being induced. Motivation could urge a provocation, a push or thrust which may denote an impelling encouragement. ACCOUNTABILITY suggests duty; what ought to be done; perhaps even a moral duty; an imperative duty, and certainly a call to duty. Within the connotation of this term is the idea of responsible answerability, even to the point of being non-exempt from liability.

Relative to personal management, inspiration and motivation in decision-making are the keys to accountability. These factors are the positive emotional lubricants that make change and planned efforts toward environmental health and safety occur smoothly, what may seem to be almost effortless.

Think of this analogy: Inspiration and motivation in management are like rivers flowing through the gates of the dam. These sources of motivation turn the wheels and dynamos of all practicality in regard to joining the ranks in this changing of the guard. Inspiration and motivation are the life-blood of improvement and the vital force of safe success. Their aim throbs and pulses in the intent of zestful, healthful living. It is through them that we can laugh in healthy recreation and play. With them flow good health, and the strength and clarity of thought to be able to work the long hours that seem but minutes in the half-forgetful absorption of self-expression, creativity, and recreation that bring us to a sense of fulfillment. We then have the opportunity to live the essence of life, the heartbeat of achievement. With our ecosystem in balance, we can enjoy the right to live safely, to experience more than just survival and premature death, hazardous and careless practices which are like the pounding of the surf eating away at the ocean shores of any helpful or positive activity.

Inspiration and motivation toward environmental achievement are the harmony that form the work song for spaceship earth's restoration. This harmony represents the strength of the draft-horse with his sweating shoulders against the cold collar, working toward remediation. Inspiration represents the melodious dream-like rhythm of the race horse's pulse as it sweeps around the track with hoofs pounding the motivational base tempo, the wind in its mane, and its heart bursting with the joy of competition as it heads for the finish line in first place. Accomplishing our restoration goals before it is too late will be crossing the finish line successfully.

Inspired, motivated accountability is the foe of mediocrity, the sister of creativity and insight, and the best defense against failure and the possible extinction of the human race.

Involvement in environmental restoration can be the subtle, subconscious feeling of the intuitive victory that a lone cyclist feels when she is one with her bike, a single unit, cornering and stretching out for the final lap. It can be a singleness of purpose that is born of an uncluttered mind whose sense of direction is accurate and whose detachment from the unsafe and the unnecessary has been completed. Its secret is the abandonment of lazy attitudes and the service of selfless self-expression set aflame. We can know what is right and that acting right is worth the fight.

Visualize this for a moment when thinking of our task: Inspiration and motivation of caring and sharing for environmental improvement are the whir of rising wings, when forward thrust overcomes resistance, where lift laughs at gravity and lofty levitation of a determined inner being changes the entire perspective of life. We will do better, we will soar higher, and we determine to do it now.

This very day, envision yourself alert, important, and involved as a member of the changing of the guard. Begin to identify personally the inspiration and motivation of the dedicated individual who expects the cooperation of a compatible, receptive spaceship earth environment. Begin to see through the eagle's eye the environmental accomplishments brought about through purposeful optimism and self-confident assurance in healthy, natural life. Begin to be receptive to the pride of participation, the dependability of teamwork, and the overflow of released life forces that rise resistless and beautiful to make the deserts of old landfills, chemical spills, and overworked farmland blossom with the verdant foliage and fruit of the manifest accomplishment of balanced restoration. Envision yourself among the ranks of the changing of the guard!

Inspired and motivated environmental accomplishment is the standard of our spaceship accountability. Be among the first to express love of healthful life. Sing the song of service and action to the purpose of salvage and preservation. It is the preservation of our own, our families', and our friends' lives, the preservation of our homes and businesses. The experience will serve as the spark of genius and the unconquerable spirit of adventure. Coupled with sincerity, earnestness, dynamic drive, and the cadence of conquest, the expression of our creative energies will form a joint venture with the creator of the universe to correct spaceship earth's environmental problems. Preservation of our lives is the cause, and this cause is worth living for. Believe it; we can and will do better!

Inspiration and motivation within corporate management form the lodestone of leadership. This lodestone attracts a dedicated work force like the fragrance and color of a flower attract a diligent swarm of bees. There can be no true leadership without inspired, motivated followers. An organization must have purposeful people as well as products. It is one thing simply to identify issues, but to progress, even to maintain, solutions must be found and implemented. In addition, you must have people-people who will work with you, fight for you, and share the enthusiasm of your plan and purpose.

It is the responsibility of inspired corporate leadership to know what it wants, when it is wanted, where it can be obtained, why it is wanted, and how to go about getting it. The leaders who know the how, why, where, and what have already built into their being the steadfastness and assurance of continued enthusiasm because their emotional drives have intelligent outlet, purpose, and direction. Their organization and circle of influence will vibrate with sureness, knowledgeable authoritativeness, and inspiration.

The atmosphere of an inspired administration tends to draw others to it. There is something contagious about earnest, sincere inspiration and motivation that alerts others who feel as well as hear the purposeful sound, see the upright attitude, and sense the vibrant tones.

There is a different sound in the inspired and motivated manager's voice. It is a sound that is heard without noise, and it challenges us to join the changing of the guard; to do meaningful, exciting things; to make life sing and shout with health and vitality; to improve our environment, our lives!

Administrative leadership must inspire others, not just by what is said or how it is said, but also by example. Administrative accountability must measure up to the stature of the positive, inspired individual who will dare to become the well-spring of inspiration and motivation for our future generations.

Inspired leadership must also condition itself to a positive reaction regardless of opposing or uncooperative circumstances. The person and the cause, not the emotion only, must always be in the driver's seat. The horse cannot sit in the saddle, and emotion, although it is a driving force, must always be directed, controlled, encouraged, held back, whipped up, or pulled to a halt when it is expedient in the mature judgment of the administrative driver. Most of all, management must lead the doers! It must, by the strength of inspired individuals, counteract the hot-air-pollution of negativity and rise above the dubious mind-smog of resistance and possible failure. If "progress" has created an environmental "mess," then as inspired, motivated leaders we must be a part of the changing of the guard to instigate "correction burns." This will be done for the preservation of our ecosystem, for the preservation of our own lives, and for the preservation of the lives of our children. It is for reasons like these that motivated and inspired individuals have been chosen as managers and leaders.

To be successful, the inspiration and motivation underlying individual accountability must be inseparably linked. Our responsibility for ourselves, our family, our home, our world is fact, not fiction. Inspiration and motivation for responsibility and accountability generate the energy to rise to the challenges of self-directed, self-assigned, self-improvement. Under the influence of motivation, tiredness gets out of bed, dresses, and "goes to town." Ill-health learns that physical action and increased awareness are more fun than reading cards of condolence. Laziness stretches farther than it intended to, opens its eyes, jumps to its feet, and joins the changing of the guard, the parade of champions! Inspiration increases mental wattage as the blood flows faster and farther, and ideas and actions cry out to be born, while asking "What can I do to help?" Thought leaps beyond the mind and telegraphs its inspiration and motivation to others. Awakened minds become unconscious centers of stimulation, control towers of positive, although unvoiced, inspirational directives that signal, "We are ready to help! Let's join the changing of the guard!"

Inspired, motivated examples must have clear-cut goals and objectives. Challenge yourself and others to be obvious examples! Crystalize your thinking; improve your methods; check your road-map along the way, a map drawn by a pen of inspiration and motivation that leads toward a goal and purpose. Inspiration and motivation will arise naturally when our conflicting directions are brought into a correlated drive of united purpose. It is here that our goals and plans play an important part. The elimination of the nonessential, the subjugation of the secondary, and the correlation of the primary purposes are the foundations of emotional release and enthusiastic living. We must aim toward a goal of doing better.

To attain and maintain enthusiasm, the inspired example must evaluate personal successes, recount personal conquests, and move on to other phases of their planned achievements. The chief focus of their attention must be in the here and now where their enthusiasm is confidence at the bat, endurance circling the bases, and courage sliding home. The inspired example will have the highest batting average and the best accountability score. Inspiration and motivation are the stuff from which champions and the changed guard are made! We are champions!

The challenge to you and to me is to be inspired, motivated examples! There is no other reasonable response to the challenge of accountability offered to us!

"Daddy, Show Me How To Do It"

A few months ago out in California, a frustrated little girl was overheard to say, "Daddy, show *me* how to do it." Have you ever been told you were doing something wrong, but knew of no option? How many television specials have you viewed in which the subject addressed, bashed you with uncertainty and fear about environmental disasters, damming public practices or willful, even criminal neglect and lack of concern?

Are you a ribbon wearer who lets the world know you care about a cause? And exactly what cause? Are you brave enough to start a friendly discussion with someone wearing a like ribbon, about ways the two of you could do more than just wear ribbons? Would the two of you actually do something about finding and practicing answers?

Are you a marcher? It is amazing how much energy is spent and how ardent and adamant some people become to raise awareness about a specific problem, but limit their assistance to marching. Many have concluded, and sadly are teaching by their action, that everything gets better if you just march for the cause. Some marchers have been interviewed who could not define the issues for which they were marching. It was just an activity, and they joined the party. Where are the people in the everyday trenches of life who apply the principles suggested by the marchers? What are all of the marchers doing the next day? Living the correction, or just marching again?

Another question: Do you complete your responsibility to environmental improvement with the payment of an annual membership in an environmental club or group? Is that nothing more than a purchase of salve for our conscience? Do you then assume that you have no further obligation but the payment of your membership fee? Remember, the problems are the problems of "we the people," and solutions for most of these problems will require the participation of "we the people."

Quite often we only wear ribbons or march because we do not really know anything else to do. To be able to respond to the plea, "Daddy, show me how to do it," as it relates to the environmental issues, we must have sound practices available. It is becoming quite evident that defining the problem is only one step. The next step is actually to set up working models: A pattern of workable solutions that would help us all, a standard for comparison and for imitation. Teach us by example! "Daddy, show me how to do it."

The Working Model Construct

As found in geometry, a "construct" includes a drawing or figure that could be used to fulfill given conditions. This construct includes a synthesis of ideas that assist the putting of parts together according to a specific plan or design. To expect an answer when we implore, "Show us how to do it," our construct must include specific (1) proposals, (2) methods, (3) organizational structures, (4) a general policy, and (5) design protocol, all of which serve as a definite plan or road map to be emulated by we the people of spaceship earth.

A "working" model includes the action of operating or producing effects. A working model will pertain to, be connected with, and used in operating the skillful working of the model into a dynamic shape or goal. The development of an energetic working model may be designed to scale in specific detail (see Chapters XII and XIII), and with such explicit directions or dimensions, as to form a guide for the workers, we the people, in the construction of our model.

Webster's Dictionary defines a model as a person or thing regarded as a standard of excellence to be imitated; to display by doing. A medical dictionary defined a model, in general, as a symbolic representation of the interrelations exhibited by a phenomenon with a system or process. An equation is analogous to a model in mathematics.

"Daddy, show me how to do it," indicates the need for each of us to understand and be able to share our working model. Be ready to teach by example.

As we design our own working model, plan for it to be followed as an example or pattern by defining the steps as simply as one, two, three. Know that this model will have positive influence as a counterpart, a facsimile designed for others to conform. This working model construct will delineate and encourage the following five general concepts:

I. PRECEPT OR RULE OF ACTION: This rule will include but not be limited to: Instruction, direction, a charge to keep, sound principles, canon, law, code, a rule of conduct, the golden rule, a working rule, a well defined standard, as well as the unwritten law of personally known oughtness.

II. REPRESENTATION: This awareness will be built around a new image, "the people of the changing of the guard" care and are involved. The movement will be identifiable as being statuary, with dignity, poise, and the salvation of spaceship earth. The change over time will serve as a monument to those courageous people who are available daily to ask, "What can I do to help?" and to be there to serve with their active involvement.

III. MEASUREMENT: Though not always widely known, there are current government standards high enough to serve as gauges for hazardous waste management improvement. These standards should and also will serve as guidelines to help prevent the generation of additional pollution. Are there valid testing measurements that will demonstrate our improvement? The following section will address some of these standards and the testing methods.

IV. VALID RESEARCH AND RECORDING: Included here is a representative design that will demonstrate a process for planning experiments and recording results accurately reflected in at least two aspects: (1) real-life environmental problems to which the working model construct will apply, and (2) reporting the existing characteristics of the present hazardous situations as related to the desired change over time, projected by the proposed working model.

From a scientific researcher's point of view, experiments are attempts to determine the effects of an independent variable. This would include, for example, treatment in the form of the practical application of the principles of a working model construct on the dependent variable. In this case the experimental example will be the short-term or the long-term effects of hazardous activities and polluting materials on our total ecosystem. Not to oversimplify, but this can be viewed as a cause/effect demonstration. We hope for a measured change over time as we apply the principles of this working model to toxic and hazardous problems of today (our data baseline.) We then can measure specific improvement or positive change.

Validity of research is determined by the extent to which a test or measurement, or any other metering device, measures what it is intended to measure. The kinds of validity include (1) content validity, (2) current validity, (3) construct validity, (4) face validity, and (5) predictive validity. If a working model is implemented, by we who are members of the changing of the guard, we can rely upon the predictable validity that our environment and the quality of our personal existence, can prove.

V. NATURE'S NOBILITY: All representations and illustrations to be found in the two working model constructs provided in the following chapters, will involve goodhearted, concerned, and worthy people. They will be made up of benefactors serving as excellent examples who will measure up to the image of assisting a friend in need, representing a true friend indeed. These helping hands will be recognizable as defenders of the working model, protectors of human health, the ecosystem guardians, and the pollution emancipators of spaceship earth.

The Author's Personal Conviction

A few years ago, I became convinced that we could do better, in regard to our environmental responsibilities. We have all heard the environmental horror stories, we have observed the pollution and the waste, and we have all experienced being victims of various deeds of society's greed. I instigated a search to find some alternative answers that could be used as illustrations of a safe substitute for various hazardous and toxic chemicals. I asked, "Is there something that has been overlooked during our scientific evolution and revolution? Must the people sacrifice personal health and the eco-balance of spaceship earth for the sake of progress? Or, might there be some way to find an example of 'how to cause' an improvement, be it ever so slight?" The search was for new formulations that were nontoxic and nonhazardous.

I am happy to report here that the search has been very rewarding! The cost of the working model is very small compared to the total cost of our past destruction. The formulas are very effective, surpassing the old systems with even greater efficiency as well as greatly improved safety. I want to make it very clear at this point that the working models presented in Chapters XII and XIII of this book are only illustrations of two extremely efficient, safe, and cost effective working models. There may be one hundred or two hundred more formulas existing in family operated laboratories, in the closed files of various chemical companies, or on the dusty shelves of university libraries. For example, Frank VanderSloot, President and CEO of Melaleuca, Inc., one of the fastest-growing, home-based businesses in America, listed in INC. 500 for the last five years, provides Melaleuca household products, free of hazardous and toxic chemicals. Just be aware that there is a better way! I challenge you, the chemical companies, and the students and scholars of our universities, to follow the example of these working model constructs with your own research efforts. There is a better way. It has been proven and is being used today!

These two working models will serve as comparative evidence by which you can judge the products you presently use. Look at the Material

Safety Data Sheets (MSDS), study the labels, read the USDA letters, and compare this information with the products you presently are using or selling. These two working models may be much better and safer than what you are using today. Now you have an option. It may be that you will develop another working model; use this working model construct, and Chapters XII and XIII for comparison. If the next working model is superior, by all means, use it. The goal is to care enough to share. Let's do everything we can to improve the ecosystem of our spaceship earth. Join the changing of the guard. Compare and share today. We will make a difference!

The intention of this book is to identify problems, suggest possible solutions, and marshall a highly-motivated and accountable workforce of those who care about solving environmental issues. There will be those who will feel an economic squeeze if their present company cannot compete by selling hazardous pollutants. Anticipate situations where successful salespersons, who have made their contacts over the years and are enjoying the good life, may now see their market cut substantially. Stand by and watch them squeal and squawk. How will they combat new, safe technology? Wait and see. One way of course, is to fight against safety and health. The other, better way is to join the changing of the guard, nature's nobility, and stay healthy, safe, and in tune with saving spaceship earth.

The lines are being drawn on our planet. There will be strong reactions and resistance by the short-sighted, comfortable, and the complacent. Watch for frustration, denial, anger, and perhaps even emotionally filed lawsuits when comfortable but greed-blinded merchants are threatened. We trust these objectors will be big enough and brave enough to care enough to join the "safe way" and become part of nature's nobility.

I have concluded that it will be a challenge and privilege to write a sequel to this book based upon the reaction of the polarized groups of people that will respond to these concepts. The battle lines have been drawn. Our spaceship earth must be preserved through as many safe and remediating working models as we can implement. The issue has come to an interesting case: GREED vs. RESTORATION and PRESERVATION!

For those individuals who observe or personally experience unsatisfactory treatment from persons not adhering to safe chemical practices or persons who continue to "hard sell" unsafe products at your expense, feel free to record your experience and send it to us, documenting the event with names and dates. If I do write a sequel to this book, "I'D RATHER FIGHT (safety) THAN SWITCH (to safety)," we may further investigate the incident, and perhaps your event can serve as an example of the need to improve the attitudes and the methods of many in recapturing a safe environment. Remember the best way for nature's nobility to win this ecological battle to preserve spaceship earth and our very own lives is to practice and teach by your own safe, successful, and responsible example.

Keep in mind, there are persons who are afraid to speak up for their safety, people who naively justify their ignorance at the risk of others, people who take payment or favors "under the table" and thus, intentionally benefit themselves at the risk of others and the environment, people who simply find themselves in a position with no training. Regardless of the reasons, many individuals wear the FATAL PATCH. Share with us by writing to:

JACKSON RESEARCH CENTER
P.O. Box 1749
Evergreen, CO 80439

Comparative Evidence

This section, Comparative Evidence, includes copies of information you can use to compare specifically with the MSDS and label information on the products you are using presently. The Comparative Evidence is organized into groups to correspond with the two working models presented in Chapters XII and XIII.

Note throughout these two working model construct chapters how simple the working model is and how many tasks can be accomplished safely with these two formulations. Best wishes with your personal, positive scrimmage.

ENVIRONMENTAL CARE & SHARE

A GENERAL MULTI-PURPOSE CLEANING CONCENTRATE

ENVIRONMENTALLY SAFE

DIRECTIONS:

1. Apply directly to the surface to be cleaned.
2. Allow adequate dwell time for penetration.
3. Scrub with sponge, cloth or brush.
4. If used to wash fruits or vegetables to remove pesticides or soil, rinse thoroughly.
5. Wipe or rinse area with water to provide clean and residue-free surface.

- NON-TOXIC
- NON-HAZARDOUS
- BIO-DEGRADABLE
- WATER SOLUBLE

CAUTION:

Keep out of reach of children. If splashed in eyes, treat as shampoo; immediately rinse with plenty of water for up to 15 minutes. If accidentally swallowed, drink water to dilute and call physician if negative symptoms occur.

MEETS EPA, OSHA AND CALIFORNIA PROPOSITION 65 STANDARDS

This product is authorized by USDA for use in official establishments operating under the Federal meat, poultry, shell egg grading, and egg products inspection programs.

Manufactured by Enviro Consultant Service, P.O. Box 1749, Evergreen, Colorado 80439.
This label is authorized by and on file with the United States Department of Agriculture, Regulatory Prog., Bldg. 306, BARC-EAST, Beltsville, MD 20705.

United States Department of Agriculture

Food Safety and Inspection Service

Regulatory Programs
Building 306, BARC-East
Beltsville, MD 20705

February 16, 1994

Dr. William R. Jackson
Enviro Consultant Service
Post Office Box 1749
Evergreen, CO 80439

Dear Dr. Jackson:

This is in reply to your request for compound authorization received on January 13, 1994 for your product Environmental Care & Share.

This product is acceptable as a general cleaning agent on all surfaces, or for use with steam or mechanical cleaning devices in all departments of official establishments operating under the Federal meat, poultry, shell egg grading, and egg products inspection programs.

Before using this compound, food products and packaging materials must be removed from the room or carefully protected. After using this compound, surfaces must be thoroughly rinsed with potable water.

Acceptance of compounds by this Department is in no way to be construed as an endorsement of the compounds or of any claims made for them.

If any change is made in the labeling information or formulation, the authorization for use in official plants becomes void immediately.

Sincerely,

John M. Damaré, Chief
Compounds and Packaging Branch
Product Assessment Division

Material Safety Data Sheet

May be used to comply with OSHA's Hazard Communications Standard, 29 CFR 1910. 1200. Standard must be consulted for specific requirements.

QUICK IDENTIFIER
Common Name: (used on label and list)
ENVIRONMENTAL CARE & SHARE (concentrat

SECTION 1 -

Manufacturer's Name	ENVIRO CONSULTANT SERVICE, INC.		
Address	P.O. Box 1749	Emergency Telephone No.	
City, State, and ZIP	Evergreen, Colorado 80439	Other Information Calls	
		Date Prepared	August 23, 1993

SECTION 2 - HAZARDOUS INGREDIENTS/IDENTITY

Hazardous Component(s) (chemical & common name(s))	OSHA PEL	ACGIH TLV	OTHER EXPOSURE% LIMITS (optional)	CAS NO.

COMPLIES WITH OSHA 29 CFR XVII-1910.1200 Section (i). AFFIDAVIT:

CONTAINS NO HAZARDOUS COMPONENTS UNDER CURRENT OSHA DEFINITIONS, EPA LISTI

This formula contains NO ingredients that are on the NPT list or registered with IAR carcinogens and the material mixture tested as a whole has been found to be:

- not toxic
- not corrosive
- not an irritant
- not a sensitiser in oral, dermal and occular tests

(see federal hazardous substance act 16 CFR 1500)

SECTION 3 - PHYSICAL & CHEMICAL CHARACTERISTICS

Boiling Point	200°F @ 1 ATM	Specific Gravity (H_2O=1)	1.017	Vapor Pressure (mm Hg)	17mm @ 68°F
		Vapor Density (Air = 1)	0.62	PH Range	10.3 - 10.6
Solubility in Water	99.94%	Reactivity in Water	REQUIRES DILUTION		
Appearance and Odor	LIGHT YELLOW LIQUID - MILD ODOR	Melting Point	NONE		

SECTION 4 - FIRE & EXPLOSION DATA

Flash Point	N/A	Method Used	P-M CLOSED CUP	Flammable Limits in Air % by Volume		LEL Lower N/A	UFL Upper N/A
Auto-Ignition Temperature	NONE	Extinguisher Media	NONE - PRODUCT DECOMPOSES WITHOUT FLAME; OK WITH DRY CHEMICAL, FOAM, WATER, SPRAY.				
Special Fire Fighting Procedures	NONE - WATER MAY BE USED TO COOL CONTAINERS INVOLVED IN FIRE.						

SECTION 5 - PHYSICAL HAZARDS (REACTIVITY DATA)

Stability — Unstable ____ Stable X — Conditions to Avoid: NONE KNOWN

Incompatibility (Materials to Avoid): THIS MATERIAL WILL NEUTRALIZE MOST ACIDS

Hazardous Decomposition Products: NONE - PRODUCT IS NOT COMBUSTIBLE

Hazardous Polymerization — May Occur ____ Will Not Occur X — Conditions to Avoid: NONE KNOWN

SECTION 6 - HEALTH HAZARDS

1. Acute: NONE KNOWN — 2. Chronic: NONE KNOWN

Signs and Symptoms of Exposure: MAY DRY OUT SENSITIVE SKIN AFTER PROLONGED CONTACT

Medical Conditions Generally Aggravated by Exposure: NONE KNOWN

Chemical Listed as Carcinogen or Potential Carcinogen — National Toxicology Program: Yes ____ No X — I.A.R.C. Monographs: Yes ____ No X — OSHA: Yes ____ No X

Emergency and First Aid Procedures: NONE

ROUTES OF ENTRY

1. Inhalation: NONE UNDER NORMAL USE IN A NORMALLY VENTED AREA
2. Eyes: RINSE THOROUGHLY WITH WATER AS ONE WOULD DO WITH REGULAR SHAMPOO
3. Skin: NONE: FOR SENSITIVE SKIN, SIMPLY RINSE WITH WATER AND APPLY HAND CREAM
4. Ingestion: DRINK LARGE AMOUNTS OF WATER

SECTION 7 - SPECIAL PRECAUTIONS AND SPILL/LEAK PROCEDURES

Precautions to be Taken in Handling and Storage: KEEP CONTAINER TIGHTLY SEALED - WILL STRATIFY AT 32°F

MAY BE THAWED AND RE-MIXED

Other Precautions: AREA OF SPILL MAY BECOME SLIPPERY - FLUSH WITH WATER TO DISPERSE

Steps to be Taken in Case Material is Released or Spilled: WASH INTO DRAIN - SAFE FOR SEWER DISPOSAL

Waste Disposal Methods (Consult federal, state, and local regulations): NO SPECIAL REQUIREMENTS

SECTION 8 - SPECIAL PROTECTION INFORMATION/CONTROL MEASURES

Respiratory Protection (Specify Type): NONE REQUIRED

Ventilation: NORMAL — Local Exhaust: NORMAL — Mechanical (General): N/A — Special: N/A — Other: N/A

Protective Gloves: NOT REQUIRED — Eye Protection: NOT REQUIRED, BUT RECOMMENDED

Other Protective Clothing or Equipment: NOT REQUIRED

Work/Hygienic Practices: NORMAL

(33) SURFACE PREPARATION is the removal of contaminants such as dust, soil, oil, grease, etc., prior to coating, adhesive, or ink applications.

(34) ULTRAVIOLET INKS are inks which dry by polymerization reaction induced by ultraviolet energy.

→ (35) VOC COMPOSITE PARTIAL PRESSURE is the sum of the partial pressures of the compounds defined as VOCs.

VOC Composite Partial Pressure is calculated as follows:

$$PP_c = \sum_{i=1}^{n} \frac{(W_i)(VP_i)/MW_i}{\dfrac{W_w}{MW_w} + \dfrac{W_e}{MW_e} + \sum_{i=1}^{n} \dfrac{W_i}{MW_i}}$$

Where:

- W_i = Weight of the "i"th VOC compound, in grams
- W_w = Weight of water, in grams
- W_e = Weight of exempt compound, in grams
- MW_i = Molecular weight of the "i"th VOC compound, in $\frac{g}{g\text{-mole}}$
- MW_w = Molecular weight of water, in $\frac{g}{g\text{-mole}}$
- MW_e = Molecular weight of exempt compound, in $\frac{g}{g\text{-mole}}$
- PP_c = VOC composite partial pressure at 20°C, in mm Hg
- VP_i = Vapor pressure of the "i"th VOC compound at 20°C, in mm Hg

(36) VOLATILE ORGANIC COMPOUND (VOC) is any chemical compound which contains the element carbon, excluding methane, carbon monoxide, carbon dioxide, carbonic acid, metallic carbides or carbonates, ammonium carbonate, and exempt compounds.

(37) WIPE CLEANING is the method of cleaning a surface by physically rubbing it with a material such as a rag, paper, or a cotton swab moistened with a solvent.

Dr. Jackson: here's the formula that the AQMD uses. if there is an easier way to determine VOC Partial Pressure they said you can solve it any way. they Need #.

VOC Partial Pressure must be 35 mm Hg or less at 20°C.

John.

industrial
LABORATORIES

THE INDUSTRIAL LABORATORIES COMPANY

Complete Consulting Chemistry Service
Bacteriological & Analytical Testing

1450 East 62nd Avenue
P.O. Box 16207
Denver, Colorado 80216

Analysis Report

To: Dr. William R. Jackson, PhD
P.O. Bos 3577
Evergreen CO 80439

JA6088

Date Received: 03/28/94
Date Reported: 05/05/94

Customer P.O.:

Attn: Dr. Jackson

Lab No.	Sample Description	Test	Result Units
IL94102382	So. Ca. Edison; Part #ECO-D050J	Vapor Pressure Determination	0.0015 mm Hg
IL94102383	Enviro Consultant Service	Vapor Pressure Determination	0.0031 mm Hg

Environmental Care and Share Degreaser

The VOC Composite Partial Pressure was calculated using the formula supplied to The Industrial Laboratories Company by Dr. Jackson (see attached photocopy) from the Southcoast Air Quality Management District; Rule 1171.

Dr. Jackson provided The Industrial Laboratories Company with the names and Chemical Abstract Service number of the five compounds present in the aqueous solution. No compound was present at greater than 1% in IL94102393 or greater than 0.5% in IL94102382. Molecular weights and vapor pressures of these compounds were obtained from references such as the Handbook of Chemistry & Physics, MSDS information and the Sigma Aldrich Library of Chemical Safety Data. Where data could only be obtained as "less than" values, the maximum number was used.

DATA:

Compound 1
Valpa Pressure (V.P.) at 20° C = 0.6 mm Hg
Molecular Weight (M.W.) = 118

Compound 2
V.P. at 20° C = 0.2 mm Hg
M.W. = 61

Compound 3
V.P. at 20° C = <1 mm Hg
M.W. = 270

Compound 4
V.P. at 20° C = <1 mm Hg
M.W. = 290

Compound 5
V.P. at 20° C = <1 mm Hg
M.W. = 1000

Water
M.W. = 18

Calculated VOC Composite Partial Pressure
IL94102382 = 0.0015 mm Hg
IL94103283 = 0.0031 mm Hg

James A. Kinsinger, PhD.

SOUTH COAST AIR QUALITY MANAGEMENT DISTRICT
21865 E. Copley Dr., Diamond Bar, CA 91765-4182

APPLIED SCIENCE AND TECHNOLOGY
REPORT OF LABORATORY ANALYSIS

TO: Edwin Pupka, Sr. Manager
Administrative Services Team
Stationary Source Compliance

LAB REPORT DATE: MAR 08 1994

LABORATORY NO. 90564-01
MR 94-0011

REFERENCE NO. SK-14-95

SAMPLE DESCRIPTION:

Industrial cleaner/degreaser

DATE SAMPLE RECEIVED: 2-24-94

SUBMITTED BY: J. Strayer

SAMPLE SOURCE: Env. Conscious Options Inc.
733 Veneto, Irvine

ANALYTICAL WORK PERFORMED, METHOD OF ANALYSIS, AND RESULTS

Volatile Organic Content (VOC) determined by SCAQMD Method 304-91.
(re. Environmental Care & Share, dispersant/degreaser)

VOC, g/L (of coating) = 260

Approved By: [signature] 3/7/94
Corazon B. Choa
Principal A.Q. Chemist

(c) Requirements

(1) Solvent Requirements

A person shall not use a solvent to perform solvent cleaning operations, including the use of cleaning devices or methods, unless the solvent complies with the applicable requirements set forth below:

(A) Substrates Cleaning During Manufacturing Processes, and Surface Preparation for Coating, Adhesive, or Ink Applications.

The solvents used on substrates for cleaning during the manufacturing process or for surface preparation prior to coating, adhesive, or ink applications shall contain VOC equal to or less than the limits specified below:

(i) On and after July 1, 1992, the limit shall be 200 grams of VOC per liter of material.

(ii) On and after July 1, 1993, the limit shall be 70 grams of VOC per liter of material.

(B) Repair and Maintenance Cleaning

On and after July 1, 1992, the solvents used for repair or maintenance cleaning shall have a VOC content of 900 grams or less of VOC per liter of material and a VOC composite partial pressure of 20 mm Hg or less at 20°C (68° F).

(C) Cleaning of Coatings and Adhesives Application Equipment

On and after July 1, 1992, the solvents used for cleaning coatings or adhesives application equipment shall have a VOC content of 950 grams or less of VOC per liter of material and a VOC composite partial pressure of 35 mm Hg or less at 20°C (68° F).

(D) Cleaning of Polyester Resin Application Equipment

On and after July 1, 1992, the solvents used for cleaning polyester resin application equipment shall comply with one of the limits specified below:

(i) The solvent shall have a VOC content of 200 grams or less of VOC per liter of material; or

(ii) The solvent shall have a VOC content of 1100 grams or less of VOC per liter of material and a VOC composite partial pressure of 1.0 mm Hg or less at 20°C (68°F); or

(iii) A solvent reclamation system shall be used if the solvent contains more than 200 grams of VOC per liter of material or the solvent has a VOC composite partial pressure of more than 1.0 mm Hg at 20°C (68°F) and contains more than 1100 grams of VOC per liter of material, and the solvent usage exceeds four (4) gallons per day per facility. The reclamation system shall operate at least at 80 percent efficiency. The solvent residues for on-site reclamation system shall not contain more than 20 percent VOC, by weight.

(E) Cleaning of Ink Application Equipment

On and after July 1, 1992, the solvents used for cleaning of ink application equipment in graphic arts shall meet the limits specified below:

(i) The solvents used in screen printing shall have a VOC content of 1070 grams or less of VOC per liter of material and a VOC composite partial pressure of 5 mm Hg or less at 20°C (68°F).

(ii) The solvents used in lithographic and letterpress printing not subject to (c)(1)(E)(iv) shall have a VOC content of 900 grams or less of VOC per liter of material and a VOC composite partial pressure of 25 mm Hg or less at 20°C (68°F).

(iii) The solvents used in graphic arts printing operations not subject to (c)(1)(E)(i), (c)(1)(E)(ii), or (c)(1)(E)(iv) shall have a VOC content of 100 grams or less of VOC per liter of material and a VOC composite partial pressure of 3 mm Hg at 20°C (68°F).

(iv) The solvents used in graphic arts printing operations, except screen printing to remove ultraviolet inks from application equipment shall have a VOC content of 800 grams or less of VOC per liter of material and a VOC composite partial pressure of 33 mm Hg or less at 20°C (68°F).

EC&S BIO-STIMULANT

May be used for ANIMAL WASTE CONTROL, DRAIN, GREASE TRAP, SEWER TREATMENT and COMPOSTING OPERATIONS

ENVIRONMENTALLY SAFE

- NON-TOXIC
- NON-HAZARDOUS
- 100% BIO-DEGRADABLE
- WATER SOLUBLE

MEETS EPA, OSHA AND CALIFORNIA PROPOSITION 65 STANDARDS

This product is authorized by USDA for use in official establishments operating under the Federal meat, poultry, shell egg grading, and egg products inspection programs.

Manufactured by Enviro Consultant Service, P.O. Box 1749, Evergreen, Colorado 80439.
This label is authorized by and on file with the United States Department of Agriculture, Regulatory Prog., Bldg. 306, BARC-EAST, Beltsville, MD 20705.

DIRECTIONS:

1. FEEDLOTS & POULTRY HOUSES: mix 1 to 10 with water and spray every 2 weeks. Misting with fogger equipment in the presence of animals is optional.
2. MANURE PONDS & LAGOONS: mix 1 to 10 with water and spray on the surface every two weeks.
3. DRAINS: pour 1 to 2 qt. down the drain as needed.
4. GREASE TRAPS: add 1 to 2 gal. every 14 days, or as needed.
5. SEWAGE TREATMENT and ODOR ABATEMENT: mix 1 to 10 with water and spray on the surface area.
6. User friendly with Environmental Care & Share multi-purpose degreaser.

CAUTION:

Keep out of reach of children. If splashed in eyes, flush with fresh water up to 15 minutes. For sensitive skin, flush with water. If accidentally swallowed, dilute by drinking water; may give milk and egg whites, and call a physician if negative symptoms occur. Do not freeze.

Material Safety Data Sheet

May be used to comply with OSHA's Hazard Communications Standard.
29 CFR 1910.1200. Standard must be consulted for specific requirements.

QUICK IDENTIFIER
Common Name: (used on label and list)
EC&S BIO-STIMULANT

SECTION 1 -

Manufacturer's Name: ENVIRO CONSULTANT SERVICE, INC.

Address: P.O. BOX 1749

Emergency Telephone No.

City, State, and ZIP: EVERGREEN, COLORADO 80439

Other Information Calls

Date Prepared: AUGUST 23, 1993

SECTION 2 - HAZARDOUS INGREDIENTS/IDENTITY

Hazardous Component(s) (chemical & common name(s))	OSHA PEL	ACGIH TLV	OTHER EXPOSURE% LIMITS (optional)	CAS NO.

COMPLIES WITH OSHA 29 CFR XVII-1910.1200 Section (i). AFFIDAVIT:

CONTAINS NO HAZARDOUS COMPONENTS UNDER CURRENT OSHA DEFINITIONS, OR EPA LIST

This material contains NO ingredients that are on the NPT list or registered with for carcinogens and the material mixture tested as a whole has been found to be:

-- non toxic

-- non corrosive

-- not an irritant

-- not a sensitiser in oral, dermal and occular tests

(see Federal Hazardous Substance Act 16 CFR 1500)

SECTION 3 - PHYSICAL & CHEMICAL CHARACTERISTICS

Boiling Point: N/A

Specific Gravity ($H_2O = 1$): N/A

Vapor Pressure (mm Hg): N/A

Vapor Density (Air = 1): N/A

PH Range: 6.5

Solubility in Water: 20%

Reactivity in Water:

Appearance and Odor: CLEAR & MILD ODOR

Melting Point: N/A

SECTION 4 - FIRE & EXPLOSION DATA

Flash Point: NONE

Method Used: NONE

Flammable Limits in Air % by Volume: NONE

LEL Lower: NONE

UEL Upper: NONE

Auto-Ignition Temperature: N/A

Extinguisher Media: DOES NOT BURN

SECTION 5 - PHYSICAL HAZARDS (REACTIVITY DATA)

Stability	Unstable ___ Stable X	Conditions to Avoid	NONE KNOWN
Incompatibility (Materials to Avoid)	STRONG OXIDIZERS		
Hazardous Decomposition Products	NONE KNOWN		
Hazardous Polymerization	May Occur ___ Will Not Occur X	Conditions to Avoid	NONE KNOWN

SECTION 6 - HEALTH HAZARDS

1. Acute NONE 2. Chronic NONE

Signs and Symptoms of Exposure: SAME AS ACUTE AND CHRONIC

Medical Conditions Generally Aggravated by Exposure: SEE ROUTES OF ENTRY

Chemical Listed as Carcinogen or Potential Carcinogen	National Toxicology Program	Yes ___ No X	I.A.R.C. Monographs	Yes ___ No X	OSHA	Yes ___ No X

Emergency and First Aid Procedures: SEE ROUTES OF ENTRY

ROUTES OF ENTRY		
	1. Inhalation	NONE
	2. Eyes	FLUSH WITH FRESH WATER; GET MEDICAL ATTENTION IF IRRITATION CONTINUES
	3. Skin	SENSITIVE SKIN - FLUSH WITH WATER
	4. Ingestion	GIVE MILK, WATER, EGG WHITES, ETC.

SECTION 7 - SPECIAL PRECAUTIONS AND SPILL/LEAK PROCEDURES

Precautions to be Taken in Handling and Storage: KEEP CONTAINER COVERED

Other Precautions: NONE

Steps to be Taken in Case Material is Released or Spilled: IF MATERIAL IS RELEASED OR SPILLED, MOP UP

Waste Disposal Methods (Consult federal, state, and local regulations): VOLUNTARY; CAUTIONS ON CONTAINER LABEL

SECTION 8 - SPECIAL PROTECTION INFORMATION/CONTROL MEASURES

Respiratory Protection (Specify Type): NONE

Ventilation	Local Exhaust	Mechanical (General)	Special	Other
	NONE	NORMAL AIR DILUTION	NO	NO

Protective Gloves: NONE Eye Protection: NONE

Other Protective Clothing or Equipment: NONE

Work/Hygienic Practices: NONE

United States Department of Agriculture

Food Safety and Inspection Service

Regulatory Programs
Building 306, BARC-East
Beltsville, MD 20705

March 04, 1994

Dr. William R. Jackson
Enviro Consultant Service
Post Office Box 1749
Evergreen, CO 80439

Dear Dr. Jackson:

This is in reply to your request for compound authorization received on December 27, 1993 for your product E C & S Bio-Stimulant.

This product is acceptable for use in sewage and/or drain lines of official establishments operating under the Federal meat, poultry, shell egg grading, and egg products inspection programs. This laboratory must be provided with records of salmonellae analysis for each new lot of this enzymatic cleaner prepared for use in such establishments. Analysis must be conducted by a qualified microbiological laboratory.

If the above condition is not fulfilled, or, if future analysis shows the presence of salmonellae and/or other pathogenic microorganisms, authorization will be cancelled.

Acceptance of compounds by this Department is in no way to be construed as an endorsement of the compounds or of any claims made for them.

If any change is made in the labeling information or formulation, the authorization for use in official plants becomes void immediately.

Sincerely,

John M. Damaré, Chief
Compounds and Packaging Branch
Product Assessment Division

XII

WORKING MODEL ONE: EC&S DISPERSANT AND DEGREASER

Chapter Outline

Introduction

Is it possible to have your shop, home, school, and commercial area safe and clean, and to eliminate most toxic and hazardous cleaning products while still watching the financial bottom line? It must be remembered that health and safety issues, as well as compliance with environmental laws, liability concerns, and insurance coverage, must be taken into consideration when a business looks at its financial bottom line. EC&S Dispersant a concentrated, commercial grade cleaner that:

- Meets all published OSHA regulatory requirements
- Meets all published EPA regulatory requirements
- Meets all published DOT regulatory requirements
- Contains no ingredients listed in California Proposition 65-The Safe Drinking Water & Toxic Enforcement Act of 1986
- Meets Air Quality Control Standards
- Has USDA approval for use under the Federal meat, poultry, shell egg grading, and egg products inspection program

In our world today, virtually everything must be cleaned for SAFETY, SANITATION, FUNCTIONAL ABILITY, or AESTHETIC reasons. As our population densities continue to increase, and health, hygiene and environmental standards are upgraded, emphasized, and enforced, there is a growing awareness of, and demand for a clean environment. A clean environment is mandatory for our survival.

Our environment includes everything that surrounds us, what we wear, touch, breathe, and all that we take into our bodies. It has been reported that people in the United States spend approximately 14 billion dollars annually for cleaning agents either by choice or government mandate. The problem is that most of the cleaning agents presently available are hazardous to the environment and to the user. In many cases the cleaning agent itself is more hazardous than the substance it is removing.

EC&S Dispersant, as referred to in this chapter, is a concentrate. For each special use, the USER must dilute it with water in a specified dilution ratio. The word "PRODUCT" in this chapter refers to EC&S Dispersant diluted to a ratio for a specified application.

Every cleaning task is different. The dilution ratios included on the product container and mentioned here are only guidelines. You may carefully analyze your intended use and experiment with dilution ratios, thus discovering and demonstrating that a specific solution is actually the best solution to use for that situation. EC&S Dispersant products are specially formulated and compounded to provide:

- CLEANER SURFACES at
- LOWER COSTS, while being
- COMPLETELY SAFE
- FOR PEOPLE and the
- ENVIRONMENT

Powerful Benefits

From the day consumers start to use EC&S Dispersant liquid cleaning products, they will begin to change the way they think about cleaning. The EC&S Dispersant range is versatile, powerful, cost-effective, and completely safe. EC&S Dispersant is a complete HYGIENE SYSTEM.

VERSATILITY: The EC&S Dispersant range of products will clean anything from heavy machinery to delicate crystal, from washing out the inside of an oil tanker to washing your hands. The product is very hygienic which makes it ideal for use in "clean" environments such as hospitals, laboratories, and electronic-component manufacturing plants. It can be used in hard, soft, and salt water, and works remarkably well even in cold water. EC&S Dispersant has minimal foaming, eliminating the problems often associated with disposal of effluent. These formulations mean you no longer have to specify, buy, store, and apply a wide range of harsh chemical cleaners. EC&S Dispersant products will replace those chemical products saving you storage and administration costs.

POWERFUL CLEANING ACTION: EC&S Dispersant achieves this wide range of successful applications due to its unique formulation. The special molecular action in EC&S Dispersant emulsifies greases, oils, and dirts while the chelating action of the product removes carbon deposits and breaks down calcium and other scaling substances. EC&S Dispersant also removes the proteins, substrates, and other invisible substances to which dirt, grease, and bacteria adhere. This means:

1. Cleaned surfaces will stay cleaner longer;
2. Subsequent cleaning becomes easier; and
3. The frequency of cleaning is reduced.

For the same reasons, using EC&S Dispersant products substantially reduces bacteria levels.

APPLICATION SAFETY: Unlike other heavy-duty cleaning products, the EC&S Dispersant materials contain no phosphates, no nitrates, no sulphates, no caustics, no enzymes, nor solvents. EC&S products are CLEAR, ODORLESS LIQUIDS, WHICH ARE NONTAINTING, NONTOXIC and NONFLAMMABLE. The products will not damage any material that can be washed in water, and will not damage animals or plants. You can use and store EC&S products wherever you like. These products can be used without protective clothing and clean soil and grease from the user's hands gently and safely, posing no threat to the cleaning staff.

EC&S Dispersant rinses off easily with water and can be washed away directly into the main drainage system without danger because it is 100% biodegradable in seven days-an ideal period from an environmental point of view, neither too slow which could lead to pollution, nor too fast, acting as a bio-stimulant, that could upset the natural cycle of decomposition in soil and water. Most cleaners on the market cannot claim to be so powerful while also being environmentally beneficial, a benefit that is especially important in this pollution-conscious era.

EQUIPMENT LIFE EXTENDED: Unlike other cleaners, EC&S Dispersant products are not caustic, abrasive, or acidic. Therefore, metals and plastics such as aluminum and vinyls can be cleaned regularly without the risk of life-shortening pitting or cracking.

RISK-FREE MACHINERY: The safe, low-sudsing EC&S Dispersant products are ideal for use in pressure washers, automatic jet and spray systems, automatic clothes washers, powered floor scrubbers, and "cleaning-in-place" systems. In fact, using EC&S Dispersant products in such equipment will prevent calcium and other scaling in lines and hoses.

COST SAVING FACTS: Using EC&S Dispersant will reduce the frequency of cleaning, even when used in diluted form. Cleaned surfaces will stay cleaner longer, reducing cleaning costs and making cleaning tasks quicker and easier. EC&S Dispersant products continue working for longer periods of time than conventional cleaners. Even though a solution of EC&S Dispersant may look dirty after performing several cleaning tasks, its molecular action is still working and it is able to continue its effectual cleaning action. This special ability leads to an added benefit while using EC&S Dispersant cleaning products. When rinsed down the drain after normal cleaning tasks, the remaining EC&S Dispersant products will clean, maintain, and de-scale all drains, sumps, grease traps, and pipe work. Therefore, you should seldom have to spend money on cleaning drains again. In addition, the purchased EC&S Dispersant is more concentrated than most cleaning products and thus provides more cleaning power per unit cost. Because this product is so safe, it will reduce hazards in the workplace and therefore reduce expenses of sick leave, accidents, fire insurance, and other safety and first aid provisions.

ENVIRONMENTAL PROTECTION: EC&S Dispersant products are environmentally beneficial. They are all 100% biodegradable within seven days and present NO HEALTH HAZARDS IN STORAGE OR APPLICATION.

EC&S DISPERSANT IS NOT:

- IS NOT hazardous to humans, animals, or the environment
- IS NOT flammable in any dilution at any temperature
- IS NOT explosive; does not possess explosive or rapid expansion characteristics
- IS NOT fuming; breathing and/or ventilation devices are not required during or after usage
- IS NOT caustic; will not burn nor irritate human skin, eyes, or internal organs; will not damage plants
- IS NOT a soap
- IS NOT a petroleum-based solvent
- IS NOT toxic or hazardous

- IS NOT an effluent problem; it is easy to dispose of because it has minimal foaming and is low-sudsing

- IS NOT a standard chemical cleaner; does not contain phosphates, nitrates, sulphates, caustic substances, enzymes, or other known pollutants

WHAT IS EC&S DISPERSANT?

EC&S Dispersant products include low-sudsing, emulsifying, degreasing suspension agents. These products are a homogenous blend of colloids, sequestrants, wetting agents, and surfactants that create a unique cleansing action as the result of ongoing random movement of atoms that separate, lift, and hold in suspension oil, dirt, and fat molecules to allow rinsing or washing away. This unique cleansing process works in a wider range of application than most known alternative and competitive products.

REMEMBER: WATER MUST BE PRESENT for the cleaning action described. The water may be hard or soft, fresh or salt water, hot or cold. Hot water adds energy and accelerates the cleaning action, but is not essential for the success of

EC&S Dispersant products. Due to the unique colloidal structure, molecular cleaning action will continue as long as moisture is present to TRANSPORT AWAY suspended oil, dirt, and biodegradable residues.

- EC&S IS EFFECTIVE FOR VIRTUALLY ALL CLEANING APPLICATIONS. It includes heavy-duty, highly concentrated, colloidal degreasing products.

- EC&S IS COMPLETELY SAFE. It holds no known risk for people or the environment in use, application, or storage.

- EC&S IS ECONOMICAL to purchase, use and store. Used with large amounts of water, it keeps working when other products would be exhausted.

- EC&S IS STABLE AND LONG-LASTING IN STORAGE.

- EC&S IS VERSATILE. Simply change the dilution for different tasks (as indicated in this chapter.)

- EC&S IS PLEASANT TO USE, leaves no unpleasant after-effects, no residue, no odor.

- EC&S IS EFFECTIVE IN HOT AND COLD WATER.
- EC&S IS DOUBLY-EFFICIENT. With regular use, it keeps drains, sumps, and grease traps clean without any additional mechanical or chemical treatment.
- EC&S APPEARS UNEQUALED BY ANY OTHER INDIVIDUAL CLEANING PRODUCT OR COMBINATION OF PRODUCTS.
- EC&S IS KIND TO HANDS; will not harm or dry out normal skin.
- EC&S IS 100% BIODEGRADABLE IN SEVEN DAYS.

How Does It Work?

A basic knowledge of other cleaning products is necessary to make correct application recommendations and to explain to users the difference between caustic and noncaustic cleaning agents. EC&S Dispersant products contain inorganic materials and do not contain carbon or carbon derivatives. Inorganic compounds clean by a saponifier action (ability to form emulsions.) Dirt, grease, and other soilage is reformed or broken down and removed from the surface where it was attached.

Chemically determined pH is a common comparison measurement of all cleaning agents. Products with a pH between 1 and 7 are very strong to mildly acidic; pure water is neutral, with a pH of thus 7; pH values between 7 and 14 are mildly to very strongly alkaline. EC&S Dispersant concentrate has a pH of 10.3 - 10.6; pH values of the various EC&S Dispersant products may range downward as low as 8 because of dilutants and additives.

COMPARATIVE EXAMPLES:

1. Heavy Duty Alkaline Cleaners: Average pH range from 11 to 14. Usually powdered, such as most laundry detergents. Generally contain some phosphates, chlorides, surfactants, etc. Many are buffered to prevent corrosion on nonferrous metals.

   EC&S Dispersant products DO NOT contain phosphates, nitrates, NTA, enzymes, sulfates, sulfonates, caustics, or any other known pollutants or irritants that are included in the majority of other cleaning products.

NOTE: EC&S Dispersant products are safe for use on any surface that is compatible with water (pH 7.)

2. <u>Heavy Duty Acid Cleaners</u>: These cleaners generally have a pH range of 3.0 to 6.6; usually liquid, normally used in processes in conjunction with other acid processes to avoid the neutralizing effect of mixing with alkaline cleaners.

3. <u>Solvent Based Cleaners</u>: These cleaners include solvents or kerosene-based, types of compounds (vapor degreasing using trichloroethylene or perchloroethylene are the most commonly used.) Emulsion types, although highly selective, for specific applications, are also included in this group. Emulsions are solvent-based products with chlorinated hydrocarbons that are <u>miscible</u> with water and as such, turn milky white in a complete water mix. Solvents can be used with or without water.

GOOD NEWS: EC&S Dispersant products may be used instead of many solvent cleaners, thereby

ELIMINATING the hazards of using flammable materials that are toxic to the user and the environment. In addition, the use of EC&S can eliminate expensive hazardous-waste disposal and EPA reporting, or air quality control monitoring.

4. Decarbonizers: Baked-on carbons from exhausts, varnishes, fuel glazes, etc. are very difficult to remove. Gunk and carburetor cleaners are common commercial decarbonizers, usually available at aircraft and automotive shops. Government and industry regulations require that all decarbonizers and cleaners used on aircraft contain natural-occurring or added buffers or inhibitors to prevent attack on nonferrous metals that could damage the aircraft through hydrogen embrittlement or other molecular action.

EC&S Dispersant products may be used instead of decarbonizers. Although the dwell time is longer than conventional decarbonizers, the trade-off is attractive because it eliminates the fire and toxic materials hazards, as well as the possibility of damage to nonferrous metal components.

SUPER WET WATER: WHY? Water is not really super wet until certain physiochemical actions occur. The following illustration is a highly simplified picture of the manner in which the colloidal particles, called micelles, perform, in reducing the surface tension of water (even in a very dilute solution.) A micelle is an electrically charged particle formed by a collection of molecules found in certain electrolyte solutions, such as cleaning agents. Each is about one ten-millionth of a centimeter (0,000,000.01 cm) in size. Although the physical action is electrical in nature, it is perhaps more understandably "hydrophilic," or having an affinity for water. The rectangular ends may be regarded as "hydrophobic" or being antagonistic to water.

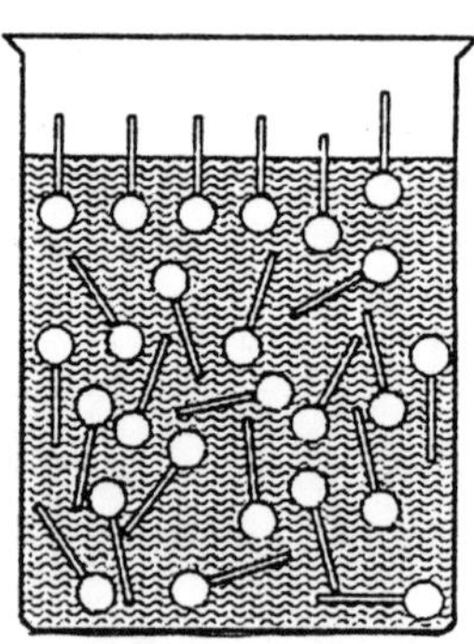

It has been demonstrated that substances such as petroleum compounds, waxes, the more complex alcohols, oil soluble dyes, and other substances that are insoluble in dilute detergent solutions WILL dissolve in a solution that contains these colloidal particles called micelles. In laboratory tests, the dyne/centimeter surface tension of tap water has been halved by adding as little as 1/3250th part of substances like EC&S Dispersant.

This documented information helps explain WHY EC&S has such a variety of uses. The diluted EC&S Dispersant products can have the properties of a soap, a detergent, a solvent, or other cleaners, AND YET BE NONE OF THESE IN ITSELF. EC&S Dispersant provides outstanding performance while maintaining its safety.

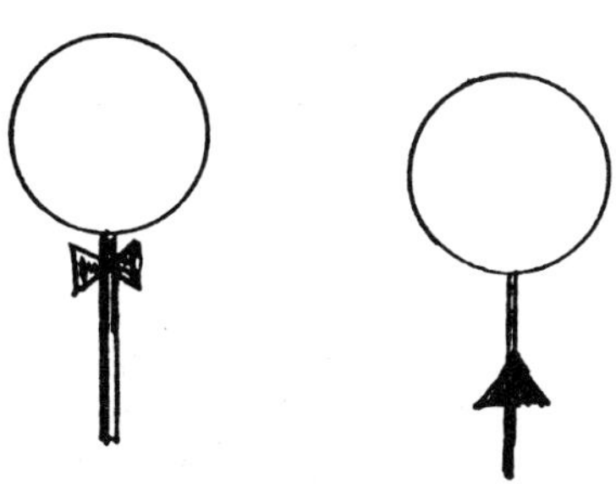

Michael & Michelle
"The **MICELLE** Twins"

The agents used in EC&S Dispersant products readily form stable micelles with oil and greases found free or bound to soil particles. The way in which the micelles are formed is illustrated in the diagram below:

WATER PHASE

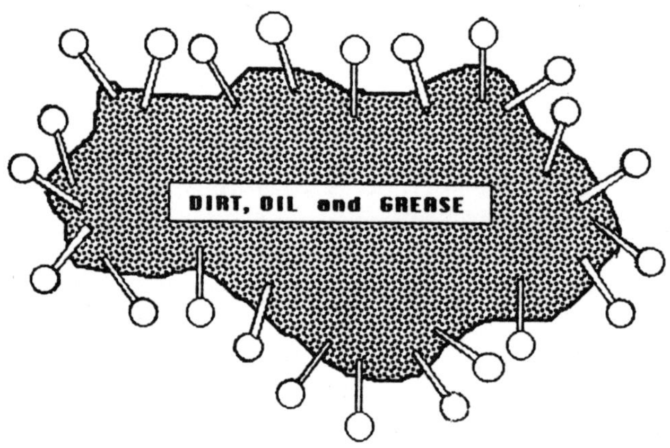

The constituents of EC&S Dispersant products integrate with dirt and grease adhering to a surface. The EC&S Dispersant molecule, which looks something like a match (○————) inserts its long stalk (——————————) into the dirt deposit. This long stalk (——————————) is hydrophobic, it does not associate with water but readily associates with dirt and grease, etc. The "match head" (○) attached to the long stalk is hydrophilic, it associates or has an affinity with water. The "match head" will protrude from the surface of the deposit, enabling the water to acquire and remove dirt and grease. Because there is a considerable quantity of water in all EC&S Dispersant products and more water is used in the rinsing process, the dirt and grease is removed. Thus the surface is cleaned. The following diagram illustrates this process:

THE CLEANING PROCESS:

Any cleaning process requires the interaction of:

1. Cleaning solution
2. Dwell time
3. Energy (heat)
4. Agitation

The Cleaning Pie

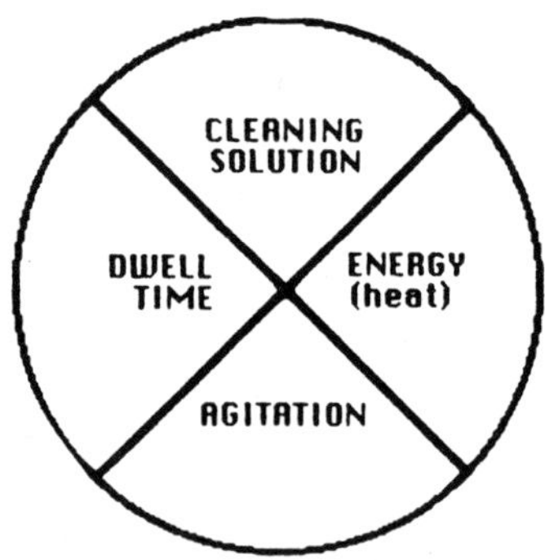

A decrease of one factor requires a balancing increase of another factor(s) to accomplish the process. Example: decreasing the volume or concentration of solution requires an increase of one or all of the remaining factors to enable the agent to clean.

1. CLEANING SOLUTION: Concentrate ratios and chemical composition determine what a product will clean and the amount of the other three factors necessary for the product to work.

The recommended EC&S Dispersant product ratios for various applications are found throughout this chapter. Remember, because EC&S Dispersant products are totally safe, there is no hazard, risk, or contingent liability if the user deliberately, inadvertently, or accidentally increases the concentration ratios, although excess concentrate will be used and cleaning costs will be increased unnecessarily.

NOTE: Chemicals, minerals, hardness, and pollutants in the water may affect optional dilution ratios. Some experimentation may be needed to determine the best dilution ratios of concentrates with water for each application and specific use.

According to manufacturers of EC&S Dispersant, the information on the label and the recommendations made are based upon product research of independent laboratories and are believed to be accurate. No guarantee of accuracy is made, however, and unless otherwise expressly provided in written contract, the product is sold without conditions or warranties, expressed or implied. Users should make their own tests to determine the suitability of such products for their particular purposes. Nothing contained herein shall be construed to be a recommendation to use, or a license to operate under, or infringe on any existing patents.

2. <u>DWELL TIME</u>: EC&S Dispersant products NEED A BRIEF PERIOD OF TIME FOR THE CEASELESS RANDOM MOVEMENT OF ATOMS TO SEPARATE, LIFT AND FORM SUSPENSION BONDS WITH THE SUBSTANCE CAUSING A SOIL. DWELL TIME is VARIABLE because of concentrations and the substance comprising the soil, but it may be as brief as 15 seconds.

DWELL TIME SHOULD BE EXPLAINED AND DEMONSTRATED to potential users as a HIGHLY-DESIRABLE TRADE-OFF to other cleaners that use highly toxic and/or caustic ingredients to shorten dwell time, and make the product work more quickly.

PICTURE IT THIS WAY: ATOMS AND MOLECULES RUNNING AROUND INTRODUCING THEMSELVES TO EACH

OTHER AND SELECTING AN APPROPRIATE COUNTERPART TO WHICH TO CLING. THIS PROCESS TAKES TIME, RANGING FROM A FEW SECONDS TO A FEW MINUTES.

3. ENERGY: Hot water (heat) accelerates the cleaning action by increasing the rate of atom movements, but is not as essential for use with EC&S Dispersant products as it is with most other cleaning agents. Consumers in many applications should be advised that they can reduce operating costs by using cold water with EC&S Dispersant products. This reduces or eliminates the use of hot water, which is normally a high-cost item that a consumer fails to consider when calculating cleaning costs.

4. AGITATION: Stirring, rubbing, brushing, etc. increases molecular contact to affect the cleaning process. Brushing may be necessary on deeply irregular surfaces, such as deep grain vinyl, to break the air barrier that forms in the bottom of the valley and prevents the cleaning product from contacting the dirt. Agitation can be used to increase effectiveness and

reduce dwell time and solution concentration.

GENERAL INFORMATION:

WE EMPHASIZE THESE FACTORS IN CERTAIN INDUSTRIES WHERE COST AND EFFICIENCY ARE IMPORTANT.

1. The product is biodegradable in the environment in the optimum desirable time of seven (7) days. EC&S Dispersant products destroy molecular bonds of oil and dirt, and facilitate biodegrading into a natural, harmless state. This is important because a substance that biodegrades too quickly is a bio-stimulant and a pollutant. Substances that biodegrade in excess of 7 days are classified as "hard" chemicals and may be hazardous to human health.

2. The product is disposable in any sewer or septic system because it is biodegradable and will not have a negative effect on the sewage treatment system. Check with your local sewage plant if there are questions. It cleans drains and traps as

it passes through and continues biodegrading residues carried out in suspension, thereby aiding instead of burdening the sewer system. Eliminating plumbing maintenance and repairs is a very important aspect of using EC&S Dispersant products because this factor is a real cost-saver to the user. This savings is in addition to the normal 30% (+ or -) the customer saves on cleaning products.

3. EC&S Dispersant products should be thought of and used as ALTERNATIVE cleaning products that achieve SUPERIOR cleaning results, yet are SAFER for the user and environment than common competitive products.

4. EC&S Dispersant products ARE NOT soaps, detergents, or petroleum solvents and therefore DO NOT display the visual actions (bubbling, foaming, or sudsing) nor give off harsh toxic odors normally associated with cleaning products. Foaming, coloring, and/or odorous additives may be added to comply with the customer's perception of a cleaning product.

However, these additives do not aid in the cleaning process. EC&S Dispersant products achieve a clean surface WITHOUT the visual activity and strong smells that users' minds are pre-programmed to expect from many years usage of caustic and toxic cleaners.

EC&S Dispersant products DO NOT CONFORM to consumers' concepts of a cleaning product. Until EC&S Dispersant products become widely used and known by the consumers, IT WILL BE NECESSARY TO DEMONSTRATE EFFECTIVELY AND EDUCATE AS MANY TIMES AS NECESSARY TO ASSURE THAT THE PRODUCT IS USED CORRECTLY. Dwell time is important.

Successful education will bring new users and repeat users. Failure to educate will prevent repeat/continued use because the individual and/or user's mind will revert to old, long-standing assumptions and expectations of cleaning products. Statistics indicate that a satisfied user tells three other people about the product, thereby multiplying the initial sales effort by three. A dissatisfied user, however, tells seven other people about the product and can negate all of your best efforts to share.

DILUTION RATES

EC&S-A	(concentrate)
EC&S-B	(one part EC&S-A + two parts water)
EC&S-C	(one part EC&S-A + three parts water)
EC&S-D	(one part EC&S-A + nine parts water)
EC&S-E	(one part EC&S-A + thirty parts water)

Where Can I Use It?

EC&S Dispersant products have already been proven valuable in many situations, including:

- Aerospace industry
- Automotive industry
- Food processing
- Hospitals and clinics
- Hotels
- Household cleaning
- Industrial cleaning
- Manufacturing industries
- Laundry
- Oil industry
- Metal Processing
- Printing
- Paper processing
- Steam & pressure washes
- Resin clean-up
- Universities
- Textiles
- Waste disposal
- Veterinary surgeries
- Laboratories
- Water treatment
- Marine and shipping industries
- Catering, general cleaning and washing
- Commercial degreasing, including office cleaning
- Glass cleaning, including windows and mirrors

Because EC&S Dispersant is PEOPLE SAFE, there is NO need for special equipment or protection when using it to clean. Of course, the best way to find out about EC&S Dispersant products' outstanding qualities is to try the products in your own cleaning tasks.

Model One: Memo Guide

Jackson Research Center

MODEL ONE: **MEMO I**

To: Environmental Health Foundation

From: William R. Jackson, Ph.D., Consultant

Subject: **Aircraft and Airports**

EC&S Dispersant is a liquid cleaner that can be applied to almost every general purpose cleaning need. Application options include:

1. Aircraft, all inside surfaces
2. Exterior of aircraft
3. Cleaning areas inside the hangar such as tire marks, grease, and general traffic spots

AIRCRAFT

EC&S Dispersant is a liquid cleaner that can be applied to almost every aircraft general purpose cleaning need.

INTERIORS

UPHOLSTERY (washable fabric):

Minimum drying time: 1) Beat EC&S-C into a foam; 2) agitate foam into fabric with a stiff brush; and 3) towel dry fabric.

Longer drying time: Follow the general instructions in the "EC&S-C" section (p. XII-502) under "General Upholstery Cleaning," Memo VI.

PLASTIC, FORMICA, AND ACRYLIC SURFACES: EC&S will not scratch, graze, or dry plastic surfaces as often happens with other cleaning products. Spray with EC&S-B, rinse thoroughly with clean, damp cloth. Dry as usual.

CARPETS: Most isolated spots can be removed by spraying with EC&C-C, agitating with a brush or cloth, rinsing with a wet cloth, and then toweling dry or drying with a vacuum cleaner. Also see the "EC&S-B" section (p. XII-474 and XII-499) under "General Commercial Use" and "General Household Use."

INSTRUMENT PANELS AND EARPHONES: Spray on EC&S-D, rinse with soft, damp cloth, and wipe dry with soft cloth.

LAVATORIES: Most aircraft lavatory cleanup can be accomplished with EC&S-D. Severe problems, however, may require EC&S-A or -B. Because EC&S is a colloidal cleaner, it breaks down and encapsulates the very substances on which bacteria rely, thus removing the substances that cause odors.

MIRRORS, WINDOWS, SHINY SURFACES, AND GENERAL GALLEY CLEANING: Spray with EC&S-E, and wipe dry with soft, clean cloth. If streaking occurs, dilute the solution or rinse with clear water and re-dry.

UNIFORMS AND LINENS: Pre-spot washable fabrics with EC&S as described in the "Fabrics-Spotting and Laundry" section (p. XII-514.)

EXTERIORS

GENERAL EXTERIOR CLEANING: EC&S will not harm aircraft surfaces or finishes, and has no limitations in terms of general cleaning. Spray, swab, brush, or wipe on EC&S-D. Agitate with a soft brush if necessary. Rinse well and dry as usual.

CARBON BUILDUP: Apply EC&S-A with a spray to exhaust and fuselage areas where there is a buildup of carbon. Allow 5 to 10 minutes dwell time. Agitate for a few minutes using a soft brush and a light, circular motion. Rinse and dry as usual.

ENGINE PARTS: Apply EC&S-A liberally, allow 5 to 20 minutes dwell time. Rinse off with full or high water pressure. Also see "Motor Vehicle" uses, Memo IX.

REMEMBER to clean from the bottom up, and rinse from the top down.

WARNING: Rinsing is important when cleaning aluminum to avoid darkening due to oxidation. If darkening occurs, simply re-clean with EC&S and rinse thoroughly.

For additional information on how EC&S can be useful, see "Motor Vehicles," Memo IX.

AIRPORT FACILITIES

(Hangars, Aprons, Landing Strips, Loading Areas)

EC&S Dispersant is a highly effective, commercial grade cleaner and degreaser that breaks-up and holds hydrocarbon based substances, such as gasoline, diesel, hydraulic oil, and lubricating oils, in suspension. In most cases, EC&S will eliminate the necessity for hazardous and toxic solvents, thus providing an environmentally safe, worker safe and thoroughly cleaned working environment. Because EC&S encapsulates oils and grease in an irreversible colloidal bond, floors, aprons, loading areas, etc. do not become as slippery as when cleaned with standard detergent or solvent cleaners.

CONCRETE SURFACES:

Pre-Spotting: Spray EC&S-A from a squirt bottle on oil and heavy spots; agitate with a broom, brush, or scrub pad. Allow 20 to 30 minutes dwell time and agitate again if needed. Rinse and dry as usual.

To Maintain Concrete Areas: Apply EC&S-D, allow 15 to 20 minutes dwell time, rinse and dry as usual. EC&S will remove organic based waxes but will not dull acrylic finishes.

NOTE: In the case of very porous surfaces or extra heavy oil and grease, more than one application may be necessary. Even though grease and oil has been removed, stains may still be visible. Time, sun, and repeated applications will continue to lighten visible stains.

REMEMBER: Removal of oil and grease from "walking surfaces" not only helps provide a clean and healthier surface with less tracking from one area to another, but it also helps prevent slipping and falling.

NOTE: Thoroughly rinse blacktop surfaces; asphalt is hydrocarbon based and may deteriorate over time if not rinsed thoroughly.

For additional information on how EC&S can be useful, see "General Household Use," Memo VI, and "General Commercial Use," Memo III.

EC&S Dispersant is:

- nontoxic
- noncaustic
- nonfuming
- nonflammable
- nonexplosive
- USDA authorized

Environmental Care & Share

Jackson Research Center

MODEL ONE: **MEMO II**

To: Environmental Health Foundation

From: William R. Jackson, Ph.D., Consultant

Subject: **Food Processing Industry and Applications**

EC&S Dispersant is the simple solution for cleaning in the food manufacturing and processing industry. It is also an ideal product to use around food, because it is nontoxic and safe for use in food processing areas.

Across industries, nowhere are cleaning tasks so varied, performance so critical, and standards so demanding, as in the food industry. No other single cleaning agent can match this product in meeting the demands for a multi-purpose, powerful, totally safe product.

EC&S Dispersant attacks the toughest jobs around-FATS, GREASE, BLOOD, and FOOD RESIDUES. Yet it is totally safe and gentle to use, leaving NO TAINTS TO TASTE, ODORS, or HARMFUL SUBSTANCES. The powerful products effectively REMOVE THE PROTEIN AND OTHER SUBSTANCES THAT HOLD BACTERIA.

EC&S Dispersant removes the substrates, proteins, and other invisible substances to which dirt, grease, and bacteria adhere. Regular use of EC&S-C, will treat the surfaces being cleaned, keeping those surfaces cleaner and reducing the frequency of cleaning.

EC&S Dispersant includes no caustics, acids, or abrasives. Therefore, it is perfectly safe on aluminum trays and plastics and gives long life to the food plant and its equipment. EC&S-C's special CHELATING action removes calcium and other scaling, thereby maintaining plumbing cleanliness very effectively. When rinsed away after normal use, EC&S-C will clean and maintain DRAINS, SUMPS, and GREASE TRAPS while removing the root causes of odors and bacterial problems associated with such areas.

EC&S Dispersant is SAFE TO USE. Unlike cleaners traditionally used for heavy-duty tasks, this product is safe on skin, is nontainting on foodstuff equipment (including dairy equipment,) and is nonflammable. When in storage, on the production line, or in the presence of MEATS and DAIRY PRODUCTS, EC&S Dispersant presents no risk to equipment, taste of food PRODUCTS, or

PERSONNEL. Even undiluted, it is a clear odorless liquid that is 100% biodegradable within seven days.

EC&S Dispersant is an EFFECTIVE, EFFICIENT, and ECONOMICAL general purpose cleaner for all types of RESTAURANT cleaning jobs. It is safe to use in FOOD PREPARATION AREAS, SERVING AREAS, and as a DISH WASHING liquid. It is 100% rinsable, REMOVING BACTERIA, GERMS, MOLD, AND MILDEW.

EC&S Dispersant WORKS WONDERS FOR CLEANING WALLS, CEILINGS, FLOORS, STAINLESS STEEL SURFACES, APPLIANCES, GLASSES, GREASE TANKS, DRAINS, DEEP FRYERS, AIR FILTERS, AND HOODS. A solution of one part EC&S-A to one part water, or EC&S-B, depending on the difficulty of the task, will clean most HEAVY GREASE and OIL FILMED surfaces, DIRTY FLOORS, and FILTERS. EC&S-E will clean WINDOWS, GLASSWARE, CHANDELIERS, and MIRRORS.

EC&S Dispersant, in a solution of one part EC&S-A to ten parts water, sprayed on ACOUSTICAL TILE and allowed to drip onto a cloth will remove nicotine accumulations, smoke, smog, and general dirt from the ceiling tile. Spray with water to rinse, using a light mist, and allow to drip dry.

EC&S Dispersant is very effective for cleaning VINYL, PLASTIC, FORMICA, LEATHER, WOOD, CERAMIC, FIBERGLASS, IVORY,

NAUGAHYDE, CHROME, CONCRETE, and any other surfaces that water will not damage. The dilution ratios will depend on the degree of soil and length of time since the surface has been thoroughly cleaned.

EC&S Dispersant also cleans COMMERCIAL FURNITURE, UPHOLSTERY, CARPETS, and FABRICS. Spot treating TABLECLOTHS, NAPKINS, etc. may also be accomplished with various concentrations of this product and may thus prevent permanent stains.

EC&S Dispersant in a 50/50 solution (1 part EC&S-A and one part water) may be used to SOAK SILVER, BRASS, and other ORNAMENTAL OBJECTS to remove light tarnish. Prolonged soaking will release and remove most tarnish so that polishes may work even better, thus bringing out a higher luster.

EC&S Dispersant can be used for SOAKING UTENSILS or FLATWARE before washing, resulting in a RENEWED SHINE and BRILLIANCE to surfaces. EC&S-E is excellent for this purpose. BURNED POTS and PANS may also be soaked in a solution of one part EC&S-A and one part water to restore appearance.

EC&S Dispersant is very effective in cleaning the EXTERIOR and INTERIOR of WALK-IN and REACH-IN REEFERS, with the additional benefit of inhibiting, and in most cases, completely ELIMINATING, THE FORMATION OF

MILDEW. An application of EC&S-B should be used in this instance. The same solution also can be used for CLEANING AND WIPING DOWN ALL STAINLESS STEEL appliances and surfaces. STEAM TABLES, STOCK POTS, and COFFEE MAKERS can also be cleaned effectively with EC&S-B. In addition, this treatment will PREVENT SCALE BUILD-UP in STEAM TABLES and reduce the RESIDUE BUILD-UP in COFFEE MAKERS as well as other equipment so cleaned.

FOR GREASE TRAPS, place one gallon of EC&S-A directly in traps at the close of the day's cleaning and leave undisturbed overnight. Repeat as often as grease builds up, or at regular intervals. Use of the product regularly on FLOORS and in sinks will normally PREVENT BUILD-UP in GREASE TRAPS (15 - 25 gallon traps.)

EC&S Dispersant can be used to clean OVENS and FRYERS. Use EC&S-A for this task. Best results occur when the unit is heated to a temperature of 200 to 300 degrees at time of application. If a heavy build-up is present, product may be left on surface overnight. If convenient, use a stiff bristle brush when necessary to clean. NO GLOVES, MASK, OR OTHER SAFETY GEAR ARE REQUIRED FOR WORKERS.

APPLICATIONS

BAKING AND DRY GOODS: Equipment such as mixers, baking trays and receptacles, ovens, and pans.

CONFECTIONERY AND PRESERVES: Effective on all surfaces such as trays, conveyors, and machinery.

DAIRY PRODUCTS: Nontainting and effective on pipes, working surfaces, rollers, and in-place systems.

FISH PRODUCTS: Aluminum and stainless steel trays and receptacles, frying vats, and smoking kilns.

FRUIT AND VEGETABLES: Removal of mud and debris at reception; blanching equipment, hoppers, elevators, peelers, and slicers.

GENERAL USE: Floors, walls, ceilings, windows, and plumbing, wherever food is present.

MEAT PREPARATION: The product effectively cleans aluminum and other vulnerable materials without caustic or abrasive action. It is ideal for cooking vessels, removing food residue and scale. These cleaning options include surfaces where meat is smoked, brine tanks, and pipe work.

POULTRY INDUSTRY: Successful on trays, floors, and incubators in hatcheries and on farms; killing and processing areas, troughs, conveyors, chillers, cutting, and packing equipment.

RETAIL: Display counters, storage areas, floors, working surfaces.

SLAUGHTERHOUSES: For stockyards, transport, and reception areas: working surfaces, belts, saws, hooks, cutting boards, mincing and cutting machinery, and trays.

WAREHOUSING & DISTRIBUTION CENTERS: Vehicle interiors and exteriors, floors, and racking and handling machinery.

Jackson Research Center

MODEL ONE: **MEMO III**

To: Environmental Health Foundation

From: William R. Jackson, Ph.D., Consultant

Subject: **General Commercial Use**

Is it possible to have your shop and commercial area safe and clean, and to eliminate most toxic and hazardous cleaning products while still watching your financial bottom line?

WITH EC&S, THE ANSWER IS YES!

It must be remembered that health and safety issues, as well as compliance with environmental laws, liability concerns, and insurance coverage, must be taken into consideration when a business looks at its financial bottom line. Not only is EC&S Dispersant a concentrated, commercial grade cleaner, it also offers the user a product that:

- Meets all published OSHA regulatory requirements

- Meets all published EPA regulatory requirements

- Meets all published DOT regulatory requirements

- Contains no hazardous ingredients listed in California Proposition 65-The Safe Drinking Water & Toxic Enforcement Act of 1986

- It is so safe, it has USDA approval for use under the Federal meat, poultry, shell egg grading, and egg products inspection program.

EC&S Dispersant offers strength, versatility, and safety. As a result, some commercial and industrial applications do not differ much from the general "household" applications. Be sure to check the index and other sections for additional application information.

In most general commercial situations, an initial, very thorough, deep cleaning is recommended. This will remove the majority, if not all, of the caked-on and layered soils that have built up over time. Begin with EC&S-A, EC&S-B, or a solution of one part EC&S-A and one part water. After the initial cleaning, solutions of EC&S-B,-C,-D or -E are usually adequate if used in a regular maintenance program.

Some industrial areas, or areas where greases and oils build up daily, may require the continued use of EC&S-A, EC&S-B, or a solution of equal parts EC&S-A and water, more dwell time, more agitation, or more energy (such as hot water or steam.) Factors such as safety considerations (i.e. slippery floor areas), time, and cost will help users determine the EC&S product best suited to their needs. THE CHOICE BELONGS TO THE USER!

HANDS AND SKIN

HEAVY GREASE AND DIRT

- Spray or splash on EC&S-A
- Rub until clean
- Wipe off with paper towel or cloth, or rinse off with water

MEDIUM GREASE AND DIRT

- Spray or splash on EC&S-C
- Rub until clean
- Wipe off with paper towel or cloth, or rinse off with water

Rinsing is not necessary if water is not readily available.

A second application may be required if soil has become deeply imbedded into pores, or if the skin has become stained. EC&S is a very safe alternative to most hand cleaners, which are solvent-based and require additional washing with soap and water to remove the solvent hazard and to eliminate the odor.

GLASS, CLEAR PLASTIC AND REFLECTIVE SURFACES

- Spray lightly with EC&S-E
- Allow 10 to 15 seconds dwell time
- Squeegee or wipe dry for a cleaner surface that stays clean longer

NOTE: Do not use a formula stronger than EC&S-E or streaking may occur. If streaking does occur, spray with WATER and dry again. Be sure paper towels or other drying materials do not have a lotion or oil content, the least expensive paper towels are usually the best. When using cloth towels, be sure fabric softener or fabric softener sheets were not used, because these products leave a residue that can be transferred to the reflective surfaces.

CONCRETE SURFACES: FLOORS, DRIVEWAYS, AND PARKING AREAS

- Apply EC&S liberally to all OIL, GREASE, or other SOILS on concrete
- Scrape thick deposits loose with scraper, hoe, or spade
- Agitate vigorously with stiff bristle brush during 5 to 10 minutes of dwell time
- Rinse well with full (or high) water pressure before cleaning solution dries
- Re-apply EC&S if concrete dries before rinsing or if soils are aged or layered.

NOTE: Due to the porosity of concrete, stains may still be visible in concrete after the surface has been cleaned. Time, exposure to sun and repeated applications of EC&S will continue to lighten visible stains.

FRESH OIL SPILLS or PETROLEUM-BASED SOILS on NONPOROUS SURFACES

- Apply sufficient EC&S to assure coverage of area
- Allow 15 to 30 seconds dwell time
- Agitate with brush or cloth if necessary
- Wipe up and rinse with damp cloth or paper towel

COMMERCIAL FLOORS

WAX REMOVAL

- Spread EC&S-B over waxed floors
- Let dwell for 10 to 25 minutes (there is no need to scrub)
- Wipe up dissolved wax
- Rinse thoroughly and let dry

NOTE: EC&S will not remove acrylic waxes.

HEEL, METAL, AND RUBBER MARKS

- Spray marks with EC&S-B
- If necessary, agitate with brush or non-scratching scrub pad and allow 5 to 10 minutes dwell time
- Wipe area with clean wet cloth; then
- Dry as usual

GENERAL FLOOR WASHING

By Hand (mop & bucket)

- For heavy soil or grease, place five quarts EC&S-A in a bucket with four gallons water
- For light soil or grease or weekly general maintenance, use five quarts EC&S-D with four gallons water
- Swab as usual
- Let stand 15 to 20 minutes
- Mop or flush with clean water
- Dry as usual

By Machine

- Add 2 cups EC&S-A per gallon of hot water

EC&S Dispersant will not cause floors to be as dangerously slippery as other cleaning products, even when removing wax. This is JUST ANOTHER SAFETY BENEFIT of EC&S Dispersant.

REMEMBER to pour any excess cleaning water down drains to keep plumbing open and flowing. This drain-cleaning is ANOTHER MAINTENANCE BENEFIT of EC&S Dispersant.

COMMERCIAL CARPET CARE

CARPET CLEANING

Spot Cleaning

- Spray EC&S-B on spot
- Agitate with brush, and using a small amount of water, "feather out"
- Allow approximately 5 to 20 minutes dwell time, depending on the spot
- With a clean cloth or sponge, absorb as much solution as possible
- Rinse with clean water
- Re-absorb remaining water with dry cloth or sponge and dry as usual

Carpet Cleaning Machines (steam and/or extraction):

- For general soil and traffic areas, fill machine with EC&S-D

- For very light soil and maintenance, use EC&S-E
- Allow 10 to 20 minutes for dwell time
- Go over carpet again with clean water

NOTE: Care must be taken never to get carpet too wet and to extract as much moisture as possible. Also, care must be taken to rinse thoroughly and to not leave concentrated cleaner in the carpet. If left in the carpet, all cleaners will continue to clean, for example, the dirt off of the bottom of your shoes.

EC&S Dispersant acts as a deodorizer by eliminating instead of covering up odors. Surfaces cleaned with EC&S Dispersant are so clean that there is little left on which odor-causing bacteria can survive.

STEAM CLEANER & PRESSURE WASH

EC&S Dispersant is nonclogging, noncaking, and nonscaling. It is highly effective for all steam cleaning applications. EC&S products keep scales from forming in the steam coils, thus reducing maintenance and nearly eliminating the need for disassembly to clear and clean the orifices and tubing.

STEAM GUNS

For general steam gun application, use four to eight quarts of EC&S-D to replace four pounds of powder, or use one cup EC&S-A per gallon at nozzle.

NOTE: EC&S Dispersant is safe on any surface that will tolerate steam.

HIGH PRESSURE WASHERS

- Use EC&S-B or C
- A 20° Vee Jet held 6 to 8 inches from the surface at a 45° angle penetrates and removes the soil as it is moved forward
- For a vertical surface, begin at the bottom and move upward
- Let stand until soil loosens
- Use a spray rinse of clear water working from the top downward

REMEMBER: The rinse does the "cleaning" because that part of the cleaning process removes the emulsified contaminant from the surface.

HAND SPRAYERS
(such as Hudson Sprayer)

Use EC&S-A to clean parking areas, garbage cans, garage storage areas, and refuse chutes. Such cleanings help to reduce odor, degrease, clean, and prevent mildew. For other sprayer applications, see specific problem or area.

CAUTION: When using EC&S Dispersant for the FIRST TIME, remove the nozzle from the gun for at least the first two minutes. This procedure allows EC&S Dispersant to clean out the coils and lines without plugging the nozzle.

DUST CONTROL

EC&S Dispersant has a SUPERIOR WATER WETTING ABILITY and is useful in areas where dust is a problem. EC&S is non-ionic and will help control the static electricity which, in turn, helps prevent dust particles from becoming airborne health and safety hazards.

- Atomize EC&S-A into the air where airborne dust particles result in potentially EXPLOSIVE CONDITIONS such as grain elevators, grain processing plants, dry fertilizer plants, and selected specific dry chemical plants.

- Heavy mist can be sprayed on asbestos dust from vehicle brake drums. See "BRAKE SHOPS" for more information, and always follow generally accepted safety procedures when asbestos is present.

- For general dust control in the WORK ENVIRONMENT, apply a light mist of EC&S-D before sweeping. EC&S is excellent for clean-up and sweeping at new construction sites, and is much more effective than oil soaked sweeping compounds.

Mix one gallon of EC&S-A with 50 gallons of water and apply by tank truck or sprayer for surface dust control on ROADS, CONSTRUCTION SITES, PATHWAYS, DIRT TRACKS, ETC. EC&S will reduce water consumption in addition to reducing the dust hazard.

Summary

Use	Product Solution
Light Degreasing	C
Medium Degreasing	B
Heavy Degreasing	A
Floors	D
Walls	B
Upholstery, Fabric, Carpet Spotting	C
Carpet Cleaning (follow specific directions)	D
Glass Cleaner	E
Steam Cleaners	D
Pressure Washers	B
Plastics	C
Heavy Equipment	B
Vehicle Washing	D
Pots & Pans	D
Hand Cleaner	A

EC&S - Dilution Rates

EC&S-A	(concentrate)
EC&S-B	(one part EC&S-A + two parts water)
EC&S-C	(one part EC&S-A + three parts water)
EC&S-D	(one part EC&S-A + nine parts water)
EC&S-E	(one part EC&S-A + thirty parts water)

Jackson Research Center

MODEL ONE: **MEMO IV**

To: Environmental Health Foundation

From: William R. Jackson, Ph.D., Consultant

Subject: **Hospitals and Elderly Care Facilities**

HOSPITALS AND ELDERLY CARE FACILITIES have a unique need for cleaning. By law, these facilities MUST be clean. Dirt is a breeding ground for bacteria, so it is imperative that the dirt be eliminated.

HOSPITALS AND ELDERLY CARE FACILITIES typically experience heavy traffic throughout, and thus require frequent scrubbing and stripping. PRIOR TO THE DAILY MOPPING OF THE FLOORS WITH EC&S, machine scrubbing is necessary to remove accumulated grime and floor finishes. In outpatient high-traffic areas which may be subjected to heavy exposure literally around the clock, the use of EC&S in an automatic scrubber has improved the cleaning and refinishing cycle by as much as 400%. In many health care facilities, floor care is performed on request, with the worst problems taking priority. With EC&S, it is possible to schedule the work, and to increase the time interval from 30 days to five months between refinishing.

According to one medical center housekeeping manager, the use of this type of cleaning agent enabled the staff to strip and refinish all hard and resilient flooring in the hospital within a one year period. Many of those floors had not been cared for in over ten years. The extended period of time between necessary maintenance afforded by this cleaning product has allowed for floor care throughout the facility that could not be accomplished in the past. While improving the quality of service and cleanliness throughout the hospital, an annual savings of more than $39,000 in cleaning supply and personnel costs was realized.

At the same hospital, nosocomial infection rate decreased significantly when the new cleaning system was implemented, from above 6% to approximately 2.5% for clean surgeries and 4.8% for clean-contaminated wounds. The normal acceptable rate is from 3 to 11%.

EC&S Dispersant products are invaluable to at least three departments within HOSPITALS AND ELDERLY CARE FACILITIES. Each department has a different assignment and need for the EC&S Dispersant system.

- ENGINEERING/PLANT SERVICES: EC&S is an effective and efficient answer to the often time-consuming problem of drainage.

- FOOD SERVICES/DIETARY: Cleaning of floors, walls, equipment, pots/pans, and employees. EC&S Dispersant will eliminate grease, smoke, and odors.

- HOUSEKEEPING: Maintaining the hygiene of the halls, walls, floors, carpeting, rooms, lavatories, etc.

APPLICATIONS

ENGINEERING: The major drainage problems experienced by engineering stems from the food services area. Wastes such as grease, oil, fat, food, and bits of packing materials flow into the drains and often accumulate in hard-to-reach areas. Unclogging these areas is time consuming and unpleasant. "Snakes" or caustic chemicals are often used, though the latter is very much discouraged, if not forbidden. In desperation, however, many of these caustic chemicals are used, because little else has proven effective. Now there is EC&S Dispersant, which has been proven to be both safe and effective.

EC&S Dispersant is most effectively applied at the major source of the problem. This application usually includes, for example, the pot sink in the Food Service kitchen where pots, pans, and utensils are washed. As the greases, oils, fats, and food particles go down the drain, they mix together and cause blockages at various points in the plumbing. Just because lines are new or made of slippery materials is no guarantee that there will be no problems. Even "New and Improved" lines have had these same problems of waste accumulation wherever there is an eddy in the flow.

EC&S Dispersant will free clogged lines of grease, oil, and fats, by eliminating the adhesive effect that holds the blockage together. EC&S Dispersant breaks down the restriction and allows the blockage to be washed away. Applying EC&S Dispersant directly to the drain usually will clear the blockage. Additionally, when pots and pans are washed with EC&S Dispersant, food services will not only have cleaner items, but the continuous flow of EC&S Dispersant through the drain lines (on a regular basis) will automatically keep the plumbing free and clean.

Food service floors are also a source of oils, fats, and grease. Cleaning these with a regular detergent produces a combination that may act like a cement in the drain. Using EC&S Dispersant and water to wash the floors will make them cleaner, safer, and the cleaning product that flows down the drains will keep the drains clear, open, and odor free. These applications will eliminate major drainage problems for the ENGINEERING department.

Drainage problems also occur in:

- NURSING STATIONS
- LAVATORY DRAINS
- SHOWERS
- TOILETS

All of these areas are constantly discharging waste into the sewer lines. Wherever there is a DRAIN THAT IS SLOW OR CLOGGED, THE FOLLOWING APPLICATION will normally clean and/or free it up.

- In the average drain having a two (2) inch outlet, apply two quarts of EC&S-A every other day for three applications. If possible, apply just prior to its most dormant time. This applies to lavatories, urinals, floor drains, and sinks. The dormant time allows EC&S Dispersant to loosen the adhesive acting materials while permitting the subsequent flow of water to wash the loosened material from the lines. If a problem area is not clean after three applications, a plumber's snake or other mechanical auger probably will be needed. Experience has proven that EC&S Dispersant applied faithfully in this manner (with dwell time) will eliminate the problem.

- To keep these drains clean and free flowing, EC&S Dispersant should be reapplied on a schedule of two quarts of EC&S-A once per week in frequently used areas or once per month in infrequently used drains.

CAUTION: If EC&S Dispersant is applied throughout the health care facility all at once, a new problem, larger than the original, might develop, if the EC&S Dispersant loosens already accumulated materials, and if the flow passage is not clean and free, the channel may clog and block the drain extensively.

SUGGESTION: Start with primary drains in one area of the system. Once the main drainage paths are clean, apply the product to drains farther and farther removed from the main drains over a period of days and weeks. Begin with the basement or first floor and work upwards to other floors. After each area or floor has been cleaned thoroughly, a Preventative Maintenance Program, applied at the perimeters on a monthly basis, should be adequate. If there is a nurses' station or lavatory that is heavily used or with a history of clogging, it is advisable to apply EC&S Dispersant more frequently, for example, once per week.

The suggested practices will help keep drains free and clear for ENGINEERING. If food services will use the product faithfully, ENGINEERING will automatically eliminate about 30% of its work. If it is used in the other areas described, another 10 to 20% work savings should be realized. The overall COST WILL BE MUCH LESS, LESS MATERIALS WILL BE USED and there will be a vast amount of TIME and LABOR SAVED.

FOOD SERVICES: It is recommended that EC&S Dispersant be used initially on the FLOORS and in the POT SINK. After this, other items can be added such as equipment, vent hoods, etc.

Floors: Start the cleaning process with a mix of one part EC&S-A to five parts water. Once EC&S Dispersant is being used regularly, the mixture can be reduced to as low as one part EC&S-A to ten parts water. The lower concentration will continue to maintain the cleanliness and odor free benefits. This odor free quality comes from EC&S Dispersant's ability to restrict bacterial growth. It leaves the surface so clean that there is little left on which bacteria can survive. This type of treated surface has proven to have a much lower rate of bacterial growth when compared to surfaces cleaned with other treatments.

Stainless Steel: Stainless steel is a highly polished piece of metal and should be cleaned in the same manner as glass. Initially, it may be quite dirty and require a heavy cleaning with a brush and EC&S-B. After it has been cleaned, however, EC&S-E will maintain the cleanliness and shine. EC&S-E is also used for chrome and glass cleaning.

Ovens: The stainless steel procedure is also applicable to ovens. Spray or wipe the product on, let stand overnight, then rinse. EC&S Dispersant will remove burned on grease with regular use. Depending upon the degree of build-up, repeated use may be necessary. Dwell time is of utmost importance.

Vent Hoods: With automatic vent hoods, EC&S-A should be poured into the reservoir provided for the cleaner. It is then mixed further in the proportioner located in the automatic hood. After it has been used for a period of time, a lower concentration may be applied.

Pot Sinks: For the washing of pots and pans in the pot sink, use EC&S-D. After the washing cycle is complete, open the drain and allow the residue water containing EC&S Dispersant to flow down through the grease trap and out to the sewer, cleaning the entire path as it flows. After EC&S Dispersant has been used for a week or more, the grease trap should be clean and remain clean, (with its only function possibly being that of an inspection point.) Some residue will normally float on the water, but the water level will be 1" to 2" lower than usual. The odor will virtually be gone, and what little is left is a result of the materials currently washing down the drain. Residue may be left in the bottom of the trap, but even heavy items such as rice and beans will continue to flush out in a regular manner. This should eliminate the need for dipping, cleaning, or pumping CREATING AN ADDITIONAL SAVINGS.

Walls and Equipment: For an initial cleaning of WALLS, an application of EC&S-C normally is sufficient. For heavy dirt, additional product strength may be needed, for example, EC&S-B. DWELL TIME is important whenever EC&S Dispersant is used. Let the cleaner remain on the surface for a short time to obtain its full effect. For EQUIPMENT, apply the cleaning product to it in the evening and wipe it off in the morning. The chef and cooks will appreciate odor free ovens, and other equipment, because the foods they cook will not have a tainted flavor, which is often a risk when other cleaners are used.

HOUSEKEEPING: Some areas of health care facilities are required by law to be cleaned with a disinfectant. EC&S Dispersant is not this type of cleaner. It is, however, a perfectly safe product that leaves all surfaces cleaner than ever before and removes materials other cleaners will not touch; for example, stains on floors and walls, marks from rubber or metals, etc. The product best suited for these purposes is usually EC&S-B or EC&S-C. BE PATIENT when stain removal is necessary. A deep rust stain under a waste basket will be partially removed with the first treatment, and each subsequent application will remove more. Ball point pen marks on painted surfaces usually will come off without damaging the paint. Deep marks may require a second or third application.

EC&S Dispersant should be used sparingly and efficiently, but used wherever there is a cleaning problem. If used in this manner, the overall results will include:

- LOWER COSTS (one product)
- COMPLETE CLEANLINESS
- NO DRAINAGE PROBLEMS

REMEMBER: EC&S Dispersant is completely SAFE FOR those PEOPLE using it as well as being SAFE FOR the ENVIRONMENT.

REMEMBER: Be patient. Recognize that the product is doing a good job the first time, and that it will be more beneficial with each application. The more it is used, the better it works. The longer it is used, the less product is required.

REMEMBER: The longer the DWELL TIME, the better it works.

For additional information, consult Memo V regarding LABORATORY GLASSWARE.

Jackson Research Center

MODEL ONE: **MEMO V**

To: Environmental Health Foundation

From: William R. Jackson, Ph.D., Consultant

Subject: **Laboratory Glassware**

EC&S Dispersant PRODUCTS CAN QUALIFY FOR A ROLE IN THE CLEAN UP TASKS AT SOPHISTICATED SCIENTIFIC LABORATORIES.

EC&S Dispersant is an effective laboratory cleaning agent for glassware contaminated with blood and protein. It maintains a buffering capacity for mineral acids. It also assists in radioactive decontamination of laboratory material.

Most modern laboratories use surface active detergent cleaning agents to clean laboratory glassware. The most convenient method of cleaning laboratory glassware is to place the used equipment into a cold solution of the detergent diluted with tap water or distilled water and allow the glassware to soak overnight. The glassware can then be removed, given a hot tap water wash, and then <u>two rinsings</u> with good quality distilled or reverse osmosis water.

AN EXPERIMENT YOU CAN TRY: Allow EC&S Dispersant to be subjected to a similar overnight cleaning procedure. Try using three different strengths of solution to see which works best. Use EC&S-A in a 3.2% strength solution, a 1.32% strength solution, and a 0.66% strength solution. The following is the specific ratio:

1. One part EC&S-A to 30 parts water (3.2%)
2. One part EC&S-A to 75 parts water (1.3%)
3. One part EC&S-A to 150 parts water (0.66%)

A liter of each of these concentrations can be made up and placed in separate beakers. In each of the three beakers, place four glass tubes which have previously been filled with clotted human blood, and from which the blood clots have been shaken out. Allow the glass tubes to fill with the solution in the beakers. The glass tubes, having been contaminated with blood, may be left in the beakers overnight, at room temperature. The next morning, the glass tubes may be removed, washed with hot tap water followed by only one rinsing with distilled water. Then, fill each glass tube with distilled water and let stand for two hours.

The distilled water contents of each tube can then be examined for the presence of blood protein by measuring the ultraviolet absorption of the water. The presence of traces of hemoglobin in solution can be determined readily by spectrophotometric absorption. Both of these tests can be carried out to determine the level of contamination following the cleaning procedure.

The results will show thorough and reproducible cleaning of protein contaminated tubes with all three dilutions. Even the third dilution, of 150 parts of water to one part EC&S-A will prove effective. The results will also reflect very low hemoglobin contamination following treatment with any of the three dilutions.

EC&S Dispersant also is very effective, having a buffering capacity at different concentrations with mineral acids. For example, it has been reported to have buffering properties with mineral acids such as hydrochloric and sulfuric acids.

EC&S Dispersant is a non-ionic cleaner that decontaminates glass, lead, and perspex, materials often found in radiochemical laboratories. The general results from surface contamination tests are impressive. A single application of the cleaning solution followed by rinsing of a heavily scratched lead surface, removed approximately 80% of the contamination. With the very smooth perspex surface, the decontamination was virtually complete, an average of 98% removal by a single application. The results demonstrate that the EC&S in a 30:1 aqueous solution is very effective as a decontamination solution.

Jackson Research Center

MODEL ONE: **MEMO VI**

To: Environmental Health Foundation

From: William R. Jackson, Ph.D., Consultant

Subject: **General Household Use**

IS IT POSSIBLE THAT YOUR HOME COULD BE MORE SANITARY THAN THE AVERAGE HOSPITAL? (See introduction to HOSPITALS AND ELDERLY CARE FACILITIES)

EC&S Dispersant is a nonpolluting, concentrated, industrial strength cleaner. Yet it is safe and ideal for multiple uses in the home. It safely cleans anything that is washable with water.

- This product can REPLACE most of the HOUSEHOLD CHEMICALS now purchased for cleaning.

- EC&S Dispersant can assure FAMILY SAFETY because of its nonhazardous, nontoxic, and noncaustic qualities.

- Because of EC&S Dispersant's unique formulation, it works equally well in hard, soft, or salt water.

- EC&S Dispersant is 100% BIODEGRADABLE in the optimum seven days.

- EC&S Dispersant is ECOLOGICALLY SAFE, PEOPLE SAFE, and ENVIRONMENTALLY SAFE.

- APPLICATION: Spray, brush, or mop an appropriate EC&S Dispersant dilute product on any washable surface, then rinse with water, or just wipe off.

- The CONCENTRATION of EC&S Dispersant may be varied to fit the specific job. To determine the best mixture for a particular job, start with a mild concentration and gradually increase the strength until the desired results are obtained.

GENERAL CLEANING: You should expect very little sudsing, and then, only when filling sinks or pails. DO NOT discard the cleaning solution because the water looks dirty; expect to wash 2 - 3 times more surface area than with other cleaners. EC&S Dispersant is absolutely safe and therefore will not feel harsh. It works any way -- all ways -- EXPECT IT!

STAIN REMOVAL: To remove coffee, tea, coke, food, and grease stains, prepare a solution of EC&S-C. Apply to the stained area and rub. Then with a brush dipped in a small amount of water, brush stained area and blend solution out into a larger area.

TO REMOVE GUM, pour a small amount of EC&S-A concentrate onto the gum. Let it remain for one to two hours, then lift gum from surface.

Care should be taken to use the proper strength for CARPETS when using any carpet cleaning concentrate on the market. Too strong of a solution may stay in the carpet because it cannot be thoroughly rinsed. If carpet cleaning material is left in the carpet, it will continue to clean, for example, the dirt off of the bottom of your shoes.

FOR WAX REMOVAL: For this task, use EC&S-B. Spread the solution over waxed floors and let it work for 10 to 25 minutes. There is no need to scrub. Rinse and let dry. EC&S Dispersant will not remove acrylic waxes.

EC&S Dispersant is <u>AT YOUR SERVICE</u>. The following is a partial list of items that can be cleaned with this product.

HEAVY-DUTY APPLICATIONS

EC&S-A

OVENS & FRYERS: Allow extended dwell time, brush and wipe heavy soils. No rubber gloves or other safety gear is required.

DEGREASING of AUTOS, BOATS, MOTORCYCLES, LAWN MOWERS and HOUSEHOLD TOOLS.

CLEAN-UP of OIL and GREASE DEPOSITS from DRIVEWAYS and GARAGE FLOORS, FIREPLACE SCREENS, BURNER TRAYS, STOVE FILTERS, etc.

MILDEW on PAINTED SURFACES, TILE, FIBERGLASS, SHOWER ENCLOSURES, etc.

GRAFFITI: Spray on, rub with nylon pad, let stand, then wipe.

MEDIUM-TO-HEAVY APPLICATIONS

EC&S-B

HEATING & AIR CONDITIONING units and fixtures; fireplace screens.

BATHROOM FIXTURES: LAVATORIES, BASINS, TILE, COUNTERS, ETC. Apply EC&S-A or EC&S-B with spray or sponge. Let stand; then wash down (rinse), and wipe dry. TOILET BOWLS - flush toilet and spray EC&S-A directly onto the bowl surface, wash around with a brush, being sure to rub under lip. Let stand. The next use of the toilet will rinse the bowl clean. EC&S-B can be used safely for tubs, sinks and showers.

KITCHEN: MICROWAVE OVENS, STOVE HOODS and FILTERS. WAX REMOVAL from FLOORS, FURNITURE, and cleaning of WOOD work.

WALLS: Clean vertical surfaces by spraying or wiping on EC&S-B solution from bottom up and rinsing or wiping off from the top down.

SPORTS & RECREATION EQUIPMENT, such as BOWLING BALLS, SHOES, GOLF BAGS, CLUBS AND BALLS. HOUSEHOLD TOOLS, SILVER and BRASS cleaning and tarnish removal: Extended dwell time, rubbing, and repeat application may be necessary in some cases. Swab or spray on, allow dwell time, brush/wipe, and rinse.

FURNISHINGS: BAMBOO, PLASTIC, NAUGAHYDE, and LEATHER FURNITURE. STAINLESS STEEL and ALUMINUM. CERAMICS and OFFICE EQUIPMENT.

MEDIUM-TO-LIGHT APPLICATIONS

EC&S-C

GENERAL UPHOLSTERY CLEANING, SPOT CLEANING of CLOTHING, FABRICS, and other articles.
WALLS, CUPBOARDS, INTERIOR SURFACES undamaged by water.
JEWELRY, personal bathroom articles, combs, brushes, hair rollers.
METAL FURNITURE, TABLES, CHAIRS

EC&S-D

MINI-BLINDS and VENETIAN BLINDS

APPLIANCES

EC&S-E

GLASS and other REFLECTIVE SURFACES: WINDOWS, PLASTIC SNEEZE GUARDS, MIRRORS, DECORATIVE GLASSWARE, CHANDELIERS, DECORATIVE STAINLESS & CHROME

APPLICATION: Spray on lightly, allow 10 to 15 seconds dwell time, squeegee or wipe dry for a cleaner surface that stays clean longer. If streaking occurs, add WATER and dry again. For crystal chandeliers, be sure power switch is off before starting, and ALWAYS follow manufacturer's recommended safety procedure. Spray EC&S-E on the crystal, allow to drip on a towel, then spray rinse water on the crystal and allow to drip dry.

DISHWASHERS

EC&S-A

AUTOMATIC DISHWASHERS: Add two ounces of EC&S-A to the load to act as a wetting agent thereby enhancing regular dish washing detergent action. This procedure will provide an excellent cleaning. Too much EC&S-A however, will cause sudsing.

HAND WASHING OF DISHES: Add two cups of EC&S-A to dish-washing water in the sink. Rinse dishes under hot water and let drip dry. Less EC&S-A

can be used if it is sprayed on, allowed dwell time, then washed off.

WASHING CAKED ON MATERIAL: Spray EC&S-A solution on caked material, and allow adequate dwell time before washing by hand.

EVAPORATIVE COOLERS

EC&S-A

To reduce odor, spray on, or soak pads in EC&S-A solution before start-up, or when new pads are installed. Add one to two gallons of EC&S-A to the reservoir to reduce vapor odor inside the house.

FOR MILDEW

EC&S-A or **-B**

Use EC&S-A or EC&S-B solution and a scrub brush to remove mildew on painted surfaces, showers, tile, etc. Either wipe off or rinse with water. Dwell time is important; allow to soak overnight if mildew is very heavy!

PET SHAMPOO

The use of EC&S Dispersant for PET SHAMPOO has many benefits. It is kind to pets' skin and eyes, it cleans exceptionally well, AND it also helps rid pets of FLEAS, FLEA EGGS, TICKS, LICE, etc. (See section on INSECT CONTROL).

INSECT CONTROL

The most common method of eliminating selected insects in recent years is by the application of extensive amounts of poisonous chemicals. There are over 45,000 different insecticide and pesticide formulas registered with the U.S. government today.

The use of poisonous materials to kill unwanted INSECTS, does so by interfering with bodily processes in a chemical way. This practice causes several other severe problems.

1. When applying the poisonous chemicals, the deadly materials frequently are spread over wide areas, and thus all living creatures, including humans are made extremely vulnerable to these poisons.

2. Poisonous insecticide and pesticide chemicals are PERSISTENT, meaning LONG-LASTING. As ANIMALS, BIRDS, or FISH eat the POISONED INSECTS, or if they ingest poisonous insecticide or pesticide because of the wide area spraying, the deadly chemicals enter the food chain and are passed on to other living creatures, including human adults and children.

3. Insects have an incredible and infinite ability to ALTER THEIR GENETIC STRUCTURE QUICKLY. No known insect variety has ever, nor will ever, be wiped out by the use of chemical insecticides or pesticides. Insects are able to BECOME IMMUNE to any poison, and thus, within a few generations, cannot be killed with any given chemical (See *U.S. News and World Report*, Sept. 14, 1992, "The Joyride is Over").

Since 1940, the United States has permitted the increased use of millions of tons of chemical insecticides and pesticides, yet we experience more insect problems than ever before. Not only do the deadly chemicals fail to solve the problems; far worse problems are created in the process. The increase in cancer, hepatitis, mental retardation, early childhood death, and many other diseases may be related to this widespread use of CHEMICAL POISONS WHICH WE CANNOT SEE, TASTE, OR SMELL.

INSECTS are not like higher forms of life. One major difference is the absence of blood vessels. INSECTS have a body cavity that holds their bodily fluids. If they lose as much as 10% of their bodily fluids, they expire. Using EC&S Dispersant helps us select which harmful or undesirable exoskeleton creatures need to lose their vital bodily fluids quickly.

HOW DOES IT HAPPEN? Most INSECTS have a WAXY coating on the outside of their bodies. This outer body shell, or exoskeleton, consists of a porous material which would allow the body fluids to escape or run out, if it were not for this WAXY coating which "seals" the shell. EC&S Dispersant REMOVES THE WAXY COATING, allowing the INSECTS' bodily fluids to drain out, thus guaranteeing the sure ELIMINATION of the INSECT. The process is actually more complicated than this brief description, and could take pages to demonstrate and describe. BUT, IT ELIMINATES UNDESIRABLE INSECTS SAFELY, WITHOUT ENDANGERING ANIMALS, PLANTS, or PEOPLE.

Take for example, the millions of dollars we spend to help rid our pets of fleas, flea eggs, ticks, lice, and/or mites. OUR PETS NEED NOT SUFFER. The use of EC&S Dispersant will eliminate those problems. The ELIMINATING PROCESS is MECHANICAL rather than a POISONOUS CHEMICAL. By direct application of EC&S Dispersant (try EC&S-C or EC&S-D) via spraying, bathing, or dipping, the INSECT cannot become immune and cannot pass on any immunity.

POTENTIAL USERS

Using this product for all the household cleaning tasks is very practical because it is nondrying to normal skin, nonirritating, nonfuming, and has a pleasant odor. IT MAKES MANY DIFFICULT TASKS A LITTLE MORE PLEASANT. The products are completely safe for use around adults, children, and pets.

Because EC&S Dispersant solutions work so well, one can eliminate almost all other household cleaners. The disposal of the used cleaning solution also cleans the drains.

Although EC&S Dispersant does not try to compete with the highly advertised household cleaning products (most of which are toxic and/or caustic), recommendations from household users and adoption for household use by industrial and commercial consumers will provide opportunities to serve and expand the household market.

Jackson Research Center

MODEL ONE: **MEMO VII**

To: Environmental Health Foundation

From: William R. Jackson, Ph.D., Consultant

Subject: **Institutional Applications**

INSTITUTIONAL APPLICATIONS

Hotels
Motels
Government Offices
Churches
Public Schools
Universities
Day Care Centers
Guest Ranches
Health Clubs
Animal Boarding Kennels
Construction Contractors
Newspaper and Printing Companies

EC&S Dispersant MAY BE USED FOR THE MAJORITY OF CLEANING REQUIREMENTS FOR A WIDE VARIETY OF INSTITUTIONS, from industrial cleaning to restaurant cleaning; from concrete parking lots to penthouses. Some of these categories are more specifically discussed in other MODEL ONE MEMOS within this chapter.

OUTSIDE AREAS

Hotel and other institutional CONCRETE PARKING AREAS (especially enclosed areas) are always a problem for management and maintenance. GREASE AND OIL MAY BE TRACKED INTO LOBBIES, ROOMS, CONFERENCE CENTERS, CONCESSION AREAS, AND OFFICES from the building's parking area. Tracked-in soil increases maintenance and cleaning costs, and presents an unsightly and unclean appearance. Because enclosed parking areas lack total "outside" ventilation, volatile cleaning compounds may not be used for safety reasons. EC&S-A, brushed onto the surface of four to five concrete stalls at a time and then mopped up, will remove surface oil and greases. A regular cleaning program will remove most of the stain and imbedded grease, eliminating the blackened dirty areas at the entrances of buildings closest to parking areas. Applying the product to a few concrete stalls before returning to mop up should allow adequate dwell time for the cleaning solution to work. An added benefit to using EC&S Dispersant around BACK PARKING AREAS, TRASH BINS, and REFUSE BARRELS is the product's ability to DEODORIZE.

For buildings with refuse chutes, EC&S Dispersant may be sprayed on the exposed areas to help eliminate odors and to prevent further accumulation of soil and dirt. Begin the process by using EC&S-A, then increase the water dilution as the area becomes cleaner, as a weaker solution is able to do the job.

Housekeepers and custodians appreciate EC&S Dispersant, because it means the elimination of many of their bottles and cans of other cleaning products. They can use EC&S Dispersant FOR EVERYTHING from baths, bedrooms, and kitchens to offices and conference rooms. EC&S Dispersant is KIND TO THEIR SKIN; it does not dry out their hands, nor are there fumes which burn their noses or make them sneeze. The product has a pleasant, nonchemical smell. Cleaning workers using EC&S can work quickly and efficiently.

WALLS, WOODWORK AND WINDOWS

As a WALL CLEANER, EC&S Dispersant does an exceptional job on virtually any surface. It is safe on paint, and will not take the plasticizers out of acrylic type wall coverings and wallpapers. For cleaning walls, it is recommended that the WASHING ALWAYS BE DONE FROM THE BOTTOM, UP, AND RINSING FROM THE TOP DOWN. This will eliminate any potential streaking. For walls, use EC&S-B. Rinse with water and wipe off.

As a WOOD CLEANER, EC&S Dispersant is completely safe with no adverse effects such as spotting, streaking, or raising the wood grain. IT CAN BE USED ON BOWLING ALLEYS, BOWLING PINS, DOORS, DESKS, TABLES, CHAIRS, CABINETS, RAILINGS, etc. For these purposes, use one part EC&S-B, and one part water. Rinse with water and wipe down.

UPHOLSTERY AND RUGS

Use EC&S-D when using cleaning machines to clean rugs and carpets. For spotting, use EC&S-E on spots and stains. Sponge it on, agitate with a soft bristled brush, and wipe with a towel. DO NOT allow the carpets to become overly saturated with water and cleaning solution. Because the cleaning product will not completely evaporate, as is true with almost all carpet cleaning compounds, and the carpets cannot be rinsed off like walls or floors, care must be taken not to use a solution that is too strong. Residue left in the carpet will continue to clean, for example, the dirt on the bottom of people's shoes, causing large dirt spots to appear where the concentrations have been too high or too wet in the cleaning. IF THIS HAPPENS, the addition of WATER to the spots will clean the areas; then towel thoroughly, fan, or vacuum out all moisture. People sometimes think that if a little is good, a lot is better. When using this product on carpets, using too much can be a headache to the maintenance people.

When dealing with upholstery and fabrics, remember the above caution. A solution of EC&S-C is a good solution for stuffed upholstery. Brush it on, then towel it off. Stains and spots may take a higher concentration, but avoid getting the furniture too wet or using any solution stronger than EC&S-B concentrate.

INSTITUTIONAL BATHROOMS

If cleaned often, use EC&S-D for bathroom floors, walls, sinks, toilet bowls, decor cleaning, lighting fixtures, etc.

FABRICS - SPOTTING AND LAUNDRY

For bedspreads, curtains, towels, sheets, or any fabrics, EC&S Dispersant is an excellent perspiration, stain, and spot remover. It is EFFECTIVE ON THE FOLLOWING TYPES OF STAINS: alcohol, food stains, milk, ammonia, fruit, mustard, beer, fruit juices, nail polish, blood, gelatin, nicotine, butter, glue, oil, candy, grass stains, ointment, chewing gum, grease, light rust, chocolate, household cement, shoe polish, cocktails, ice cream, smoke stains, coffee, inks, soft drinks, cologne, perfume, iodine, soot, colored pencil, ketchup, sugar, cooking oil, lipstick, tar, cosmetics, mayonnaise, tea, medicine, water colors, crepe paper, metal polish, water stains, dyes, methylate, non-acrylic waxes, egg, mildew, wine, and many, many more.

EC&S-A may be used for difficult stains. Apply and allow dwell time of approximately 15 minutes. Agitate the cleaning product into the stain, then rinse. If it is an old stain, or very stubborn, repeat the process, allowing the product to remain on the stain for another 15 to 20 minutes following agitation. Rinse again. Several applications may be necessary, but usually the stain can be removed after one application. For less difficult stains, EC&S-B may be used. Follow the above procedure.

FURNITURE

EC&S Dispersant is safe for use on plastic, wood, cane, bamboo, metal, chrome, leather, and fabric. The best solution for cleaning all of your furniture is EC&S-D or -E. (See special instructions for upholstery - Model One: Memo VII, p. XII-512).

APPLIANCES

EC&S Dispersant is an effective cleaner of all APPLIANCES, large or small, inside or outside. Use EC&S-D for this cleaning purpose, including the exteriors of refrigerators, washers, dryers, ranges, small appliances, air conditioners, etc. Where heavy accumulations of grease and oil exist, use a solution of one part EC&S-A and one part water. The cleaning solution may be applied by spray or sponged on the appliance. The best results will be obtained when cleaning with a cloth or sponge, by cleaning from the bottom, up, while removing (rinsing) from the top, down. Be certain appliances are unplugged, and follow manufacturer's recommended safety procedures when cleaning any electrical appliance. Do not forget the value of dwell time.

Jackson Research Center

MODEL ONE: **MEMO VIII**

To: Environmental Health Foundation

From: William R. Jackson, Ph.D., Consultant

Subject: **Marine Use**

EC&S Dispersant is a concentrate that may be diluted with either fresh water or salt water. It is completely safe to use throughout ships, boats, and other vessels.

EC&S Dispersant is NONFLAMMABLE, NONEXPLOSIVE, NONTOXIC, NONHAZARDOUS, and has NO HAZARDOUS VAPORS OR ODORS. This cleaning agent requires no special handling or clothing and can be utilized with normal ventilation because there are no harmful vapors. It is well suited for use in enclosed areas such as engine rooms and ship interiors.

EC&S DISPERSANT WORKS EQUALLY WELL WHEN DILUTED WITH FRESH OR SALT WATER. THE PRODUCT WILL NOT HARM MARINE AQUACULTURE, FLORA, OR FAUNA. EC&S DISPERSANT CONTAINS NO NITRATES, PHOSPHATES, SULFONATES, CAUSTICS, OR CHLORINES.

APPLICATIONS

EC&S is effective for HEAVY DUTY CLEANING of engine room boilers, fireside washdowns of cargo tanks, of refrigerator containers, piping, pumps and valves, without toxic or polluting properties.

For REMOVAL OF CRUDE OIL AND OTHER PETROLEUM PRODUCTS from cargo tankers, (check with the consultants) a modified EC&S Dispersant may be sprayed into the cargo area by low volume high pressure pumps. This procedure should be done through the use of revolving spinner heads which can be lowered into the cargo tanks. This type of operation suggests the use of a 5° VEE jet nozzle, and these jet nozzles should be placed in the spinner heads. The process of spraying should begin as soon as possible after the ship is empty, thereby preventing the formation of volatile gases from the remaining crude oil or other petroleum residue. Continue the pumping until the cleaning solution has covered the entire surface. For best results, this solution should remain in place for about one hour. Following the dwell time of one hour, the Butterworth system should be used for 30 to 45 minutes.

An additional benefit is that EC&S Dispersant can be left on the INTERIOR OF THE CARGO TANKS, piping, pumps, and valves for periods of time longer than one hour with no negative effects. The initial one hour is the minimum recommended dwell time which will give the cleaning agent adequate time to begin breaking down the crude oil or other petroleum-like products. The longer dwell time will not decrease its efficiency, because complete evaporation will not occur. Thus, the results would be the same if Butterworthing is delayed as it would be if the process were done in sequence. After the procedure has been completed, the hold should be clean and gas free. In the event any gases do remain however, spray the interior of the cargo tanks with a solution of one part EC&S-A and six parts water, pressured through the revolving spinner heads. This spraying will make the tank gas free.

Because EC&S Dispersant holds a petroleum product in suspension and breaks it down to such a degree that it cannot come back together to its original state, the procedure can be completed without fear of creating an oil slick in the wake of a ship. ONCE THE REACTION HAS OCCURRED,

THE OIL LOSES ITS IDENTITY AS AN OIL and TAKES ON THE CHARACTERISTICS OF A WATER SOLUBLE SOLUTION. There are NO REVERSE EMULSIONS with EC&S Dispersant.

Cleaning ENGINE ROOMS with EC&S-A will emulsify the grease and act as a fire preventative. The product is nonflammable and nonexplosive.

REFRIGERATOR CONTAINERS may be cleaned with a 50/50 solution: one part EC&S-A and one part water. A greater dilution with water may be used for lighter soil. Using EC&S Dispersant for cleaning purposes will help to eliminate and control odors. In addition, successive cleanings will be easier once all the grease and dirt has been removed.

For BILGE CLEANING, approximately one gallon of EC&S-A will disperse one gallon of oil from a ship's bilges. Agitate with 80 to 100 gallons of fresh or salt water. If at sea, the roll of the ship will agitate the solution sufficiently. If in the harbor, agitate with high pressure water until the oil goes into solution. When EC&S Dispersant has completely absorbed the oil, the mixture will look milky. At this point, it can be disposed of without creating an oil slick. EC&S Dispersant is very efficient on Bunker "C" type fuel oil.

EC&S Dispersant is very effective as a MIDSHIPS cleaner. In the engine room where fuel oil, smoke, etc. are problems, apply a solution of one part EC&S-A and six parts water, then wipe down the area with a cloth. No rinsing or further wiping is necessary.

EC&S Dispersant is excellent for swabbing down BULKHEADS and DECKS. It will not damage paint or wooden surfaces, and if it is not rinsed off, it assists in preventing rust on exposed surfaces. For these applications, use EC&S-D.

Small amounts of the cleaning material may be introduced into the ship's VENTILATION SYSTEM by means of an atomizing spray, to dispel foul air or odors.

A solution of EC&S-C or EC&S-D effectively removes STACK GASES.

EC&S Dispersant can remove TARNISH and CORROSION from copper, brass, and silver. In addition, it will remove LIGHT RUST from iron and steel when used in a soak tank operation with a solution of one part EC&S-A and one part water. Dwell time will depend upon the degree of contamination.

An application of EC&S-A or EC&S-B effectively removes mildew from LINES, CANOPY SAILS, RIGGING, UPHOLSTERY, and KEELS.

The same application, EC&S-A or EC&S-B, removes oil from BILGES, DECKS, HULLS, ENGINE, and ENGINE COWLING. Salt water and salt water spots from windshields, decks, and hulls may also be cleaned.

EC&S Dispersant is completely safe to use throughout marine vessels because it has NO

INGREDIENTS TO DISTURB THE GRAIN OF FINE WOOD. There is no chlorine to bleach PAINTED SURFACES and NO PETROLEUM SOLVENTS TO CRAZE OR WARP PLASTIC OR FIBERGLASS MATERIALS.

Jackson Research Center

MODEL ONE: **MEMO IX**

To: Environmental Health Foundation

From: William R. Jackson, Ph.D., Consultant

Subject: **Motor Vehicles: Autos, Trucks, Buses, and Trains;**
Service Station Maintenance
Brake Shops
Heavy Equipment Shops

MOTOR VEHICLES: AUTOS, TRUCKS, BUSES, and TRAINS

EC&S Dispersant is a uniquely versatile cleaner that will safely and effectively clean and degrease while breaking down and biodegrading oil and dirt.

EC&S Dispersant may be used under all conditions, and because it is nontoxic, free of enzymes, sulphates, nitrates and known pollutants, it can be used with no special or protective clothing. Only normal ventilation is needed.

After the cleaning project is complete, the dirt, oil, and grease materials are sewer treatable. EC&S Dispersant may be diluted with either cold or warm water. Most cleaning work will require only one application. However, the cleaning process may be facilitated by a longer dwell time and agitation if necessary.

POTENTIAL USERS

Bus operators	Body shops
Car & truck washers	Fleet owners
Dealers - all vehicles	Mechanic shops
Government motor pools	Motorhome sales
Public transit authorities	Railroads
Service stations & repair garages	Rapid transit
Taxi & limousine operators	Rental car agencies

SPECIAL FEATURES & BENEFITS

- Single product that cleans and degreases, thus eliminating from four to six other products from the inventory.

- Breaks down and biodegrades oils and dirts for safe disposal and sewage treatment.

- Safe products that eliminate the need for special clothing or protective devices. EC&S Dispersant will not contribute to fire hazards.

- Mild, pleasant odor is not offensive to people when used to clean passenger compartments.

- Restores like-new appearance of interior upholstery and trim.

- Safely cleans up oils, fuel, gas spills, and leaks commonly associated with motor vehicles.

- Mechanic health risk and owner liability are reduced through use of environmentally safe products that reduce health and safety hazards. This would encourage lower insurance rates.

APPLICATIONS

HAND CLEANER: Apply, rub until clean, and rinse off or just wipe dry.

ENGINE & VEHICLE COMPONENT DEGREASING

Light to moderate grease: Apply EC&S-A liberally, allow 5 to 20 minutes dwell time. Rinse off with full or high water pressure. Do NOT allow EC&S-A to dry before rinsing, because a hot engine will further bake the hydrocarbon mixture.

Heavy grease: Apply EC&S-A to all greasy areas. Allow 5 to 15 minutes dwell time. Scrape off thick deposits with scraper or other tool when grease becomes softened by the solution. Re-apply solution. Allow 5 to 20 minutes more dwell time and agitate with stiff bristle brush if needed. Rinse off with full or high water pressure before cleaning solution dries.

ENGINE BLOCK: Liberally spray EC&S-A over cool engine block. Allow 5 to 15 minutes dwell time. Rinse off with full or high water pressure.

TIRES/WHITEWALLS, and HUBCAPS: Apply with stiff bristle brush, then rinse.

VEHICLE EXTERIORS-EC&S WILL REMOVE COSMOLINE (PETROLATUM)

General cleaning: With soft cloth or sponge, wipe on EC&S-B. Allow dwell time, then rinse with full or high water pressure. Dry as usual.

Heavy Cosmoline coating: New vehicles and equipment may be shipped to dealers with a heavy coating of Cosmoline (petrolatum), especially foreign imports. If such a coating exists, spray vehicle with a fine mist of EC&S-A, starting at the bottom and working up. Allow 5 to 10 minutes dwell time (approximate time to work your way around the vehicle), and then wash as indicated above and dry as usual.

VEHICLE INTERIORS: Spray on, brush or wipe after 15 seconds dwell time; rinse with damp cloth. Vacuum upholstery when dry if loose dirt remains on the surface.

AUTO RADIATORS: Pour one part EC&S-A and nine parts water in the radiator and allow to circulate for four days. Drain, flush, and refill with antifreeze and water.

RADIATOR and ENGINE BLOCK CLEANING for **TRUCKS and BUSES**: Place one part EC&S-A and nine parts water in the radiator. Drive the vehicle for one day. Drain the radiator water. Fill the radiator 1/2 full with water and run the engine until the temperature reaches approximately 140 degrees. Turn off the engine. Drain the radiator. Flush the radiator until the water is clear. When cleaning engine blocks with EC&S-A, allow adequate dwell time and remove before running the engine excessively to avoid baking the EC&S solution on to the block.

WINDOWS, MIRRORS, and INSTRUMENT PANELS: Spray on, wipe off. If there is streaking, wipe with a wet cloth or dilute the cleaning solution.

SERVICE STATION MAINTENANCE

EC&S Dispersant products are very useful for service station maintenance.

PRE-SPOTTING (before cleaning service drives): Take a squirt bottle and fill with EC&S-A. Spray oil and heavy spots, then agitate. Let set, and then clean the service drive.

SERVICE DRIVES: Use a mop bucket containing EC&S-C. Apply with mop and let stand 5 -10 minutes if possible. Rinse and squeegee dry.

FOAMER: Fill concentrate, EC&S-A to second line on foamer and fill container with water. Apply with a hose, and brush with a broom. Let stand 5 - 15 minutes if possible. Rinse and squeegee dry.

GENERAL MAINTENANCE of PUMPS, WALLS, etc.: Place EC&S-B in a squirt bottle. Spray on and rinse or wipe off.

SERVICE ISLAND: Place one part EC&S-A and 30 parts water in windshield-washing container.

WINDOWS, GLASS, STAINLESS, etc.: Place EC&S-E in a squirt bottle. Spray on and rinse or wipe off. In the event of streaking, dilute the solution.

BRAKE SHOPS

WETTING AGENT (Control of hazardous asbestos brake dust): Research has shown that the inhalation of asbestos dust increases the risk of asbestosis and cancer. A 1985 television documentary disclosed a high incidence of lung cancer caused by breathing in asbestos dust when doing brake jobs. In some cases, death occurred within four months of doing a brake job. For information concerning the identification and abatement of asbestos hazards, contact the Consumer Protection Safety Commission, Washington, DC at 1-800-638-2772 or U.S. EPA Toxic Substance Control Act (TSCA) hotline, Washington, DC at 1-202-554-1404. (Note: telephone numbers were correct at the date of publication but are subject to change).

EC&S is non-ionic and will help control the static electricity that may cause brake dust to become airborne. Immediately wet dust from brake drums and wet or wash surfaces of drum and brake assemblies to help prevent asbestos dust from "flying." Wipe up residues with paper towels or rags and dispose of in approved, enclosed containers. Brake dust should NEVER be removed by blowing or brushing.

NOTE: Protective clothing and breathing equipment should be worn at ALL TIMES when working around areas where asbestos may be present.

HEAVY EQUIPMENT SHOPS

EC&S Dispersant HEAVY EQUIPMENT SOLUTION is a superior performing concentrate designed for typical dirt and soils found on HEAVY FIELD EQUIPMENT IN OIL FIELD RIGS, HEAVY EARTH MOVING MACHINERY, ETC. It can be applied by soak tank or pressure spray with or without water proportioning. It can also be mixed with kerosene, stoddard solvent, diesel fuel, or used alone, depending upon the soil conditions, temperature, and severity.

EC&S Dispersant, HEAVY EQUIPMENT SOLUTION is an effective degreaser for swab, spray, or soak tank applications, for use on painted or unpainted surfaces, ferrous to nonferrous metals.

- OIL FIELD EQUIPMENT, ENGINE BLOCKS, HEAVY EQUIPMENT, FLOORS or any other surface where extra heavy grease deposits occur: Mix two parts EC&S-A to one part kerosene, solvent, or diesel fuel. This will make an emulsion that gets thicker without repeated stirring. This thickness serves a very important function in that it causes the cleaner to cling to a vertical surface long enough to increase dwell time and accomplish the cleaning task. Once the solution becomes smooth in consistency, apply by a spray method. A three to five gallon hand-pump type sprayer is ideal for this purpose. EC&S Dispersant HEAVY EQUIPMENT SOLUTION in a solvent emulsion usually works in about 20 - 30 minutes. WHEN GREASE STARTS TO SLIDE, RINSE OFF WITH HIGH PRESSURE WATER.

- For light to medium-heavy degreasing, use EC&S-B or EC&S-A.

EC&S Dispersant HEAVY EQUIPMENT SOLUTION has a UNIQUE QUALITY as a degreaser. When it is left on a surface, it will not completely evaporate. Leave the solution on the surface overnight, and wash it down with high pressure water the next day. The results will be the same as if you had completed the job in sequence.

EC&S Dispersant HEAVY EQUIPMENT SOLUTION INHIBITS RUST AND CORROSION of metals as long as there remains an adequate amount of the agent on the metal surface. In the event that all product is rinsed off thoroughly with water, the metal is left exposed and therefore subject to rusting and corrosion as usual. To inhibit this occurrence, a light oil film may be applied to the surface.

EC&S Dispersant HEAVY EQUIPMENT SOLUTION deals with those areas where MILDEW is a problem. It is extremely effective in MILDEW removal under a hot water, high-power pressure spray application. Once the surface has been cleaned thoroughly, MILDEW is somewhat inhibited from returning.

SUMMARY OF MODEL ONE: MEMO GUIDE APPLICATION

EC&S-A

- Carbon removal from aircraft exteriors
- Concrete surface cleaning
- Dust control (for roads - 50:1)
- Degreasing
- Engine and greasy vehicle components
- Evaporative coolers/pads
- Graffiti
- Greasy grills
- Hand cleaner after automotive grease or printers' ink use
- Oven and fryer cleaning
- Pre-treatment of stains prior to washing
- Refuse chutes
- Refuse containers
- Sidewalks, parking areas
- Sprinkler stains
- White walls of tires

EC&S-B

- Bowling balls
- Ceilings
- Fryer hood/vents/filters
- Garden tools/mower
- General cleaning of interiors of houses, autos, trucks, transportation vehicles, stores, and commercial buildings

Glue: Soften and loosen dried school glue
Allows removal of undried high-strength glues (resorcinol - carpenters glue)
Golf carts/bags/clubs/balls
Household appliances - inside/outside (very dirty)
Kitchen counters/tables/chairs
Lavatories
Microwave ovens
Mildew control
Oil on surfaces
Refrigerator ship containers
Refrigerators, commercial walk-in
Shower/bathtubs/sinks (in hard water areas)
Silver/brass cleaning
Tire or shoe marks
Trash containers
Veterinary/animal bathers

EC&S-C

Bowling alley
Desks/tables/cabinets
Doors
General household - furniture, fixtures, personal items (combs, brushes, jewelry, etc.), appliances, personal use (sink, tub, or shower)

	Railings Spot cleaning of carpets Upholstery cleaning Vents/hoods (light use) Wood surfaces
EC&S-D	Acoustical tile Aircraft exteriors Aircraft instruments, earphones, and lavatories Aluminum & stainless steel surface cleaning Appliances (with regular use) Auto exteriors Auto radiators Carpet cleaning by machine Floors/mopping (or 10 oz per gallon) Furniture (all types) Laundry Loading dock areas Pots and pans (or 10 oz per gallon) Stainless steel (very greasy) Venetian, mini blinds, and window covers
EC&S-E	Clear plastic surfaces Decorative stainless steel Glass cleaning

Lamps/chandeliers
Mirrors
T.V. and computer screens

The question again is: Is it possible to have your shop, home, school, and commercial area safe and clean, and to eliminate most toxic and hazardous cleaning products while still watching the financial bottom line? The answer is YES! With EC&S, an outstanding working model!

XIII

WORKING MODEL TWO: EC&S BIO-STIMULANT

Chapter Outline

EC&S Bio-Stimulant
Overview and Data Sheet

SPECIFICATIONS:

- Highly concentrated, multi-component, bio-ecosystem in translucent aqueous solution
- Chemical analysis reveals almost pure water with a number of common trace elements detected spectrographically
- Contains 100% organic materials
- Able to exist and thrive in waters with wide variations of salt content

- Classified nonhazardous and poses no health hazard either internally or externally

- Produced according to Federal Regulations 1910.1200

- See MSDS included in Chapter XI.

APPROVALS:

- USDA authorization for use under the Federal meat, poultry, shell egg grading, and egg products inspection program for bio-remediation

- Meets all published OSHA regulatory requirements

- Meets all published EPA regulatory requirements

- Meets all published DOT regulatory requirements

- Contains no ingredients listed in California Proposition 65-The Safe Drinking Water and Toxic Enforcement Act of 1986

EC&S Bio-Stimulant contains a carefully developed system that keeps its water medium in a constant state of oxygen saturation. This system revitalizes the indigenous microorganisms that are already present in living and previously living matter, in hydrocarbon based toxic contamination, and natural (in situ) remediation sites, which have descended to a state of dormancy due to unfavorable and/or toxic conditions. According to J.S. Baskt, as referenced in the article "Impact of Present and Future Regulations on Bioremediation," 1991, Journal of Industrial Microbiology, 8:13-22, it was confirmed that if live microorganisms were imported and used on a job site, especially genetically cultured or modified microbial organisms, TOXIC SUBSTANCES CONTROL ACT (TSCA) and FEDERAL PLANT PEST ACT (FPPA) approval would usually be required.

Unlike single strain bio-remediation imported microorganisms, EC&S Bio-Stimulant is a biochemical product containing a complete system of several vitamin precursors of both plant and animal origin, in an ecologically-balanced and highly concentrated mass of autotrophic, aerobic, and anaerobic enzymes, coenzymes, exoenzymes, and multifactorial inducer molecules. The product stimulates a broad spectrum of flocculative and specialized natural microorganisms. This nontoxic, non-pathogenic suspension of bio-stimulants remains active over a wide range of temperatures and other environmental influences. The bio-stimulants have been selected for maximum efficiency in stimulating specific bio-ecosystems that have a high rate of efficiency at bio-degrading a wide range of toxicants in the industrial and commercial waste arenas.

PETROLEUM HYDROCARBON BIO-REMEDIATION

EC&S Bio-Stimulant, a complete system of microorganism stimulation, serves as multifactorial inducer molecules to accelerate the rapid reproduction of microorganisms such as bacteria, fungi, algae, and actinomycetes, and thus greatly expands the process governing bio-degradation. EC&S Bio-Stimulant enhances the capability of a bacterium to degrade hazardous waste materials by controlling the actions that catalyze a specific oxidation. Petroleum products such as diesel, motor oil, and gasoline, various solvents, and complex combinations of pollutants are metabolized. The final products of the enzyme-stimulated, bacterial-degradation of this waste matter are modified cells, H_2O and CO_2. Coupled with bio-venting, the in-situ process of EC&S Bio-Stimulant enhanced bio-degradation can reach under buildings and other surface obstructions as an inexpensive remediation method. For more specific information, see Jackson Research Center Memo V, Petroleum Hydrocarbon Remediation within this chapter.

MUNICIPAL and INDUSTRIAL WASTE BIO-RESTORATION

EC&S Bio-Stimulant alters the physical structure of suspended organic solids, causing more efficient separation for improved digestion rates and terminal flocculation. Fats, oils, and greases are rapidly solubilized through the enzymatic and exoenzymatic hydrolysis stimulated by EC&S Bio-Stimulant. Cellulose materials from products such as cotton, paper, fruit, and vegetable pulps, and cigarettes are rapidly hydrolyzed and degraded by native cellulose digesting microorganisms when the sewage material is inoculated with EC&S Bio-Stimulant's carefully balanced enzyme, exoenzyme coenzyme, and multifactorial inducer molecule system. This inoculation also assists the process by which microbial life breaks down the many components in synthetic detergents that alter the efficiency of an activated sludge plant. This increases the overall efficiency of the aerobic waste treatment system and reduces the sludge volume. For more specific information, see Jackson Research Center Memo IV in this chapter, Municipal and Industrial Wastewater Bio-Restoration.

ANIMAL WASTE BIO-TRANSFORMATION

EC&S Bio-Stimulant enzymatically alters the physical structure of the suspended organic solids.

The completely balanced bio-ecosystem of EC&S Bio-Stimulant provides a significantly greater concentration of highly effective enzymes, coenzymes, exoenzymes, and multifactorial inducer molecules that improve digestion rates and terminal flocculation. Cellulose materials are rapidly degraded and hydrolyzed by the stimulation of naturally occurring cellulose digesting microorganisms. This process results in a more complete liquefaction and gasification, and a reduction in sludge volume. The ammonia concentration in wastewater is also reduced, thus reducing or eliminating the retrograde step of ammonium nitrate/nitrite conversion in the overall denitrification process. In situ microbial treatment of animal waste utilizes the indigenous biota conditioned by EC&S Bio-Stimulant to form a natural reactor for the bio-degradation of animal waste. For more specific information, see Jackson Research Center Memo III in this chapter, Animal Waste Bio-Transformation.

ODOR CONTROL - BIO-DISSIPATION

EC&S Bio-Stimulant contains high amounts of free and dissolved oxygen. It not only will assist in replenishing oxygen in stagnant ponds or other polluted mediums; it also will eliminate much of the odor causing substances. EC&S Bio-Stimulant's balanced formula instantly goes into solution to produce great amounts of self-generating, dissolved, and free-oxygen that restricts odor-causing anaerobes and stimulates the eutrophic process. When applied as specified for individual condition requirements, EC&S Bio-Stimulant can reduce odor remediation time by 20% to 75%. For more specific information, see Jackson Research Center Memo II in this chapter, Odor Control and Bio-Dissipation.

AGRICULTURAL BIO-APPLICATION

With the accelerated use of commercial farm chemicals thought to be necessary to modern agriculture, the study and use of soil microbes becomes increasingly important in revitalizing the soil rapidly, safely, and economically. For more specific information, see Jackson Research Center Memo I in this chapter, Agricultural Bio-Stimulant.

APPLICATION METHODS

1. INOCULATION for use in waste remediation systems such as wastewater treatment facilities, animal waste wash-down water, grease traps, etc.

2. SPRAY OR MIST for use on animal waste ponds, compost piles, feed lots, poultry houses, and in wastewater treatment facilities, etc.

3. PRESSURE INJECTION for use in subterranean areas

APPLICATION PARAMETERS

1. pH: Optimum of 7, minimum of 4.5, maximum of 9.0

2. DO (dissolved oxygen): Optimum 3 PPM+, minimum of 2 PPM

3. C/N (carbon/nitrogen ratio): Optimum 10:1, maximum 20:1

4. Temperature: Maximum 49° C, optimum 30° C., minimum 19° C

5. Increased surface area or solubility allows for more rapid oxidation and stimulated metabolism of the biota in the waste being treated.

SOME SUGGESTED SPECIFIC TREATMENT SYSTEMS

1. Activated sludge systems

2. Tickling filters

3. Oxidation lagoons

4. Wastewater treatment tanks

5. Mist/Spray systems

6. Pressure injection/Bio-venting systems

APPLICATION RATES

Dilution rates, frequency of application, and duration of treatment are determined by individual situation requirements as recommended by your professional consultant.

Introduction to Working Model Two

Bio-Stimulant application converts the transformation, remediation, and restoration tasks from those of Herculean brute force to those involving a sly but powerful strategy. These tasks are accomplished by drafting nature's invisible army! This massive army, faithfully and quietly eats away at nature's various assignments. It is possible to command this powerful force of microbes to convert to water (H_2O) and carbon dioxide (CO_2), to respond, to enrich worn soil, and to digest the nastiest, most troublesome pollutants.

The mode for employing the powerful force of microorganisms and restoring natural environmental conditions is available, and it is not the "Blob That Ate Detroit." The numerous one-celled life forms known as microorganisms include bacteria, fungi, algae and others. Their job is very basic, as related by Dr. Carl Oppenheimer of the University of Texas at Austin: Microorganisms "recycle the components of organic matter, or once living organisms, and convert them to the nutrient chemicals used by plants in photosynthesis and chemosynthesis."

Data substantiates the following: The majority of microorganisms (bacteria, etc.) retreat into a spore form. Picture this result as hibernation, or a type of suspended animation. When these microorganisms are confronted with hostile conditions (e.g., lack of nutrients, excessive heat, cold, pH change, or lack of adequate moisture), the microorganism will retreat and become dormant. Dormant microbial life forms (various spores) were found in recent years in Egyptian pyramids. Many were not dead; they were just "asleep."

Can microbial life be awakened on cue? Is it possible to "bring them back," to rekindle their dynamic usefulness? What can be done to control their environment efficiently? Is there a way to stimulate their rapid reproduction, and thus increase this army's powerful effectiveness? Thereby, indigenous microbial life would be sufficient, and the imported, questionable live microbial life would not be required.

The microorganisms in our environment act by initiating humification through biochemical transformation of complex carbonaceous substances. They are involved in a series of reactions caused by their enzymes' actions and reactions that decompose dead plant and animal tissues, thus disintegrating parts from complex polymers into simple segments. All biochemically produced organic compounds can be digested by microorganisms.

Basically, all living tissue is made up of a collection of biomolecules that are unstable in use and production of heat (thermodynamics). When no longer engaged in the life process (including secretions, excretions, or the death of the organism), bio-molecules usually lose their original composition and are ultimately transformed into simple stable components. This breaking down of organic compounds involves physicochemical processes such as oxidation, photolysis, and thermolysis. However, the majority of these changes are initiated biologically.

Is nature's action of disintegration and transformation related to the cycle that includes the overall food chain? For example, does this involve the food source for the billions and billions of microorganisms that work for us in the soil? How do other elements such as oxygen, or the lack of it, affect the biological changes of disintegration and transformation, referred to as humification? How does nature establish a menu to serve all life that comes to her table?

Biological transmutations may include microorganisms breaking down existing elements or atoms and actually making new elements. Is there something outstanding and astonishing happening when microbial life proliferates in accord with nature itself? Is it possible that through biological transmutation, bio-agriculture and even bio-remediation can become more effective? With its own natural balancing ability, nature can heal itself when left alone. Nature practices multiple methods of preventing deficiencies subject to the availability of natural microbial life. What threatens the existence of microorganisms? In many cases microbial life may be removed from the soil, or forced into a state of dormancy by various toxic chemicals which may include the over-application of herbicides, pesticides or any other application of fertilizer salts in the form of chemical fertilizers.

It has been suggested that EC&S Bio-Stimulant is involved in assisting nature in its natural steps of transmutation. Is it possible that some of the measurable results of remediation are related to chemistry while the unknown, unobservable phenomenon is that of transmutation? Is it even possible that some of the measurable results of remediation are related to chemistry while the unknown, unobservable phenomenon is that of transmutation? Is it even possible that bio-life could function as an "atom smasher," allowing microorganisms to exist as the power source to maintain balance? How else do we expect to achieve balance in nature if we are not willing to allow it to happen naturally? For example, would this natural balance make our crops less susceptible to harmful insects and parasites, thus affording more freedom from the required use of pesticides? Have we developed a collection of problems which are actually man-made consequences of biological imbalance?

Microorganism activity in one acre of soil uses about the same amount of energy in soil preparation as 10,000 people would burn for the same work, for the same period of time.* Microorganisms must be protected, nourished, and further stimulated when required.

MICROBIAL RESIDENTS

Some microorganisms like a fairly specific selection of organic compounds, and others have the ability to find a source of energy and food value for their metabolic survival from a large menu of carbon compounds. Through humification, complex

---

*Jackson, William R., Ph.D. (1993). *Humic, Fulvic and Microbial Balance: Organic Soil Conditioning*. Evergreen, CO: Jackson Research Center, p. 33 and 409.

polymers are disintegrated into simpler segments. Then the microorganisms remanufacture or recombine those simple segments or units into altogether different sequences, thus forming a complete series of new and different complex polymers and eventually forming humic molecules.

In general, four major types of microorganisms can be found in soil and in the marine environment:

1. Algae
2. Bacteria
3. Fungi
4. Actinomycetes

Under favorable circumstances, all four of these categories of microorganisms are present in the soil in very large numbers. For example, 1 gram of soil (1 cubic centimeter) may contain 300,000 algae, 4 billion bacteria, 1 million fungi, and 20 million actinomycetes.* All of these microorganisms are of significant value in the decomposition of organic materials. This process releases elements of nutrient value and captures nitrogen from the atmosphere.

Soil microorganisms perform many activities that make powerful contributions to our ecosystem. The fertility level of the soil and spaceship earth's remediation depends so heavily upon microorganism

---

*Jackson, 34.

activity that if they were to fail, life for higher plants, animals, and humans would cease.

ALGAE are very important plants, and most algae are microscopic. They function in the decomposition of organic residues and thereby make nutrients available for plant growth. The cyanobacteria called blue-green algae, for example, are presumed to have developed from bacteria during the prehistoric upper Onverwacht period. The Carboniferous period of history included an abrupt change in the make-up of organic matter. At this time, organic carbon became strongly enriched with heavy carbon isotopes. An increase of algae and available carbon as a plant food source is noted during this era when dense plant life covered the continents. It is assumed that the climate conditions during this period were humid and favorable for growth of terrestrial vegetation. It was during this Carboniferous time that large amounts of biomass or humic materials were developed. The accumulation of land plants making up this mass of organic matter has been preserved in the rocks of this historic age.[*] Then, as now, microflora played a major role in the breakdown of organic materials to serve as plant food.

---

[*]Jackson, 34.

There are many families of BACTERIA, the most predominant collection of marine microorganisms. Bacteria can be either aerobic, requiring air or free oxygen for life, or anaerobic, capable of growing or existing in the absence of free oxygen (for example, fermentation in the absence of air.) The majority of aquatic or water bacteria have the capacity as anaerobes to grow in the presence or absence of free oxygen. Bacteria are so versatile that they can survive under extreme environmental conditions, including variations of salinities, pH conditions, temperatures, or barometric pressures. They can exist under pH conditions ranging from 4 to 9, but do best in the range of 6.5 to 8.5. Bacteria are second only to fungi in their digestive ability, and they will attack and break down almost any organic compound for use as food. They not only digest proteins and sugars, but also fats, oils, and cellulose, among many other carbonaceous compounds.[*]

When conditions are acceptable, bacteria multiply very rapidly. Their generation time ranges from 20 minutes to a few hours, depending on the family to which they belong.[*] Bordovskiy reported that the number of bacterial cells in marine

---

[*]Jackson, 35.

[*]Jackson, 35.

sediments varies, ranging from 5.7×10^7 to 1.2×10^{10} per gram (or 570 million to 120 billion per gram), depending on the environmental situation.* According to him, very few groups of marine microorganisms can compare with bacteria in:

1. Rapid multiplication
2. Growth
3. Diversity of function
4. Magnitude of activity

This bacterial biomass makes a forceful impact in contributing organic matter.

FUNGI are extensively distributed throughout our environment. All fungi are aerobic, needing free oxygen for life, and are heterotrophic, capable of utilizing only organic materials as food. Fungi are very tolerant of pH variation, living in environments ranging from acidic to alkaline. However, they seem to do best in an acidic environment.*

Fungi adapt well to complex food systems, specifically the polymeric compounds that are not easily decomposed by bacteria and actinomycetes.

---

*Jackson, 35.

*Jackson, 36.

Such materials as cellulose, hemicellulose, protein, chitin, and other polymers are degraded and digested by these microorganisms.[*]

When the numbers of fungi are compared to bacteria, fungi are fewer. However, fungi contribute a significant amount of biomass because of the extensive development of their filaments.

ACTINOMYCETES are numerous, and their distribution is extensive. They are found in oceans, lakes, ponds, sediments, and soils. Their abundance is second only to bacteria, and they exist in a very wide array of distinctly different family groups.[*] Alexander reported that in certain parts of the Pacific Ocean, actinomycetes make up 95% of the microorganisms present. In soil they may range from 1 million to 1 billion per gram of soil.[*] These microorganisms are EFFICIENT IN BREAKING DOWN THE RESISTANT COMPOUNDS OF BOTH PLANTS AND ANIMALS. Their diet ranges from simple, organic acids and sugars to complex organic compounds, including polysaccharides, lipids,

---

[*]Jackson, 36.

[*]Jackson, 36.

[*]Jackson, 36.

proteins, paraffins, phenols, steroids, chitins, and pyrimidines.

OVERVIEW OF MICROBIAL DISINTEGRATION AND TRANSFORMATION

The microorganism population is an assemblage of several general families, including algae, bacteria, fungi, and actinomycetes. There are many other groups and families of microorganisms, but these four make the most important contribution in humification. These microorganisms are so versatile in their diet that they can actually attack and decompose almost any complex matter. In this process, they transform carbon into new protoplasm and thereby create the energy required for their metabolic functions. In spite of the high degree of complexity and diversity found in organic compounds manufactured in the cell, all compounds, even the complex polymers, are disintegrated by the microbial population, their enzymes, and other bio-stimulants. Each bio-stimulant is involved in a specific role, following particular steps in a well defined process on a substrata backdrop or stage. These critical bio-stimulants and collection of multifactorial inducer molecules play a unique role in the biochemistry of organisms in the full range of life, from bacteria to humankind.

Environmental disadvantages may create conditions that change the rate and the direction of the microorganisms' metabolism. However, microorganisms are exceptionally capable of adapting themselves in order to overcome environmental change and stress.* Bio-stimulants may be used to increase productivity toward various tasks to be accomplished.

Humification by microorganisms involves complex carbon compounds being digested and disintegrated into simple forms. These simple forms are then remanufactured, transformed, resynthesized, and recombined into altogether new and different combinations and sequences of now new complex polymers. As the original material is broken down and new combinations are assembled, these new multiple combinations are forming humic molecules.

It has been concluded that the addition of a simple substratum to the soil (e.g. glucose, which is readily usable by microorganisms as a source of energy) causes a notable and immediate increase in the metabolism of the biomass. This process is followed by a decrease as the substratum becomes depleted.* It has been calculated that much of the added glucose is not utilized as an energy source because much of the carbon from the glucose enters

---

*Jackson, 37.

*Jackson, 39.

microbial tissue.[*] Along with glucose and other carbohydrates serving as a food source, soil microorganisms may also utilize substituted aromatic carboxylic acids, phenols, and amino acids.

It should be noted again that humic substances participate with vigor in the life cycles of flora as well as do microorganisms. Humic acids exert a specific influence on soil microorganisms by means of the carbon cycle. Carbon makes up approximately 50% of the soil organic matter. Compared to most types of inorganic compounds, these materials seem resistant to the degradation of microorganisms. Inasmuch as the majority of soil inorganic matter is resistant to degradation, its carbon source is only slightly usable, suggesting there is limited carbonaceous material available in inorganic matter to be utilized by microorganisms or by photogenic organisms.

On the other hand, the basis of the nitrogen cycle involves the mineralization of nitrogen bound in organic molecules and then the immobilization of inorganic nitrogen by its transformation to organic compounds. Nitrogen functioning as a macronutrient has a powerful influence on the growth of microorganisms, plants, and eventually on animals.

---

[*]Jackson, 40.

Chemical composition of living matter. The basic sources of living matter are:

1. Phytoplankton
2. Zooplankton
3. Microorganisms
4. Higher plant and animal life

The living cells of all organisms are capable of manufacturing a variety of heterogeneous and highly complex organic compounds. This collection of individual compounds manufactured by living organisms is incredibly large. The chemical composition of both marine and terrestrial living matter is highly variable and depends upon many factors. For example, within the carbohydrates, cellulose makes up 15% to 60% of the dry weight. This wide variation may be explained by the nature of the organisms, the nutrition available, the nature of their surroundings, and many other environmental variables. On the other hand, the majority of the compositional characteristics of all organisms are very much alike inasmuch as they all are composed of a variety of proteins, carbohydrates, lipids, and minerals. Their differences are based upon the variable concentration and proportion of these compounds. For example, marine phytoplankton are mainly made up of protein with a small and variable mixture of lipids and carbohydrates.

The chemical composition of higher plants is more diverse than that of marine living matter. Terrestrial plants are mainly composed of carbohydrates, lignins, and proteins. Carbohydrates are the most plentiful compound in higher land plants, making up 50% to 70% of their dry weight.* Knowledge of the chemical composition of the biomass helps us understand the action of humification.

Cellular makeup and microbial breakdown. During humification, all cellular makeup undergoes a pattern of transformations, modifications, and structural rearrangements, resulting in highly complex polymeric humic compounds. Although some of these modifications are chemical, most are biochemical and develop through the enormous numbers of enzymes. Some bio-stimulants are released by the microorganism population. Because of this action, microorganisms are credited for the breakdown of cellular formations. As described earlier, A LIVING CELL IS A UNIQUE BIOCHEMICAL LABORATORY WHERE A TREMENDOUS NUMBER OF ORGANIC COMPOUNDS ARE MANUFACTURED. Reviewing some of these major groups of compounds and understanding some of the products developed

---

*Jackson, 42.

by the degradation of the microorganisms will assist in our working knowledge of humification.

The protein family and microbial breakdown. Proteins are the foundational component of all living organisms. These organic compounds are directly associated with all physiological functions of living organisms and are the common polymers in all plants and animals. They are derived from amino acids combined with peptides and contain approximately 16% nitrogen. This fact is important because nitrogen is a very critical element in all living organisms. Lower plants most often have high concentrations of nitrogen, and these nitrogen containing compounds account for about 40% of the organic matter associated with marine sediment. Rashid reported that a protein molecule may contain from a few dozen to several thousand individual amino acids and that amino acids are the building blocks of all peptides and proteins. Multiple amino acids and related compounds are found in sea water sediments and sedimentary humic compounds. It is believed that many amino acids can remain stable over millions of years.*

In addition to proteins, peptides, and amino acids, cells contain substantial amounts of nucleic acids. The nitrogen containing compounds of nucleic acids directly include nucleic acids in the

---

*Jackson, 45.

biochemistry of humification. Microorganisms actively participate in biochemical reactions that develop into the remanufacturing of humic compounds. Although amino acids may be the most important compounds containing nitrogen, nucleic acids and amino sugars are also of high precedence.

The two most emphasized nucleic acids are RNA (ribonucleic acid) and DNA (deoxyribonucleic acid). RNA and DNA are found in the protoplasm of all plant and animal tissues. Bacteria, fungi, and actinomycetes are involved in the decomposition of nucleic acids, and thus the large molecules are converted into smaller units. Protein also makes nitrogen available for all microbial flora active in the humification process.[*]

Carbohydrates and microbial disintegration. Carbohydrates are involved in a significant portion of marine and terrestrial life, including all microorganisms within that biomass. These organic compounds serve as an energy base and assist in cell structure. Simple carbohydrates are known as monosaccharides, and the more complex polymers are called polysaccharides. Whether naturally manufactured or synthesized, carbohydrates and the monosaccharides and polysaccharides transformed by microorganisms are major contributors to humification.

---

[*]Jackson, 45.

Lipids and related resources. The lipid family includes fats, oils, waxes, and related compounds. These organic substances are types of triglycerides. Oxidative coupling of both phenolic compounds and some aromatic amines occurs during humification, caused by enzyme activity, bio-stimulants, inducer molecules, as well as chemical reactions. The oxidation of phenols stimulates the formation of radicals.

Review. Different types of products can be found in the different stages of this process, including (a) products resulting from the initial degradation, (b) the intermediate products of transformation, and (c) the end products of metabolism. The probable formation of humus begins with reactions involving the most abundant and reactive components such as:

1. Phenols, polyphenols, and related compounds

2. Proteins, amino acids, peptides, and other nitrogen containing compounds

3. Carbohydrates, sugars, and various products of their transformation*

---

*Jackson, 46.

Microbial transformations of cellular makeup result in many chemical and biochemical reactions leading to the vast number of products of decay and disintegration. This activity eventually results in the beginning of a group of compounds commonly known as humic substances.

Humification is the most universal biogeochemical phenomenon in the biosphere, and humic compounds are among the most plentiful organic compounds on and around our spaceship earth. These organic materials exist in our soils, sediments, peats, shales, lignites, coals, and all marine environments.

Model Two: Memo Guide

Jackson Research Center

MODEL TWO: **MEMO I**

To: Environmental Health Foundation

From: William R. Jackson, Ph.D., Consultant

Subject: **Agricultural Bio-Application**

Microorganisms and Soil Rebuilding

Microorganisms granulate the soil and thus aerate it to facilitate the infusion of water and air. The depth of the aerated top soil determines the quantity and quality of the local microorganisms and the life compounds they make available to plants.

Except for a plant's invagination of nutrients by absorption, plants seldom can take up substances of high molecular weight. Because the majority of soil organic matter consists of high-molecular-weight materials, the value of soil microorganisms becomes apparent. Soil microorganisms break down high-molecular-weight material, so that these biodegradable substances can better serve as a major food source for plants.

SOIL MICROORGANISMS STIMULATE THE REBUILDING OF THE SOIL and often have been observed to do so at a more rapid rate than many other known methods such as crop rotation, mulching, and other soil treatments. Under favorable conditions of moisture, temperature, and the proper balance of soil microorganisms, the following influences can be observed:

1. Faster and more thorough DECOMPOSITION OF CROP RESIDUE and other organic materials.

2. GRANULATION OF THE SOIL, DECREASED CRUSTING, AND A DECREASE IN MASSIVE CLODDING (as observed on some untreated soils) facilitating easier plowing, cleaner harvesting of root crops, and development of stronger and deeper plant root systems.

3. INCREASED CROP QUALITY and YIELD:
    a. plants better able to withstand disease;

b. faster and greater germination percentages;

c. more evenly spaced stands of crops;

d. faster fruiting; and

e. notable improvement in flavor and texture of many fruits and vegetables.

4. Greater response in soils previously treated with fertilizers and then treated with additional cultured micro-organisms, indicating better utilization of many soil compounds.

5. These effects have been observed to increase as the growing season progressed even though one might expect soil nutrients to decrease in availability.

Effects of EC&S Bio-Stimulant and Humus

The ecological significance of the biological effects of humic substances becomes more meaningful when we consider the overall impact of these humic materials on the productivity and fertility of soil and water ecosystems.[*] In addition to facilitating the dissolution of most otherwise insoluble metallic salts, humic substances are involved in a variety of reactions in soils, sediments, and water with major nutrients such as ammonia, nitrates, phosphates, and silicates. Research indicates that these interactions not only considerably increase the retention and residence time of the nutrients in the growing media, but also enrich and biologically condition the growing media. These interactions and effects together have a profound influence on the biological production process.

When a growing medium is enriched with humic material, both direct and indirect effects can be observed on the growth of plants.[*] Indirect effects result because humic materials act as suppliers and regulators of plant nutrients. The indirect processes are concerned mainly with modifications of physical and chemical components of the soil and generally take place outside the plant. On the other hand, the direct effects involve entry of the humic material through the plant roots, affecting the metabolic processes of the plant.

Generally speaking, the productivity or crop yield of soil enriched with humic materials increases.

---

[*]Jackson, 174.

[*]Jackson, 174.

The high-molecular-weight humic materials, humic acids, alter the physical characteristics of the soil, while the low-molecular-weight humic substances, fulvic acids, are involved in chemical reactions in the soil that in turn influence plants' metabolic processes. EC&S Bio-Stimulant activates these chemical reactions within the soil.

T.L. Senn, K.D. Westwood, G.H. Huffman,[*] and an article in the January 1981 issue of the *California Farmer* generalized several categories of the FUNCTIONS OF ORGANIC MATTER and HUMIC SUBSTANCES that are woven into the following outline. The first three categories are functions exhibited external to plants. The other two categories are more directly related to the growth of plants.

A. PHYSICAL CONDITIONS OF THE SOIL
   1. Desirable structure, texture, and looseness or friability and crumbliness, of particular importance in tight clay soils.
   2. Adequate drainage.
   3. Suitable aeration.
   4. Water holding capacity.

---

[*]Jackson, 174.

5. Heat absorption (in the event of darker colored substances).
6. Buffering properties (that is, the prevention of rapid changes in soil acidity and alkalinity, which is accomplished by the humic substance readily assisting the soil in accepting or donating free hydrogen ions).
7. Openness for easy surface absorption of water, thus reducing surface water runoff and soil erosion, and soil water accumulation.

B. MECHANICAL CONDITIONS. In this category of soil humic substance values, the following can be listed:

1. A more favorable medium for plant root system development, which is especially important in the production of root crops.
2. A desirable environment for beneficial microorganism development.

C. SOIL CHEMICAL ACTIVITY. Humic substances are of essential value in:

1. The further active disintegration of soil rock, thus releasing additional supplies of important plant nutrients.
2. Soil chemical reactions that convert a number of important plant elements, including chemical compounds available for plant root uptake (for example, the conversion of phosphorus into a form available for plant use, the chelating of soil iron compounds to a form suitable for plant utilization in leaf chlorophyll development -- yellowing of leaves, known as chlorosis, is the result of iron starvation, generally speaking).
3. A reduction of the "locking up" of P_2O_5 (phosphorus) in the soil, especially soil with a clay base.
4. The liberation of carbon dioxide from soil calcium carbonate, thus increasing the availability of this important plant nutrient through plant roots for carbohydrate synthesis.

5. The neutralization of soil chemical substances that may cause plant toxicity.
6. A high ion exchange capacity in soils. This benefit allows better retention and utilization of various elements, including minerals and soil nitrogen, by preventing excess losses of these ingredients through drainage water leaching from plant root zone areas. In the presence of an adequate amount of humic substance, the plant food nutrients are held in the soil and made available to the plant roots upon demand.
7. The storage of plant nutrients. The gradual decomposition of organic matter/humic substance by soil microorganism actions results in the availability of:
    a. carbon dioxide;
    b. nitrogen as ammonia quickly changed to nitrites and nitrates by select bacteria;
    c. phosphorus and other elements essential for

plant growth, such as sulphur and potash.

8. Through soil biochemistry and microorganisms, the high-molecular-weight organic materials are broken down, making up to 5,000 calories per gram of energy available to be used by plants until further bio-degradation takes place.*
9. A retardation of the growth of soil organisms injurious to plants.
10. The promotion and conversion (chelation) of a number of elements into "food" forms; nutrient uptake is thus available to plants.

D. BIOCHEMICAL VALUES. More directly, the following general effects have been claimed by plant botanists, plant physiologists, and horticulturists around the world:

1. The stimulation of plant cellular growth and division, including accelerated growth due to the

---

*Jackson, 176.

presence of auxin type reactions.

2. The effective development of plant circulatory systems.
3. The most favorable functioning of plant respiration and transpiration systems.
4. The decrease of plant stress and premature deterioration.

The above listed plant physiological activities are further benefitted by humic acids because they contribute to the formation of plant stimulating substances known as auximones. These substances seem to be absorbed by plant roots and bring about desirable plant physiological activities in greater degree by increasing plant cellular membrane and plasma permeability. This permeability promotes the uptake of plant nutrients by increasing the development of polyphenols that function as respiratory catalysts, thereby causing an increase in living plant metabolism. Thus, there is a contribution to the complete plant enzyme system that is intensified, accelerating plant cell division. This introduces us to the fifth, generalized function of humic substances and the application of EC&S Bio-Stimulant.

E. PRAGMATIC RESULTS. As a result of the factors listed above, plant growth is stimulated, as reflected in these observations:

1. Improved seed germination.
2. Greater growth of fibrous roots.
3. Increases in legume root nodule formation (numbers and size).
4. Greater resistance to insects.
5. Greater plant resistance to drought and effects of frost damage.

These effects are of economic value as contributors to increased yields and to improved crop quality, including the storage life of perishable crops.

In addition to increasing plant dry weight, EC&S Bio-Stimulant and humic substances have been found to accelerate the differentiation of growing points, intensify the effects of auxins, and positively influence morphogenesis, respiration, chlorophyll content, and metabolism when applied to either soil or foliage. EC&S Bio-Stimulant and humic substance may also alter the penetrability of plant membranes and thus change the viscosity of protoplasm.*

Upon entering the plant, humic substances may serve as supplementary sources of polyphenols that function as respiratory catalysts. Quinone (a

---

*Jackson, 178.

carbon ring arrangement) groups may serve as hydrogen acceptors and oxygen activators, thus regulating oxygen reactions.[*]

These results have been explained on the basis of stimulation of physiological and biochemical processes associated with cellular metabolism brought about by EC&S Bio-Stimulant.[*] Several studies have pointed out that humic matter acts as a specific sensitizing agent, increasing the permeability of the plant cell membrane and thereby increasing the uptake of nutrients. Other important but subtle effects have been observed in plants treated with these humic materials, although the effects have not been fully explained. Such effects include:

1. Increased activity of a number of enzymes, coenzymes, endoenzymes, and exoenzymes;
2. Altered oxidation-reduction processes;
3. Altered protein and carbohydrate metabolism; and
4. Enhanced chlorophyll synthesis.[*]

---

[*]Jackson, 178.

[*]Jackson, 178.

[*]Jackson, 178.

The role of EC&S Bio-Stimulant in increasing productivity includes more complete utilization by plants of nutrients such as nitrogen, phosphorus, and potassium. In addition, the solubility, mobility, migration, recycling, and accumulation of trace metals through the chelation processes of humic compounds play a very meaningful role in the mineral nutrition of soil grown plants. The participation of these humic substances in plant respiration occurs either through functioning as respiratory catalysts or through other mechanisms that increase oxygen absorption by plant tissue. Increased oxygen absorption is ecologically significant because it enables plants to withstand better the adverse effects of higher and lower temperature exposures.*

Physiological Stimulation Effect

In addition to the nutritional benefits of stimulated substances, EC&S Bio-Stimulant affects the growth of plant life by stimulating various physiological and biochemical processes related to cellular metabolism. Bio-Stimulants and various complex inducer molecules, developing low-

---

*Jackson, 179.

molecular-weight humic compounds, penetrate the roots and then are translocated to the shoots of plants. The volume of humic material translocated to the shoots generally is very small and consists of only humic material small enough to be transported through the plant: low-molecular-weight supportive nutrients. Other authors have proposed that humic compounds also are taken up by the vascular system.* These compounds have been used to augment cellular activity by increasing metabolism. Some of the stimulations and mechanisms associated with the use of bio-stimulants, including multifactorial inducer molecules, are:

1. Respiratory catalysts
2. Increased cell permeability
3. Effects on roots and shoots
4. Plant metabolism

Soil organic ligands are a functional group, ion, or molecule bound to a central atom, such as a metal, in a complex between chemical species referred to as a coordination complex. Ligands such as fulvic acids are complex mixtures possessing polyelectrolytic properties.* These polymers, or

---

*Jackson, 276-279.

*Jackson, 281.

complex electrolyte mixtures, play an important role in natural systems (lakes, streams, and soil solutions), influencing the speciation (forming of new species) of metal ions, binding with organic pollutants (for example, pesticides and herbicides), and catalyzing the breakdown of toxic pollutants. A recent study of the binding of a donor molecule to humic substance in solution revealed direct evidence for donor-acceptor charge-transfer mechanisms involving groups on the humic material.[*]

At the University of Amsterdam, G.G. Choudhry studied humic substances and found them to be rich in stable free radicals. It was concluded that these free radicals probably play important roles in polymerization-depolymerization reactions, in reaction with other organic molecules, including pesticides and toxic pollutants, and in other physiological effects. According to R.W. Rex, some free radicals are formed or polymerized into lignin by either acid or fungal attack, which produces the dehydrogenation or oxidative removal of hydrogen. These free radicals are trapped in the humic polymers and thus protected from their macro-environment.[*]

---

[*]Jackson, 281.

[*]Jackson, 281.

An impressive number of field observations and substantial experimental evidence indicate that EC&S Bio-Stimulant and the inducer molecule fractions of organic compounds directly and/or indirectly influence the chemistry, physics, and biology of spaceship earth's plant life. At the same time, the detoxification of pollutants also is related to this phenomenon.

The elements of Working Model Two, EC&S Bio-Stimulant include the participants in many oxidation-reduction, electron transfer, and catalytic reactions. The production and consumption of oxygen and carbon dioxide are related to the quantitative and qualitative distributions of humic and other organic compounds, as are pH buffering capacities.

THE pH OF THE SOIL DIRECTLY AFFECTS THE GERMINATION, HEALTH, AND GROWTH OF PLANT LIFE inasmuch as it affects the availability of ALL plant nutrients. The system that supplies plants with all the essential nutrients from organic decomposition or from the breakdown of rocks depends to some degree on soil pH. The population of microorganisms that changes organic nitrogen to the ammonium form of nitrogen and then to the nitrate form that is used by the plants depends on a balanced pH in the soil. These processes illustrate the importance of soil pH. It is advisable in problem situations to take soil samples for microbial analysis and root samples to determine the numbers and kinds of organisms present.

In general, multiple biochemical and geochemical processes develop as a result of physical and chemical modifications to the environment. The EC&S Bio-Stimulant phenomenon is responsible for a surprising number of positive modifications. Spaceship earth is empowered by this type of phenomenon. With the magic and the miracle of a dynamic electrolyte, bio-stimulant, inducer molecules and humic substance create a natural balance for many life processes.

AFFINITY FOR WATER: The glutinous, thick, sticky, and adhesive polysaccharides produced by microorganisms are important in conserving the moisture content of the soil. The mucilage added to the soil as plant roots exude is highly hydrated and functions to PREVENT DEHYDRATION OF THE ROOTS.*

E.M. Burdick suggested that humates supply growing plants with food, but they serve in many more important ways to make soils more productive, and thus farming more profitable.* They INCREASE THE WATER HOLDING CAPACITY

---

*Jackson, 393.

*Jackson, 393.

of soils, and thus soils containing relatively large amounts of humate material resist droughts more effectively and produce better yields where rainfall or irrigation may be insufficient. HUMATES IMPROVE TILTH, OR WORKABILITY, OF THE SOIL. With humic substances, heavy clay soils can be worked into satisfactory seed beds and marginal soils can be turned into profitable ones. Soils are more friable and suitably sized particles are formed in the aggregate. Humic substance reduces soil erosion while at the same time retains water soluble inorganic fertilizers* and releases them to the growing plants as needed.

It has been reported repeatedly* that changes in viscosity and specific gravity can be brought about in soils through the addition of small amounts of humates, a byproduct of stimulated microbial action.

Water soluble, low-molecular-weight trace minerals, with the aid of stimulated microbial life in very low concentrations, have been shown to STIMULATE SEED GERMINATION and viability, FACILITATE ROOT RESPIRATION and FORMATION, and STIMULATE ROOT

---

*Jackson, 393.

*Jackson, 394.

GROWTH, especially lengthwise.* Significantly increased yields have been scientifically researched and reported for many crops, such as cotton, potatoes, wheat, tomatoes, mustard, and nursery stock. These reports also have demonstrated stimulated growth and proliferation of desirable soil microorganisms, as well as algae and yeasts.* Researchers have reported that EC&S Bio-Stimulant microbial life has assisted the development of humic and fulvic acids, and with the further assistance of water, can solubilize and make available to plants certain materials that are otherwise unavailable, such as rock phosphates, as reported by R.W. Teasley.

This combination seems to play an important role in plant utilization and metabolism of the phosphates.* This treatment can liberate carbon dioxide from soil calcium carbonates and thus make it available to the plants through the roots for continued photosynthesis. It is further reported that this situation is known to stimulate various plant enzymes. The following are highlights of this concept:

---

*Jackson, 394.

*Jackson, 394.

*Jackson, 395.

- Under drought conditions, EC&S Bio-Stimulated humic and fulvic acids help balance water and assist plant TRANSPIRATION, the transport of water and nutrients of the cell tissues.

- The balancing phenomenon of this process produces a REDUCTION IN THE AMOUNT OF WATER required.

- The reactions of the treatment of EC&S Bio-Stimulant assist the balance of water under drought conditions by increasing PLANT RESPIRATION, thus helping the plant "breathe" better while under stress.

- The EC&S Bio-Stimulant treatment will aid water in assisting the PENETRATION AND PERMEATION OF PLANT CELLS and thus assist in nutrient uptake and water storage within the plant cells during dry times.

- EC&S Bio-Stimulation of microbial life can assist plants during drought to accumulate soluble sugars and thus help to PREVENT WILTING.

- EC&S Bio-Stimulant, as it develops humus, has a very positive effect on the WATER HOLDING CAPACITY of the SOIL. These humic substances also allow the reduced supply of water in its very thin film to be MORE EASILY RELEASED during drought conditions, and thus be made AVAILABLE TO THE ROOTS of the plants.

- EC&S Bio-Stimulated microbial life also assists in the development of BETTER, STRONGER, AND LARGER ROOT STRUCTURES, which improves the uptake of water and nutrients.

- Electrolytes, aided by EC&S Bio-Stimulant in water solution, conduct electrical current for life giving energy.

- WATER DISSOLVES, TRANSPORTS, AND AMPLIFIES EC&S Bio-Stimulant, and transports its electric action throughout the plant.

- Water vapor or humidity tends to CLUSTER around and BOND to various trace minerals, which is referred to as SORPTION.

- Humic substance aided by EC&S Bio-Stimulation of microbial life reduces SOIL EROSION by increasing sorption and increasing the binding force of the very fine soil particles to the electrolytically charged water.

Humic acid, fulvic acid, and microbial activity stimulated by EC&S Bio-Stimulant combined with water provide a highly productive material with many very unique properties. The value of this unique combination of nature is in its productivity and its natural safety.

Nitrogen and Microorganism Activity

Microorganisms impregnate nitrogen with three major elements, oxygen, carbon, and hydrogen, on behalf of all living cells. This courtship provides approximately 90% of the activity in converting inert nitrogen gas into inorganic nitrogen compounds for organic use. In this process of nitrification, microorganisms transform soil ammonia into nitrates and nitrites that plants can incorporate into their own system.

Bacteria are the principal agents of courtship by which nitrogen in the air is converted to biologically useful compounds. Some bacteria, known as symbiotic, have the power to enter plant tissue and cooperate with plants in the fixation of atmospheric nitrogen. Others, known as nonsymbiotic organisms (including aerobic and anaerobic groups depending on whether they require atmospheric oxygen or obtain oxygen from its compounds), are also able to fix atmospheric nitrogen.

The nitrogen courting bacteria associated with legumes are symbiotic. In this case, the BACTERIA INVADE THE ROOT HAIRS OF HOST PLANTS, where they multiply and stimulate formation of root nodules, enlargements of plant cells and bacteria in intimate association. Within the nodules, the bacteria convert free nitrogen to nitrates and then to amino acids that the host plant can utilize for its development.

The most impressive amount of nitrogen courtship is accomplished by symbiotic organisms in root nodules. By way of comparison, it is reported that nonsymbiotic bacteria probably add as much as 10 pounds of fixed nitrogen to each acre of soil per year, while the fixation by legumes alone through the action of symbiotic organisms is approximately 50 to 100 pounds per acre per year. It is further assumed that as much as two thirds of the total plant nitrogen used by such crops comes from the air. It is a common practice to inoculate/bio-stimulate legumes if the microorganisms of the required type are not adequately abundant in the soil. Microorganisms living in the roots of legumes such as peas, beans, clover, alfalfa, and peanuts assimilate atmospheric nitrogen, but certain other free-living anaerobic bacteria also extract nitrogen from the air. Other microorganisms in soil convert ammonium salts to nitrates and nitrites.

REMEMBER: BACTERIA ARE THE AGENTS BY WHICH 90% OF NEEDED NITROGEN OF THE AIR IS CONVERTED TO USEFUL COMPOUNDS. Following is a diagram of the nitrogen cycle in nature.

THE NITROGEN CYCLE IN NATURE*

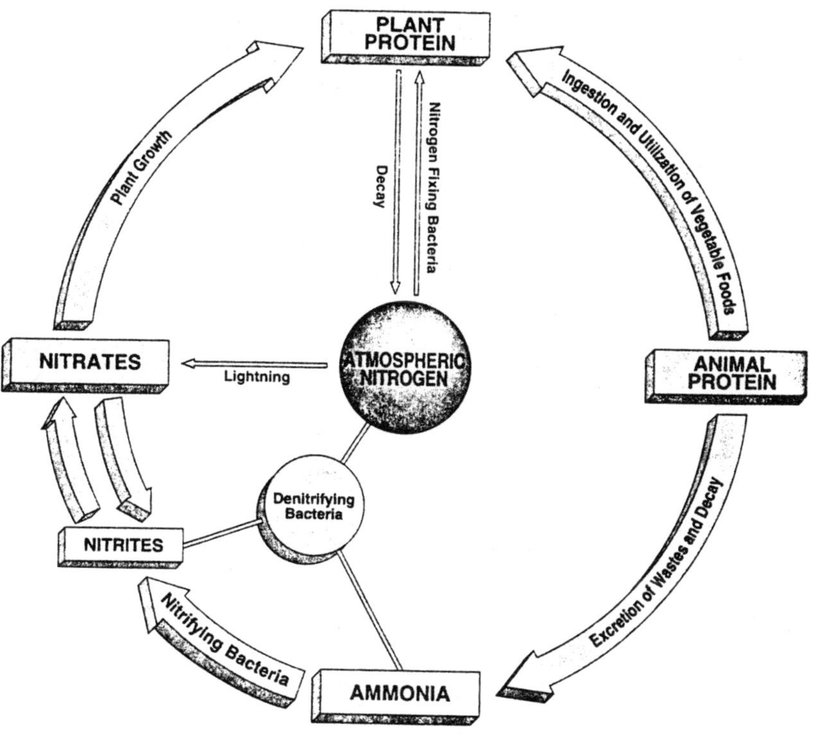

*Jackson, 404.

ARTIFICIAL FERTILIZER: In 1909 the German chemist Fritz Haber discovered that nitrogen from the atmosphere could be combined with hydrogen, a forced courtship with another plentiful element. Under special conditions, nitrogen and hydrogen are brought into a union of ammonia, the beginning point for the production of a wide range of nitrogen compounds. The process described, made feasible by Karl Bosch, has been known as the Haber-Bosch process of artificial fertilizer.

Nitric acid is a principal commercial nitrogen compound that can be involved in an artificial fertilizing. It is a colorless, highly corrosive liquid employed extensively in the production of artificial fertilizers. Ammonium nitrate (NH_4NO_3), a salt of ammonia and nitric acid, is the most common nitrogen component of artificial fertilizers.

The industrial procedure used to change atmospheric nitrogen (N_2) to nitrates (NO_3^-) for use as artificial fertilizers requires an energy input that must at least equal the eventual increase in crop yield. Ammonium nitrate nitrogen is mobile in the soil, and thus it can move with soil water to plant roots where uptake can proceed. Nitrite nitrogen, on the other hand, is somewhat bound to the surface of each soil particle and therefore cannot move into our water supply. Over-application of ammonium nitrates can exceed nature's system of balance, leading to chemically toxic soil conditions and water pollution.

Artificial fertilizer production has served many crop yield benefits in the past. The industry fixes several million tons of nitrogen each year in the form of various nitrogen fertilizers. However, there are several concerns about this process:

1. COST OF THE PRODUCTION, including the excessive involvement of fossil fuel in the production process of the fertilizer

2. Possible DAMAGE TO THE ORIGINAL MICROORGANISM BASE

3. The application of artificial fertilizer, which has been PROVEN TO CONTRIBUTE TO WATER POLLUTION

Because nitrogen-fixing microorganisms do not require fossil fuel energy and do not cause pollution, soil science is now directing its research toward developing a way to make all plants capable of forming nodules. Genetic work in the field of DNA techniques also is underway so plants can contain the biochemical ability to fix nitrogen on their own. EC&S Bio-Stimulant serves to assist in this conversion without having to affect the genetic factors for the development of nodules.

DENITRIFICATION: Denitrification is the process by which nitrates or nitrites in the soil or in organic deposits are reduced to lower oxides of nitrogen by the action of denitrifying microorganisms (various bacteria) in both aquatic and terrestrial environments. The process results in the escape of nitrogen back into the atmosphere. So, what happens if too much nitrogen is converted to nitrates? As designed by nature, denitrifying bacteria counter-balance the process of nitrogen fixation to assure balance. However, a problem can develop in the event of excess nitrogen fixation due, for example, to the overuse of artificial chemical fertilizers. The soil could become chemically toxic, reducing or eliminating microorganism life. In such cases, nature's balancing system is destroyed. This destruction could be reversed or drastically reduced with the assistance of EC&S Bio-Stimulant. A good example of this would be experienced when treating for animal waste remediation.

NITRIFICATION SUBCYCLE: After plants have absorbed nitrogen in a usable form, they can synthesize or manufacture proteins and nucleic acids. Some of the newly courted organic nitrogen quickly returns to the soil as fallen foliage or as animal waste, known as humus. The remaining organic nitrogen reserve returns to the soil only when plants and animals die. Decomposing mechanisms then break down these organic nitrogen compounds through decay and release ammonia. Under this scenario, the ammonia often is turned into oxidized nitrate by nitrifying bacteria; this process is referred to as nitrification. Thus, there is a subcycle among members of food chains that does not involve atmospheric nitrogen (N_2) at all.

This courtship of nitrogen sometimes makes nitrogen available to crops from organic matter through two additional reactions. Protein and allied compounds are broken down into amino acids through a reaction called aminization. Soil microorganisms acquire energy from this digestion. They also utilize some of the available amino-nitrogen in their own cell structure. Ammonia-nitrogen is formed by a second reaction that converts amino compounds into ammonia (NH_3) and ammonium (NH_4^+) compounds. The remains of all living tissues and their waste products are decomposed by microorganisms in this process. This reaction is called ammonification. The ammonia that was just yielded can now leave the soil or be converted into other nitrogen compounds, depending to some degree on the soil conditions. The dual reaction of aminization (proteins to amino acids) and ammonification (amino compounds to ammonia, NH_3, and ammonium, NH_4^+) is referred to as mineralization.

Recorded in U.S. Bureau of Mines Report 7203 and U.S. Bureau of Mines Circular 8471, this subcycle within the nitrogen cycle allows nitrogen compounds to be released naturally over the entire growing season rather than a shocking dose of a limited duration as experienced with an artificial substance applied periodically.* A serious concern surfaces about chemically abused and toxic, crop-worn soils that have been stripped of basic humic substances and left sterile of active microbial life. Again, EC&S Bio-Stimulant, Working Model Two, can be called upon to awaken the abused, often dormant indigenous microbial life.

REMEMBER: MICROORGANISM ACTIVITY IN ONE ACRE OF SOIL USES ABOUT THE SAME AMOUNT OF ENERGY IN SOIL PREPARATION AS 10,000 PEOPLE WOULD BURN FOR THE SAME WORK, FOR THE SAME PERIOD OF TIME. MICROBIAL LIFE MUST BE PROTECTED, NOURISHED AND FURTHER STIMULATED WHEN REQUIRED.

Biological Growth Functions: How Many Inducer Molecules Can You Name?

What are some of the biological functions that naturally cause a plant to develop? Are these

---

*Jackson, 409.

functions related to the time required for the plant to mature? Does maturation time affect the quality and quantity of the crop yield? Is the plant's nutritional value to humans and animals influenced by the various activities of this development? The following includes a discussion of a number of plant metabolism patterns, relative to bio-stimulants.

Amino acids and proteins. Amino acids are the molecules that, through condensation, become proteins. These proteins are described as very large molecules active in both structural functions and metabolic functions. Included among the categories of proteins are multitudes of enzymes, which serve as organic catalysts to increase the speed with which chemical reactions can take place within the cells. Enzymes, or globular protein molecules, make "warm chemistry" unnecessary. In our chemical laboratory, it is often necessary to heat the elements in a reaction flask to bring about chemical change. So, do you heat the growing plant to cause these various chemical reactions? No, the same chemical reactions may take place very rapidly because a specific enzyme is present for each and every reaction. Thereby, "cold chemistry" is possible. NO REACTION CAN OCCUR IN A CELL UNLESS

ITS OWN PERSONALIZED ENZYME IS PRESENT AND ACTIVE.*

Energy for activation. Energy for activation is often required when molecules will not react with one another. For example, the log in the fireplace will not burn unless it is heated to a higher temperature. The heating reaction causes the number of effective collisions between molecules to increase, thus allowing them to react with one another more frequently. This activity is known as the energy of activation. Enzymes lower the necessary energy of activation for cellular chemical activity. Consider the speed at which enzymes function by observing the example of the breakdown of hydrogen peroxide into water and oxygen: it can occur 600,000 times a second when the enzyme catalase (peroxisome) is present. This rapid breakdown can be compared to little, if any, breakdown in the absence of enzymes. Enzymes can function even more rapidly at optimum temperatures and acceptable pH levels. Now add multifactorial inducer molecules, the immediate "on switches," plus the proper nutrient diet, and watch the EC&S Bio-Stimulant process begin!

Enzymes, coenzymes, and exoenzymes. Enzymes are made up of protein substances produced by living cells that can change the rate of chemical

*Jackson, 513.

reactions. They are organic catalysts that can be introduced to other inducer molecules listed in this chapter, and they speed up reaction rates of all living systems. Sometimes enzymes require nonprotein molecules known as coenzymes to assist them in performing their reactions. Coenzymes are organic molecules that attach to enzymes and function as carriers for either chemical groups or electrons. Most often, coenzymes are involved directly in reactions. Exoenzymes are enzymes that are formed within the cell and then excreted into the surrounding medium. Endoenzymes are enzymes that remain within the cell that produced it.

- Amino acids and proteins, for example, are enzymes that increase the speed of the cold chemical reactions within cells.

- No reaction can occur in a growing plant cell unless its own personalized enzymes are present and active.

- Heat or warm chemistry causes an increased number of effective collisions between molecules, thus chemical reactions occur more frequently when the energy of activation is available. Enzymes lower the amount of energy necessary for activation. Enzymes are most effective at optimum temperature and acceptable pH.

- Coenzymes, nonprotein organic molecules, attach to enzymes and function as carriers for both chemical groups and electrons.

- Working Model Two, EC&S Bio-Stimulant, is a complete and functional microbial stimulant that is totally natural, remarkably efficient, and effectively inexpensive. With the synergistic cooperation of enzymes, endoenzymes, exoenzymes, coenzymes, natural plant hormones, a balanced diet of microbial nutrients, and inducer molecules, this microbiological, multifactorial treatment can become an almost unbelievable stimulant, perhaps involving biological transmutation, assisting the balancing of problematic situations of our spaceship earth.

External and internal growth patterns. Most plants respond to both external and internal energizing which affect their growth patterns. Examples of external elements that regulate growth are:

1. Light
2. Length of day
3. Temperature
4. Gravity

The principal internal growth regulators are plant hormones. A plant hormone is a natural chemical messenger that is produced in very small amounts by one part of the plant and becomes active in another part of the plant. S.S. Mader explained that, generally, these hormones are produced by the meristematic (rapidly growing or actively dividing) regions of a plant and are transported to the vascular tissue. A response to plant hormones probably will be observed in almost every part of the plant's structure. Plant hormones sometimes interact to control specific physiological processes; various combinations produce different effects. Each naturally occurring growth-regulating hormone has a particular chemical structure.[*] EC&S Bio-Stimulant activates natural plant growth regulators.

Natural plant hormones that promote growth. Three basic groups of natural plant hormones, AUXINS, GIBBERELLINS, and CYTOKININS, foster plant growth activities. Various plant hormones produce different plant responses,

---

[*]Jackson, 514.

depending on soil type, type of plant, climate variations, and microbial life.

AUXINS: The term auxin means "to increase." The main function of these plant hormones is to promote the elongation of cells and other growth effects on young leaves, flowers, and fruits, for example. Auxins function by controlling light reception and causing the affected cell to degrade some of the polysaccharides in the cell wall. Polysaccharide degradation causes the cell to then elongate because it is less able to resist the expansion caused by the movement of water into the cell. The direction of cell expansion or growth is related to the weakest part of the cell wall. By way of further description, when a plant is exposed to light, auxins are transported up the plant along the side exposed to the sunlight and then laterally over the shaded side of the stem. As the plant "stretches" toward the light, the auxins move over to the elongated, shady side. The unequal accumulation of auxin causes the cells on the shady side to elongate or develop more quickly than those on the sunny side. As the sunlight moves, the plant moves and the auxins move laterally and slowly over to the other side. This "stretching" and elongation of the cells result in the binding of the plant's parts back and forth toward the light source, allowing the cells to develop first on one side and then on the other side of the plant.

Research has confirmed that the contact of a weak solution of auxins to a woody cutting will stimulate root growth. Seeds treated with auxins evidence increased fruit growth. S.S. Mader indicated in her writings that when auxins are applied on leaves and fruits rather than the stem, the leaves and fruit do not fall off prematurely.[*] Trees can be sprayed with a mild foliar application of auxins to prevent preharvest drop of fruit, to increase fruit set, produce seedless fruits, give some weed control, and stimulate flower formation.

Plant physiological developments are accentuated by EC&S Bio-Stimulant treatment that contributes to the formation of plant stimulating auximones or substances functioning like auxins. In addition, this treatment is absorbed by plant roots, encouraging plant physiological activities leading to greater plant cellular membrane and plasma permeability. The uptake of plant nutrients is promoted through:

1. Increasing the development of polyphenols, which function as respiratory catalysts, thus causing an increase in living plant metabolism

2. Intensifying the plant enzyme system

---

[*]Jackson, 515.

3. In some cases, assisting the cytokinins in accelerating plant cell division

Auxins are natural plant hormones that promote the growth of plant cells in roots, shoots, leaves, flowers, and fruits by controlling light reception and making sugars available to the plant. EC&S Bio-Stimulant includes auxins, or functions as auxins, and thus has a positive effect on plant metabolism.

GIBBERELLINS. Gibberellins are natural plant hormones. They are likely to be present in newly growing plant organs because they are growth stimulators that will cause cell division and enlargement of the affected cells. When applied externally to plants, gibberellins promote stem elongation. It is often the BALANCE of natural plant hormones in a plant cell that determines the effect, rather than the presence or absence of a specific hormone. Gibberellins, as well as auxins, help regulate the balance of plant development. It is assumed that gibberellins trigger the DNA gene code of enzymes necessary for the breakdown of starch within the plant, which helps break seed and bud dormancy.* EC&S Bio-Stimulant includes the

*Jackson, 516.

"trigger" to induce the DNA gene natural actions and reactions.

CYTOKININS. Cytokinin means "cell division." The cytokinin hormones are part of the purine adenine, one of the nitrogen bases in DNA and RNA. Cytokinins promote cell division; they also prevent leaf aging, initiate growth in higher plants, and work with auxins to control the growth and development of plants in general. Cytokinin activity is enhanced notably by the application of EC&S Bio-Stimulant.

Natural Plant Growth Regulating Hormones

Type	Function
Auxins	Cell elongation
Gibberellins	Stem elongation
Cytokinins	Cell division

Growth regulator effects of organic compounds. EC&S Bio-Stimulant affects compounds that are phytoactive in various manners. Organic growth regulators, organic nucleic acids, organic glycosides, organic porphyrins, and organic morphogens are among these compounds. Although auxins, gibberellins, and cytokinins are called growth regulating hormones, cytokinins are not to be thought of in the same way as animal tissue hormones. Instead they are a unique and highly physiologically active plant substance.*

Lehninger stated that because plant hormone compounds are active for some time after application, they may be categorized as enzymatic and metabolically stimulating in nature.* Their effect on seed germination, root and top growth, flowering, and impact of nitrogen applications signifies both catalytic and hormonal properties of humic substances, which must liberate their action through what has been referred to as the "cascade effect." In this scenario, a minimal amount of hormone liberates a chain reaction by attaching to target cells with which it is involved. Then the affected cells produce a group of specialized enzymes that stimulate the production of additional enzymes, with the possibility of affecting even more levels of specific enzymes until the final reaction is a greatly amplified physiological response within both the plant cells and tissue. This total function was initiated from a very minute initial plant hormone.

---

*Jackson, 517.

*Jackson, 517.

Organic growth regulators involve certain functions of DNA, probably activating and accelerating the production of specific enzymes, exoenzymes, coenzymes, and various inducer molecules, which in turn cause the cellular growth and cell division observed by R. Horgan. Horgan identified seven effects when cytokinins were externally applied to plants:

1. CELL DIVISION ENHANCEMENT.

2. REGULATION OF THE STRUCTURAL DEVELOPMENT of the plant or its parts, specifically, when combined with auxins to stimulate roots, cell walls, buds, and various other plant organs. Crown gall bacteria (Agrobacterium tumefaciens) inject a large bacterial plasmid (a self-duplicating ring of accessory DNA in the cytoplasm of bacteria) into a plant cell genome and directly influence the basic development of plant tissue.*

3. ENHANCEMENT OF CELL ENLARGEMENT. According to D.S. Letham, cell volume can be specifically

---

*Jackson, 518.

enhanced by adding cytokinins, which is the basis of the radish cotyledon bioassay.*

4. DELAY OF DEGENERATE AGING. Chlorophyll and protein degradation may be delayed by cytokinin influence through the stabilization of polysome aggregates and reduction in several membrane-associated chloroplast activities, including the suppression of respiration rate changes and mitochondrial coupling, according to M.V. Berridge and R.K. Ralph, H. Thomas, and R.M. Tetley and K.V. Thimann.*

5. ACTIVATION OF METABOLISM OR HORMONE DIRECTED TRANSPORT. The higher metabolism and delay of degenerate aging influenced by cytokinins creates a "sink" toward which metabolites flow. Locally green areas in yellowing leaves can therefore be produced by this plant

---

*Jackson, 518.

*Jackson, 518.

hormone application, as confirmed by R.K. Wood and K. Mothes.*

6. SUBSTITUTION FOR OR INTERACTION WITH LIGHT. Seed germination, pigment synthesis, and chloroplast development may be affected. C.O. Miller noted that cytokinin can substitute for the red light required for germination, thereby influencing phytochrome activity. These substances also stimulate the synthesis of certain chloroplast materials during light-dependent development and can restore chloroplast structures and restart chlorophyll synthesis in detached yellowing leaves, as outlined by T.A. Dyer and D.J. Osborne. According to V.A. Khokhlava, chlorophyll development is speeded up after exposure to light. This major effect of cytokinins is achieved through an increase of chloroplast internal membranes.*

---

*Jackson, 519.

*Jackson, 519.

7. INCREASE IN STOMATAL OPENING AND TRANSPIRATION in various species. M.J. Cooper et al. and N.L. Biddington and T.H. Thomas stated that both synthetic and naturally occurring cytokinins have been shown to increase stomatal opening by 50%.*

Organic growth regulators involve certain functions of DNA, including specific enzymes that cause cellular growth and cell division as follows:

1. Cell division enhancement
2. Regulation of the structure of the plant
3. Enhancement of cell enlargement
4. Delay of plants' degenerate aging
5. Activation of metabolism-directed transport
6. Substitution for or interaction with light
7. Increase in stomata opening and transpiration

ORGANIC NUCLEIC ACIDS. The nucleic acids of DNA and RNA are the hereditary material in the chromosomes of all living matter. They are

---

*Jackson, 519.

made up of chains of pentose sugars joined by the molecules of the phosphate group, to which purine and pyrimidine bases are attached. The chains are double in the spiral structure; each of the two chains bears its set of complementary bases: adenine paired with thymine, and guanine with cytosine.* These sets are joined by weak hydrogen bonds that hold the two spirals together.

It has been pointed out that, theoretically, cytokinins can be formed rather easily from subunits of nucleic acids.* If DNA units found in bio-stimulants could be incorporated into the cellular mechanism of treated plants and their associated rhizospheric microorganisms, we would have more complete answers as to how these cells operate. As the plant cellular mechanisms are stimulated to produce higher levels of chlorophyll, exoenzymes, enzymes, and coenzymes, plus other substances in the cells, greater plant growth results along with better overall health and vigor. The stimulation of rhizosphere microorganism cellular substances also has indirect effects in causing more minerals, hormones, vitamins, and other growth factors to be released and absorbed by the plant root system. This procedure of DNA transfer from viruses to normal

---

*Jackson, 520.

*Jackson, 520.

cells for control of their reproduction is well defined and possibly more extensive in nature than previously concluded.

Organic nucleic acids of DNA and RNA form the basic foundation of all hereditary materials. Cytokinins can be rather easily formed from subunits of nucleic acids, allowing humic acids and EC&S Bio-Stimulant to stimulate the production of high levels of chlorophyll, specialized indigenous endoenzymes and enzymes, etc., thus encouraging greater plant growth and general plant health.

ORGANIC GLYCOSIDES. Glycosides are compounds found widely throughout nature. They are made up of a sugar and another attached molecule, for example, an alcohol or phenol. Glycosides are found predominately in leaves, buds, and young shoots where metabolism is active, and in the bark and seeds, according to D.M. Considine.*
When the sugar is glucose, the compound is referred to as glycoside, which is highly soluble in water and can be transported easily through the vascular cell tissues of plants.

Glycosides have a high capacity for reactions of condensation and self-condensation and may thereby serve as the basic source for the formation of complex synthetic substances. Glycosides are

---

*Jackson, 521.

important stimulators of cell respiration and often include sterols as structural and active components of membranes. Sterols are the initial materials for the synthesis or manufacturing of various hormones and ergosterol, a minor part of plant sterols. F.B. Salisbury and C.W. Ross stressed that these are especially important, because they are converted by ultraviolet radiation to vitamin D_2. Flavonoids are usually present in plant tissues, especially in flowers and plastids or single cell masses of protoplasm. They appear as colorful water soluble pigments and are classified as glycosides. Besides attracting insects and birds to insure pollination, they may also help plants resist disease. M.M. Cardwell noted that they help protect leaf cells from ultraviolet light damage by filtering out these harmful rays. According to P. Hanchey-Bauer, PLANT PATHOGENS (DISEASE PRODUCING ORGANISMS) MAY BE INHIBITED BY PHENOLIC GLYCOSIDES, PREVENTING FUNGAL SPORE GERMINATION.* These and other phenolic compounds readily oxidize the quinones that could easily oxidize to sulfhydryl groups on enzymes and disrupt the normal oxidation-reduction balance in cells. Phytoalexins (Greek for "plant warding-off compounds") may be glycosides that are not normally present in healthy plant tissues, but are synthesized

*Jackson, 521.

or manufactured in a local area in response to an infection.*

Organic glycosides are widely found in nature and are made up of sugars or glucose, plus the natural plant alcohol or phenol molecule. Glycosides are found where plant metabolism is active. GLYCOSIDES INCLUDE PLANT STEROLS AND NATURAL HORMONES THAT AFFECT PLANT GROWTH AND HELP WARD OFF HARMFUL INSECTS, FOREIGN ORGANISMS, AND PLANT INFECTIONS.

ORGANIC PORPHYRINS. EC&S Bio-Stimulant positively affects various porphyrins that originate from pyrrole ring structures of chlorophyll molecules of plants and are extracted for the plants' production use. These molecules are supplied by the decomposition of hematin and chlorophyll and may involve iron and magnesium pyrrole components. Pyrroles occur in all plant and animal protoplasm. C.R. Noller reported that porphyrins derived from natural humate pigments (that were provided by chlorophyll a and b) in various plant extracts have substituents on the eight beta-position of the pyrrole nuclei.* These natural pigments (occurring as

---

*Jackson, 521.

*Jackson, 522.

chlorophyll) consist of metal chelate complexes of the porphyrins. For plants, the application of humic and fulvic substances (and thus porphyrin as well) assists in the trapping of light energy and its transfer of energy through the electron transport system, accelerating various growth mechanisms of plants in photosynthesis.

It is concluded by many that organic porphyrins, encouraged by EC&S Bio-Stimulant, does assist plants in trapping light energy and then assist in the transfer of that energy through the electron transport system. This light energy-trapping process accelerates the various growth mechanisms of plants through improved photosynthesis.

ORGANIC MORPHOGENS AND VITAMIN A. Organic morphogens act on specific tissues during specific periods of development in the plant. Morphogens stimulate the end of dormancy of fungal spores or stimulate heterocyst development of cyanobacteria and thus increase nitrogen fixation. According to M.F. Hopkins, vitamin A and closely related retinol and carotenoid compounds are critical for the light reactions and energy transport in higher plants.[*] B.V. Milborrow continued that carotenoids and other pigments play an important role in intermolecular excitation of energy transfer, allowing

---

[*]Jackson, 523.

wavelengths of light that chlorophyll cannot absorb to contribute to photosynthesis.* As an added benefit, carotenoids are precursors of the synthesis of abscisic acid in plant tissue, thereby influencing growth regulator production.

Organic morphogens assist in ending plant dormancy, while also stimulating the development of cyanobacteria, thus increasing nitrogen fixation. Vitamin A is critical to light reaction and energy transport in higher plants. These pigments serve to cause intermolecular excitation of the energy transfer through control of wavelengths of light, which assists in the development of chlorophyll and contributes to photosynthesis.

Water as a growth regulator. You may look at the heading "Water as a Growth Regulator" and say, "Sure, if you have water, things grow; without water they die; if there is too little water, growth may be retarded. Therefore, of course, water is acting as a growth regulator." However, water should be considered as more than just water for plant transpiration and as a carrier of organic and mineral compounds in living cells. Often, humic substances are diluted in water from streams for purposeful applications through irrigation. How can water be so effective when in some cases it is carrying as little as

---

*Jackson, 523.

500 to 1,000 parts per million of electrolytes. This dilute solution is nearly 100% water!

It has been confirmed that water itself may be activated to stimulate plant metabolism through being vigorously shaken or otherwise effectively blended so that polymers are formed via succussion. Through this process, the structure of the water is determined by the original structure of the solution (fulvic acids, for example) that caused special changes in the solvent (water). G.P. Barnard and J.H. Stephenson emphasized that these polymers are believed to induce growth and splitting through the energy provided within the structured water.[*] Thus, the water polymers could impregnate further blending of solutions and act as TEMPLATES for the generation of more polymers. The concept of WATER CARRYING INFORMATION ABOUT THE CONTENT OF THE SOLUTION has been reinforced further by the work of Smith and Boericke, Gibson, Unger, Rawson, Kumar, and Jussal, Bioron and Luu, and Jones and Jenkins. Gibson and Jones and Jenkins specifically emphasized the merits of effectively blending water with electrolytes in order to PROPAGATE THE INFORMATION CONTENT ON WATER. Jones and Jenkins, after evaluating recent research on water, also suggested that rather than long chains

---

[*]Jackson, 524.

there may be closed chains of cyclic clusters of two to six molecules.* Thus, short, three-dimensional polymers would serve as TEMPLATES, PASSING INFORMATION into the mass of water.

How do information-carrying water polymers affect plants? Are porphyrins, glycosides, or any other growth regulators involved? Barnard and Stephenson alluded to the probability that bacteria and other pathogens may develop polymers in body fluids, and the water polymers available may act as neutralizers. A similar function was defined by Gibson et al., who compared it to antibody-antigen reactions and suggested that perhaps the effect of an introduced type of polymer on a defect or a deficiency is analogous to a lock and key. In another more recent research report, Barnard and Stephenson suggested that while plants are in a diseased state of any sort, there are large excursions of entropy, or unavailable energy in a thermodynamic system, and that the added information carrying polymers could somehow serve in an anti-entropic manner.* G. Vithoulkas also suggested that structured water may influence plants when the energy pattern surrounding the organism, being

---

*Jackson, 524.

*Jackson, 524.

distorted by a pathogen or deficiency, is corrected or rebalanced in some manner.*

In the presence of natural organic electrolytes, the nuclei of atoms within the water may be magnetized. This possibility was discussed by A.L. Buchachenko who discovered that the magnetic properties of the nucleus of an element play a role in chemical reactions. Buchachenko argued that it is much more important to differentiate substances by magnetization than by isotopes. The dynamics of biochemical reactions are effective through this "magnetic isotope effect." Cope added that water activation through magnetization is very likely based on the detection of magnetic monopoles.* These magnetic monopoles are actually particles that have only one magnetic pole, either positive or negative, and not both. Keep in mind, a normal magnet or particle has both north and south poles. Cope went on to explain that under certain conditions a dipole can dissociate into a pair of separate monopoles. Some of these monopoles are called TACHYONS, or particles with a speed faster than light. This monopole-tachyon theory explains how metal plates may absorb some sort of sun energy and conduct this energy through metal wires to another location,

---

*Jackson, 524.

*Jackson, 524.

allowing plants to sprout and grow sturdy and green under this influence with no direct sunlight available.

Is the unwinding of the sun's energy into the form of carbon, which is then stored in the form of humic and fulvic acids, related to the monopole-tachyon concept? Is water the conductor, transporter, and amplified activator of the electrolytes within fulvic acids, for example? Or other trace mineral combinations? Is this electrolyte energy then duplicated in multiple templates or patterns of energy and dumped into the mass of water to distribute the information of growth energy through the plant's DNA? Does this energy message actually become part of the growth-regulator balance?

The literature indicates that tachyons and monopoles, either or both, can move from molecule to molecule through water, or metal plate to plate through wires, to be re-radiated to growing plants. Perhaps photosynthesis may not be tied to visible photons as much as it directly involves monopoles and tachyon or other systems involving particles yet to be recognized. Natural electrolyte substances contain minerals and compounds with specific magnetic configurations. These materials, derived from sun energy early on, are now further activated when exposed to more sunlight. Thus, even better absorption of magnetic monopoles can then be transmitted to the water to assist in the structuring and magnetizing of the water. In this manner more energy would be transferred to the plants' natural growth extracts as a further aid to their maximum vitalization, allowing the minute concentrations of humic and fulvic acids applied to the crop treated with EC&S Bio-Stimulant to exert their full potential.

WATER AS A BALANCED GROWTH REGULATOR:

1. Water polymers are templates or patterns for the generation of more polymers.

2. Water carries the informational content of the solution which influences the plant DNA.

3. The effective blending of water with electrolytes, for example fulvic acids, propagates the information content of various trace mineral combinations by way of the templates which pass this information on to the water mass.

4. Water soluble trace minerals, for example, have an influence on water in that the nuclei of atoms within the water are charged or magnetized; thus, minerals and compounds are involved in a specific magnetic configuration,

assisting in the informational message to the plant's DNA.

Organic Substance Activators:

DNA and RNA

The positive effects of EC&S Bio-Stimulant observed in plants and soil indicate activation of DNA and/or RNA. The combination of compounds found in these substances (including various growth regulators, porphyrins, and glycosides, to name a few) is assumed to be involved in the activation of specific regions of the DNA stacked within the chromosomes of cell nuclei. This activation process may also affect the RNA within the cells to serve as an "on switch." Through the effects of DNA and RNA, the essentials for additional growth are experienced. DNA is the nucleic acid found in the NUCLEUS OF CELLS; it is responsible for transmitting hereditary characteristics and for building proteins. RNA is the nucleic acid found in the CYTOPLASM OF CELLS. Both DNA and RNA carry an electric charge: DNA has a negative charge, while RNA carries a positive charge.

Plant science literature has reported that in minimal amounts EC&S Bio-Stimulant and humic substances activate the functions of several enzymes, involving alkaline phosphates, transaminase, and invertase, and intensify the metabolism of proteins, RNA, and DNA.* By activating the nucleic acids and the significant results of duplication, transcription, and translation, the additional metabolic activities of plants and rhizosphere organisms can be more clearly observed and better understood. Multifactorial inducer molecules found in EC&S Bio-Stimulant affect plants and soil and activate DNA and RNA. This activity has a positive growth regulating effect on the cells of plants and microorganisms.

---

*Jackson, 527.

SIMPLIFIED SCHEME FOR THE ROLE OF NUCLEIC ACIDS
IN PROTEIN MANUFACTURE
DNA
REPLICATION
(enzymes)
TRANSCRIPTION
MESSENGER RNA
TRANSFER RNA
RIBOSOMAL RNA
TRANSLATION
PROTEIN
STRUCTURE
CARRIERS
ENZYMES

*Jackson, 528.

Working Model Two: EC&S Bio-Stimulant

The following pages of this memo include the agricultural plant and soil applications for Model Two: EC&S Bio-Stimulant.

A COMPILATION

of

General Product and Application Information

from various sources

Table of Contents

General Product Information

How should products be stored?

Keep container tightly closed. Avoid freezing. Store at temperature below 104° (40°C). Do not store in sunlight. DO NOT STORE DILUTED PRODUCT. KEEP OUT OF REACH OF CHILDREN.

How long is product active?

Product can stay active for two to three years if stored properly.

When should broadcast and banded applications be used?

Application recommendations are based upon product effectiveness and cost-benefit ratios. Research has shown banded application to be more efficient and costs less than broadcast application. If it is more convenient, however, apply product by broadcast application method. For broadcasting application, use twice as much product as recommended for banded application unless otherwise noted.

How critical is the time for Foliar Bio-Stimulant application?

The timing of application is crucial for good plant response:

If a vegetative stage (4-6 leaf, etc.) is recommended, application should be completed within 10 days of the plant reaching that recommended stage of growth.

If a generative stage (flowering, fruit set, etc.) is recommended, application should be completed within 5 days of the plant reaching that recommended stage of growth.

Apply earlier rather than too late. Keep application time as close as possible to those recommended.

How many product applications must be applied to obtain good response?

Generally, all three applications give the best response. Beneficial responses, however, can be obtained from any combination of Soil, Seed and Foliar Bio-Stimulant.

How have dosage rates and application time been established?

Dosages and application time have been established by research of field trials, laboratory experiments and the theoretical knowledge of the plants.

Is research in these two areas continuing?

Research is ongoing and written reports from growers of application results are welcome.

Field Crop Index

ALFALFA & CLOVER

PRODUCT	APPLICATION RATE	APPLICATION TIME	DILUTION RATE Parts Product : Parts Water	METHOD OF APPLICATION	FIELD OBSERVATIONS
SOIL BIOSTIMULANT	Fertile Soil: (16 fl. oz./acre) Moderate Soil: (24 fl. oz./acre) Problem Soil: (32 fl. oz./acre)	On new crops: Preplanting. On established crops: In the Spring	For best results: Aerial - 1:20, 1:50 Ground - at least 1:100 Dilution rate may vary depending on the spray equipment used. Dilute to obtain uniform and accurate coverage.	Broadcast: Aerial or Ground Spray product evenly on soil using conventional spray equipment. On New Crops: Incorporate product into the soil. On Established Crops: Product must be applied when soil is moist and rain is expected within 3-5 days	INCREASED: Soil tilth; Organic matter content; Water holding capacity and drainage; Soil aeration; Neutralization of soil pH.
SEED BIOSIMULANT	FOR NEW CROPS (2 fl. oz/ 110 lbs of seeds)	At planting	1:5	Spray diluted product in a fine mist to obtain thorough coating of seeds. Use any conventional spray equipment. Mix seeds until dry and they do not stick together. Do not keep treated seeds in direct sunlight. Plant seeds as usual.	IMPROVED: Plant emergence; Root development; Resistance of seedlings to stress (low temperature, drought, diseases, etc.).
FOLIER BIOSTIMULANT	(16 fl.oz./acre)	Twice: At first growth and; After every second cutting at 4-6 leaf stage.	For best results: Aerial - 1:20, 1:50. Ground - at least 1:100 Dilution rate may vary depending on the spray equipment used. Dilute to obtain uniform and accurate coverage.	Broadcast. Aerial or ground. Mix with water. Spray mixture evenly on crop using any conventional spray equipment. For best uptake apply product in the evening or early morning. Heavy rain or aerial irrigation within 24 hours of application will diminish product effectiveness.	IMPROVED: Vigor of plant; Regrowth; Maturation; Protein content; Yield.

CEREALS (Small Grains): BARLEY, OATS, RYE, WHEAT

PRODUCT	APPLICATION RATE	APPLICATION TIME	DILUTION RATE Parts Product : Parts Water	METHOD OF APPLICATION	FIELD OBSERVATIONS
SOIL BIOSTIMULANT	Fertile Soil: (12 fl.oz./acre) Moderate Soil: (16 fl.oz./acre) Problem soils: 24 fl. oz./acre)	Preplanting	For best results: Ground - at least 1:100 Dilution rate may vary depending on the spray equipment used. Dilute to obtain uniform and accurate coverage.	Banded. Ground. Spray diluted product evenly in furrows using conventional spray equipment. After application, incorporate product into soil. Rain or irrigation after application will inprove product performance.	INCREASED: Soil fertility; Organic matter content; Water holding capacity & drainage; Soil aeration.
SEED BIOSTIMULANT	(2 fl.oz./ 110 lbs.seeds.)	At Planting	1:4	Spray diluted product in a fine mist to thoroughly coat seeds. Use any conventional sprayer. Mix seeds until dry and they do not stick together. Do not keep treated seeds in direct sunlight. Plant seeds as usual.	IMPROVED: Plant emergence; Vigor of seedlings; Root development; Resistance of seedlings to stress (low temperature, drought, disease, etc.)
FOLIER BIOSTIMULANT	(12 fl.oz/acre)	For winter varieties: At first growth in Spring. For Spring varieties: At 6-8 leave stage.	For best results: Aerial - 1:20, 1:50 Ground - at least 1:100 Dilution rate may vary depending on spray equipment used. Dilute to obtain uniform and accurate coverage.	Spray diluted product evenly on foliage using convention spray equipment. For best uptake, apply product in the evening or early morning. Heavy rain or aerial irrigation within 24 hours of application will diminish product effectiveness.	IMPROVED: Maturation time; Yield; Protein content.

CORN (MAIZE)

PRODUCT	APPLICATION RATE	APPLICATION TIME	DILUTION RATE Parts Product : Parts Water	METHOD OF APPLICATION	FIELD OBSERVATIONS
SOIL BIOSTIMULANT	Fertile Soil: (12 fl.oz./acre) Moderate Soil: (16 fl.oz./acre) Problem soils: (24 fl.oz/acre)	Preplanting	For best results: Aerial - 1:20, 1:50 Ground - at least 1:100 Dilution rate may vary depending on the spray equipment used. Dilute to obtain uniform and accurate coverage	Banded. Ground. Spray product evenly in furrows using conventional spray equipment, irrigation lines or ditches. After application, incorporate product into the soil. Rain or irrigation after application will improve soil bio-performance	IMPROVED: Soil tilth; Soil fertility; Organic matter content; Water holding capacity and drainage; Soil aeration.
SEED BIOSTIMULANT	(2 fl.oz/ 90 lbs seeds)	Planting	1:4	Spray diluted product in a fine mist to thoroughly coat seeds. Use any conventional sprayer. Mix seeds until dry and they do not stick to each other. Do not keep treated seeds in direct sunlight. Plant seeds as usual	IMPROVED: Plant emergence; Vigor of seedlings; Root development; Resistance of seedlings to stress (low temperature, drought, disease, etc.).
FOLIER BIOSTIMULANT	(12 fl.oz./acre)	At 6-8 leaf stage.	For best results Aerial - 1:20, 1:50. Ground - at least 1:100 Dilution rate may vary depending on the spray equipment used. Dilute to obtain uniform and accurate coverage.	Spray diluted product evenly on foliage using conventional spray equipment. For best uptake apply product in the evening or early in the morning. Heavy rain or aerial irrigation within 24 hours of application will diminish product effectiveness.	IMPROVED: Plant vigor; Maturation time; Yield; Quality of seeds.

COTTON

PRODUCT	APPLICATION RATE	APPLICATION TIME	DILUTION RATE Parts Product : Parts Water	METHOD OF APPLICATION	FIELD OBSERVATIONS
SOIL BIOSTIMULANT	Banded:: (16 fl.oz./acre) Broadcast: (24 fl.oz./acre)	Preplanting	For best results: Aerial - 1:20, 1:50 Ground - at least 1:100 Dilution rate may vary depending on spray equipment used. Dilute to obtain uniform and accurate coverage.	Banded or Broadcast. Ground or Aerial. Spray diluted product evenly in furrows (banded) or apply to the total field (broadcast). Use any conventional spray equipment. After application, incorporate product into the soil. Rain or irrigation after application will improve performance.	INCREASED: Soil tilth; Soil fertility; Organic matter content; Water holding capacity and drainage; Soil aeration; Neutralization of soil pH.
SEED BIOSTIMULANT	(2 fl.oz./ 110 lbs.seeds)	Planting	1:4	Spray diluted product in a fine mist to thoroughly coat seeds. Use any conventional sprayer. Mix seeds until dry and they do not stick together. Do not keep treated seeds in direct sunlight. Plant seeds as usual. Do not store treated seeds.	IMPROVED: Plant emergence; Vigor of seedlings; Root development; Resistance of seedlings to stress (low temperature, drought disease, etc.).
FOLIER BIOSTIMULANT	(12 fl.oz./acre)	At the beginning of flowering (5-10% open flowers)	For best results: Aerial - 1:20, 1:50 Ground - at least 1:100 Dilution rate may vary depending on the spray equipment used. Dilute to obtain uniform coverage.	Spray diluted product evenly on foliage using conventional spray equipment. For best uptake, apply product in the evening or early morning. Heavy rain or aerial irrigation within 24 hours of application will diminish product effectiveness.	IMPROVED: Plant vigor; Maturation time; Yield; Quality of cotton fibers and seeds.

FLAX

PRODUCT	APPLICATION RATE	APPLICATION TIME	DILUTION RATE Parts Product : Parts Water	METHOD OF APPLICATION	FIELD OBSERVATIONS
SOIL BIOSTIMULANT	Moderate Soil: Banded: (16 fl.oz./acre) Moderate soil Broadcast: (24 fl.oz./acre) Problem soil: Banded: (16 fl.oz./acre) Problem soil Broadcast: (25 fl.oz./acre)	Preplanting	For best results: Aerial - 1:20, 1:50 Ground - at least 1:100 Dilution rate may vary depending on the spray equipment used. Dilute to obtain uniform coverage.	Banded or Broadcast. Ground or Aerial. Spray diluted product evenly in furrows (banded) or apply to the total field (broadcast). Use any conventional spray equipment. After application, incorporate product into the soil. Rain or irrigation after application will improve performance.	INCREASED: Soil tilth; Soil fertility; Organic matter content; Water holding capacity and drainage; Soil aeration; Neutralization of soil pH.
SEED BIOSTIMULANT	(2 fl.oz./ 110 lbs seeds)	Planting	1:5	Spray diluted product in a fine mist to obtain thorough coating of seeds. Use any conventional spray equipment. Mix seeds until dry and they do not stick together. Do not keep treated seeds in direct sunlight. Plant seeds as usual.	IMPROVED: Plant emergence; Vigor of seedlings; Root development; Resistance of seedlings to stress (low temperature, drought; disease, etc.).

GRASS (PASTURES, HAY, LAWNS)

PRODUCT	APPLICATION RATE	APPLICATION TIME	DILUTION RATE Parts Product : Parts Water	METHOD OF APPLICATION	FIELD OBSERVATIONS
SOIL BIOSTIMULANT	Fertile soil: (24 fl.oz./acre) Moderate soil: (32 fl.oz./acre) Problem Soil: (40 fl.oz./acre)	For established pastures and lawns: In early spring. For new lawns: Before planting	For best results: Aerial - 1:20, 1:50 Ground - at least 1:100 Dilution rate may vary depending on the spray equipment used. Dilute to obtain uniform and accurate coverage.	Broadcast. Aerial or ground. Spray diluted product evenly on soil using any conventional spray equipment. On new crops: Incorporate product into the soil. On established crops: Product must be applied when soil is moist and rain is expected in 3-5 days.	INCREASED: Soil fertility; Water holding capacity and drainage; Organic matter content; Neutralization of soil pH.
FOLIAR BIOSTIMULANT	(12 fl.oz./acre.)	Twice: 1st at first growth in spring; 2nd in 4-6 weeks.	For best results: Aerial - 1:20, 1:50 Ground - at least 1:100 Dilution rate may vary depending on the spray equipment used. Dilute to obtain uniform and accurate coverage.	Broadcast. Aerial or ground. Spray diluted product evenly on soil using any conventional spray equipment. For best uptake apply in the evening or early morning. Heavy rain or aerial irrigation within 24 hours of application will diminish product effectiveness.	IMPROVED: Vigor of plant; Regrowth; Greener and thicker leaves; Yield; Protein content.

PEANUTS (GROUNDNUTS)

PRODUCT	APPLICATION RATE	APPLICATION TIME	DILUTION RATE Parts Product : Parts Water	METHOD OF APPLICATION	FIELD OBSERVATIONS
SOIL BIOSTIMULANT	Fertile soils: (12 fl.oz./acre) Moderate soils: (16 fl.oz./acre) Problem soils: (24 fl.oz./acre)	Preplanting	For best results: Ground - at least 1:100 Dilution rate may vary depending on the spray equipment used. Dilute to obtain uniform and accurate coverage.	Banded. Ground Spray diluted product evenly in furrows using any conventional spray equipment, irrigation lines, ditches or overhead sprinklers. After application plant seeds and cover furrows with soil. Rain or irrigation after application will improve performance.	INCREASED: Soil tilth; Soil fertility; Organic matter content; Water holding capacity and drainage; Soil aeration; Neutralization of soil pH.
SEED BIOSTIMULANT	(2 fl.oz./ 110 lbs. seeds)	Planting	1:4	Spray diluted product in a fine mist to obtain thorough coating of seeds. Use any conventional spray equipment. Mix seeds until dry and they do not stick together. Do not keep treated seeds in direct sunlight. Plant seeds as usual.	IMPROVED; Plant emergence; Vigor of seedlings; Root development; Resistance of seedlings to stress (high temperature, drought, disease, etc.).
FOLIER BIOSTIMULANT	(12 fl.oz./acre)	About 80 days after sowing.	For best results: Aerial - 1:20, 1:50 Ground - at least 1:100 Dilution rate may vary depending on the spray equipment used. Dilute to obtain uniform and accurate coverage.	Spray diluted product evenly on foliage using conventional spray equipment. For best uptake, apply product in the evening or early morning. Heavy rain or aerial irrigation within 24 hours of application will diminish product effectiveness.	IMPROVED: Pod formation; Yield; Oil content.

JUTE

PRODUCT	APPLICATION RATE	APPLICATION TIME	DILUTION RATE Parts Product : Parts Water	METHOD OF APPLICATION	FIELD OBSERVATIONS
SOIL BIOSTIMULANT	Fertile Soils: (12 fl.oz./acre) Moderate soils: (16 fl.oz./acre) Problem soils: (24 fl.oz./acre)	Preplanting	For best results: Ground - at least 1:100 Dilution rate may vary depending on the spray equipment used. Dilute to obtain uniform and accurate coverage.	Banded. Ground. Spray diluted product evenly in the furrows using conventional spray equipment. After application, incorporate product into soil. Rain or irrigation after application will improve performance.	INCREASED; Soil tilth; Soil fertility; Organic content; Water holding capacity and drainage; Soil aeration; Neutralization of soil pH.
SEED BIOSTIMULANT	(2 fl.oz./ 110 lbs. seeds)	Planting	1:4	Spray diluted product in a fine mist to thoroughly coat seeds. Using any conventional sprayer. Mix seeds until dry and they do not stick to each other. Do not keep treated seeds in direct sunlight. Plant seeds as usual.	IMPROVED: Plant emergence; Vigor of seedlings; Root development; Resistance of seedlings to stress (high temperature, drought, diseases, etc.)

LUPINE

PRODUCT	APPLICATION RATE	APPLICATION TIME	DILUTION RATE **Parts Product : Parts Water**	METHOD OF APPLICATION	FIELD OBSERVATIONS
SOIL BIOSTIMULANT	Moderate Soil: (32 fl.oz./acre) Problem Soil: (40 fl.oz./acre)	Preplanting	For best results: Aerial - 1:20, 1:50 Ground - At least 1:100 Dilution rate may vary depending on the spray equipment used. Dilute to obtain uniform and accurate coverage.	Broadcast. Aerial or Ground Spray diluted product evenly on the ground using any conventional spray equipment. After application incorporate product into the soil. Rain or irrigation after application will improve performance.	INCREASED: Soil tilth; Organic matter content; Water holding capacity and drainage; Soil aeration; Neutralization of soil pH
SEED BIOSTIMULANT	(2 fl.oz./ 110 lbs. seeds.)	Planting	1:5	Spray diluted product in a fine mist to thoroughly coat seeds. Use any conventional sprayer. Mix seeds until dry and they do not stick together. Do not keep treated seeds in direct sunlight. Plant seeds as usual.	IMPROVED: Plant emergence; Vigor of plant; Root development; Vegetative growth.

MILLET

PRODUCT	APPLICATION RATE	APPLICATION TIME	DILUTION RATE Parts Product : Parts Water	METHOD OF APPLICATION	FIELD OBSERVATIONS
SOIL BIOSTIMULANT	Fertile Soils: (12 fl.oz./acre) Moderate soils: (16 fl.oz./acre) Problem soils: (24 fl.oz./acre)	Preplanting	For best results: Ground - at least 1:100 Dilution rate may vary depending on the spray equipment used. Dilute to obtain uniform and accurate coverage.	Banded. Ground. Spray diluted product evenly in the furrows using conventional spray equipment. After application, incorporate product into soil. Rain or irrigation after application will improve performance.	INCREASED: Soil tilth; Soil fertility; Organic matter content; Water holding capacity and drainage; Soil aeration; Neutralization of soil pH.
SEED BIOSTIMULANT	(2 fl.oz./ 110 lbs. seeds)	Planting	1:4	Spray diluted product in a fine mist to thoroughly coat seeds. Using any conventional sprayer. Mix seeds until dry and they do not stick to each other. Do not keep treated seeds in direct sunlight. Plant seeds as usual.	IMPROVED: Plant emergence; Vigor of seedlings; Root development; Resistance of seedlings to stress (high temperature, drought, diseases, etc.)
FOLIER BIOSTIMULANT	(12 fl.oz./acre)	At 6-8 leaf stage.	For best results Aerial - 1:20, 1:50. Ground - at least 1:100 Dilution rate may vary depending on the spray equipment used. Dilute to obtain uniform and accurate coverage.	Spray diluted product evenly on foliage using conventional spray equipment. For best uptake apply product in the evening or early in the morning. Heavy rain or aerial irrigation within 24 hours of application will diminish product effectiveness.	IMPROVED: Plant vigor; Maturation time; Yield.

OIL PALM

PRODUCT	APPLICATION RATE	APPLICATION TIME	DILUTION RATE Parts Product : Parts Water	METHOD OF APPLICATION	FIELD OBSERVATIONS
SOIL BIOSTIMULANT	(32 fl.oz./acre)	Once a year. Before new growth after final harvest.	For best results: Ground - at least 1:100 Dilution rate may vary depending on the spray equipment used. Dilute to obtain uniform and accurate coverage.	Spray diluted product in a ring around the trunk of a tree, at a distance of 3 to 4 feet, using any conventional spray equipment. After application, incorporate product into soil. Rain or irrigation after application will improve performance.	INCREASED: Soil fertility; Water holding capacity and drainage; Soil aeration; Organic matter content.
SEED BIOSTIMULANT	FOR TRANSPLANTED SEEDLINGS ONLY (7 fl.oz./acre)	At Transplanting	1:100	Dip the roots of seedlings in diluted product immediately after removing from seedbed and transplant to prepared holes. Water transplanted seedlings with remaining solution	IMPROVED: Survival of seedlings; Regeneration and growth of root system; Resistance of seedlings to stress (high temperature, drought, disease, etc.).
	OR - AFTER SEEDLINGS ARE TRANSPLANTED (7 fl.oz./acre)	At Transplanting	Not less than 1:20	Calculate dilution rate so recommended amount of product will be used per acre.	
FOLIAR BIOSTIMULANT	(12 fl.oz./acre)	At the beginning of intensive plant growth. (1-2 new leaves developed)	For best results: Aerial - 1:20, 1:50. Ground - at least 1:100. Dilution rate may vary depending on the spray equipment used. Dilute to obtain uniform and accurate coverage.	Spray diluted product evenly on tree leaves using any conventional spray equipment. For best uptake apply product in the evening or early morning. Heavy rain within 24 hours of application will diminish product effectiveness.	IMPROVED: Plant vigor; Fruit set; Yield; Oil content.

POTATOES

PRODUCT	APPLICATION RATE	APPLICATION TIME	DILUTION RATE Parts Product : Parts Water	METHOD OF APPLICATION	FIELD OBSERVATIONS
SOIL BIOSTIMULANT	(16 fl.oz/acre)	At planting	For best results: Ground - 1:100 Dilution rate may vary depending on spray equipment used. Dilute to obtain uniform and accurate coverage.	Banded. Ground. Spray diluted product evenly in furrows using conventional spray equipment. Plant potatoes and cover furrows with soil. Rain or irrigation after application will improve performance.	INCREASED: Soil tilth; Soil fertility; Organic matter content; Water holding capacity and drainage; Soil aeration; Neutralization of soil pH.
	OR - See TUBER TREATMENT IN FURROWS below				
SEED on seed BIOSTIMULANT	TUBER TREATMENT ONLY IMPROVED: (1 quart/16,200 lbs seed potatoes)	At planting	water, but not more then necessary, to thoroughly coat tubers.	At least 1:100. Use enough potatoes in a fine mist to thoroughly coat all tubers. Use any convention spray equipment.	Spray diluted product Plant emergence; Plant vigor; Root development; Resistance of plants to stress (low temperature, drought, disease, etc.).
	OR - TUBER TREATMENT IN FURROWS	At planting	1:100	Plant tubers in furrows and spray evenly with diluted product. Cover furrows with soil immediately after treatment.	
FOLIER BIOSTIMULANT	(12 fl.oz/acre)	6-8 leaf stage	For best results: Aerial - 1:20, 1:50 Ground - at least 1:100 Dilution rate may vary depending on spray equipment used. Dilute to obtain uniform and accurate coverage.	Spray diluted product evenly on foliage using conventional spray equipment. For best uptake, apply product in the evening or early morning. Heavy rain within 24 hours of application will diminish product effectiveness.	IMPROVED; Plant vigor; Tuber growth; Yield; Quality of tubers.

RAPE

PRODUCT	APPLICATION RATE	APPLICATION TIME	DILUTION RATE Parts Product : Parts Water	METHOD OF APPLICATION	FIELD OBSERVATIONS
SOIL BIOSTIMULANT	(16 fl.oz./acre)	Preplanting	For best results: Ground - at least 1:100 Dilution rate may vary depending on the spray equipment used. Dilute to obtain uniform and accurate coverage.	Banded. Ground. Spray diluted product evenly in the furrows using conventional spray equipment. After application, incorporate product into soil. Rain or irrigation after application will improve performance.	INCREASED: Soil tilth; Soil fertility; Organic matter content; Water holding capacity and drainage; Soil aeration; Neutralization of soil pH.
SEED BIOSTIMULANT	(2 fl.oz./ 110 lbs. seeds)	Planting	1:4	Spray diluted product in a fine mist to thoroughly coat seeds. Using any conventional sprayer. Mix seeds until dry and they do not stick to each other. Do not keep treated seeds in direct sunlight. Plant seeds as usual.	IMPROVED: Plant emergence; Vigor of seedlings; Root development; Resistance of seedlings to stress (high temperature, drought, diseases, etc.).
FOLIER BIOSTIMULANT	(12 fl.oz./acre)	For winter varieties: At first growth in the spring. For spring varieties: At 6-8 leaves stage	For best results Aerial - 1:20, 1:50. Ground - at least a:100 Dilution rate may vary depending on the spray equipment used. Dilute to obtain uniform and accurate coverage.	Spray diluted product evenly on foliage using conventional spray equipment. For best uptake apply product in the evening or early in the morning. Heavy rain or aerial irrigation within 24 hours of application will diminish product effectiveness.	IMPROVED: Plant vigor; Maturation time; Yield; Oil content..

RICE

PRODUCT	APPLICATION RATE	APPLICATION TIME	DILUTION RATE Parts Product : Parts Water	METHOD OF APPLICATION	FIELD OBSERVATIONS
SEED BIOSTIMULANT	(2 fl.oz./ 110 lbs seeds)	Seeding	1:4	Spray diluted product in a fine mist to thoroughly coat seeds. Using any conventional sprayer. Mix seeds until dry and they do not stick to each other. Do not keep treated seeds in direct sunlight. Plant seeds as usual.	INCREASED: Plant emergence; Vigor of seedlings; Root development; Resistance to stress.
	(2 fl.oz./acre)	Transplanting time	At least 1:20. Use enough water, but not more than necessary, to dip the roots of plants to be planted on one acre. Calculate dilution rate so recommended amount will be used per acre.	Dip the roots of the transplanted plants in dilution immediately after removing from seedbed and transplant them in field..	IMPROVED: Survival of seedlings; Regeneration and growth of root system; Resistance of seedlings to stress.
FOLIER BIOSTIMULANT	(12 fl.oz./acre)	At panicle initiation (40-50 days after transplanting)	For best results Aerial - 1:20, 1:50. Ground - at least 1:100 Dilution rate may vary depending on the spray equipment used. Dilute to obtain uniform and accurate coverage.	Spray diluted product evenly on foliage using conventional spray equipment. For best uptake apply product in the evening or early in the morning. Heavy rain or aerial irrigation within 24 hours of application will diminish product effectiveness.	IMPROVED: Amount of panicles; Maturation time; Yield; Quality of seeds.

SORGHUM, MILO

PRODUCT	APPLICATION RATE	APPLICATION TIME	DILUTION RATE Parts Product : Parts Water	METHOD OF APPLICATION	FIELD OBSERVATIONS
SOIL BIOSTIMULANT	Fertile Soils: (12 fl.oz./acre) Moderate soils: (16 fl.oz./acre) Problem soils: (24 fl.oz./acre)	Preplanting	For best results: Ground - at least 1:100 Dilution rate may vary depending on the spray equipment used. Dilute to obtain uniform and accurate coverage.	Banded. Ground. Spray diluted product evenly in the furrows using conventional spray equipment. After application, incorporate product into soil. Rain or irrigation after application will improve performance.	INCREASED: Soil tilth; Soil fertility; Organic matter content; Water holding capacity and drainage; Soil aeration; Neutralization of soil pH.
SEED BIOSTIMULANT	(2 fl.oz./ 110 lbs. seeds)	Planting	1:4	Spray diluted product in a fine mist to thoroughly coat seeds. Using any conventional sprayer. Mix seeds until dry and they do not stick to each other. Do not keep treated seeds in direct sunlight. Plant seeds as usual.	IMPROVED: Plant emergence; Vigor of seedlings; Root development; Resistance of seedlings to stress (high temperature, drought, diseases, etc.).
FOLIER BIOSTIMULANT	(12 fl.oz./acre)	At 6-8 leaf stage.	For best results Aerial - 1:20, 1:50. Ground - at least a:100 Dilution rate may vary depending on the spray equipment used. Dilute to obtain uniform and accurate coverage.	Spray diluted product evenly on foliage using conventional spray equipment. For best uptake apply product in the evening or early in the morning. Heavy rain or aerial irrigation within 24 hours of application will diminish product effectiveness.	IMPROVED: Plant vigor; Maturation time; Yield; Quality of seeds.

SOYBEANS

PRODUCT	APPLICATION RATE	APPLICATION TIME	DILUTION RATE Parts Product : Parts Water	METHOD OF APPLICATION	FIELD OBSERVATIONS
SOIL BIOSTIMULANT	Moderate soils: (12 fl.oz./acre) Problem soils: (16 fl.oz./acre)	Preplanting	For best results: Ground - at least 1:100 Dilution rate may vary depending on the spray equipment used. Dilute to obtain uniform and accurate coverage.	Banded. Ground. Spray diluted product evenly in the furrows using conventional spray equipment. After application, incorporate product into soil. Rain or irrigation after application will improve performance.	INCREASED: Soil tilth; Soil fertility; Organic matter content; Water holding capacity and drainage; Soil aeration; Neutralization of soil pH.
SEED BIOSTIMULANT	(2 fl.oz./ 110 lbs. seeds)	Planting	1:4	Spray diluted product in a fine mist to thoroughly coat seeds. Using any conventional sprayer. Mix seeds until dry and they do not stick to each other. Do not keep treated seeds in direct sunlight. Plant seeds as usual.	IMPROVED: Plant emergence; Vigor of seedlings; Root development; Resistance of seedlings to stress (low temperature, drought, diseases, etc.).
FOLIER BIOSTIMULANT	(12 fl.oz./acre)	At 7-8 trifoliate (having 3 leaflets) leaf stage.	For best results Aerial - 1:20, 1:50. Ground - at least a:100 Dilution rate may vary depending on the spray equipment used. Dilute to obtain uniform and accurate coverage.	Spray diluted product evenly on foliage using conventional spray equipment. For best uptake apply product in the evening or early in the morning. Heavy rain or aerial irrigation within 24 hours of application will diminish product effectiveness.	IMPROVED: Plant vigor; Maturation time; Yield; Quality of beans.

SUGAR BEETS

PRODUCT	APPLICATION RATE	APPLICATION TIME	DILUTION RATE Parts Product : Parts Water	METHOD OF APPLICATION	FIELD OBSERVATIONS
SOIL BIOSTIMULANT	Fertile Soils: (12 fl.oz./acre) Moderate soils: (16 fl.oz./acre) Problem soils: (24 fl.oz./acre)	Preplanting	For best results: Ground - at least 1:100 Dilution rate may vary depending on the spray equipment used. Dilute to obtain uniform and accurate coverage.	Banded. Ground. Spray diluted product evenly in the furrows using conventional spray equipment. After application, incorporate product into soil. Rain or irrigation after application will improve performance.	INCREASED: Soil tilth; Soil fertility; Organic matter content; Water holding capacity and drainage; Soil aeration; Neutralization of soil pH.
SEED BIOSTIMULANT	(2 fl.oz./ 110 lbs. seeds)	Planting	1:4	Spray diluted product in a fine mist to thoroughly coat seeds. Using any conventional sprayer. Mix seeds until dry and they do not stick to each other. Do not keep treated seeds in direct sunlight. Plant seeds as usual.	IMPROVED: Plant emergence; Vigor of seedlings; Root development; Resistance of seedlings to stress (low temperature, drought, diseases, etc.).
FOLIER BIOSTIMULANT	(12 fl. oz./acre)	At 6-8 leaf stage.	For best results Aerial - 1:20, 1:50. Ground - at least a:100 Dilution rate may vary depending on the spray equipment used. Dilute to obtain uniform and accurate coverage.	Spray diluted product evenly on foliage using conventional spray equipment. For best uptake apply product in the evening or early in the morning. Heavy rain or aerial irrigation within 24 hours of application will diminish product effectiveness.	IMPROVED: Plant vigor; Maturation time; Yield; Quality of beans.

SUGARCANE

PRODUCT	APPLICATION RATE	APPLICATION TIME	DILUTION RATE Parts Product : Parts Water	METHOD OF APPLICATION	FIELD OBSERVATIONS
SOIL BIOSTIMULANT	Good and Moderate soils (16 fl.oz./acre) Problem soils: (24 fl.oz./acre)	Planting	For best results: Ground - at least 1:100	Banded. Ground. Plant sugarcane pieces as usual. Spray diluted product uniformly in furrows with sugarcane pieces using any conventional spray equipment. After application cover furrows with soil., Rain or irrigation after application will improve performance.	INCREASED: Soil fertility; Water holding capacity and drainage; Soil aeration; Neutralization of soil pH.
FOLIER BIOSTIMULANT	(12 fl.oz./acre)	Twice: 1st application when plants are approx. 36 inches high. 2nd application 30-45 days before harvest.	For best results: Aerial - 1:20, 1:50 Ground - at least 1:100 Dilution rate may vary depending on the spray equipment used. Dilute to obtain uniform and accurate coverage.	Spray diluted product evenly on foliage using conventional spray equipment. For best uptake apply product in the evening or early in the morning. Heavy rain or aerial irrigation within 24 hours of application will diminish product effectiveness.	IMPROVED: Vigor of plants; Yield; Sugar content.

SUNFLOWER

PRODUCT	APPLICATION RATE	APPLICATION TIME	DILUTION RATE Parts Product : Parts Water	METHOD OF APPLICATION	FIELD OBSERVATIONS
SOIL BIOSTIMULANT	Good and Moderate: Soils: Banded: (16 fl.oz./acre) Broadcast: (24 fl.oz./acre) Problem soil: Banded: (16 fl.oz./acre) Broadcast: (32 fl.oz./acre)	Preplanting	For best results: Aerial.- 1:20, 1:50 Ground - at least 1:100 Dilution rate may vary depending on the spray equipment used. Dilute to obtain uniform coverage.	Banded or broadcast. Ground or aerial. Spray diluted product evenly in furrows (banded) or apply to the total field (broadcast). Use any conventional spray equipment. After application, incorporate product into the soil. Rain or irrigation after application will improve performance.	INCREASED: Soil tilth; Soil fertility; Organic matter content; Water holding capacity and drainage; Soil aeration; Neutralization of soil pH.
SEED BIOSTIMULANT	(2 fl.oz./ 110 lbs. seeds)	Planting	1:4	Spray diluted product in a fine mist to obtain to thorough coating of seeds. Use any conventional spray equipment. Mix seeds until dry and they do not stick together. Do not keep treated seeds in direct sunlight. Plant seeds as usual.	IMPROVED: Plant emergence; Vigor of seedlings; Root development; Resistance of seedlings to stress (high temperature, drought; disease, etc.).
FOLIAR BIOSTIMULANT	(12 fl.oz./acre)	At star formation	For best results: Aerial.- 1:20, 1:50 Ground - at least 1:100 Dilution rate may vary depending on the spray equipment used. Dilute to obtain uniform coverage.	Spray diluted product evenly on tree leaves using any conventional spray equipment. For best uptake apply product in the evening or early morning. Heavy rain within 24 hours of application will diminish product effectiveness.	IMPROVED: Plant vigor; Yield; Maturation time; Quality of seeds.

TEA

PRODUCT	APPLICATION RATE	APPLICATION TIME	DILUTION RATE Parts Product : Parts Water	METHOD OF APPLICATION	FIELD OBSERVATIONS
SOIL BIOSTIMULANT	Moderate Soils: (24 fl.oz./acre) Problem Soils: (32 fl.oz./acre)	1-2 weeks before first flush growth.	For best results: Ground - at least 1:100 Dilution rate may vary depending on the spray equipment used. Dilute to obtain uniform and accurate coverage.	Banded. Ground. Spray diluted product uniformly along tea bushes using any conventional spray equipment. After application, incorporate product into the soil. Rain or irrigation after application will improve performance	INCREASED: Soil fertility; Water holding capacity and drainage; Soil aeration.
SEED BIOSTIMULANT	FOR TRANSPLANTED SEEDLINGS ONLY (7 fl.oz./acre)	Planting	1:100	Dip the roots of seedlings in diluted product immediately after removing from seedbed and transplant to the field. Water transplanted seedlings with remaining solution	IMPROVED: Survival of seedlings; Regeneration and growth of root system.
FOLIAR BIOSTIMULANT	(8 fl.oz./acre)	Three times: 1st at first flush growth; 2nd, 7-9 weeks after first application; 3rd, 7-9 weeks after second application.	For best results: Aerial - 1:20, 1:50. Ground - at least 1:100. Dilution rate may vary depending on the spray equipment used. Dilute to obtain uniform and accurate coverage.	Spray diluted product evenly on plant foliage using any conventional spray equipment. For best uptake apply product in the evening or early morning. Heavy rain within 24 hours of application will diminish product effectiveness.	IMPROVED: Growth of shoots; Yield; Quality of tea.

TOBACCO

PRODUCT	APPLICATION RATE	APPLICATION TIME	DILUTION RATE Parts Product : Parts Water	METHOD OF APPLICATION	FIELD OBSERVATIONS
SEEDLING BIOSTIMULANT	(24 fl.oz./acre)	Planting	At least 1:20. Use enough water, but not more than necessary, to dip the roots of plants to be planted on one acre. Calculate dilution rate so recommended amount will be used per acre.	Dip the roots of the seedlings in dilution immediately after removing from seedbed and transplant them to the field. Water transplanted seedlings with remaining solution.	IMPROVED: Survival of seedlings; Regeneration and growth of root system; Soil fertility around roots.
FOLIAR BIOSTIMULANT	(12 fl.oz./acre)	Twice: 1st,S 30-35 days after planting; 2nd, 30-35 days after first application.	For best results: Aerial - 1:20, 1:50. Ground - at least 1:100. Dilution rate may vary depending on the spray equipment used. Dilute to obtain uniform and accurate coverage.	Spray diluted product evenly on tree leaves using any conventional spray equipment. For best uptake apply product in the evening or early morning. Heavy rain within 24 hours of application will diminish product effectiveness.	IMPROVED: Plant vigor; Fruit set; Yield; Oil content.

Vegetable Crop Index

VEGETABLES - LEAF, STEM, AND FLOWER

Artichoke, Asparagus, Broccoli, Brussel Sprouts, Cabbage, Cauliflower, Celery, Chard, Chicory, Chives, Cress, Endive, Kale, Kohlrabi, Lettuce, Parsley, Parsnips, Radishes, Rutabagas, Spinach, Turnips

PRODUCT	APPLICATION RATE	APPLICATION TIME	DILUTION RATE Parts Product : Parts Water	METHOD OF APPLICATION	FIELD OBSERVATIONS
SOIL BIOSTIMULANT	Fertile soils: (12 fl.oz./acre) Moderate Soils: (16 fl. oz./acre) Problem Soils: (24 fl.oz./acre)	Preplanting	For best results: Ground - at least 1:100 Dilution rate may vary depending on the spray equipment used. Dilute to obtain uniform and accurate coverage.	Banded. Ground. Spray diluted product evenly the trunk using any conventional spray equipment. After application incorporate product into soil. Rain or irrigation after application will improve performance.	INCREASED: Soil tilth; Soil fertility; Water holding capacity and drainage; Soil aeration; Neutralization of soil pH.
SEED BIOSTIMULANT	(2 fl.oz./ 110 lbs. seeds)	Planting	1:4	Spray diluted product in a fine mist to obtain to thorough coating of seeds. Use any conventional spray equipment. Mix seeds until dry and they do not stick together. Do not store treated seeds in direct sunlight. Plant seeds as usual.	IMPROVED: Plant emergence; Vigor of seedlings; Root development; Resistance of seedlings to stress (low temperature, drought, disease, etc.).
	OR - FOR TRANSPLANTED SEEDLINGS (7 fl.oz./acre)	At transplant	At least 1:20. Use enough water, but not more than necessary, to dip the roots of plants to be planted on one acre. Calculate dilution rate so recommended amount will be used per acre.	Dip the roots of the transplanted plants in dilution immediately after removing from seedbed and transplant them in field.	IMPROVED: Survival of Regeneration and growth of root system; Resistance of seedlings to stress.
FOLIAR BIOSTIMULANT	(12 fl. oz./acre)	At 6-8 leaf stage	For best results: Aerial - 1:20, 1:50. Ground - at least 1:100. Dilution rate may vary depending on the spray equipment used. Dilute to obtain uniform and accurate coverage.	Spray diluted product evenly on plant foliage using any conventional spray equipment. For best uptake apply product in the evening or early morning. Heavy rain within 24 hours of application will diminish product effectiveness.	IMPROVED: Plant vigor; Vegetable growth; Yield; Quality of vegetable.

VEGETABLES - SEED

Beans, Peas, Soybeans

PRODUCT	APPLICATION RATE	APPLICATION TIME	DILUTION RATE Parts Product : Parts Water	METHOD OF APPLICATION	FIELD OBSERVATIONS
SOIL BIOSTIMULANT	Moderate soils: (12 fl.oz./acre) Problem soils: (16 fl.oz./acre)	Preplanting or Planting	For best results: Ground - at least 1:100 Dilution rate may vary depending on the spray equipment used. Dilute to obtain uniform and accurate coverage.	Banded. Ground. Spray diluted product evenly in the furrows using conventional spray equipment. After application, plant seeds and cover furrows. Rain or irrigation after application will improve performance.	INCREASED: Soil tilth; Soil fertility; Organic matter content; Water holding capacity and drainage; Soil aeration; Neutralization of soil pH.
SEED BIOSTIMULANT	(2 fl.oz./ 110 lbs. seeds)	Planting	1:4	Spray diluted product in a fine mist to thoroughly coat seeds. Using any conventional sprayer. Mix seeds until dry and they do not stick to each other. Do not keep treated seeds in direct sunlight. Plant seeds as usual.	IMPROVED: Plant emergence; Vigor of seedlings; Root development; Resistance of seedlings to stress (low temperature, drought, diseases, etc.).
FOLIER BIOSTIMULANT	(12 fl.oz./acre)	At 7-8 trifoliate (having 3 leaflets) leaf stage.	For best results Aerial - 1:20, 1:50. Ground - at least 1:100 Dilution rate may vary depending on the spray equipment used. Dilute to obtain uniform and accurate coverage.	Spray diluted product evenly on foliage using conventional spray equipment. For best uptake apply product in the evening or early in the morning. Heavy rain or aerial irrigation within 24 hours of application will diminish product effectiveness.	IMPROVED: Plant vigor; Maturation time; Yield; Quality of beans.

VEGETABLES - ROOT

Beet (red), Carrots, Parsnips, Radishes, Rutabagas, Turnips

PRODUCT	APPLICATION RATE	APPLICATION TIME	DILUTION RATE Parts Product : Parts Water	METHOD OF APPLICATION	FIELD OBSERVATIONS
SOIL BIOSTIMULANT	Fertile Soils: (12 fl.oz./acre) Moderate soils: (16 fl.oz./acre) Problem soils: (24 fl.oz./acre)	Preplanting	For best results: Ground - at least 1:100 Dilution rate may vary depending on the spray equipment used. Dilute to obtain uniform and accurate coverage.	Banded. Ground. Spray diluted product evenly in the furrows using conventional spray equipment. After application, incorporate product into soil. Rain or irrigation after application will improve performance.	INCREASED: Soil tilth; Soil fertility; Organic matter content; Water holding capacity and drainage; Soil aeration; Neutralization of soil pH.
FOLIER BIOSTIMULANT	(12 fl. oz./acre)	Twice: 1st, 6-8 leaf stage; 2nd, 4-6 weeks later.	For best results Aerial - 1:20, 1:50. Ground - at least a:100 Dilution rate may vary depending on the spray equipment used. Dilute to obtain uniform and accurate coverage.	Spray diluted product evenly on foliage using conventional spray equipment. For best uptake apply product in the evening or early in the morning. Heavy rain or aerial irrigation within 24 hours of application will diminish product effectiveness.	IMPROVED: Plant vigor; Yield; Quality of vegetables.

SWEET CORN

PRODUCT	APPLICATION RATE	APPLICATION TIME	DILUTION RATE Parts Product : Parts Water	METHOD OF APPLICATION	FIELD OBSERVATIONS
SOIL BIOSTIMULANT	Fertile Soils: (12 fl.oz./acre) Moderate soils: (16 fl.oz./acre) Problem soils: (24 fl.oz./acre)	Preplanting	For best results: Ground - at least 1:100 Dilution rate may vary depending on the spray equipment used. Dilute to obtain uniform and accurate coverage.	Banded. Ground. Spray diluted product evenly in the furrows using conventional spray equipment. After application, incorporate product into soil. Rain or irrigation after application will improve performance.	INCREASED: Soil tilth; Soil fertility; Organic matter content; Water holding capacity and drainage; Soil aeration; Neutralization of soil pH.
SEED BIOSTIMULANT	(2 fl.oz./ 90 lbs. seeds)	Planting	1:4	Spray diluted product in a fine mist to thoroughly coat seeds. Using any conventional sprayer. Mix seeds until dry and they do not stick to each other. Do not keep treated seeds in direct sunlight. Plant seeds as usual.	IMPROVED: Plant emergence; Vigor of seedlings; Root development; Resistance of seedlings to stress (low temperature, drought, diseases, etc.).
FOLIER BIOSTIMULANT	(12 fl.oz./acre)	At 6-8 leaf stage.	For best results Aerial - 1:20, 1:50. Ground - at least a:100 Dilution rate may vary depending on the spray equipment used. Dilute to obtain uniform and accurate coverage.	Spray diluted product evenly on foliage using conventional spray equipment. For best uptake apply product in the evening or early in the morning. Heavy rain or aerial irrigation within 24 hours of application will diminish product effectiveness.	IMPROVED: Plant vigor; Maturation time; Yield.

FRUIT VEGETABLES

Cucumbers, Eggplant, Peppers, Pumpkin, Squash, Tomatoes, Zucchini

PRODUCT	APPLICATION RATE	APPLICATION TIME	DILUTION RATE Parts Product : Parts Water	METHOD OF APPLICATION	FIELD OBSERVATIONS
SOIL BIOSTIMULANT	Fertile soils: (16 fl.oz./acre) Moderate Soils: (24 fl. oz./acre) Problem Soils: (36 fl. oz./acre)	Preplanting	For best results: Aerial - 1:20, 1:50 Ground - at least 1:100 Dilution rate may vary depending on the spray equipment used. Dilute to obtain uniform and accurate coverage.	Broadcast, Ground or Airplane Spray diluted product evenly the trunk using any conventional spray equipment. After application incorporate product into soil. Rain or irrigation after application will improve performance.	INCREASED: Soil tilth; Soil fertility; Water holding capacity and drainage; Organic matter content; Soil aeration; Neutralization of soil pH;
SEED BIOSTIMULANT	(2 fl.oz./ 110 lbs. seeds)	Planting	1:4	Spray diluted product in a fine mist to obtain to thorough coating of seeds. Use any conventional spray equipment. Mix seeds until dry and they do not stick together. Do not store treated seeds in direct sunlight. Plant seeds as usual.	IMPROVED: Plant emergence; Vigor of seedlings; Root development; Resistance of seedlings to stress (low temperature, drought; disease, etc.).
	FOR TRANSPLANTED SEEDLINGS (7 fl.oz./acre)	At transplant	At least 1:20. Use enough water, but not more than necessary, to dip the roots of plants to be planted on one acre. Calculate dilution rate so recommended amount will be used per acre.	Dip the roots of the transplanted plants in dilution immediately after removing from seedbed and transplant them in the soil.	IMPROVED: Survival of seedlings: Regeneration and growth of root system; Resistance of seedlings to stress.
FOLIAR BIOSTIMULANT	(12 fl.oz./acre)	Twice: At early bloom (10-30% of blossoms) and For multiple picking: after each harvest	For best results: Aerial - 1:20, 1:50. Ground - at least 1:100. Dilution rate may vary depending on the spray equipment used. Dilute to obtain uniform and accurate coverage.	Spray diluted product evenly on plant foliage using any conventional spray equipment. For best uptake apply product in the evening or early morning. Heavy rain within 24 hours of application will diminish product effectiveness.	IMPROVED: Plant vigor; Yield; Maturation; Quality of vegetables.

VEGETABLES - TUBER

Potatoes, Jerusalem Artichokes, Yams

PRODUCT	APPLICATION RATE	APPLICATION TIME	DILUTION RATE Parts Product : Parts Water	METHOD OF APPLICATION	FIELD OBSERVATIONS
SOIL BIOSTIMULANT	(16 fl.oz./acre)	Planting	For best results: Ground - at least 1:100 Dilution rate may vary depending on the spray equipment used. Dilute to obtain uniform and accurate coverage.	Banded. Ground. Spray diluted product evenly in the furrows using conventional spray equipment. Plant potatoes and cover furrows with soil. Rain or irrigation after application will improve performance.	INCREASED: Soil tilth; Soil fertility; Organic matter content; Water holding capacity and drainage; Soil aeration; Neutralization of soil pH.
	<u>OR</u> -See SEED POTATO TREATMENT IN FURROWS below				
SEED BIOSTIMULANT	SEED POTATO TREATMENT ONLY (1 qt../16,200 lbs. seeds potatoes)	At Planting	1:100	Spray diluted product in a fine mist to thoroughly coat seed potatoes using any conventional sprayer.	IMPROVED: Plant emergence; Plant vigor; Root development; Resistance of seedlings to stress (low temperature, drought, diseases, etc.).
	<u>OR</u> - SEED POTATO TREATMENT IN FURROWS (same)	At Planting	1:100	Plant tseed potatoes in furrows and spray uniformly with diluted product. Cover furrows with soil immediately after treatment.	
FOLIER BIOSTIMULANT	(12 fl.oz./acre)	At 6-8 leaf stage.	For best results Aerial - 1:20, 1:50. Ground - at least a:100 Dilution rate may vary depending on the spray equipment used. Dilute to obtain uniform and accurate coverage.	Spray diluted product evenly on foliage using conventional spray equipment. For best uptake apply product in the evening or early in the morning. Heavy rain or aerial irrigation within 24 hours of application will diminish product effectiveness.	IMPROVED: Plant vigor; Yield; Quality of tubers and bulbs.

VEGETABLES - BULB

Celeriac, Garlic, Leeks, Onions, Shallots

PRODUCT	APPLICATION RATE	APPLICATION TIME	DILUTION RATE Parts Product : Parts Water	METHOD OF APPLICATION	FIELD OBSERVATIONS
SOIL BIOSTIMULANT	(16 fl.oz./acre)	Preplanting or Planting	For best results: Ground - at least 1:100 Dilution rate may vary depending on the spray equipment used. Dilute to obtain uniform and accurate coverage.	Banded. Ground. Spray diluted product evenly in the furrows using conventional spray equipment. Plant potatoes and cover furrows with soil. Rain or irrigation after application will improve performance.	INCREASED: Soil tilth; Soil fertility; Organic matter content; Water holding capacity and drainage; Soil aeration; Neutralization of soil pH.
SEED BIOSTIMULANT	(1 qt./ 110 lbs. seeds)	Seeding	1:4	Spray diluted product in a fine mist to thoroughly coat seeds using any conventional sprayer. After application incorporate product into the soil. Rain or irrigation after application will improve performance.	IMPROVED: Plant emergence; Vigor of seedlings; Root development; Resistance of seedlings to stress (high temperature, drought, diseases, etc.).
	OR - FOR BULB PLANTING ONLY (7 fl.oz./ 1,100 lbs bulbs	Planting	1:50	Spray diluted product in a fine mist to obtain thorough coating of bulbs. Use any conventional spray equipment. Plant bulbs as usual. Do not store treated bulbs.	IMPROVED: Plant emergence; Vigor of seedlings; Root development; Resistance of seedlings to stress (high temperature, drought, diseases, etc.).
FOLIER BIOSTIMULANT	(12 fl.oz./acre)	At 6-8 leaf stage.	For best results Aerial - 1:20, 1:50. Ground - at least a:100 Dilution rate may vary depending on the spray equipment used. Dilute to obtain uniform and accurate coverage.	Spray diluted product evenly on foliage using conventional spray equipment. For best uptake apply product in the evening or early in the morning. Heavy rain or aerial irrigation within 24 hours of application will diminish product effectiveness.	IMPROVED: Plant vigor; Yield; Quality of tubers and bulbs.

Fruits and Nuts Index

FRUIT TREES

Apple, Apricot, Avocado, Cherry, Mango, Mulberry, Nectarines, Papaya, Peach, Pear, Plum, Quince

PRODUCT	APPLICATION RATE	APPLICATION TIME	DILUTION RATE Parts Product : Parts Water	METHOD OF APPLICATION	FIELD OBSERVATIONS
SOIL BIOSTIMULANT	Moderate Soils: (24 fl.oz./acre) Problem Soils (32 fl.oz./acre)	At beginning of intense plant growth.	For best results: Ground - at least 1:100 Dilution rate may vary depending on the spray equipment used. Dilute to obtain uniform and accurate coverage.	Banded. Ground. Spray diluted product evenly around the trunk using any conventional spray equipment. After application, incorporate product into the soil. Rain or irrigation after application will improve performance	INCREASED: Soil fertility; Water holding capacity and drainage; Soil aeration; Organic matter content.
SEED BIOSTIMULANT	DURING SEEDLING TRANSTLANT ONLY (7 fl.oz./acre)	At transplanting	At least 1:20. Use enough water, but not more than necessary, to dip the roots of plants to be planted on one acre. Calculate dilution rate so recommended amount will be used per acre.	Dip the roots of seedlings in diluted product immediately after removing from seedbed and transplant to the field. Water transplanted seedlings with remaining solution	IMPROVED: survival of seedlings; Regeneration and growth of root system; Resistance of seedlings to stress (low temperature, drought, disease, etc.).
	OR - AFTER SEEDLINGS ARE TRANSPLANTED (7 fl.oz./acre)	At transplanting	At least 1:100	Water transplanted plants with diluted product.	
FOLIAR BIOSTIMULANT	(16 fl.oz./acre)	Twice: 1st, at fruit set; 2nd, 4-6 weeks before harvest.	For best results: Aerial - 1:20, 1:50. Ground - at least 1:100. Dilution rate may vary depending on the spray equipment used. Dilute to obtain uniform and accurate coverage.	Spray diluted product evenly on plant foliage using any conventional spray equipment. For best uptake apply product in the evening or early morning. Heavy rain within 24 hours of application will diminish product effectiveness.	IMPROVED: Plant vigor; Fruit set; Yield; Quality of fruit.

CITRUS

Grapefruit, Lemon, Lime, Mandarin, Oranges

PRODUCT	APPLICATION RATE	APPLICATION TIME	DILUTION RATE Parts Product : Parts Water	METHOD OF APPLICATION	FIELD OBSERVATIONS
SOIL BIOSTIMULANT	Moderate Soils: (24 fl.oz./acre) Problem Soils (32 fl.oz./acre)	At beginning of intense plant growth.	For best results: Ground - at least 1:100 Dilution rate may vary depending on the spray equipment used. Dilute to obtain uniform and accurate coverage.	Banded. Ground. Spray diluted product evenly around the trunk using any conventional spray equipment. After application, incorporate product into the soil. Rain or irrigation after application will improve performance	INCREASED: Soil fertility; Water holding capacity and drainage; Soil aeration; Organic matter content.
SEED BIOSTIMULANT	DURING SEEDLING TRANSPLANT ONLY (7 fl.oz./acre)	At transplanting	At least 1:20. Use enough water, but not more than necessary, to dip the roots of plants to be planted on one acre. Calculate dilution rate so recommended amount will be used per acre.	Dip the roots of seedlings in diluted product immediately after removing from seedbed and transplant to the field. Water transplanted seedlings with remaining solution	IMPROVED: survival of seedlings; Regeneration and growth of root system; Resistance of seedlings to stress (low temperature, drought, disease, etc.).
	OR - AFTER SEEDLINGS ARE TRANSPLANTED (7 fl.oz./acre)	At transplant	At least a:100	Water transplanted plants with diluted product.	
FOLIAR BIOSTIMULANT	(16 fl.oz./acre)	Twice: 1st, at fruit set; 2nd, 4-6 weeks before harvest	For best results: Aerial - 1:20, 1:50. Ground - at least 1:100. Dilution rate may vary depending on the spray equipment used. Dilute to obtain uniform and accurate coverage.	Spray diluted product evenly on plant foliage using any conventional spray equipment. For best uptake apply product in the evening or early morning. Heavy rain within 24 hours of application will diminish product effectiveness.	IMPROVED: Plant vigor; Fruit set; Yield; Quality of fruit.

MELONS

Cantaloupe, Casaba, Crenshaw melon, Honeydew, Muskmelon, Watermelon

PRODUCT	APPLICATION RATE	APPLICATION TIME	DILUTION RATE Parts Product : Parts Water	METHOD OF APPLICATION	FIELD OBSERVATIONS
SOIL BIOSTIMULANT	Fertile soils: (16 fl.oz./acre) Moderate Soils: (24 fl.oz./acre) Problem Soils: (36 fl.oz./acre)	Preplanting	For best results: Aerial - 1:20, 1:50 Ground - at least 1:100 Dilution rate may vary depending on the spray equipment used. Dilute to obtain uniform and accurate coverage.	Broadcast, Ground or Airplane Spray diluted product evenly the trunk using any conventional spray equipment. After application incorporate product into soil. Rain or irrigation after application will improve performance.	INCREASED: Soil tilth; Soil fertility; Water holding capacity and drainage; Organic matter content; Soil aeration; Neutralization of soil pH.
SEED BIOSTIMULANT	(2 fl.oz./ 110 lbs. seeds)	Planting	1:4	Spray diluted product in a fine mist to obtain to thorough coating of seeds. Use any conventional spray equipment. Mix seeds until dry and they do not stick together. Do not store treated seeds in direct sunlight. Plant seeds as usual.	IMPROVED: Plant emergence; Vigor of seedlings; Root development; Resistance of seedlings to stress (low temperature, drought; disease, etc.).
FOLIAR BIOSTIMULANT	(12 fl.oz./acre)	At visible plant set.	For best results: Aerial - 1:20, 1:50. Ground - at least 1:100. Dilution rate may vary depending on the spray equipment used. Dilute to obtain uniform and accurate coverage.	Spray diluted product evenly on plant foliage using any conventional spray equipment. For best uptake apply product in the evening or early morning. Heavy rain within 24 hours of application will diminish product effectiveness.	IMPROVED: Plant vigor; Yield; Maturation time; Fruit set; Quality of fruit.

BERRIES

Blackberry, Blueberry, Cranberry, Gooseberry, Raspberry, Currant (Red), Strawberry

PRODUCT	APPLICATION RATE	APPLICATION TIME	DILUTION RATE Parts Product : Parts Water	METHOD OF APPLICATION	FIELD OBSERVATIONS
SOIL BIOSTIMULANT	Moderate Soils: (24 fl.oz./acre((32 fl.oz./acre)	On new crop: Before planting. In the spring.	For best results: Ground - at least 1:100 Dilution rate may vary depending on spray equipmen used. Dilute to obtain uniform and accurate coverage.	Banded. Ground. Spray diluted product evenly in furrows or along bushes using any conventional sprayequipment, irrigation lines or ditches. After application incorporate product into the soil. Rain or irrigation after application will improve performance	INCREASED: Soil fertility; Water holding capacity and drainage; Soil aeration; Neutralization of soil pH.
SEED BIOSTIMULANT	FOR TRANSPLANTED SEEDLINGS ONLY (7 fl.oz./acre)	Planting	At least 1:20. Use enough water, but not more than necessary to dip roots of plants to be planted on one acre. Calculate dilution rate so recommended amount will be used per acre.	Dip the roots of seedlings in diluted product immediately after removing from seedbed and transplant in soil. Water transplanted seedlings with remaining solution	IMPROVED: Survival of seedlings; Regeneration and growth of root system; Resistance of seedlings to stress (low temperature; drought, disease, etc.).
FOLIAR BIOSTIMULANT	(12 fl.oz./acre)	Twice: At early bloom to 30% bloom; and For multiple picking: After each harvest.	For best results: Aerial - 1:20, 1:50. Ground - at least 1:100. Dilution rate may vary depending on the spray equipment used. Dilute to obtain uniform and accurate coverage.	Spray diluted product evenly on plant foliage using any conventional spray equipment. For best uptake apply product in the evening or early morning. Heavy rain within 24 hours of application will diminish product effectiveness.	IMPROVED: Plant vigor; Yield; Quality of fruits.

NUTS

Almonds, Cashews, Chestnuts, Coconuts, Hazelnut, Pecans, Pistachios, Walnuts

PRODUCT	APPLICATION RATE	APPLICATION TIME	DILUTION RATE Parts Product : Parts Water	METHOD OF APPLICATION	FIELD OBSERVATIONS
SOIL BIOSTIMULANT	Moderate Soils: (16 fl.oz./acre) Problem Soils (24 fl.oz./acre)	At beginning of intense plant growth.	For best results: Ground - at least 1:100 Dilution rate may vary depending on the spray equipment used. Dilute to obtain uniform and accurate coverage.	Banded. Ground. Spray diluted product evenly around the trunk using any conventional spray equipment. After application, incorporate product into the soil. Rain or irrigation after application will improve performance	INCREASED: Soil fertility; Water holding capacity and drainage; Soil aeration; Neutralization of soil pH.
SEED BIOSTIMULANT	DURING SEEDLING TRANSPLANT ONLY (7 fl.oz./acre)	At transplanting	At least 1:20. Use enough water, but not more than necessary, to dip the roots of plants to be planted on one acre. Calculate dilution rate so recommended amount will be used per acre.	Dip the roots of seedlings in diluted product immediately after removing from seedbed and transplant them to soil. Water transplanted seedlings with remaining solution	IMPROVED: Survival of seedlings; Regeneration and growth of root system; Resistance of seedlings to stress (low temperature, drought, disease, etc.).
	<u>OR</u> - AFTER SEEDLINGS ARE TRANSPLANTED (7 fl.oz./acre)	At transplanting	At least 1:100	Water transplanted plants with diluted product.	
FOLIAR BIOSTIMULANT	(16 fl.oz./acre)	Twice: 1st, at pre-bloom stage; 2nd, 4-6 weeks prior to harvest	For best results: Aerial - 1:20, 1:50. Ground - at least 1:100. Dilution rate may vary depending on the spray equipment used. Dilute to obtain uniform and accurate coverage.	Spray diluted product evenly on plant foliage using any conventional spray equipment. For best uptake apply product in the evening or early morning. Heavy rain within 24 hours of application will diminish product effectiveness.	IMPROVED: Plant vigor; Fruit set; Yield; Quality of fruit.

OLIVES

PRODUCT	APPLICATION RATE	APPLICATION TIME	DILUTION RATE Parts Product : Parts Water	METHOD OF APPLICATION	FIELD OBSERVATIONS
SOIL BIOSTIMULANT	Moderate Soils: (16 fl oz./acre) Problem Soils: (24 fl.oz./acre)	In the Spring	For best results: Ground - at least 1:100 Dilution rate may vary depending on the spray equipment used. Dilute to obtain uniform and accurate coverage.	Banded. Ground Spray diluted product evenly around the trunk using any conventional spray equipment. After application incorporate product into soil. Rain or irrigation after application will improve performance.	INCREASED: Soil fertility; Water holding capacity and drainage; Soil aeration; Neutralization of soil pH.
SEED BIOSTIMULANT	DURING SEEDLING TRANSPLANT ONLY (7 fl.oz./acre)	At transplant	At least 1:20. Use enough water, but not more than necessary, to dip the roots of plants to be planted on one acre. Calculate dilution rate so recommended amount will be used per acre.	Dip the roots of the transplanted plants in dilution immediately after removing from seedbed and transplant them in soil.	IMPROVED: Survival of seedlings; Regeneration and growth of root system; Resistance of seedlings to stress (low temperature, drought, disease, etc.).
	OR AFTER SEEDLINGS ARE TRANSPLANTED	At transplant	At least 1:100.	Water transplanted plants with diluted product.	
FOLIAR BIOSTIMULANT	(7 fl.oz./acre)	Twice: 1st at intensive plant growth (one month before bloom); 2nd at fruit formation (approx. one month after bloom).	For best results: Aerial - 1:20, 1:50. Ground - at least 1:100. Dilution rate may vary depending on the spray equipment used. Dilute to obtain uniform and accurate coverage.	Spray diluted product evenly on tree leaves using any conventional spray equipment. For best uptake apply product in the evening or early morning. Heavy rain within 24 hours of application will diminish product effectiveness.	IMPROVED: Plant vigor; Fruit set; Yield; Oil content.

GRAPES

PRODUCT	APPLICATION RATE	APPLICATION TIME	DILUTION RATE Parts Product : Parts Water	METHOD OF APPLICATION	FIELD OBSERVATIONS
SOIL BIOSTIMULANT	Moderate Soils: (16 fl. oz./acre) Problem soils: (24 fl. oz./acre)	At the beginning of spring plant growth.	For best results: Ground - at least 1:100 Dilution rate may vary depending on the spray equipment used. Dilute to obtain uniform and accurate coverage.	Banded. Ground Spray diluted product evenly along the vines using any conventional spray equipment. After application incorporate product into the soil. Rain or irrigation after application will improve performance.	INCREASED: Soil fertility; Water holding capacity and drainage; Soil aeration; Neutralization of soil pH.
FOLIER BIOSTIMULANT	(12 fl.oz/acre)	At fruit set.	For best results: Aerial - 1:20, 1:50 Ground - at least 1:100 Dilution rate may vary depending on the spray equipment used. Dilute to obtain uniform and accurate coverage.	Spray diluted product evenly on plant leaves using any conventional spray equipment. For best uptake apply product in the evening or early morning. Heavy rain or aerial irrigation within 24 hours of application will diminish product effectiveness.	IMPROVED: Fruit set; Maturation; Yield; Quality of grapes.

BANANAS, DATES, FIGS, PINEAPPLE

PRODUCT	APPLICATION RATE	APPLICATION TIME	DILUTION RATE Parts Product : Parts Water	METHOD OF APPLICATION	FIELD OBSERVATIONS
SOIL BIOSTIMULANT	(24 fl.oz./acre)	Once a year; Before new growth	For best results: Ground - at least 1:100 Dilution rate may vary depending on the spray equipment used. Dilute to obtain uniform and accurate coverage.	Banded. Ground Spray diluted product evenly around the trunk using any conventional spray equipment. After application incorporate product into soil. Rain or irrigation after application will improve performance.	INCREASED: Soil fertility; Water holding capacity and drainage; Soil aeration; Neutralition of soil pH.
SEED BIOSTIMULANT	FOR TRANSPLANTED SEEDLINGS ONLY (7 fl.oz./acre)	At transplanting	At least 1:20. Use enough water, but not more than necessary, to dip the roots of plants to be planted on one acre. Calculate dilution rate so recommended amount will be used per acre.	Dip the roots of the transplanted plants in dilution immediately after removing from seedbed and transplant them in soil.	IMPROVED: Survival of seedlings; Regeneration and growth of root system; Resistance of seedlings to stress (low temperature, drought, disease, etc.).
FOLIAR BIOSTIMULANT	(12 fl.oz./acre)	Twice: 1st at intensive plant growth; 2nd at the beginning of fruit set.	For best results: Aerial - 1:20, 1:50. Ground - at least 1:100. Dilution rate may vary depending on the spray equipment used. Dilute to obtain uniform and accurate coverage.	Spray diluted product evenly on tree leaves using any conventional spray equipment. For best uptake apply product in the evening or early morning. Heavy rain within 24 hours of application will diminish product effectiveness.	IMPROVED: Plant vigor; Fruit set; Yield; Quality of fruit.

Complete Crop Index

D

E

F

T

U-V

W

X-Y-Z

Environmental Care & Share

Jackson Research Center

MODEL TWO: **MEMO II**

To: Environmental Health Foundation

From: William R. Jackson, Ph.D., Consultant

Subject: **Odor Control and Bio-Dissipation**

Animal Odor Remedy for Homes, Kennels, Barnyards, Commercial Feed Lots, Etc.

Concentrated EC&S Bio-Stimulant almost instantly neutralizes animal odors in homes, zoos, kennels, and wherever animals are kept. There is little problem with this easy to apply, nontoxic product because it is completely safe for use around humans and animals. It is not a bacteriological culture or a masking agent. It consists of a self-generating living bio-system that immediately goes into solution to produce multiplied amounts of dissolved and free oxygen which neutralize odor-causing anaerobes. This process includes nature's own balancing: an odor-neutralizing process recreated and captured in a balanced micro-ecosystem. Other derivations of this system are currently in use by industry and by sewage treatment plants to eliminate odors. Many of these additional uses are included throughout this chapter.

Description

EC&S Bio-Stimulant is an aqueous compound containing extremely high amounts of oxygen in the forms of dissolved oxygen (DO) and free oxygen (O_2). It neutralizes odor-causing anaerobic life forms through oxidation saturation. This bio-system consists of an ecologically-balanced combination of plant and animal microorganism stimulants, which can remain active over wide ranges of temperatures and other environmental influences. Applied according to directions to animal cages or living quarters, it will overcome odor-causing anaerobes by using the sulfur and mercaptan odor sources as nutrition for the now stimulated indigenous microbial life. This process continues the generation of oxygen. In addition to eliminating odors, it actually provides environmental benefits to animals by inhibiting the growth and spread of fungi and helps to provide an aerobic layer that is aversive to ticks, fleas, lice and other pests.

Application

EC&S Bio-Stimulant is easily applied to odorous areas as either a rinse or a post-wash coat. In an enclosed area or building, it is recommended that the entire area be fogged or sprayed with EC&S Bio-Stimulant once prior to the start of a routine cleaning schedule. The bio-stimulant should be applied to all cage walls, floors, ceilings, within animal caves (zoos), and other areas where odors originate and emanate and may be missed in normal cleaning.

It is not necessary to remove animals or their food while applying EC&S Bio-Stimulant. Some disinfectants will reduce the effectiveness of a portion of the odor neutralizing microorganism enzymes and coenzymes found in the product, but disinfectants cannot reduce the oxygen content. If a disinfectant has been applied, a somewhat heavier coat of EC&S Bio-Stimulant should be used.

Normal dilution of the odor remedy product ranges from nine parts water to one part EC&S Bio-Stimulant (9:1), to 200:1. A good practical means of application is to create a 10:1 dilution and introduce through a conventional hose-siphon, which will further dilute to 20:1. In the event particularly strong odors persist, the user need only re-spray after a short time or strengthen the mix of EC&S Bio-Stimulant by reducing the dilution.

Keep in mind, free oxygen in the odor remedy product will help kill many odors almost immediately. However, conversion of odor-causing mercaptans and sulfur compounds may take as long as an hour.

Odor Remedy Review

EC&S Bio-Stimulant is a biochemical product containing several vitamin precursors of plant and animal origin in a highly concentrated mass of different autotrophic, aerobic, and facultative enzymes and coenzymes, exoenzymes, humic nutrients, and various multifactorial inducer molecules. So combined, these components are able to withstand a wide range of environmental conditions while decomposing and deodorizing plant, animal and commercial residues. This is accomplished by dispensing OXYGEN and deriving energy from the oxidation of simple mineral compounds and organic gases such as ammonia, hydrogen sulfide, carbon monoxide, sulfur dioxide and others.

EC&S Bio-Stimulant produces a biologically balanced stimulant for the ecosystem in water, air, soil, and plant and animal niches by increasing available nutrients through the increase of OXYGEN. The enzymes and coenzymes, etc. found in this product are able to exist and thrive in waters with wide variations in salt content.

EC&S Bio-Stimulant has made it possible for agriculture, industry, and commerce to obtain a faster biologically balanced recovery of wastewaters, solid wastes, and plant and animal residues.

EC&S Bio-Stimulant is safe to use on plants and animals as a natural biological deodorant. This material is USDA AUTHORIZED for use in sewage and/or drain lines of official establishments operating under the Federal meat, poultry, shell egg grading, and egg products inspection programs.

Jackson Research Center

MODEL TWO: **MEMO III**

To: Environmental Health Foundation

From: William R. Jackson, Ph.D., Consultant

Subject: **Animal Waste Bio-Transformation**

Microorganisms and Animal Waste

Animal waste, and even up to 90% of the chemical substances considered hazardous, can be bio-degraded. To accomplish this transformation, nature requires a relatively small proportion of indigenous (native) microorganisms found in a contaminated matrix that have the intrinsic (genetic) ability to degrade the contaminant. Generally speaking, the process involved in bio-transformation develops through a complex series of enzymatically related reactions, which may or may not be expressed by a specific bacterial species or group of bacteria (consortium). The animal waste environment, for example, plays an important role in determining not only the percentage of microorganisms that have the ability to act upon a contaminant, but also whether the ability will be expressed under site-specific conditions. Long-term exposure to a contaminant generally results in an increased number of "adapted" contaminant-degrading strains.

We have yet to encounter the need for exogenous (foreign) or recombinant (the formation in offspring of genetic combinations not present in parents) bacterial species to perform the necessary bio-degradative task. With very few exceptions, bio-remedial specialists rely upon the tremendous diversity and capability exhibited by naturally occurring microbial populations.

Microbial life is pervasive in any ecosystem, existing for example, in all geological soils and animal waste, and under all climatic conditions. This microbial life is extremely aggressive under the appropriate circumstances and with adequate stimulation. These microorganisms were created to be very competitive in performing nature's assigned tasks. This process is how ecological balance is maintained for a specific location. As excessive foreign-organic materials, such as large amounts of animal waste matter, are introduced into a specific ecosystem, a natural process begins to occur to eliminate the overload problem. As the continuous additions of this foreign (overload) of material occur, the surplus begins to burden the natural processes and serious contamination results. This problem can be corrected by a balancing addition of EC&S Bio-Stimulant. When the overload or foreign matter is eliminated, the revived natural and native ecosystem resumes its normal process as structured by nature. After the task is complete, the additional microbiota that were induced are phased out and allowed to become dormant again. In other words, upon completion of the remediation, the treated site returns to the original indigenous (original existing microbial life that represented balance) microbiota system. Bio-remediation is powerful and demonstrates dynamic benefits.

This enzyme recruitment system made available by EC&S Bio-Stimulant offers the potential for the acquisition and evolution of new degradative pathways. This ability to create new pathways suggests a great flexibility in the capability of communities of microbes to degrade complex materials. This includes animal waste substances that are unfamiliar to those microbes.

Animal Waste Treatment: Cellulose

Animal waste containing high levels of cellulose is among the compounds that are difficult to liquefy and decompose. Cellulose is bio-degraded by certain bacterial and fungal strains capable of secreting cellulose enzymes that convert the tough-fibrous structure of cellulose into a soluble fluid state. This cellulose material is able to benefit from the rapid hydrolyzing capabilities of EC&S Bio-Stimulant. EC&S Bio-Stimulant contains selected inducer molecules for microbial ecosystems that are capable of efficiently degrading native cellulose by secreting a variety of select cellulose digestive enzymes within the microbiota. A limited quantity of cellulose digesting enzymes are produced by the normal flora of the average animal waste disposal system, and some of those have been forced into dormancy. More microbial life needs to develop and dormant microbiota must be activated to meet the demands of many of our overloaded systems. The inoculation of animal waste products with EC&S Bio-Stimulant reactivates many trillions of cellulose enzyme-secreting, inducer-molecule triggering microorganisms that are able to hydrolyze and bio-degrade efficiently the various forms of waste and cellulose found in animal waste treatment systems.

The bio-stimulant applications may be 1) added to an influent line of a biological treatment section of a waste treatment system, 2) added into a lagoon on a water-slurry pond, 3) added through a primary clarifier or process pump, or 4) sprayed over the surface of a lagoon or holding pond. When EC&S Bio-Stimulant is applied to fields or stockyards, a spray application is best; however, when applied to this situation, adequate moisture must be maintained because microbial life is moisture sensitive.

In situ microbial treatment may be the ideal animal waste treatment technique. The areas where the waste products are found serve as a reactor structure. Commercial waste treatment sites have activated naturally occurring microorganisms with naturally occurring hormonal enzymes and coenzymes, thus accentuating or promoting microorganism growth through the addition of nutrients or oxygen. The additional nutrients or oxygen, in turn, accelerates natural bio-degradation properties, without a formal reactor. Using this approach, the natural (in situ) environment itself becomes a giant reactor, accentuated by the use of EC&S Bio-Stimulant.

Nitrification Process in Animal Waste Treatment

Ammonia concentration in wastewater is reduced by treating the wastewater with a suspended growth microbial system such as an activated sludge, containing organisms stimulated by a collection of enzyme and coenzyme stimulants found in the EC&S Bio-Stimulant system. This process subjects the ammonia-containing wastewater to a bio-stimulated microbial system. As a result, this retrograde step of ammonium nitrate/nitrite conversion in the overall denitrification process is reduced or eliminated, with consequent energy and cost savings.

The EC&S Bio-Stimulant treatment of enzymes and coenzymes is a method directed toward the natural microbial population. This method conditions the biota population to enhanced bio-conversion or bio-degradation of a given substrate. Subsequently, greater bio-conversion of a substrate is possible even when the microbial population is exposed to fluctuations of conditions including particular shock loads of the substrate. The microbial population is able to adjust to such fluctuations because of biota exposure to a nontoxic or non-inhibitory amount of bio-stimulant activated enzymes and coenzymes, and is biochemically or structurally activated and thus beneficial to the substrate being treated. This method of bio-stimulation is applicable for systems where the production of useful metabolites is the objective. The method also applies to waste treatment where degradation of a waste into a more acceptable form is to be achieved.

It is during aerobic respiration that organic carbon is converted to carbon dioxide, nitrogen to nitrates, sulfur to sulfates, and phosphorus to phosphates. The presence of excessive amounts of organic matter causes a great demand for oxygen due to the intense activity of the microorganisms. If this demand for oxygen exceeds its supply, the metabolic processes become anoxic rather than occurring with a normal amount of oxygen. Microflora and microorganisms exist in different metabolic types. When there is a change of chemistry in the substrate and its environment, different types of organisms take over. When the oxygen supply becomes depleted, anaerobics become active. At this juncture, nitrates, phosphates, and sulfates become the basic oxidants and terminal acceptors of the electrons generated in the degradation of organic matter.[*]

Application parameters for bio-stimulant

1. pH: Optimum of 7, minimum of 4.5, maximum of 9.0

2. DO (dissolved oxygen): Optimum 3 PPM+, minimum of 2 PPM

3. C/N (carbon/nitrogen ratio): Optimum 10:1, maximum 20:1

4. Temperature: Optimum 30° C, minimum 19° C, maximum 49° C

---

[*]Jackson, 267-268.

5. Free of toxic metals, such as hexavalents and chromium, and reasonable dilution of organic and inorganic cyanide wastes and normally toxic compounds

6. Increased surface area or solubility allows for more rapid oxidation and stimulated metabolism of the biota of the animal waste being treated

Specific treatment systems

1. Activated sludge systems

2. Trickling filters

3. Oxidation lagoons

4. Wastewater treatment tanks

Animal Waste Transformation

The capacity of a bacterium to degrade animal waste materials is controlled by enzyme stimulation that catalyzes a specific oxidation. Even though a bacterium contains the information to synthesize enzymes in its genetic material, the cell may not spend the energy to produce the enzymes necessary for rapid reproduction and thus accelerate the degrading of a specific waste matter. The application of EC&S Bio-Stimulant enzyme treatment with various additions, serves as a trigger, an "on switch" of the genetic material of a bacterium and thus serves as an inducer molecule. The multifactorial inducers may then serve as a degradation product of the substrate molecule. Relative to metabolic pathways, each oxidation step is catalyzed by highly specific enzymes experiencing complex multifactorial inducer activity. The final products of the enzyme-stimulated, bacterial-degradation of this animal waste matter are reduced cells of H_2O and CO_2.

What to Look For in Model Two Production

EC&S Bio-Stimulant is a highly concentrated multi-component bio-ecosystem. Dispersible in liquids, EC&S Bio-Stimulant contains enzymes, coenzymes, exoenzymes, natural nutrients, and inducer molecules as explained in the introduction of this chapter. This combination of components stimulates a broad spectrum of specialized natural microorganisms that are composed of aerobic and facultative (capable of adaptive response to varying environment) anaerobic microbial strains selected for maximum efficiency within conditions existing in industrial, animal, and municipal waste treatment systems. EC&S Bio-Stimulant, with its unique bio-ecosystem, has a higher rate of efficiency at bio-degrading various toxicants within waste treatment systems than isolated strains of imported microorganisms. This system offers the user the advantage of immediate activity within indigenous microorganisms at pre-computed levels of biochemical capability, always capable of working with indigenous microorganisms only.

The use of EC&S Bio-Stimulant, being a well balanced bio-ecosystem, results in the secretion of significantly greater concentrations of highly effective substances which improve digestion rates and terminal flocculation, thereby, increasing the overall efficiency of the aerobic waste treatment system. When EC&S Bio-Stimulant is added properly to almost any organic waste treatment system, higher concentrations of waste can be accommodated because of the more rapid bio-degradation. EC&S Bio-Stimulant "ENZYMATICALLY" ALTERS THE PHYSICAL STRUCTURE OF THE SUSPENDED SOLIDS, causing those substances to separate more efficiently. The reduced sludge volume that follows more thorough digestion is due to the more complete liquefaction and gasification of the organics in the waste stream and the destruction of waste-binding molecules.

EC&S Bio-Stimulant contains a carefully developed system which keeps its water medium in a constant state of oxygen saturation. It includes an ecologically-balanced combination of stimulants that serve as bio-activators or "triggers" and remain active over wide ranges of temperature and other environmental influences. Continuous treatment of water or waste material with EC&S Bio-Stimulant will completely clear the effluent under treatment of any objectionable odors, and will at the same time, regenerate the natural eutrophic in these liquids. Over a period of time (relative to BOD/COD ratios and contact periods), effluent being treated may be totally returned to life-supporting oxygenated water.

Remediation Review

EC&S Bio-Stimulant is a biochemical treatment containing several vitamin precursors of plant and animal origin in a highly concentrated mass of different autotrophic, aerobic, and facultative components. So combined, the components are able to withstand a wide range of environmental conditions while decomposing and deodorizing plant, animal, and commercial residues. Decomposing and deodorizing are accomplished by dispensing OXYGEN and deriving energy from the oxidation of simple mineral compounds and organic gases such as ammonia, hydrogen sulfide, carbon monoxide, sulfur dioxide, and others.

EC&S Bio-Stimulant produces a biologically balanced stimulant for the ecosystem in water, air, soil, and plant and animal niches by increasing available nutrients through the increase of OXYGEN. EC&S Bio-Stimulant has made it possible for industry, agriculture, and commerce to obtain a faster biologically balanced recovery of wastewaters, solid wastes, and plant and animal residues.

EC&S Bio-Stimulant is safe to use on plants and animals for natural biological remediation and is USDA AUTHORIZED for use in sewage and/or drain lines of official establishments operating under the Federal meat, poultry, shell egg grading, and egg products inspection programs.

EC&S Bio-Stimulant Application

Apply EC&S Bio-Stimulant by simply diluting one part product with nine parts of clean water. To initiate the treatment, the diluted (1:9) EC&S Bio-Stimulant should be sprayed over the surface of the area to be treated at a rate of 10 gallons of the diluted solution to each foot/acre of animal waste. This application may need to be doubled as a shock treatment for the initial treatment. Repeated application should then be made once every two weeks until the pond or lagoon is liquefied. Observe the directions for application on the label.

Continuous application of EC&S Bio-Stimulant is most effective when applied as a spray, either over the surface of an aeration pond or directly at the top of a pipe mouth. It is best to cover as much water area as possible. Over time, the eutrophic process will penetrate deeper; however, initially, most of the odor control will be through the surface layers.

Environmental Care & Share

Jackson Research Center

MODEL TWO: **MEMO IV**

To: Environmental Health Foundation

From: William R. Jackson, Ph.D., Consultant

Subject: **Municipal and Industrial Wastewater Bio-Restoration**

Bio-restoration of contaminated sites, such as sewage treatment plants, has been used for several decades. Over the years, the technology has been modified, adapted, and improved.

The selection of a specific bio-restoration strategy is determined by a number of important considerations:

1. Factors that can impede the bio-degradation process.

2. Problems related to the transport of any contaminants within that specific environment.

3. The biological/chemical reactivity of a specific contaminant.

4. Time required for degradation.

5. Client's future liability.

6. What the client can afford.

Special effort is required to determine which choices are correct. This special effort involves the integration of the principles of geochemistry, hydrogeology, microbiology, engineering, and job costing.

Bio-restoration usually provides the best answers, particularly as it relates to budget and future liability considerations. At the same time, it may be necessary to employ other technologies in concert with bio-restoration to satisfy the unique demands of a given project.

EC&S Bio-Stimulant treatment recommendations have cut restoration time from 20% to 75%. The system is environmentally clean, functionally safe, and complies with all published EPA and OSHA regulatory requirements. The treatment materials are USDA authorized for wastewater and sewage treatment.

What You Can Expect from EC&S Bio-Stimulant

- Greatly improved digestion rates and terminal flocculation.
- Markedly reduced solidified fats, oils, and grease, thereby eliminating "cake" or matting in anaerobic digesters.
- Significantly accelerated bio-degradation of synthetic detergents, thus decreasing the time required to achieve the overall BOD (Biological Oxygen Demand) reduction.
- Rapidly hydrolyzes and bio-degrades the various forms of cellulose usually present in waste treatment plants, thus increasing the overall digestive efficiency.
- Bio-degrades up to 200 ppm of inorganic and organic cyanide compounds, thereby reducing the toxic

shock loading effects on industrial waste treatment systems.

- Highly phenol-cyanide tolerant; therefore able to reduce concentrations to near zero levels, thus eliminating excessive capital expenditures for costly equipment.

About the Product

EC&S Bio-Stimulant is classified nonhazardous and is produced according to Federal Regulations 1910.1200. Because it is an aqueous solution, there are no fire or explosive hazards. EC&S Bio-Stimulant poses no health hazard either internally or externally (see MSDS, Chapter XI). After being emptied, the product container can be rinsed with water and reused.

EC&S Bio-Stimulant is a biochemical product containing several vitamin precursors of plant and animal origin in a highly concentrated mass of autotrophic, aerobic, and facultative enzymes, exoenzymes and coenzymes, along with other additives. So combined, these constituents are able to withstand a wide range of environmental conditions while decomposing and deodorizing plant, animal, and commercial residues. Decomposing and deodorizing are accomplished by dispensing OXYGEN and deriving energy from the oxidation of simple mineral compounds and organic gases such as ammonia, hydrogen sulfide, carbon monoxide, sulfur dioxide, and others.

EC&S Bio-Stimulant produces a biologically balanced stimulant for the ecosystem in water, air, soil, and plant and animal niches by increasing more available nutrients through the increase of OXYGEN. The enzymes and coenzymes found in this product are able to exist and thrive in waters with wide variations in salt content.

EC&S Bio-Stimulant is a highly concentrated, multi-component, bio-ecosystem. Dispersible in liquids, EC&S Bio-Stimulant contains a system that stimulates a broad spectrum of specialized natural microorganisms composed of aerobic and facultative (capable of adaptive responses to varying environment) anaerobic microbial strains. Components of the product were selected for maximum efficiency in conditions existing in industrial, animal, and municipal waste treatment systems. EC&S Bio-Stimulant, with its unique bio-ecosystem, has a higher rate of efficiency at bio-degrading various toxicants within waste treatment systems than isolated strains of imported microbial life. This system offers the user the advantage of immediate activity at pre-computed levels of biochemical capability.

EC&S Bio-Stimulant, being a well balanced bio-ecosystem, provides an improved digestion rate and terminal flocculation, thereby, increasing the overall efficiency of the aerobic waste treatment system. When EC&S Bio-Stimulant is added properly to a waste treatment system, higher concentrations of waste can be accommodated because of the more rapid bio-degradation.

EC&S Bio-Stimulant ENZYMATICALLY ALTERS, CHEMICALLY COMBINES, AND MOLECULARLY MODIFIES THE PHYSICAL STRUCTURE OF THE SUSPENDED ORGANIC SOLIDS, causing those substances to separate more efficiently. The reduced sludge volume that follows more thorough digestion is due to the more complete liquefaction and gasification of the organics in the waste stream and the destruction of waste-binding molecules.

EC&S Bio-Stimulant is a water medium including extremely high proportions of free and dissolved oxygen, as described in more detail earlier in this working model. This product was designed with specificity to keep its water content in a constant state of oxygen saturation. Continuous treatment of an aqueous effluent with EC&S Bio-Stimulant will eliminate the materials that are giving off objectionable odors. Thus, treatment of industrial and municipal sewage results in effluent that will meet most local, state, and federal standards for discharge onto land or into lakes and rivers.

EC&S Bio-Stimulant is not a bacterial culture. It is a nontoxic, non-pathogenic suspension of aerobic, facultative, oxygen-producing bio-stimulants.

Degradation of Animal Fats & Oils

Annually, millions of gallons of greases, fats, cooking and industrial wastes, and oils from personal care products are introduced to waste treatment plants. These materials create an overload on the plant, and the normal microbial flora are unable to degrade these substances. In many situations these insoluble greases, fats, and oils contribute as much as 25% to 50% of the actual organic matter in the domestic sewage plant. These insoluble fatty acids accumulate in the activated sludge treatment plants due to the inability of the resident microbial biota to degrade these materials properly within the allotted processing time. Solid grease is usually skimmed from the clarifiers and pumped directly to the anaerobic digesters. This cycle bypasses the aerobic liquefaction and bio-degradation process. Anaerobic digesters, then exposed to this overload of compacted grease, generate floating mats or layers, often two to five feet thick. This situation results in digester malfunction and costly repairs.

EC&S Bio-Stimulant includes a natural addition to and stimulation of a microbial ecosystem capable of secreting higher concentrations of lipase enzymes, exoenzymes, and coenzymes that solubilize fats, oils, and greases through rapid enzymatic and exoenzymatic hydrolysis. The programmed addition of EC&S Bio-Stimulant to activated sludge systems significantly reduces the emulsified grease solids, thereby assisting in the elimination of digester "cakes" or matting within the sewage plant anaerobic digesters.

Degradation of Cellulose

Municipal treatment plants accommodate industrial wastes that contain high levels of cellulose. Among the cellulose waste are such materials as cotton, cigarettes, and various forms of paper. These materials are among the most difficult compounds within the municipal and industrial waste treatment systems to liquefy and decompose. Fortunately, cellulose is bio-degradable by certain bacterial and fungal strains that are capable of secreting cellulose enzymes that convert the tough, fibrous structures of cellulose to a soluble fluid state. Municipal waste treatment plants that receive overloads of paper, cotton, fruit and vegetable pulps, cereal fibers, and various other forms of cellulose substances can benefit from the rapid hydrolyzing capabilities of EC&S Bio-Stimulant.

EC&S Bio-Stimulant contains selected enzymes, exoenzymes, coenzymes, and other components which trigger the microbial ecosystems capable of efficiently degrading native cellulose by further secretion of a variety of cellulose enzymes, exoenzymes, and inducer molecules. Limited quantities of cellulose digesting enzymes are produced by the normal flora of the average waste disposal system. Inoculation of sewage materials with EC&S Bio-Stimulant generates many trillions of additional, active cellulose-secreting microorganisms. This new microbial life is able to hydrolyze and biodegrade efficiently the various forms of cellulose materials found in waste treatment plants.

Degradation of Detergents

Municipal wastewater treatment includes many synthetic detergents, including nonylphenol ethoxylates, N-alcohol ethoxylates, and sodium N-dodecyl benzene sulfonate. These materials, due to the ability to reduce both surface and interfacial tension, alter the efficiency of sewage treatment systems by reducing the oxygen transfer rate of these systems. Such a reduction of oxygen transfer reduces the operating capacity of an activated sludge plant by as much as 30% to 40%, thus increasing the amount of time required to process the sewage and to obtain overall BOD reduction and final flocculation.

The goal is to reduce the injurious effects of these detergents and other closely related syndets. This goal can be accomplished with the aid of EC&S Bio-Stimulant, which serves as a tonic and a "trigger" to the natural microbial ecosystems which have been isolated or have become dormant. It assists the existing microbial life to bio-degrade a wide variety of detergents effectively and to cause the bio-degradation of higher concentrations of these detergents with less residence time. EC&S Bio-Stimulant is USDA authorized for use in sewage and/or drain lines of official establishments operating under the Federal meat, poultry, shell egg grading, and egg products inspection programs.

Odor Remedy for Industrial Use and Municipal Sewage Treatment

Heavy-duty industrial application of EC&S Bio-Stimulant is designed to neutralize odors from municipal sewage treatment plants and in industrial processes in which large quantities of odor-producing water must be remediated. It is also useful in replenishing oxygen and thus eliminating odors in stagnant ponds or other standing or polluted water.

The remedy is easy to apply, nontoxic, and completely safe for use around humans and animals. This model is not a bacterial culture or odor masker. It is a balanced formula that instantly goes into solution to produce great amounts of self-generating, dissolved and free-oxygen that restricts odor-causing anaerobes and stimulates the eutrophic process (natural waters to develop with high nutrient loading, thus with high primary production of organic materials with natural microorganism activity.)

Description

EC&S Bio-Stimulant contains a carefully developed system that keeps its water medium in a constant state of oxygen saturation. It includes an ecologically balanced combination of enzymes, coenzymes, exoenzymes and multifactorial inducer materials, that serve as a bio-stimulant, and remain active over wide ranges of temperature and other environmental influences. Continuous treatment of water or waste material will clear completely the effluent under treatment of any objectionable odors and will, at the same time, regenerate the natural eutrophic in these liquids. It has been confirmed that over a period of time (relative to BOD/COD ratios and stagnancy periods) effluent being treated may be returned totally to life-supporting, oxygenated water.

Application

Often the most effective usage for odor remedy of sewage or a specific industrial odor abatement need may require a tailor-made system to meet that individual requirement. In general, however, the following guide may be followed:

Apply EC&S Bio-Stimulant by simply diluting one part product with nine parts of clean water. Spray or sprinkle evenly over the entire odor area. Repeat application if necessary or whenever more odorous material is added.

EC&S Bio-Stimulant will generate great gas pressure when reacting with anaerobic life forms and should not be used in enclosed vessels. In sewage plants, it should be added to the system after initial digesting, in an oxidation pond or trickling filter where it is outside in sunlight and where it may exist on the surface of the material being treated.

Initial shock treatment usually will be required. To initiate treatment, the odor remedy should be sprayed over the surface of the area to be treated at a rate of 10 gallons of the diluted product (1 part EC&S Bio-Stimulant and 9 parts water) per foot/acre of sewage. The odor should begin to diminish within a few minutes. This treatment should be repeated at one to two week intervals.

Repeated application of EC&S Bio-Stimulant is most functional when applied as a spray, either over the surface of an aeration pond or directly at the top of a pipe mouth. It is best to cover as much water area as possible and to allow the odor remedy to be applied at the surface of the sewage as long as possible. Over time, the eutrophic process will penetrate deeper; initially, however, most of the odor control will be through the surface layers.

EC&S Bio-Stimulant is applied continuously in a 200:1 dilution at a rate of 360 gallons diluted product to 1 million gallons of effluent. There are several acceptable ways to accomplish this treatment. For treatment with a volume near 1 million gallons per day, the easiest and least costly means is with the use of a 200-gallon tank of 10:1 dilution that is rediluted with water 20:1 upon application. Thus, treating 1 million gallons/day would require replenishing the tank with 20 gallons EC&S Bio-Stimulant concentrate every ten days. Other application rates for different effluent volumes may be linearly calculated by this example.

Jackson Research Center

MODEL TWO: **MEMO V**

To: Environmental Health Foundation

From: William R. Jackson, Ph.D., Consultant

Subject: **Petroleum Hydrocarbon Bio-Remediation**

Consider the present energy system and the energy storage on spaceship earth. Included are power from the sun, life in the oceans, the living action within the soil, and the accumulated reserve of power in carbon. Microorganisms can be considered one of the most successful representatives of life on our planet, and when and where allowed, microbial life continues to abound. It has been estimated that the combined weight of microbial cells on spaceship earth is about 25 times that of the earth's other animal life. While their individual size is incredibly small, one cubic inch of pure typical bacteria would contain over nine trillion microorganisms. Even today, microorganisms continue to cleanse this planet effectively .

Environmental Bio-technology and Bio-remediation

The concept of bio-remediation is used to describe operationally the process of using living organisms, microorganisms, to decontaminate a polluted system effectively. Some of the microorganisms used are bacteria, fungi, algae, actinomycetes, and various other plants. Several techniques use microorganisms to degrade a number of pollutants. One method uses the microorganisms that can already be found in the soil. These microbes may be stimulated to grow by introducing nutrients, bio-stimulants, and humic materials into the soil, thereby enhancing the bio-degradation process. This process is referred to as bio-stimulation. Another method involves culturing the microorganisms independently and adding the culture to the polluted site. This process is known as bio-augmentation.

An advantage of bio-remediation is that the process may be implemented on site, involving a minimum amount of space and equipment. When the treatment takes place on the original location, the overhead costs and the liability factors are greatly reduced when compared to off-site treatments that require transporting large volumes of polluted material. On-site and off-site treatments have advantages and disadvantages, and the decision to use one method of treatment versus the other is usually dictated by the economic and efficiency factors of each unique scenario.

MICROORGANISMS CONTINUE TO CLEANSE SPACESHIP EARTH EFFECTIVELY. THROUGH BIO-REMEDIATION, THESE MICROBES ASSIST IN EFFECTIVELY DECONTAMINATING POLLUTED SITES AND SYSTEMS.

No book would include all of the possible solutions for each ugly pollution problem. However, an attempt has been made here to give a few general categories of problems that have been successfully addressed with bio-technology involving microbial action. These situations serve as limited examples, and if you have a pollution problem, you are encouraged to know your local, state, and federal regulations and to work with a competent consultant in that field to assist you with his or her experience, advice, and up-to-date laboratory analysis of your specific pollution problem. Most hazardous waste problems require individualized engineering, advice, and in many cases bonding and special permits.

The following are a few examples of the bio-cultural answers presently available:

1. EC&S Bio-Stimulant activates the indigenous microorganisms found in

sewage treatment plants and collection lines, including municipal wastewater treatment facilities. This technology can handle a variety of waste problems including heavy grease loadings, cosmetics, salad oils, petroleum products and byproducts, and many industrial waste products. Foul odors and hydrogen sulfide emission are controllable. Overall treatment plant efficiency can be improved while sludge volume is reduced.

2. Bio-remediation through the use of EC&S Bio-Stimulant, treats high concentrations of carbohydrates, starch wastes, and aliphatic chemical wastes such as acrylics, vinyl acetates, and a variety of solvents using the indigenous microbial life, present on site. This approach also is beneficial for canning companies, soft-drink bottlers, and manufacturers of corn products, starches, glue products, and chemicals. This treatment category effectively enhances settleability.

3. Another category of bio-degradation treats wastewaters with very high lipid content, such as animal, fish, and

vegetable oils. Here again, EC&S Bio-Stimulant is effective in activating the indigenous microorganisms. It improves the performance of wastewater treatment systems including lagoons, activated sludge systems, trickling filters, and oxidation ditches. The microorganisms degrade gasoline, light weight mineral oils, and most petrochemical products.

4. Some indigenous microbes combat heavy tar-like oils, coal tars, and organic sludge in waste streams, tanks, and land spills which react to the triggering effect of EC&S Bio-Stimulant. Indigenous microbes are particularly effective in degrading diesel fuel, bunker oil, and crude oil. Also included in this category is treatment of waste containing phenolic and other aromatic chemical structures. These microbes are capable of breaking down diverse organic materials, including coke wastes, as well as wood preservative wastes such as creosote and pentachlorophenol that are associated with railroad ties and telephone pole facilities, refinery bottoms, and asphalt.

5. Some EC&S Bio-Stimulants function as a bio-treatment, successfully treating industrial wastes with exceptionally high protein contents such as blood and fat. High protein wastes generated by dairy processing, and meat packing and processing companies can be heated effectively. Treatment of nitrogenous compounds generated by petrochemical firms is reported to form excellent flocs. Here again, no foreign microbial life is imported.

6. Bio-remediation with EC&S Bio-Stimulant improves the performance of anaerobic systems. The already present microbes, highly stimulated and multiplied, aid the breakdown of problematic organic material in septic systems, Imhoff tanks, digesters, and anaerobic lagoons. Percolation in leach fields and seepage pits is restored, while sludge volumes are reduced and odors controlled. This category of microorganism stimulation is specifically effective with anaerobic treatment of domestic wastes containing heavy amounts of salad oils, detergents, and grease.

7. The final indigenous microorganism category in this list consumes many of the components found in industrial waste streams. They treat wastes containing detergents, various petroleum and petrochemical byproducts, and protein and lipid structures. These EC&S Bio-Stimulated microbes treat pulp, paper, and forest products in wastewaters.

These functional descriptions are only examples of some of the tasks bio-remediation can accomplish. EC&S Bio-Stimulant, functioning as a triggering microorganism activator, reactivates or revitalizes microbes present in soil, water, and out-of-balance toxic wastes. Once activated, the microbes stimulate naturally existing microbes as well as perhaps the bio-augmented microbe family. Microorganisms may be further stimulated by nutrients such as humic matter to promote healthy organic activity. Environmental bio-technology complements bio-remediation and contributes to the healing of our lands.

The Role of Microorganisms

Bio-degradation makes various elements available to other living organisms in nature's constant cycle of decomposition and regeneration. The microorganisms that help "earth recycle earth" are being used more and more today as natural biological remedies to humankind's pollution. Up to 90% of the chemical substances considered hazardous, can be bio-degraded. Nature requires a relatively small proportion of indigenous (native) microorganisms found in a contaminated matrix that will have the intrinsic (genetic) ability to degrade the contaminant. Generally speaking, the process involved in bio-transformation develops through a complex series of exoenzymatic inducer molecule and enzymatic reactions which may or may not be expressed by a specific bacterial species or group of bacteria (consortium). The chemical and hazardous waste environment, for example, plays an important role in determining not only the percentage of microorganisms that have the ability to act upon a contaminant, but also whether the ability will be expressed under site-specific conditions. Long-term exposure to a contaminant will generally result in an increased number of "adapted" contaminant-degrading strains.

We have yet to encounter the need for exogenous (foreign) or recombinant (the formation in offspring of genetic combinations not present in parents) species to perform the necessary bio-degradative task. With very few exceptions, bio-remedial specialists rely upon the tremendous diversity and capability exhibited by naturally occurring microbial populations.

REVIEW: Microbial life exists, for example, in all geological soils, and petroleum hydrocarbon waste, under all climatic conditions. This microbial life is extremely aggressive under the correct circumstances and with adequate stimulation. These microorganisms were created to be very competitive in performing nature's assigned tasks. This is how ecological balance is maintained for a specific location. As excessive foreign hydrocarbon materials, such as large amounts of hazardous waste petroleum hydrocarbon contaminations, are introduced into a specific ecosystem, a natural process begins to occur to eliminate the overload problem. As the continuous addition of these foreign materials (overload) occurs, the surplus begins to burden the natural processes, and serious contamination results. This problem can be corrected by a balancing addition of EC&S Bio-Stimulant, a natural activator. When the overload or the foreign matter is eliminated, the revived natural and native ecosystem resumes its normal process as structured by nature. Once the task is complete, the additional microbiota that were induced are phased out; they are allowed to become dormant again. In other words, upon the completion of the remediation, the treated site returns to the original indigenous (original existing microbial life that represented balance) microbiota system. Bio-remediation is powerful and demonstrates dynamic benefits.

This "enzyme recruitment" ecosystem of EC&S Bio-Stimulant offers the potential for the acquisition and evolution of new degradative pathways. This potential suggests great flexibility in the capability of communities of microbes to degrade complex materials, including hazardous waste substances that are unfamiliar to the EC&S ecosystem. Inoculation of hazardous waste products with EC&S Bio-Stimulant generates many trillions of active coenzyme, exoenzyme, enzyme-secreting microorganisms, and indigenous molecules that are able to hydrolyze and bio-degrade efficiently the various forms of hazardous materials found in the remediation systems. When EC&S Bio-Stimulant is applied to this situation, adequate moisture must be maintained because microbial life is moisture sensitive.

In situ microbial treatment sites may be the ideal hazardous waste treatment technique. The various areas where the waste products are found serve as a reactor structure. In these commercial waste treatment sites, naturally occurring microorganisms are cued up with naturally occurring hormonal exoenzymes, enzymes and coenzymes, plus a selection of inducer molecules, thus accentuating or promoting their growth through the addition of nutrients or oxygen. This growth, in turn, accelerates their natural bio-degradation properties, yet does not require a formal reactor. **Using this approach, the natural (in situ) environment itself becomes a giant reactor.**

The bio-stimulant use of selected exoenzymes, enzymes, and coenzymes, etc. is a method directed toward the natural microbial population, conditioning the biota population to enhanced bio-conversion or bio-degradation of a given substrate. This bio-degradation usually assists the survival and performance of greater bio-conversion of a substrate when the microbial population is exposed to fluctuations in conditions, including particular shock loads of the substrate. The balancing ability of the microbial population becomes more adaptable by exposing this biota to a nontoxic or inhibitory amount of EC&S Bio-Stimulant that is biochemically or structurally similar. This method of bio-stimulation is applicable for systems where the production of useful metabolites is the objective.

Application Parameters for Bio-Stimulant

1. pH: Optimum of 7, minimum of 4.5, maximum of 9.0

2. DO (dissolved oxygen): Optimum 3 PPM+, minimum of 2 PPM

3. C/N (carbon/nitrogen ratio): Optimum 10:1, maximum 20:1

4. Temperature: Optimum 30° C, minimum 19° C, maximum 49° C

Hazardous Waste Bio-Remediation

Bio-remediation is defined as the utilization of a multifactorial ecosystem to stimulate naturally occurring bacteria to break down undesired organic compounds into harmless compounds by the enhancement of the stimulated microorganism ecology.

The following is a quote from the *Smithsonian Magazine*, April 1993:

> Typical EPA Nightmare: An underground gas plume of volatile organic compounds threatens to waft into an aquifer that supplies drinking water. Conventional treatment calls for sinking small shafts, perhaps in the

> hundreds, to trap the VOC (volatile organic compounds) and route them to expensive extraction equipment. But it's time-consuming and still leaves much of the VOC mass underground. Another way: dig a few narrow wells and force air through them. Underground the VOCs are forced to rise to the surface, where most are captured via extraction wells. Meanwhile, the hollow spaces beneath the surface, now filled with fresh air, become dining rooms for bacteria. Bugs and nutrients, pumped in through the same air wells, serve as a sort of janitorial crew by filtering out the remaining VOCs.

Picture for a moment a green meadow or lawn area dotted every few feet with white plastic well pipes thrust above the surface like cemetery markers. Some of these pipes transport fresh air down to the polluted aquifer below. Shorter pipes draw air up through the soil. This is a simplified picture of bio-venting.

How does it function? The fresh air pumped down to the soil and ground water picks up the contaminant. Vacuum pumps then draw the unclean air back up. As the hazardous waste contaminants filter up through the in situ soil, they are digested by native microorganisms. These microbes, or bacterium, can be stimulated by EC&S Bio-Stimulant, and are further encouraged when suitable bio-nutrients are added.

The capability of a bacterium to degrade hazardous waste materials is controlled by EC&S Bio-Stimulation that catalyzes a specific oxidation. Even though a bacteria contains the information to synthesize various enzymes, for example, in its genetic material, the cell will not spend the energy to produce these enzymes necessary for rapid reproduction and, thus, accelerate the degrading of a specific waste matter. The application of EC&S Bio-Stimulant serves as a trigger, for the genetic material of various categories of microbial life, including chemically and light-sensitive active and reactive bacteria, and thus serves as an inducer molecule. The inducer may then serve as a degradation product of the substrate molecule. Relative to metabolic pathways, each oxidation step is catalyzed by highly specific exoenzyme, enzyme, and coenzyme ecosystems. The final products of the enzyme-stimulated, chemically activated, molecularly mobile bacterial-degradation of this waste matter now take the form of H_2O and CO_2 cells. The following are examples of EC&S Bio-Stimulant microbial degradation.

Examples of EC&S Bio-Stimulant Bacterial Degradation

SAMPLE 1:

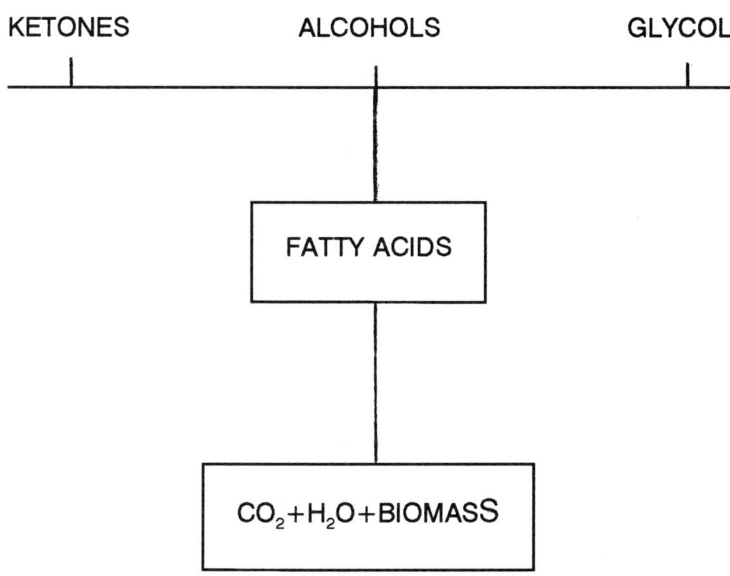

SAMPLE 2:

ETHYL
BENZENE TOLUENE BENZENE XYLENES PHENOLS NAPHTHALENE
C_6H_6 C_7H_8 C_8H_{10} C_8H_{10} C_6H_6O $C_{10}H_8$
CATECHOL
FATTY ACIDS
$CO_2+H_20+BIOMASS$

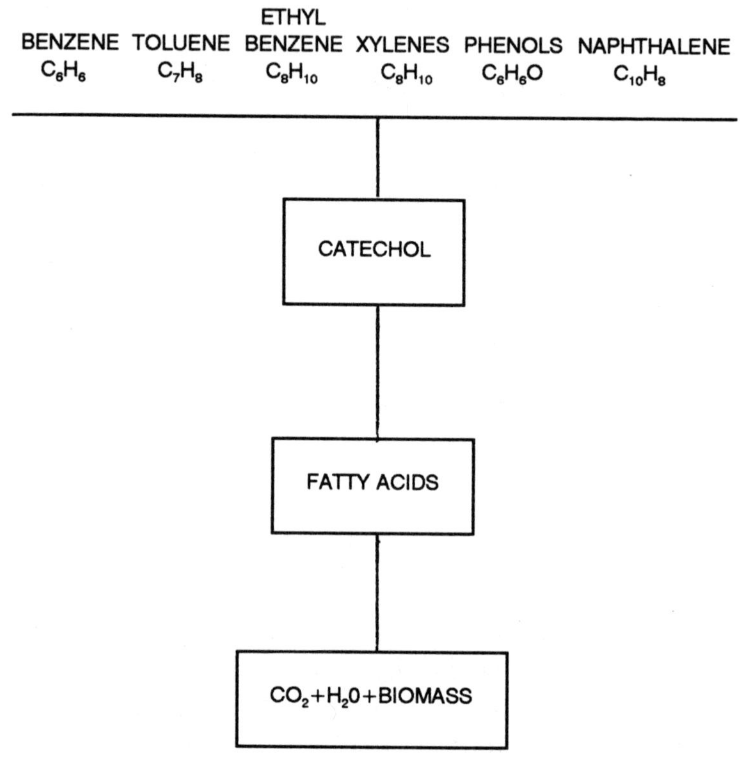

SAMPLE 3:

Degradation of Trichloroethylene (TCE) Under Aerobic Environment (Co-Metabolic Processes)

1. TCE+METHANE+BACTERIA+O_2+NUTRIENT = CO_2+H_2O+BIOMASS
(C_2HCl_3) (CH_4)

2. TCE+TOLUENE+BACTERIA+O_2+NUTRIENT = CO_2+H_2O+BIOMASS
(C_2HCl_3) (C_7H_9)

OR

TCE+PHENOL+BACTERIA+O_2+NUTRIENT = CO_2+H_2O+BIOMASS
(C_2HCl_3) (C_6H_7O)

Because these contaminants have basically been converted to H_2O and CO_2, the air samples analyzed at the surface are clean. The army of microorganisms has turned the in situ soil into a bio-reactor. Bio-stimulation, enhanced by bio-venting, is an inexpensive method of bio-remediation and can reach under buildings and other surface obstructions and is showing signs of being a significant remediation technology of the future.

What to Look for In a Bio-Stimulant Product

EC&S Bio-Stimulant is a highly concentrated, multi-component, bio-ecosystem. Dispersible in liquids, EC&S Bio-Stimulant contains enzymes, coenzymes, exoenzymes, multifactorial inducer molecules, and suitable organic nutrients that synergistically stimulate a broad spectrum of specialized natural microorganisms that are composed of aerobic and facultative (capable of adaptive responses to varying environment) anaerobic microbial strains selected for maximum efficiency in hazardous waste treatment systems conditions. EC&S Bio-Stimulant, with its unique bio-ecosystem, has a higher rate of efficiency at bio-degrading various toxicants within waste treatment systems than isolated strains of imported microorganisms. This system offers the user the advantage of immediate activity within indigenous microorganisms at pre-computed levels of biochemical capability.

EC&S Bio-Stimulant, being a well balanced bio-ecosystem, results from having secreted significantly greater concentrations of highly effective enzymes, coenzymes, and exoenzymes that improve digestion rates, thereby increasing the overall efficiency of the aerobic waste treatment system, along with other actions and reactions, which were presented earlier in the Working Model Two, introduction. Higher concentrations of waste can be accommodated when coupled with the more rapid bio-degradation that can be obtained through the proper use of EC&S Bio-Stimulant in the waste treatment system.

EC&S Bio-Stimulant enzymatically and chemically triggers various results that alter the physical structure of the suspended organic solids, causing them to separate more efficiently. The reduced hazardous waste volume that follows more thorough digestion is due to the more complete liquefaction and gasification of the petroleum hydrocarbons contained in the hazardous waste and the destruction of waste-binding molecules. EC&S Bio-Stimulant is USDA authorized for bio-remediation tasks as defined and stated on its label.

Description

EC&S Bio-Stimulant contains a carefully developed system that keeps its water medium in a constant state of OXYGEN SATURATION. It includes an ecologically-balanced complex multifactorial system that serves as a bio-stimulant, and remains active over wide ranges of temperature and other environmental influences. Continuous treatment of hazardous waste material will clear the area under treatment and will regenerate the natural eutrophic conditions in these locations. Over a period of time (relative to BOD/COD ratios), the area being treated may be restored totally to life-supporting, oxygenated balance.

Remediation Review

EC&S Bio-Stimulant is a biochemical product containing several vitamin precursors of plant and animal origin in a highly concentrated mass of autotrophic, aerobic, and facultative enzymes, coenzymes, and exoenzymes, including various inducer molecules. So combined, the constituents are able to withstand a wide range of environmental conditions, including salt contents, while decomposing commercial hazardous waste residues. This decomposing process is accomplished by dispensing OXYGEN and deriving energy from the oxidation of simple mineral compounds and organic gases. EC&S Bio-Stimulant produces a biologically balanced stimulant for the ecosystem in water, air, and soil by increasing available nutrients through the increase of OXYGEN.

EC&S Bio-Stimulant has made it possible for industry and commerce to obtain a faster, biologically balanced recovery of wastewaters, solid wastes, and hazardous waste residues. EC&S Bio-Stimulant is USDA authorized for specific bio-remediation tasks.

XIV

EPILOGUE

Throughout this book, an environmental question has been asked: Are toxic, out-of-balance waste and pollution, the use of harmful chemicals, and an "I don't know, I don't care" attitude inevitable parts of our society? Take the example of pesticides: Doesn't having 45,000 different chemical pesticide formulations registered in the United States alone, alarm you? Well, there is good reason for alarm because harmful chemical compounds, when present in excess, not only cause toxic deterioration in nature, but also function as deadly toxins for inhabitants of spaceship earth. This unwholesomeness and destruction, however, can be remedied. Chapters XI, XII and XIII serve as examples of working models that may be used as a possible standard for comparison when you look for safer products. With a determined resolve to see remediation happen, the assistance of natural processes, and adequate information from which to choose safe chemicals, microbial balance and sound, functional, purposeful reclamation can be accomplished. With balance, the toxicity of harmful chemicals may be neutralized, hydrocarbons and oils dissolved and digested, heavy metals and inorganic pollution impounded, the ill effects of some radioactive materials reduced, and the possibility of having toxic wastewater pollution eliminated.

Through bio-remediation, indigenous microorganisms continue to cleanse spaceship earth effectively. Their ability to decontaminate polluted sites and systems is used in various methods, including bio-stimulation and bio-augmentation. Natural microbial activity may be further encouraged by nutrients found in humic matter, thus promoting healthy organic action and providing healing for our lands. Nature holds the answer for its own redemption from toxic conditions. The plea to the inhabitants of spaceship earth is: Be responsible, responding, informed people, foregoing selfish greed while honorably playing by nature's rules of preservation. Each of us then will have had a part in the healing process and the productive future of spaceship earth. Hear again the paraphrase of Oliver Wendell Holmes used in John F. Kennedy's Presidential inaugural address of January 20, 1961, which rang out, "Ask not what your country can do for you, but what you can do for your country." We suggest today that as trustees of spaceship earth, that our paraphrase might be: "Ask not what else I can take, nor which of nature's rules may I break, but rather, in my environment, what can I do to help?"

What are you willing to pay for environmental safeguards? How convinced are you that we have out-of-balance problems? How determined are you to be a soldier in the battle for overcoming these potentially fatal problems? Can we count on your service in the ranks of the changing of the guard? Will you participate in this synergism for balance? Can you now visualize being involved as part of the solution to the situation right where you live? Napoleon Hill stated that what the mind can conceive and believe, it can achieve. Do we understand the problem? Do we believe there is a functional answer to this dilemma? And so we ask ourselves again, "What can I do to help?"

Friends and relatives of mine have died in recent years because toxicity accumulated as the result of a lack of balance in their systems. It affected their health and ultimately cost their lives. My life has been blessed with beautiful children and precious grandchildren. I love them and care very much about their well-being; thus I am highly motivated to CONCEIVE and understand our dilemma, to BELIEVE there is a solution to this destruction, and to work to see answers ACHIEVED. I love you; and as cohabitants of our spaceship earth, I care about the safety and well-being of each of us, and I care about the preservation of our planet. Are we yet so convinced that the problem must be solved, that we are willing to set aside some of our own "personal rights" (for example, greed, convenience, old habits) to help return balance to spaceship earth?

Can we achieve this great task? Can we reverse the attitudes of ignorance and the greed of the past? **YES**. We must develop a strong philosophy of life, rearrange our priorities, and resolve our will to win. W. Clement Stone stated on many occasions at sales meetings, "If you have nothing to lose by trying, and everything to gain, by all means, TRY."

Inspiration and motivation can make environmental books and pleas come alive, throwing a luster on the printed page and making the words and thoughts easier to read, to hear, and to understand. This goal to preserve our spaceship earth inspires and motivates obedience, stimulates the comprehension, and evokes the cooperation of sincere people like you and me. This goal makes learning, decision-making, and taking action, adventures and true pleasures.

Inspiration and motivation stimulate the will to achieve. Inspired environmentalists must face, deep within themselves the battle of life's accountability and the necessity of continuous self-improvement. We must will to win. We must have some great goals and some personal, significant causes and relationships which have special meaning to each of us individually and collectively. We must come to the conclusion that it is actually easier to earn and enjoy the fruits of the accountable and creatively courageous life than to endure and be a part of the pain of spaceship earth's failure. We must aspire to a safe and balanced life and have the will to live it. If we mesh gears with reality and find somewhere to begin, further directions will arise from the nature of our circumstances as we move out along the line of our inspired action.

May I count on you as my fellow traveler, my co-inhabitant, to do your part in allowing this great ecosystem to rebalance? We can do more than just survive; we can live! Beautiful lives. Fulfilled lives. Healthy lives. And we can ensure such lives for future generations. The self-discipline is worth the price. You are a part of the changing of the guard. Nature's nobility! And we the people of spaceship earth will do better!